Victorian Noon

Victorian Noon

English Literature in 1850

Carl Dawson

THE JOHNS HOPKINS UNIVERSITY PRESS
Baltimore and London

Manufactured in the United States of America

The Johns Hopkins University Press, Baltimore, Maryland 21218
The Johns Hopkins Press Ltd., London

Library of Congress Catalog Number 78-13939
ISBN 0-8018-2110-X

Library of Congress Cataloging in Publication data will be found on the last printed page of this book.

Illustration Credits

Thomas Carlyle, a medallion by Thomas Woolner, courtesy of The Scottish National Portrait Gallery, Edinburgh
Alfred Tennyson, portrait by Samuel Laurence, courtesy of the National Portrait Gallery, London
William Thackeray, a chaulk sketch by Samuel Laurence, courtesy of Mrs. Belinda Norman Butler
Thackeray, "Editors of the *Leader*," courtesy of the National Portrait Gallery, London
Matthew Arnold, a photograph, reproduced by permission of the Trustees of Dove Cottage, Grasmere, England
Robert Browning, portrait by D. G. Rossetti, 1855-56, copyright © by the Fitzwilliam Museum, Cambridge, England; reprinted by permission of the museum
John Newman, a portrait, courtesy of the Radio Times Hulton Picture Library
John Ruskin, portrait by George Richmond, courtesy of the National Portrait Gallery, London
Charles Dickens, an 1849 photograph, reproduced by permission of The Huntington Library, San Marino, California
J. M. W. Turner, "Yarmouth Sands," reproduced by permission of the Yale Center for British Art, Paul Mellon Collection (J. M. W. Turner, R. A., [1775-1851]: *Yarmouth Sands*, ca. 1840-42, watercolor, 9 3/4 X 14 3/8 in. [247 X 260 mm])
Charlotte Brontë, a portrait by George Richmond, courtesy of the National Portrait Gallery, London
Charles Kingsley, an 1851 portrait, courtesy of the Historical Society of Pennsylvania
D. G. Rossetti, portrait by Holman Hunt, courtesy of the Birmingham Art Gallery, England

To Hanne
and
to the memory of Lorna Dawson

Contents

	Preface	xi
I	Introduction	1
II	Poetics: *The Hero as Poet*	16
III	In Memoriam: *The Uses of Dante and Wordsworth*	36
IV	Dramatic Elegists: *Arnold, Clough, and Browning at Mid-Century*	63
V	Phases of the Soul: *The Newman Brothers*	105
VI	"The Lamp of Memory": *Wordsworth and Dickens*	123
VII	Men of Letters as Hacks and Heroes	153
VIII	Polemics: *Charles Kingsley and* Alton Locke	179
IX	The Germ: *Aesthetic Manifesto*	203
X	Postscripts: *On the Eve of the Great Exhibition*	224
	Notes	241
	Index	257

Illustrations

Title page from *Punch* 53
Crystal Palace: Western entrance 54
Crystal Palace: Interior of the transept 54
Crystal Palace: Southern entrance to the transept 55
Crystal Palace: The transept from the north side 56
Thomas Carlyle: A medallion by Thomas Woolner 57
Alfred Tennyson: Portrait by Samuel Laurence 57
William Thackeray: A chaulk sketch by Samuel Laurence 58
Thackeray: "Editors of the *Leader*" 58
Thackeray: "The overburdened author" 59
Matthew Arnold: A photograph 59
Robert Browning: Portrait by D. G. Rossetti 60
Francis Newman: A photograph 60
John Newman: A portrait 61
John Ruskin: Portrait by George Richmond 61
Charles Dickens: An 1849 photograph 145
"The River" from *David Copperfield* 145
Title page from *David Copperfield* 146
Ruskin: "Chamouni" 147
J. M. W. Turner: "Yarmouth Sands" 147
Title page from *Pendennis* 148
Hill and Adamson: "The McCandlish Children" 148
Charlotte Brontë: A portrait by George Richmond 149
Charles Kingsley: An 1851 portrait 149
Richard Doyle: Drawing for *The King of the Golden River* 149
George Cruikshank: An illustration from *Frank Fairlegh* 149
D. G. Rossetti: Portrait by Holman Hunt 150
Title page from *The Germ* 150
First page of *The Household Narrative* 151

Preface

Victorian Noon requires a preliminary word. It is an odd title for what may well be an odd book. I have borrowed the title, or rather adapted it, from G. M. Young, who speaks of mid-nineteenth-century England as "the Victorian noon-time."[1] Since Young recommends that historians of the Victorian period concentrate on the social and political developments, the public events and the private dramas within a particular year, it may also seem that I have borrowed from Young my reasons for the book as well as its title. And certainly I have had his suggestion in mind for some time. The truth is, however, that *Victorian Noon* grew unprompted and uninvited. As I read for a study of Matthew Arnold and his nineteenth-century critics, I found myself taking notes about writers at mid-century. When checking on the biography of a friend or critic of Arnold I would soon be asking: Was he (or she) alive, or how old was he in 1850? Whom did he know? What was he reading? Was he writing? The person might be a journalist or a poet, old or young, famous or unremembered.

Quite simply, I became intrigued by the richness and diversity of the literature of mid-nineteenth-century England. Eighteen fifty, like 1859, was an extraordinary year. I began to think—and with moments of vacillation have thought since—that *Victorian Noon* ought to be written, that it could show much about the Romantic heritage, about the mid-nineteenth-century literary world, while it offered new ways of looking at certain English classics.

I have also come to realize why few writers have followed G. M. Young's suggestion, or at least what pitfalls he invites us into. For whatever is said by way of explanation, the focus on a given year will seem arbitrary. History's categories rarely confine themselves to a single year. Things sprawl in time, and cause and effect move us backward and forward. My own topic involves literature rather than social or political history, but it also raises difficult questions. Is there, after all, any intrinsic connection between the literary events of a given year? Would demonstrated relationships prove more convenient than meaningful?

My justification for the book and responses to such questions will, I hope, become clear soon enough. I want to say first that the focus on the historical, thematic, or biographical relationships of a single year seems to me at once a fitting response to the Victorians' own preoccupation with the patterns of time—and with 1850 as a pivotal or "transitional" year—and also an appropriate study for a literary historian today. Although I am not a structuralist, I have thought in terms of a favorite structuralist distinction: that between a synchronic and diachronic approach to a subject. If literary history tends to be diachronic, or chronological, perhaps it is worthwhile to look at our subject in a synchronic or contemporaneous way, considering works in their immediate context and weighing the forgotten with the great. I suspect that such a broad invitation might take us back to traditional critical methods as well as push us to semiotics. An exhaustive critique of Baudelaire's "Les Chats" or of a Balzac short story may be understood as an outgrowth of the New Criticism and a study of the potential plot elements of fiction as a neo-Aristotelian approach. Even discussions of formal intellectual contexts may be seen as extensions of the Arthur Lovejoy studies in the history of ideas. Whatever the practical effect of structuralist aesthetics, I have accepted the reminder to include materials beyond an accepted canon. On the other hand, I have resisted the temptation to dwell on more than a few individual works and have felt free to play with temporal metaphors, moving back and forth as well as across.

A study of the literature of a particular year might be approached in a variety of ways. It would, for example, be illuminating to discuss the connections between English and European or American literature. In America too 1850 was a watershed. Hawthorne published *The Scarlet Letter*; Emerson published *Representative Men*; Poe's "Poetic Principle" appeared posthumously; Melville published *White Jacket*, shortly after publishing *Redburn*; and *The Whale*, soon to be *Moby Dick*, would appear the following year. Melville went to England in the fall of 1850 to sell new books to English publishers. American works were read in England, just as English works were read—and pirated—in America. To attempt a study of international literary relations would, however, be another venture altogether, and I have limited my attention to English works in

England, unless making a quick comparison or discussing (as in chapter III) the uses to English writers of a Dante or Goethe.

Even with the geographical limitation, various possibilities would be open. I might have followed the example of John Dodds in *The Age of Paradox*, who writes a kind of diary of mid-century years. The chronological sweep of literature reviewed in the *Athenaeum* or *Examiner* or Dickens's *Household Narrative* could serve for a month-by-month discussion of what books were available and how they were being read. I have chosen instead to group my chapters around well-known or representative works and to discuss them in terms of contemporary responses, historical circumstances, and pertinent traditions or parallels, mentioning chronology only where it seems appropriate.

Apart from asserting the extraordinary range and quality of the literature at mid-century, *Victorian Noon* has no overriding thesis. I am dubious about reductive theses and interested, to put this positively, in doing justice to the subject. My aim is firstly descriptive. I want to know how *The Prelude* was received, what relation there might be between Dickens and the Pre-Raphaelites, how contemporary reviewers spoke to new directions in fiction and poetry, or how they handled inherited assumptions. But a description of mid-century literature raises broader, theoretical issues about the status of imagination, the uses of myth and memory, the significance of heavily used words like *nature*, the impact of religious and scientific inquiry on literary works. I address these issues in changing contexts and in relation to authors whom we might otherwise think of as unrelated.

After a general, introductory chapter which offers a framework for discussion and places the literature briefly in its historical setting, I move on to a chapter entitled "Poetics," which comments on the defense of imaginative works in a society obsessed by mechanical power and committed to historical schemes of progress. Chapter III continues the discussion of critical vocabulary with reference to the two recognized great poets of the time: Wordsworth and Tennyson. The chapter explores the Victorian homage to Dante in terms of poetic autobiography. Chapter IV broadens the discussion of poetry, its norms and expectations, by turning to Arnold, Clough, and Browning, whom I call "dramatic elegists." In chapter V I turn more centrally to religious issues, concentrating on John Henry and Francis Newman, and reading them in light of contemporary poets. Religious autobiography leads back to Wordsworth and also to Dickens's autobiographical *David Copperfield*, which I introduce with

Ruskin's chapter "The Lamp of Memory" in chapter VI. My commentary on Wordsworth and Dickens speculates on the importance of Romantic conventions for writers of the time, novelists no less than poets.

Chapter VII plays with a wide range of authors. This is an omnibus chapter, mentioning contemporary reviews of fiction, prefaces by novelists, and other contemporary remarks about the stature of fiction. I refer to George Henry Lewes's reviews of Charlotte Brontë to clarify the mid-century emphasis on literary figures who are at once unprepossessing and, in Carlyle's phrase, "men-of-letters as heroes." Chapter VIII focuses on one writer, Charles Kingsley, whom I take as an index to the age, commenting on his religious views, his critical principles, and on his polemical writings. Chapter IX is a discussion of the Pre-Raphaelites and *The Germ*. The Pre-Raphaelites serve to pull together theories about *nature* and *tradition*, and I compare the short-lived *Germ* with Dickens's enormously successful *Household Words*.

Chapter X raises further questions about mid-century tastes and about the possibility of, or the recognition of, a literary culture. Entitled "Postscripts," it explores again the relationship between the public optimism of the time, expressed in plans for the Great Exhibition, and the melancholic strain in so much of the literature. There was, in Dickens's words, clearly a "summer-dawn" of literature of mid-century, but the literature seems at odds with the nationalism, the pride, even the tastes epitomized in what *Punch* promptly labeled "the Crystal Palace."

The range of these contents will indicate how much of *Victorian Noon* must be indebted to the work of other scholars. My borrowings should be clear in footnotes, although the vast range of scholarship addressed to Tennyson, Dickens, Arnold, Browning, Thackeray, Wordsworth, John Henry Newman, and other writers who enter this study, would make it at best unwieldy to list all pertinent works. I have tried at various points to debate specific arguments of what I take to be representative views. Apart from incidental borrowings, I must point to some evident models for *Victorian Noon*. I refer to *1859: Entering an Age of Crisis*, a work by several hands and without the intent of unity, but an obvious forerunner; to *Mid-Victorian Studies*, a collection of reviews and essays by Kathleen and Geoffrey Tillotson; and especially, perhaps, to Kathleen Tillotson's *Novels of the Eighteen-Forties*, from which I have learned much. Other pertinent studies include Jerome Buckley's *Victorian Temper*, a work of greater scope than mine, but a helpful model, John Dodds's study, *The Age of Paradox*, mentioned above, and Masao Myoshi's "The Colloquy of the Self: 1850" in *The Divided Self*.

My indebtedness here goes beyond my reading. I want to express thanks to the John Simon Guggenheim Memorial Foundation and its president, Gordon Ray, who sponsored another topic, but who made the writing of this book possible, and also to Deans Raymond Erickson and William Drew and the Central University Research Council of the University of New Hampshire, who provided funds for travel and typing. Mr. Hugh Pritchard and the staff of the University of New Hampshire Library have been patient and cooperative, despite excessive requests for inter-library loans. I am also grateful to the staff of the Huntington Library, who are always very helpful, and to the British Library. Throughout the writing of the book, Mary Dargon, English graduate secretary at the University of New Hampshire, not only has found time to type illegible drafts, but has worked with unflagging good will on the administrative chores we have shared. I want to thank, too, John Quimby, who prepared the photographic plates, Trixie McLean, who typed the final manuscript, and Peter Johnson and Patricia Rooney, who saved me time and error.

Professor Michael V. De Porte has read several of the chapters as they grew, and Professor Seamus Deane has read the completed book. I am grateful to them for their generosity, insight, and needed support. Finally, I owe belated thanks to Professor Carl Woodring, who has not read this manuscript, but who long ago read my first. His early encouragement made me aware of things that might be done, his kindness reminds me of what we are about.

C. D.
Barrington, N.H., 1977

Victorian Noon

I

Introduction

1

That unquestioning optimism, that yet unarrested drive, that naivety in overlooking bleak problems, belong wholly to 1850.—Sir Nikolaus Pevsner, *High Victorian Design*[1]

There must be a new world, if there is to be any world at all! . . . These days of universal death must be days of universal new birth, if the ruin is not to be total and final.—Thomas Carlyle, *Latter-Day Pamphlets* (1850)[2]

Victorian Noon is an approach to English literary culture in 1850, the year Tennyson published *In Memoriam* and Wordsworth's widow issued the poem called, for convenience, *The Prelude*. Thackeray, at the height of his popularity after writing *Vanity Fair*, finished *Pendennis* in 1850 and published *The Kickleburys on the Rhine*. Thackeray generously recommended to others a work he thought, at times, superior to his own: Dickens's *David Copperfield*, the mid-century saga of Micawber, Uriah Heep, Steerforth, and David himself, the author-protagonist in a story of success. Carlyle also was active in 1850, publishing the angry and despondent *Latter-Day Pamphlets*, a stinging indictment of English life. One of many who learned from Carlyle, Charles Kingsley, wrote "Cheap Clothes and Nasty," an exposure of Englishmen's mistreatment of other Englishmen, and published *Alton Locke*, his account of the tailor-poet who grows up in London slums. Matthew Arnold, Arthur Clough, George Lewes, George Meredith, the Brownings, and Dante Gabriel Rossetti were all writing in 1850, which saw publication of "Memorial Verses," *Christmas-Eve and Easter-Day*, *Sonnets from the Portuguese*, and "The Blessed Damozel." Rossetti and his Pre-Raphaelite Brotherhood began their short-lived *The Germ* to celebrate their views, and Dickens launched his

Household Words, which included a Philistine assault on the Pre-Raphaelites.

Not all the great Victorians made an appearance in 1850. Some, like Thomas Hardy, William Morris, Walter Pater, A. C. Swinburne, and Lewis Carroll, were simply too young. Leslie Stephen, Walter Bagehot, and Frederic Harrison were all soon to enter their careers in journalism. A writer like Benjamin Disraeli wrote before and after. *Coningsby*, *Sybil*, and *Tancred* belong to the mid-forties, and Disraeli was not to publish his next novel for another two decades. George Eliot had already translated Strauss's controversial *Life of Jesus* (1846) but had yet to begin her career as editor and novelist. Among the Brontë sisters, Charlotte alone was still alive, although *Wuthering Heights* like *Jane Eyre* was reissued in 1850, and the Brontës were frequently reviewed. From Ruskin, only the fairy tale *King of the Golden River* appeared; Ruskin had, however, made his reputation with the early parts of *Modern Painters* and with *The Seven Lamps of Architecture* (1849). He was hard at work on *The Stones of Venice* (1851), a study he felt had bearing on civilization in modern London.

Some writers published uncharacteristic works this year. Trollope, soon to embark on the Barchester novels, published *La Vendée*, an antirevolutionary romance. He also wrote letters for the *Examiner* on the social and political state of Ireland. Wilkie Collins published his first work of fiction, *Antonina, or the Fall of Rome*, which hardly foretold the fine melodrama of *A Woman in White*. The works of other writers were in the air, among them the first volume of Macaulay's *History of England* (1848), Carlyle's *Past and Present* (1843) and *Heroes and Hero-Worship* (1841), and Newman's tracts and sermons. But the list of works actually published in 1850 remains impressive in itself. Although the *Apologia* belongs to a later date, Newman published in 1850 the lectures *On Certain Difficulties Felt by Anglicans*. His brother Francis published *Phases of Faith*, an autobiography. There are works by Herbert Spencer, William Allingham, Elizabeth Gaskell, Thomas De Quincey, Leigh Hunt, John Stuart Mill, Walter Savage Landor, and posthumous works by Coleridge and Thomas L. Beddoes. The list could go on.

When Dickens, writing in *Household Words*, spoke of "this summer-dawn of time,"[3] he may have had in mind the vigor of mid-century literature. More likely, he was expressing a sense of well-being, of hope and promise, which he shared for a time with his countrymen, and which was probably independent of the political events of the year. With one large exception, those events were inauspicious. In June, Sir Robert Peel died, thrown from his horse. Pope Pius IX stirred old antipopery sentiments when he reestablished the Catholic hierarchy in England, appointing Nicholas Wiseman cardinal. Within the Anglican Church itself there arose a controversy called the Gorham Case, which preoccupied the Cabinet and puzzled laymen; it involved questions of church authority that had been raised by Newman and the Tractarians. If no longer vigorous, no longer really a movement as such, the Oxford Movement continued its influence. When his friend Manning converted to the Roman Church in 1851, Gladstone said he felt as if Manning had murdered his mother by mistake.[4]

Abroad, there were disruptions in Schleswig-Holstein and minor problems in Greece, but the revolutionary ferment of 1848 had gone. England's most trying international problems were perhaps those fomented by Palmerston, who was soon to attain his greatest power, and who infuriated the royal couple and embarrassed Lord John Russell, the prime minister, by his independent handling of foreign affairs.[5] From California reports continued to flow in about Sutter's Fort and the lures and pitfalls of the hunt for gold. And apart from gold, English and Irishmen were still crowding inhospitable ships for the immigration to new worlds. Dickens's *Household Words*, among other magazines, openly endorsed emigration as a partial cure for social ills, which included, at mid-century, the recurrent threat of cholera in the cities; the overcrowding in "the Rookeries" (the subject of an 1850 book); the disquiet caused by "Navvies," who were building the now octopus-like railways; and the almost institutionalized problems of Sanitation, Crime, and Prostitution.

But in spite of such problems, the worst starvation and depression of the forties seemed to be over. The Corn Laws had been repealed; the harvests were improving. England began to enjoy the first acknowledged economic "boom" in history. By 1850, as Asa Briggs points out, England's "output of coal had reached 56 million tons a year; pig iron output was over two million tons—half the total world output; there were 1,800 cotton factories employing 328,000 workers and using steam engines with 71,000 total horsepower, and there were over 5,000 miles of railway." Sixty percent of the world's tonnage in 1850 was English.[6] Such statistics, intriguing in their own right, also reflect the mid-century Englishman's pleasure in statistical evidence, which can be seen in the ecstatic accounts of what was possibly the most important event in mid-century England. In 1850, Prince Albert and Henry Cole (and before his death, Sir Robert Peel) were planning their triumphant industrial fair, the Great Exhibition. The opening of the Exhibition took place in May of 1851, but its creation was of 1850. With the "hungry forties" over and Chartism discredited, the mood of the country seems to have been, if not jubilant, then at least confident, Paxton's Crystal Palace testifying to English hegemony in manufacturing and trade.

Many people objected to the Exhibition. Some, like Ruskin, thought it an abomination; others, like Dickens, soon grew tired of hearing about it. But as the regular and detailed accounts in newspapers and weeklies, art magazines and humor papers make clear, the Exhibition emerged as a symbol of national direction, even of hope for humanity. "Nobody who has paid any attention to the peculiar features of the present era [wrote Prince Albert in 1850] will doubt for a moment that we are living at a period of most wonderful transition, which tends rapidly to accomplish that great end, to which, indeed, all history points—the realization of the unity of mankind."[7] More obviously chauvinistic was G. R. Porter, who updated his *Progress of the Nation* in 1851. "It must at all times be a matter of interest and utility to ascertain the means by which any community has attained to eminence among nations. To inquire into the progress of circumstances which has given preeminence to one's own nation would almost seem to be a duty."[8]

Here in both passages, with the "transition" and the "great end," the "utility," "progress," and "duty," we can see the self-confidence and the self-consciousness of the new times. It is a quality in the lightest as well as most earnest of comments. A squib from *Punch* shows how such assumptions lent themselves to readily understood humor. Already nine years old and dedicating "the fulness of [its] Ninth Year to Nine Pins," *Punch* speaks of the policeman as "'that great embodiment of progress' because he says 'Move on!'"[9] Actually, as Mr. Punch was well aware, the policeman *was* an embodiment of progress, an instance of social reform, a sign of the times. Periodicals less radical and less satiric than *Punch* are replete in 1850 with summings-up and with golden prognoses for the years to come. There are articles in the conservative *Quarterly* and *Blackwood's*, contrasting the new equilibrium of English society with the chaos of 1848, often referred to as "the worst year in history."

2

> Literature has ever been the surest reflex of a people.—John Stores Smith, *Social Aspects* (1850)[10]

To some extent the literature of the time expresses the optimism of public opinion—and, indeed, how are we to separate public opinion from the pages of the popular press? We are faced in any historical inquiry with the voiceless feelings of the many perhaps conflicting with the highly vocal expressions of the few. Still, we can recognize in the sales of magazines and books as well as in contemporary reviews that confidence in economic prosperity is matched by a confidence about literature. If fiction still lacked the acknowledged stature of poetry in critical discussions, the praise of "Dickens and Thackeray, Thackeray and Dickens" became almost universal, and reviewers consistently pointed out the achievement of their two novelists in relation to Fielding, Scott, and other giants of the past. Few doubted that, whatever the pitfalls of serial fiction, the novel had found its masters. (This would change somewhat with the response to later books of both Dickens and Thackeray.) Similarly in poetry: despite a common refrain about the vast amounts of poetic dribble being published and the expectation of a greater age of poetry to come, there seemed a general acknowledgment that Tennyson in particular represented a high order of writing. Assessments of literature like the assessments of society tended to be as favorable as they were hopeful, and—for good or ill—a sense of "progress" extended into the arts.

Nevertheless, the mood of the literature often differed from the optimism of its reviewers. Carlyle, though damned for the ferocity of *Latter-Day Pamphlets*, knew that he was not alone in his distressed assessment of the "Condition of England." For "in spite of our Statistics, Unshackled Presses, and Torches of Knowledge," the age reveals itself as "one of boundless misery and sorrow."

> The deranged condition of our affairs is a universal topic among men at present; and the heavy miseries pressing, in their rudest shape, on the great dumb inarticulate class, and from this by sure law, spreading upwards, in a less palpable but not less certain and perhaps still more fatal shape on all classes to the very highest, are admitted everywhere to be great, increasing and now almost unendurable.[11]

Carlyle's polemics find their counterpart—as they show their influence—in fiction of the time. Yet there was at mid-century perhaps a different kind of borrowing from Carlyle. Just as in *Household Words* Dickens carefully balances bad tidings with good, so in *David Copperfield* he only touches on the social and political nightmares that preoccupy Carlyle. Written at the mid-point of Dickens's career, and providing a kind of hiatus between *Dombey and Son* and *Bleak House*, *David Copperfield* is a long, retrospective assessment in Carlyle's terms of "the hero as man-of-letters."

At a time when he was learning most from Carlyle, Dickens writes anything but an angry book. The same may be said of both Elizabeth Gaskell and William Thackeray, both of whom write not uncharacteristic but strongly pastoral novels. Mrs. Gaskell's *The Moorland Cottage*, coming after *Mary Barton* (1848), takes place in the Lake District and scarcely mentions the world of Manchester and mill owners and operatives. But Mrs. Gaskell will later return to the polemical art by which she is best remembered. And Dickens, if sanguine about the "summer-dawn," has not forgotten the awful equation between the sufferings of the poor and the wholesale contamination of society. Drawing on his own experiences as well as on Carlyle, he will soon begin (in 1851) his terrible anatomy of English law, English classes, and English public life.

Along with Dickens and Carlyle, Charles Kingsley, Joseph Kay, and Henry Mayhew discuss the other England, that of the downtrodden and dispossessed. Mayhew and his collaborators began in October 1849 their incomparable articles for the *Morning Chronicle* about the "London Labour and the London Poor."[12] As "Parson Lot," Kingsley drew from Mayhew to write "Cheap Clothes and Nasty," and he attempted in *Alton Locke* the exposure of a thoughtless capitalist society. Joseph Kay, brother of Kay-Shuttleworth, published his disturbing report, *The Social Conditions of the Working Classes*, which showed how exploited and uneducated the English poor were, even by comparison with small nations of Europe. Another polemic caused no stir at all in 1850. The "Communist Manifesto" of Marx and Engels made its first English appearance in *The Red Republican*, a new, left-wing paper. Marx, an exile, had settled in London in 1849, condemned to the squalid housing and humiliating poverty described by Mayhew and Kingsley.

Marx's assessment of "the condition of the working classes" was no more accurate, and certainly no more irate, than Mayhew's and Kingsley's. His prophecy—and this may explain his almost total isolation in London—presupposed a different world. Revolutionary visions that might have had some application in 1848 had little or none in 1850, and even in 1848, Marx would have seemed strange and possibly mad to most Englishmen. For if reviewers of *Latter-Day Pamphlets* were to find Carlyle offensively pessimistic and frightening, they were hardly ready for Marxist dialectics. This is as true of intellectuals as of ordinary men and women. "The English intelligentsia," writes Asa Briggs, "was neither rootless nor rebellious; at its centre, it was stable and assured, with enough property to buy leisure and independence."[13] Briggs clarifies the lack of rebelliousness, but he overstates the economic and emotional stability of contemporary writers. One intellectual—later to be known for his trenchant criticisms of

English culture—clearly worried about his leisure and independence, despite serving as secretary to the Whig statesman Lord Lansdowne and anticipating a career as Inspector of Schools. A member of the establishment though he was, Matthew Arnold could write, in "Memorial Verses," about "this iron time/Of doubts, disputes, distractions, fears."[14] His urbane, even dandyish manner contrasted so radically with the melancholy in his poems that close friends and members of his family were surprised by *The Strayed Reveller* (1849). The point is that Arnold, beneath his urbanity and in spite of his career, *was* somehow "rootless." His poems express that "ache of modernism," the disaffection, or—to use a mid-century term appropriated by Marxists—the *alienation* of many intellectuals, who remained nonetheless far from thoughts of revolution.

Arnold helps to illustrate that underlying doubts or melancholy in mid-century literature bear a peculiarly tangential relationship to social or political issues, to what Marx, like Benjamin Disraeli, conceived as the warring of "two nations." "This iron time" implies problems that may never be solved, problems of a society in which organic metaphors no longer obtain, where "democracy" raises a specter of conformity, uniformity, and a possible end to "civilization," and where an individual becomes an unwitting part of a social mechanism. John Henry Newman addresses himself to such questions in *Certain Difficulties*; so does Francis, his erudite brother, in *Phases of Faith*. From their antithetical viewpoints, these men come to an awareness of large historical processes, of real or potential threats to the values of culture and of faith (see chapter V). They typify a widespread preoccupation in mid-century writers, for embattled faith and the precariousness of certitudes are at least implicit subjects in many works of the time. T. S. Eliot speaks about the lack of "serenity," the tragic quality of Tennyson's *In Memoriam*,[15] and contemporary reviewers recognized this side of the poem, though they preferred to think of it as a noble hosannah of faith.

Arthur Clough, who considered *In Memoriam* magnificent, must have seen its somber side. His Faustian dialogue "Dipsychus" shares with Tennyson's and Arnold's lyric laments an account of religious and emotional tribulation. Even Browning, after success with more impersonal or "dramatic" poetry, returned to an apparently private vehicle in *Christmas-Eve and Easter-Day*. The voices in his strange companion poems, no less than the voice of the Duke of Ferrara, may be dramatic projections, but they record the poet's intimate struggles with questions of God, faith, and personal immortality—with what Tennyson aptly called "the way of a soul."

Tennyson spoke of *In Memoriam* not only as "the way of a soul" but also as "a kind of *Divina Commedia*, ending with happiness." "It is . . . the cry of the whole human race. . . . In the poem . . . private grief swells out into thought of, and hope for, the whole world."[16] Small wonder that Tennyson became Poet Laureate in 1850 at the instigation of Prince Albert, who was sponsoring his Great Exhibition for the benefit of the whole world. Like the broad English public, the prince saw in Tennyson a voice for the time. Did Tennyson, who struggled for answers and certitudes that were assumptions to Dante, invoke *The Divine Comedy* to move beyond the merely autobiographical or elegiac, to avoid what Carlyle called "self-consciousness"? In any case (and I raise the question in chapter III), we can speculate why, in the nineteenth century, Dante's long poetic journey appealed to English poets, who had no conception of Purgatory, only a metaphoric notion of Hell, and scarcely any hope of a multifoliate vision.

Tennyson, Clough, Browning, and Arnold typify a large proportion of mid-century writers who expressed themselves autobiographically. William Aytoun's coinage "Spasmodics," to describe poets like Alexander Smith, indicated the contempt with which certain critics dismissed self-indulgent writing—as well as the commonplace nature of that writing. And what is true in religious essays and in poetry is also true in a large number of novels. *David Copperfield* and *Pendennis* may be Dickens's and Thackeray's most personal novels, and *Copperfield* draws on what Dickens had in earlier years drafted as autobiography. Thackeray narrates *Pendennis* in a third-person style that develops from *Vanity Fair*, but Thackeray seems in this later novel to speak more intimately with his reader, as though sharing the experience of Pen's unfolding life; and Thackeray's next major novel, the historical *Henry Esmond*, takes an autobiographical guise.

Lesser novelists followed the example of the giants. Even *Alton Locke*, which grows out of the polemical novels of the forties, is told as autobiography; so, too, Francis Smedley's *Frank Fairlegh* and Eliot Warburton's costume novel of the Civil War, *Reginald Hastings*. George Borrow, each of whose books is fundamentally autobiographical, was at work in 1850 on *Lavengro* (1851), a novel that began as autobiography and became the characteristic mixture of self-praise and exuberance that makes up Borrow's fiction. To name an altogether different figure, Bulwer-Lytton, in 1849, published *The Caxtons*, a novel that reviewers rightly called eclectic. It hero-narrator, drawing parallels with Tristram Shandy, plays his own David Copperfield and proves himself both a self-made man and a gentleman.

As Bulwer would indicate, autobiographical forms do not imply a necessary indebtedness to Wordsworth. Yet some debt seems likely. Kingsley said that his soul "had been steeped from boyhood" in Wordsworth's poetry, from which Kingsley had learned how to "feel with nature" and to avoid "shallow and materialistic views."[17] In each of the novels I have mentioned the central characters learn a comparable lesson.

Whatever the reasons for the shift to autobiographical forms, there can be no question about their importance in the literature of mid-century England. Autobiography is not, of course, a nineteenth-century discovery; but the term *autobiography* barely anticipates the new century.[18] It served to identify a genre that multiplied by staggering proportions throughout the century and that had its effect on fiction, poetry, and nonfictional prose. The mere popularity of autobiography can be seen in an announcement of the relatively staid *Art-Journal*, which ran a series of biographical and autobiographical accounts of *artists* (another term that had come to have broad application): "In autobiography there is a charm which narrative in the third person does not possess."[19] The charm derived from the intimate record, but so might *truth*. Frequently quoted at the time was Sir Charles Lyell's remark that rocks and fossils reveal the earth's autobiography. To the seeing eye, as poets like Wordsworth no less than scientists like Lyell knew, ordinary objects assume extraordinary significance, offering new dimensions of awareness. This is Ruskin's point in his defense of Turner and the Pre-Raphaelites (see chapter IX). In several of his works Ruskin observes that the art of a people is its most revealing and worthy autobiography.[20] Kingsley says much the same thing in his lectures at the new institution for women, Queen's College: "The literature of every nation is," he says, "its autobiography." And for Kingsley the converse is equally true: "The history of each individual [is] more or less the history of the whole human race."[21] As I shall try to show, the autobiographical impulse and autobiographical forms of mid-century literature are related to new theories of perception (including the mechanical eye of photography), new theories of history, new literary idols, and new permutations of Romantic literary styles.

3

> Meanwhile, since it is the spiritual always that determines the material, this same man-of-letters hero must be regarded as our most important modern person.—Thomas Carlyle, *Heroes, Hero-Worship and the Heroic in History*[22]

In an age increasingly enamored of the captains of industry, as Carlyle himself called them, Carlyle's account of the hero as man-of-letters might have seemed as quaint as it was strident. But Carlyle reflected his times as much as he influenced them. His sense of the man-of-letters came to be widely shared, and we can see one of its manifestations in Dickens's and Thackeray's mid-century novels, both of which record the lives of aspiring writers. Carlyle's pronouncement about "our most important person" points to his own substantial position as man-of-letters and to the periodicals of the age, in which Carlyle and other writers found their main outlets.

It is, in fact, hard to overestimate the importance of periodical literature at mid-century.[23] True, some of the best magazines, like the *Contemporary* and *Fortnightly* reviews, had not been founded by 1850; the *Saturday Review* and the *Daily Telegraph* were still five years away (as was repeal of the newspaper tax). But the *Edinburgh* and *Quarterly* continued to flourish, if not quite with their old energy, and so did *Blackwood's*, the *Westminster* (soon to be edited by George Eliot), and the two powerful weeklies, the *Spectator* and the *Athenaeum*. The *Athenaeum*, that "mirror of Victorian culture," was bought by as many as twenty thousand readers a week.[24] Among the daily papers, of which London alone had over a hundred, the *Times* was the dean of respectable journalism and the *Morning Chronicle*, though in its final years, perhaps the most vigorous inquirer. Quarterlies, monthlies, fortnightlies, weeklies, dailies, magazines for women, magazines for political groups, for children, for religious sects, for the arts–dozens and dozens of publications came and went or lingered during the period. Eighteen forty-nine saw publication of the popular *Eliza Cook's Journal*, along with the *Journal of Design*, and, beginning its long history, *Notes and Queries*. Eighteen fifty added *The Germ* and *Household Words*, another *Journal* by Leigh Hunt (who published his *Autobiography* in this year), Kingsley's and Maurice's *Christian Socialist*, and George Lewes's *Leader*.

Together, such publications contained innumerable articles by legions of anonymous writers, the bulk of whom were never publicly known or have been, across the years, slowly forgotten. Yet, as Walter Houghton and his collaborators for the *Wellesley Index* have shown, many anonymous writers were not forgettable hacks: they included John Stuart Mill and George Eliot, Charles Kingsley and Coventry Patmore, George Lewes and W. E. Gladstone. Gladstone, by way of example, wrote a substantial review essay in 1850 on the poet Leopardi.

Gladstone did not make his living from his pen; other writers did.

Money as well as influence was to be had for such work. George Lewes, active as editor and journalist in 1850, recorded in his Receipts Book an income from writing of about £300.[25] But this was modest. "There are many men now," wrote J. W. Kaye (anonymously), "in London, Edinburgh, and other parts of the country, earning from £1000 to £3000 per annum by their literary labours." Thanks mainly to periodicals, literature had become a "profession." "Take it for all in all, with all its drawbacks, and all its abuses, it is a great, a noble, and delightful profession."[26] Kaye may have protested too much. Regardless, however, whether mid-century men of letters deserved the title of profession (and it has been denied them in our time as in their own), they enjoyed a higher standing than their forerunners earlier in the century, possibly because they included in their ranks the "mid-century clerisy," university dons and other non-journalists like Gladstone.[27] They were proud of their accomplishments. F. Knight Hunt, whose *The Fourth Estate* (1850) borrowed its title from Carlyle, praised periodical writers as the preservers of England's freedom. Again, there were doubters. Kaye's essay, which began as a review of Thackeray's *Pendennis*—notorious for its satire on literary men—was apology as much as description. But Thackeray himself, retracting some of his strictures in *Pendennis*, could write: "Putting the money out of the question, I believe that the social estimation of the man of letters is as good as it deserves to be, and as good as that of any other professional man." "The words in *Pendennis* are untenable, be hanged to them."[28]

If today we are inclined to think the satire in *Pendennis* entirely tenable and to accept (too hastily) Ruskin's and Arnold's impatience with the critical biases and puerilities of so many of the periodicals, Thackeray's vacillation points to mixed attitudes of the time. John Henry Newman offers a further instance. In "Christ upon the Waters," a sermon of 1850, Newman writes that Englishmen turn to magazines for intellectual sustenance as well as guidance and that the anonymous pontifical dribble of magazines actually determines English taste. Much like Arnold later on, Newman equates the freedom of the press with unbridled liberalism, or anarchy. On the other hand, Newman was to edit the *Rambler* (in 1859), and to give up the post under pressure and with regret. If he could not approve the influence of magazines, he was aware of their potential use.

Because of their influence, magazines are indispensable for an understanding of mid-nineteenth-century literature. I recur throughout the following chapters to reviews by men like George Lewes and David Masson and William Michael Rossetti not only because these are often shrewd assessments but also because they tell us a good deal about the interrelationships of mid-century writers and about the climate in which they wrote. For reasons, however, of space and convenience, I limit my discussion of periodicals as such to one chapter and—while glancing for contrast at Dickens's *Household Words* and George Harney's *Red Republican*—to only one publication: the Pre-Raphaelite *Germ*.

The Pre-Raphaelites founded their Brotherhood in 1848, the year of European revolutions, and their intent was a revolution in taste, just as Harney's was a revolution in fact. In 1850 the Pre-Raphaelites published four numbers of *The Germ*, the title itself asserting a metaphor of growth as well as an allegiance to "nature." Ruskin admired the Pre-Raphaelites, arguing that, with Turner excepted, they were the only artists who offered welcome alternatives to the bad drawing and false colors of the Royal Academy. Although people disagreed about the virtues of the Pre-Raphaelites, the intent of the group coincided with the lifelong intent of Wordsworth and Ruskin, and with the intent of others who categorically disapproved of Rossetti, Hunt, and Millais. The respect for nature affected even the planners of the Great Exhibition, who accepted the greenhouse design of Paxton and preserved the great elms of Hyde Park in their new glass palace.

Dickens's magazine, enormously successful throughout the 1850s, addressed itself to a broad public, so much so that Dickens constantly worried, revising and tampering to insure its appeal. Dickens contributed articles on the slaughter yards, on London's waterworks, on the post office, on policemen, and on the Rookeries, those warrens of the underworld, where filth, crime, and disease offended the sensibilities of well-heeled Londoners.[29] If *The Germ* was a kind of artists' manifesto, aspiring to a review, *Household Words* was a magazine for ordinary men and women, cutting across barriers of religion and to some extent of class.

4

> What we call literature, and what we teach, is what the middle class—and not the working class—produced. Our definition of literature and our canons of taste are class bound.—Martha Vicinus, *The Industrial Muse*[30]

To think of *The Germ* and *Household Words* in relation to the bulk of mid-century periodicals is to see the impossibility of an exhaustive account of the literature available to an Englishman living in 1850, let alone the impossibility of mentioning all the literature being written. In only its second year of operation (1849), the new W. H. Smith bookstall at Paddington Station offered one thousand titles, and those mainly novels, to railway travelers.[31] Even the most avid reader of the time could have known but a part of the fiction, poetry, translations, books from America, novels from France, books of exploration and travel, classical editions, scientific or historical treatises, critical studies, reprints, or new editions. If books did not appear in floods as they did in the late nineteenth century, they came fast enough. Moreover, they came in a variety of forms for a variety of audiences.

In a study she properly describes as ground-breaking, Martha Vicinus calls attention to "the Industrial Muse," the literature of working-class people, which finds no place in middle-class studies of middle-class literature. While I agree with Professor Vicinus about the importance of working-class entertainments, from broadsides to music hall (which was reaching its height at mid-century), I don't agree that nineteenth-century books that have remained popular have been preserved by academies, which have, in effect, established a canon. Enthusiasm of a wide public has brought writers like Dickens into the academy—just as lack of enthusiasm has kept others, middle- and working-class, among the unremembered. And we may delude ourselves about some of the remembered. Where is the public that still reads Arnold, Browning, even Tennyson? How many now read Carlyle and Ruskin? In any meaningful sense, is there a canon? Despite the appreciation of scholars, and quite apart from questions of class, most Victorian writers are probably more written about than read.

It remains true that various sorts of literature for the poor flourished at mid-century. My reasons for a largely middle-class focus have something to do with preference, more to do with the limits of space and with the simple fact that the bulk of mid-century literature came from the Philistines. But in fact a number of working-class writers—the not-so-mute inglorious Miltons—make at least a scattered appearance in *Victorian Noon.* In addition to George Harney and his communistic *Red Republican,* I touch on Thomas Cooper, "the Cockney Poet," and his appeal for a working-class literature, on Thomas Prest, purveyor of cheap melodramas, who died poor after publishing over sixty works in the 1840s alone. My interest in Prest centers on *The String of Pearls,* because this grotesque bestseller bears on melodramatic tendencies in other works of fiction. Similarly, I am interested in Ebeneezer Elliott ("The Corn-Law Rhymer," who died in 1850 and received much attention), less as a working-class poet than as a lecturer who asserted "The Principle of Self-

Communion in Poetry" and therefore allied himself with major poetic movements of the day.

Elliott might remind us that 1850 saw the introduction of the first Public Library Act—at the time a wholly symbolic gesture. Efforts were being made to introduce reading materials into working-class lives, in years when older attempts, that of the Society for the Diffusion of Useful Knowledge among them, were failing. Louis James has described how reading habits and reading materials "for the working man" changed dramatically from 1830 to 1850.[32] During the years when Smith's railway stalls and Mudie's Circulating Library became established middle-class institutions, the penny dreadful tended to give way to the kind of reprints offered (for the first time in the 1840s) by publishers like George Routledge and Charles Knight, who catered to readers hungry for books in a society now about half literate.[33] But entire studies could be written about Charles Knight and his work in publishing for the poor; or about the inexpensive reprints made available by Routledge and other pioneers in the long tradition "from Aldine to Everyman";[34] or about the implications of Smith's bookstalls or Mudie's Library for Victorian reading tastes. These topics are simply beyond my scope.

Another significant omission is the drama, which was, in spite of popular mid-century theaters, far less vigorous than other genres. Except for Douglas Jerrold (whose *The Catspaw* appeared in 1850), few mid-century playwrights are remembered at all. And few were acknowledged then. A writer for *Bentley's Miscellany*, describing "the Stage as it is in 1850," concluded that the theater had neither writers nor managers of consequence and that, with the retirement of Macready (which came in 1851), "we shall be in utter darkness."[35] This and any number of comparable discussions illustrate the low estimate of the drama, along with the time-worn prejudice against the theater as connected with actors and audiences of dubious morality. Scott had expressed such opinions earlier in the century. Thackeray plays on the sentiment in his treatment of theaters and of "the Fotheringay" in *Pendennis.*

George Lewes approached the "decline of the drama" from a different perspective. Agreeing about the deplorable state of modern drama, Lewes argued that playwrights were at fault. Instead of imitating seventeenth-century plays, modern dramatists must "create a new form." "The escape into the Old Drama was a brilliant fallacy: it was the Young Englandism of Art: disgusted with the Present, yet without faith in the Future." For Lewes, who published his own Jacobean *The Noble Heart* in 1850—

a melodramatic tragedy, set in Spain—the drama should use a modern idiom "to move the general heart of men."

If literature is "the reflex of the age," for Lewes "drama [is] a reflex of our life."[36] And for some mid-century writers this was in part the case. The *Bentley's* writer mentions the "fashionable prestige" of private theatricals, which interested, for example, Queen Victoria and Bulwer-Lytton. Charles Dickens, always attracted by the stage, spent a great deal of energy while editing *Household Words* and finishing *David Copperfield*, planning, directing, and acting in a variety of plays. But plays, for Dickens or for any of his contemporaries, are not the remembered works. This is not to dismiss drama. It is to say that, public or private, the drama is a field in itself, involving theater history, architecture, acting styles, accounts of managers, and so on.[37]

The limited comments on working-class literature, publishing history, and the drama may help to clarify my purpose, which is anything but an exhaustive survey. As one reader's account of mid-nineteenth-century literature, *Victorian Noon* is a compromise between description of the available literature and what I see as its lasting qualities. Again, my intent is the sketching of relationships, the assessment of the great and remembered in terms of the climate in which they wrote.

One further point is appropriate here. Implicitly, and for good reason, most readers respond to books in the way E. M. Forster advocates in *Aspects of the Novel*. Forster imagines the world's great novelists divorced from history and sitting in the same timeless room, as though their own contemporaries. To the extent that a book is worth reading, it will establish its world, drawing us away from the local or temporal—and from what Keats called the "irritable reaching after fact and reason." Not to read with abandon is to invite both a failure of imagination and a loss of enjoyment. But once we have read, our interests change. We may want to think of a poem or a novel in any number of different ways, ways that are related to but also distinct from the initial reading. For this study I prefer to imagine, not the timeless and ordered reading room, but the variety, richness, and immediacy of real relationships and crowds of books. Perhaps we can immerse ourselves in a collective literature as well as in individual works.

II

Poetics

The Hero as Poet

1

> Poetry with them [the "Lake Poets"] is a religion; they, like the bards of the heroic age, are not artists only, but priests and hierophants. In Wordsworth, poetry, which is but another name for the reverent study of nature, embraces all knowledge, all sanctity, all truth.—Thomas Shaw, *Outlines of English Literature* (1849)[1]

In March 1850, George Lewes and Thornton Hunt began to edit a new periodical they had helped to found. The *Leader* was a liberal, even radical weekly, an example of some of the best and most vigorous mid-century journalism, which offered full reviews of cultural events and recent publications. In an early number of the *Leader*, an anonymous reviewer, but probably Lewes himself, speculated about the reputation of William Bowles, the minor poet whom we remember because of Coleridge's early admiration. Bowles not only outlived Coleridge, he died in the same year as Wordsworth, well into the reign of Victoria. The reviewer says that Bowles, in a sense, died at an inappropriate time. Had he died thirty years before, he would have enjoyed a better leave-taking, with high-sounding obituaries and full honors. In 1850 he died almost unnoticed. "What does this mean? It means that the general intelligence of the nation is such that no man of ordinary thews and sinews can be mistaken for a hero; the democracy of literature, like the democracy of Society, though it in nowise prevents Great Men, renders the 'Throne and the Sceptre' less easy of attainment."[2]

If Lewes did write the Bowles obituary, he was not at his best. The pomp of "thews and sinews" implies the kind of critical patronage that Lewes elsewhere deplored, and the glib comparison with an earlier literary climate does not in itself make much sense. Of course Bowles might have died a literary hero thirty years before—at the time, roughly, of Keats's death—but only because he would then have been better remembered. And it is unlikely that reputations came more easily in earlier decades of the century when Byron made his ironic call for a hero, though "every year and month sends forth a new one." Literary reputations may have been easily made, but no more easily than at mid-century, when Martin Tupper won enormous popularity for his *Proverbial Philosophy* (1842), a work that was to sell, worldwide, millions of copies.

But if this was not the most thoughtful article of a very competent critic, it remains a piece of characteristic writing, a clue to shared assumptions of the time. If we ask what Lewes is saying about poets and the climate for poetry, we can posit these answers: Lewes assumes, for example, that there *is* a literary climate, a national condition supportive of or adverse to the writing of poetry. He assumes a potential opposition between the poet and society—an opposition that may force a poet into the role of hero. He thinks of literary heroism in terms both of stature and of fame, of intrinsic quality and public recognition. He accepts the inevitability of the democratizing of society, and he associates democracy directly with literature. Whether he means by "the democracy of literature" simply the increased sophistication of large numbers of readers, or the greater accessibility of literature (through new mediums of duplication and through increased numbers of publications), or whether he means that writers have made themselves more available to wider audiences is unclear. He may be equating political liberty with the common assumption of the poet's freedom from generic or thematic restraint, implying that the poet, like the ordinary citizen, has his right to speak out. Whatever his specific intent, Lewes touches on several issues that concerned mid-century critics. And like so many of his contemporaries, he is contrasting his age with Regency England, asking what has happened in the intervening years, what distinguishes his age from the age of Wordsworth or Byron. I want to suggest in this chapter why Lewes might argue along the lines he does and to speculate about the assumptions and the terms of literary debate at mid-century. The central question of literary heroism, or the poet-as-hero, can best be addressed by stepping back the thirty years that Lewes uses for his contrast.

Almost exactly thirty years earlier, T. L. Peacock had written his ironic "Four Ages of Poetry," in which Wordsworth, Coleridge, Scott, Byron, and their contemporaries come in for a verbal drubbing. These poets have projected themselves into a kind of unaware bathos; they are self-created heroes, poets who use their verse for confessional purposes, misunderstanding both the nature of poetry and their own personal limitations. According to Peacock, "A poet in our times is a semi-barbarian in a civilized community. He lives in days that are past. . . . The march of his intellect is like that of a crab, backward. The brighter the light diffused around him by the progress of reason, the thicker is the darkness of antiquated barbarism, in which he buries himself."[3] Peacock argues, not so much that poetry is defunct (although that is a possibility), but rather that its practitioners are bringing it to dotage. Like Byron, whose satire in *English Bards* and *Don Juan* runs along similar lines, Peacock recognizes that Wordsworth's poetry is the dominant literary force of the time, and he deplores what he sees as a self-congratulatory earnestness, an ignorance of healthy classical or neoclassical models, and an escape into a childish world. Among the immature modern poets, however, Peacock includes Byron, who is trivial and self-indulgent.

The issues lurking in Peacock's essay went further than impatience with false heroes and self-important poetasters. When Shelley received a copy of "The Four Ages," he sensed immediately that Peacock's criticism involved fundamental questions about the nature of poetry, its intrinsic qualities, its relation to society, its uses and possibilities. Shelley's "Defense of Poetry" is a rebuttal of Peacock's overt arguments, but it also isolates Peacock as an apologist for new and troubling attacks on poets and poetry. For Shelley, Peacock expresses an essentially utilitarian position. The "march of intellect" reduces poetry to the status of a child's toy, so that it becomes no more important to society than—to use Bentham's notorious comparison—the game of push-pin. Shelley's defense is probably the finest, most eloquent apology for poetry in modern times, but it also illustrates the very claims for poets that Peacock and Byron had denied. Shelley elevates the poet to a role of eternal utility, for the poet is, above all men, seer, prophet, bringer of joy, source of light. No less than for Kant and Coleridge, Shelley's poet knows an ultimate reason that makes Peacock's seem the mere "gew-gaw." If in private Shelley could agree with Peacock's estimate of some of his contemporaries, and if Peacock could himself write poems about the magic of Thessaly or the realms of Pan, the public rhetoric of the two friends was quite absolute. And their basic positions were to represent poles of critical opinion for years to come.

By mid-century the debate illustrated by Peacock and Shelley had not so much progressed as widened and intensified. Review essays of the time are characterized by gestures toward large perspectives and by extreme statements of position. Even in a limited review, the intent often points toward a hoped-for aesthetic, a means of dealing with critical chaos. This may explain the increased appeals to virtues like "seriousness" and "morality," which can imply the emotional stature of a poet and can carry over to the poet's effect on his audience, but which, even for the most sophisticated writer, raise almost insuperable barriers to the text at hand. Expressive theories of literature, which are by mid-century the dominant theories, do not, in fact, fit comfortably with theories of social utility, and early Victorian critics struggle with apparently irreconcilable premises.

Poe's "Poetic Principle" (appearing in America in 1850) argues the impossibility of a long poem, given the intrinsically lyric nature of poetry, and Poe's theories, drawn from Wordsworth and Coleridge, look forward both to the cryptic qualities of the French symbolists and to the fragmentary, nondiscursive verse of Eliot's *Waste Land.* And as Poe leaned in one direction, John Keble leaned in another. Keble is no less an exponent of expressive theories, but Keble's influential Oxford lectures (in the 1830s) presuppose the inadequacy of short works for revealing the fullness of the individual. Anticipating Freud's understanding of literary composition, Keble sees literature as disguised autobiography, which is necessarily comprehensive if it serves its cathartic function.[4] Poe, then, demands what is quintessentially lyric; Keble finds lyric poetry inadequate. Both reflect major directions in Victorian poetry, which experimented with lyric modes and developed new forms of verse fiction.

Keble expresses other late Romantic tendencies. Honoring Wordsworth, he also thinks of Wordsworth as a religious spokesman, specifically a High Church spokesman, whose poetry serves religious ends. While mid-century Englishmen looked back to Wordsworth for a variety of purposes, Keble's sense of a personal tradition was well grounded. In the *Essay* of 1815, Wordsworth had written:

> The concerns of religion refer to indefinite objects, and are too weighty for the mind to support them without relieving itself by resting a great part of the burthen upon words and symbols. The commerce between Man and his Maker cannot be carried on but by a process where much is represented in little, and the Infinite Being accommodates himself to a finite capacity. In all this may be perceived the affinity between religion and poetry.[5]

If at mid-century the directions of religious poetry were many—one thinks of Browning, Tennyson, Arthur Clough—the assumption that poetry could or should deal with religious questions was widespread.

Wordsworth's feeling that spiritual aspiration must be "represented in little" points to a further dilemma for his theoretical followers. The problem of the matter-of-fact or the trivial as opposed to the significant and the eternal raised puzzling questions. I shall suggest in later chapters how the association of the novel with external things made it difficult for readers to respect "realistic" tendencies in verse, while at the same time it hindered useful comparisons between fiction and poetry. As light entertainment, fiction might escape the responsibilities assumed for literature; poetry could not. For poetry was understood as charged language, a kind of spiritual shorthand with social effect.

The sense of responsibility for poetry developed at the same time as new historical inquiries into the English language and new historical estimates of literature—at the same time, that is, as the growth of an implicit cultural relativism. The poet and critic Aubrey De Vere, in an 1850 review of Walter Savage Landor, typically speaks of his subject in relation to changing theories of nature, and De Vere looks back in his survey to the poetry of the Greeks, to eighteenth-century English writers, and to Landor's own generation. He ascribes Landor's lack of popularity to inadequate expectations on the part of his readers: Landor is, essentially, a classical poet in democratic and romantic times.[6] Although De Vere is a representative student of the literature of his age, assuming certain expressive qualities in poetry and seeing the poetry as a product of evolution, he also shares apprehensions about the state of the art. Like Dickens and so many others, he thinks of himself living in a utilitarian age, and he finds the age hostile to imagination. De Vere writes twenty-five years after the founding of the *Westminster Review*, which set out, under the auspices of the Mills and John Bowring, to offer a political alternative to the established quarterlies. But just as the *Quarterly Review* silently judged fiction—by seldom noticing its existence—so the *Westminster* reflected a threat to poetry. By mid-century, the overt hostility to poetry by men like Bowring had waned appreciably, but *Westminster* writers did continue to assume that poetry must move with the times, that it was, along with social institutions, subject to growth and decay. Such assumptions led, often enough, to notions about literary determinism; more importantly, they led to fears for the existence of literature itself.

When Alba Warren, in his survey of early Victorian literary theory, speaks of critics recapitulating diverse ideas "from Plato to Shelley," he suggests some of the variety and range of literary interests.[7] But the phrase *from Plato to Shelley* indicates a central quality of the criticism that Warren more or less ignores. For mid-century England still experiences a crisis in criticism generated by expressive theories of literature and by the circumstances in which they developed. At least one reason for the interest in Plato and Shelley (Bacon, because of his view of imagination, was a common third) is the recurrent problem of defending imaginative literature; and the problem remains acute for many mid-century commentators. George Lewes's concern with literary heroism is drawn from Carlyle, though it echoes Shelley. Like De Vere, Lewes is asking about the formal and generic aspects of literature, but also about its reason for being. How do we justify it? What are its purposes? Of what use is a poet?

To illustrate the importance of literary apology, two writers, both historians and part-time critics, serve especially well. By mid-century neither Thomas Babington Macaulay nor Thomas Carlyle was writing much about literature, but the influence of both was still felt. These men extend, at times to the point of unwitting parody, the context of literary debate introduced by Shelley and Peacock, and they seem to set the terms of discussion used by Lewes in his obituary of William Bowles. Both Macaulay and Carlyle illustrate how intimately views about poetry reflect assumptions about the individual and his role in a changing society. Because they are historians, sharing certain premises while apparently at odds about most issues, they show why technical considerations of literature became for mid-century writers subordinate to questions of science and progress and to the related matters of "civilization" and "culture." For both men, historical change involves a threat to imaginative literature.

2

> Poetry produces an illusion on the eye of the mind, as a magic lantern produces an illusion on the eye of the body. And, as the magic lantern acts best in a dark room, poetry effects its purpose most completely in a dark age.—T. B. Macaulay, "Milton"[8]

Macaulay's essay on "Milton" (1825) appeared, like most of Macaulay's influential essays, in the *Edinburgh Review*. At once lucid, combative, and overstated, it is polemical with a commercial purpose. "Periodical work like ours . . . , whose whole life is month or two, may, I think, be allowed to be sometimes even viciously florid."[9] The life of Macaulay's *Edinburgh* essays turned out to be far more than a month or two, but his style—achieved, in John Stuart Mill's estimate, at the expense of truth—remained, as Macaulay put it, "bold" and "dashing." In "Milton," as in the later essays on Herodotus, Machiavelli, Dryden, and Macaulay's contemporary Robert Montgomery, Macaulay speculates about the historical development of literature. Sometimes covertly, sometimes baldly, he urges his own kind of historical writing as the proper literature for his age, while finding little hope for poetry. Like Peacock, Macaulay loved older poetry and wrote verse himself. His theories of literature may have led him to set the *Lays of Ancient Rome* in what he considered a heroic age and to employ a ballad measure to suggest a less "philosophical" poetry.

Echoing Peacock, Macaulay says: "We think that, as civilisation advances, poetry almost necessarily declines" (153). Whereas even utilitarian critics had been able to assume that poetry could progress with civilization, Macaulay tacitly agrees with Bentham in equating poetry with lies. This is in fact the English empirical tradition against which Coleridge and Shelley had reacted: a distrust of rhetoric as deceit and ornament, and of poetry as rhetoric. We can find it in Sprat, Locke, and their followers, and it is summed up in Bentham's remark that "between poetry and truth there . . . must be a natural opposition."[10] Macaulay and Peacock both assume that the "natural opposition" is aggravated by the "progress," the advancement of society. Macaulay says categorically that there is an inverse relationship between the development of poetry and the development of accurate and scientific truth: "Language, the machine of the poet, is best fitted for his purpose in its rudest state. Nations, like individuals, first perceive, and then abstract. They advance from particular images to general terms. Hence the vocabulary of an enlightened society is philosophical, that of a half-civilised people is poetical" (153).

This argument, or versions of the argument, indicated to many writers that poetry was in trouble. For if *progress* implies improvement as well as change; if civilization advances and knowledge grows, then science becomes increasingly the modern means to understanding, and the functions of poetry become suspect. "We have seen on our own time," Macaulay writes, "great talents, intense labour, and long meditation, employed in this struggle against the spirit of the age, and employed, we will not say absolutely in vain, but with dubious success and feeble applause" (156). He seems here to turn around defenses like Wordsworth's that fame must wait for the great talent. Not only will the poet not create the taste by which he is to be enjoyed, his whole creative endeavor may be in vain. And why? Because poetry itself is at odds with "the spirit of the age." Macaulay speaks—is it inadvertently?—of language as the poet's "machine."[11] Evidently it is a machine as appropriate for modern civilization as the hand-loom is for the Manchester weaving shed.

No doubt the "mechanical fallacy" of Macaulay's argument would have been easy enough to rebut. An order of words is not an instrument of production; art has its own laws of development. A young painter, John Orchard, wrote this for *The Germ*: "The fine arts, poetry, painting, sculpture, music, and architecture, as thought, or idea, Athene-like, are complete, finished revelations of wisdom at once. Not so the mechanical arts and sciences: they are arts of growth. . . . On all sides they are the exact opposites of each other."[12] Unfortunately, this line of argument presents difficulties of its own.

The opposition of the mechanical and organic had led John Stuart Mill, for example, to useful but inadequate conclusions. Mill's seminal essays on Bentham and Coleridge (1838, 1840) isolate radical intellectual tendencies, which Mill uses to characterize his age and which we know (from the *Autobiography*) represent a temperamental split within Mill himself.

> No two thinkers can be more entirely at variance [he says of hypothetical followers of Bentham and Coleridge] than the two we have supposed—the worshippers of Civilization [progress] and of Independence, of the present and the remote past. Yet all that is positive in the opinions of either of them is true; and we shall see how easy it would be to choose one's path, if either half of the truth were the whole of it, and how great may be the difficulty of framing . . . a set of practical maxims which combine both.[13]

Here, as in the *Autobiography*, Mill implies the need for a synthetic approach that fuses the thesis and antithesis represented by the two men he admired so much. Yet his synthesis seems more a compromise. Mill's whole attempt is to honor and combine the truth of opposing values. He sees his own life as a movement from emotional starvation toward the cultivation of feelings. Like Orchard and so many writers who followed him, he thinks of himself defending the arts while honoring what he calls "civilization." One might, however, argue that Mill's wholly expressive theory of art separates art from other mental activities and in effect reduces it. He has the variant truths within him, just as he acknowledges them in his society, and, profoundly as he learns the truths of civilization and independence, he articulates rather than solves the problems he faces. In the recorded "Crisis" in the *Autobiography*, Mill recognizes his need for literature; yet for purely therapeutic results, the undistinguished Marmontel serves just as well as Wordsworth and Coleridge. Does Mill after all draw from the Romantic verse he admires any new way of organizing his experience or addressing social problems? Whether or not we accept Carlyle's feeling that the *Autobiography* tells the story of a steam engine, we may want to acknowledge that the retrospective Mill still *thinks* as he was trained to think, remaining "nearer to Bentham than to Coleridge."[14] In poetry he honors a necessary "culture of the feelings," but also a separate way of understanding. Such a line of defense could be construed as admission of defeat, another concession to "the spirit of the age."

Often enough, if writers rejected the historical determinism adumbrated by Macaulay, they subscribed to some other historical arguments and saw the influence of science and industry in no less disheartening ways. Assertions that "Pan is dead" or that "there are no Naiads in the Regent's Canal" are common from early in the century, but the lament seems especially plaintive by mid-century, even though great amounts of poetry were being published and read. Matthew Arnold, already espousing in private the classicism that was to become public in the 1853 preface to his *Poems*, brushed aside Macaulay as a second-rate mind. But Arnold's sense of historical development led him, if not to assert the diminished function of poetry, then to feel that the spirit of the age was hostile to poetry. In an 1849 letter to Arthur Clough, whom he unbraided for a preoccupation with issues, with the *Zeitgeist*, he wrote: "Reflect too . . . how deeply *unpoetical* the age and all one's surroundings are. Not unprofound, not ungrand, not unmoving:—but *unpoetical.*"[15] Arnold's letter is remembered and sometimes cited as a lonely cry of dissent. In fact, the notion that the age was "unpoetical" was as common as that of the necessary superannuation of poetry by science. In the William Bowles obituary, George Lewes speaks of the unpoetical lament as a cliché. He could not have read Arnold's private letter, but he has heard the sentiment often enough: "Poets who feel themselves equal, if not superior [to earlier writers], and disgusted at receiving no ovations themselves, declare the age is unpoetical."[16] If we ignore the possibility that Arnold, like the poets Lewes mocks, might have been apprehensive about his reputation in the year he published *The Strayed Reveller*, we have his overwhelming conviction that the age is inimical to poetry against Lewes's assertions that poetic success merely comes harder in more enlightened times. Thus, Lewes has in a sense accepted Macaulay's assumption about social progress while rejecting the common corollary about poetic decline; Arnold is skeptical about progress, but he admits historical influence, just as he shares some of Macaulay's strictures about the literature of his age.

Macaulay's appallingly absolute categories involve questions about literature and science and art and society that have preoccupied critics from Coleridge to Eliot—with Arnold standing squarely between. Certainly by mid-century his arguments seemed to lurk in most critical discussions. As John Orchard's dialogue indicates, discussions *of* art usually involved some sort of apology *for* art. Poetry remained on the defensive. And yet, direct attacks on poetry were anything but common. If the foremost Utilitarian, John Stuart Mill, could think of poetry as soliloquy and admit the healing effects of Wordsworth and Coleridge, where were the announced enemies of poetry? Did poetry no longer warrant a direct assault? Had it come to assume an accepted but diminished role? In his later claim for the immense future of poetry, Arnold answered these questions in one way. Macaulay answered them in another.

One of Macaulay's charges (anticipated by Peacock) was to become a recurrent theme in the discussion of Romantic literature. It may have reached its pitch in Irving Babbitt's notorious denunciations in *Rousseau and Romanticism* (1919). Macaulay ostensibly uses the theory about the advance of civilization to urge Milton's greatness, since Milton has accomplished his work against the tide of history. The theory leads Macaulay to an extreme and devastating conclusion beyond the needs of the argument. "Perhaps no person can be a poet, or can even enjoy poetry, without a certain unsoundness of mind" (154). While this is the traditional Platonic charge about the madness of poets and the ill-effects of poetry on its listeners, it receives in Macaulay a characteristically nineteenth-century extension: "He who, in an enlightened and literary society, aspires to be a great poet must first become a little child" (156).

Macaulay seems to take as inevitable the preoccupation with childhood, whether the child as muse in Blake, or the child as father to the man in Wordsworth, because he sees the measure of literature in his century in its reversion from mature thought. Appropriately, he was to speak of *The Prelude* (in 1850) as so much "twaddle" and dismissed *David Copperfield* as self-indulgence.[17] But whatever his tastes, Macaulay did of course recognize a profound current in the literature of his age. This was not only the century of writers like Wordsworth and Dickens, whose works for adults extol the virtues of childhood; it was also the century that spawned vast industries of children's literature, including fairy tales, "nonsense" verse, stories of "wonderland," moral exempla, children's hymns, and children's periodicals. However diverse the social or philosophical or commercial reasons for the growth of children's literature, it had as one impetus the self-scrutiny and preoccupation with childhood that Macaulay objects to in the poetry of his age. If post-Wordsworthians would accept the re-creation of one's childhood as a search for understanding, Macaulay sees it as infantilism: not necessarily bad (witness Milton) but certainly regressive and anti-intellectual. He speaks of the modern poet taking "to pieces the whole web of his mind" (156) in what amount to an imaginative leap backward in time.

In Macaulay's judgment is reflected a widespread tendency to think of nineteenth-century poetry as immature. It lies in Goethe's remark that Byron became a child whenever he thought; it recurs in Matthew Arnold, who finds fault with Romantic writers for their intellectual immaturity; later it receives polemical force in T. E. Hulme, Ezra Pound, and T. S. Eliot, as well as in Babbitt. Eliot's "dissociation of sensibility" is, after the manner of Macaulay, a historical theory to explain the character of modern verse, and Eliot argues from on high the mental limitations of poets writing since the seventeenth century. His concern with a poet's maturity and his conviction as to the failings of nineteenth-century poets, is a defense of the classically minded, the adult poet (like Vergil), who can write without becoming a child.

Whether critics at mid-century remembered Macaulay's essay on Milton or whether they knew him better as the author of the early volumes of the *History of England* (1848), they were certainly familiar with his arguments. Indeed Macaulay was a popular writer. In a survey of modern literary figures, George Gilfillan called him (in 1850) one of the two most popular writers of the time, his rival being Dickens.[18] But apart from the fact that history was appreciated as a branch of literature and that publishers' lists usually carried diverse historical studies, Macaulay owed some of his popularity to his self-consciously broad appeal. Just as he wanted the *Edinburgh* to reach a large audience—with whatever "bold" and "dashing" means—so he envisaged his history as a work for vast numbers of people. Macaulay was a popularizer, both reflecting and influencing his readers, and his theories of literature, like his theories of history, politics, society, were very much in the air.

The kind of historical scheme that Macaulay outlined in "Milton" had become fairly common. English writers like Lewes and Harriet Martineau were already advocating the theories of Auguste Comte, whose positivistic philosophy conceived of a progression from *theological* to *metaphysical* to *positivistic* or *scientific* times; and Comte's own scheme, whether or not indebted to Giambattista Vico, emerged in an era of growing interest in Vico's writings. The Rugby historian Thomas Arnold was a proponent of Vico's theories, which he passed on to Matthew Arnold, but which did not, either for himself or for his son, lead to the optimistic conclusions arrived at by Vico himself.[19] Some of Matthew Arnold's own worries about the future of poetry may have come from Vico's assumption that poetry had outlived its historical function.

Unlike Vico, Comte and his English followers argued that poetry shared it and benefited from the progress of society, because its strengths and its uses could be more clearly seen. Surprisingly, this was also an early view of Karl Marx. Though still unknown in England, Marx was already adapting the Hegelian dialectic (and perhaps Hegel's speculations about the development of art) toward a materialistic interpretation of society. Marx struggled with the question of the role of art in a world he saw determined by material forces. At one time he felt that great art might be exempted from historical necessity; later—perhaps for clarity or consistency—he argued that art, too, must be determined by material causality. It could have no independent life.[20]

Herbert Spencer, one of the pioneers of sociology, and a man who was shortly to have enormous popularity in both England and America, shared presuppositions of both Comte and Marx. He discovered later that the phrase used for the title of his first book, *Social Statics* (1850), had been anticipated by Comte, and like Comte he wanted what he called "a system of social and political morality" (the subtitle of *Social Statics*), or "a kind of Natural History ethics."[21] Spencer envisaged the ultimate perfectibility of man, the final "adaptation of human nature to the social state." Like Marx, he anticipated the withering away of the political state, which would become useless. Spencer's philosophy, while it insists on historical progress, argues a radical individualism (hence its attraction to men like Andrew Carnegie), and *Social Statics* introduced the phrase that we have come to associate with Darwin, "survival of the fittest." Following Mill as well as Comte, Spencer conceived of a special role for art, as the cultivator of feeling. He was later to scoff at Arnold's pedagogic notion of poetry as "a criticism of life." But if more generous than Macaulay and Marx, Spencer still seems to think of art as an awkward category, something to be disposed of when other problems are solved. He may be an apologist, but he leaves to literature a diminished place.

3

> Sincerity, I think, is better than grace.—Carlyle, *Heroes, Hero-Worship, and the Heroic in History*[22]

It is against collectivist and materialistic views of history that we have to understand both the continuation of Romantic theories of art and Carlyle as their major interpreter. By 1850 Harriet Martineau (in the *History of the Thirty Years' Peace*) can speak of Carlyle as perhaps the most influential thinker of the time.[23] Critics are full of Carlyle. His interests are their interests, his terms their terms, even when they deplore his intemperance or complain about *Latter-Day Pamphlets*, in which the man-of-letters serves as doomsday prophet.

If Macaulay is a lover of poetry who finds poetry inappropriate for his age, Carlyle is an apologist for poetry whose aesthetic interests are minimal. Already by 1830, Carlyle was asking himself whether he truly liked poetry and confessing: "I sometimes fancy almost, not."[24] Over the years he addressed himself less and less to poetry as such (he never cared for the visual arts, in which "meaning" was of secondary importance), and he clearly drew from Schiller, Fichte, and his other German sources only a part of their aesthetic thinking. What interested Carlyle was the spiritual impetus behind poetry, its power to symbolize or mythologize, which derived from the soul of the poet. "As the importance of emotion is enhanced [writes G. S. R. Kitson-Clark], so necessarily is the importance of the human being who entertains the emotion. If feeling is to be the test, then the history of the man who feels is peculiarly interesting and significant, and so is the moment at which he experiences the emotion at its strongest."[25] Kitson-Clark is describing in this passage the continuity of "The Romantic Element" in England through 1850. And about the inheritance of Wordsworth, Coleridge, Shelley, and Keats, he is quite right. Although rival theories arose to counter "subjective" literature (as my following chapters suggest), critics as well as poets seem convinced that poetry is a form of *self-communion*, that its true subject, in George Lewes's words, is the history of "the Human Soul."[26] The problem for so many writers, however, was their acceptance of such assumptions about art at a time when theories of history seemed to militate against art, or at least against its importance and social purpose. This was perhaps the fundamental issue in Carlyle's aesthetics.

With all his reservations about poetry and his inadequate appreciation of poetry, Carlyle nevertheless emerges as its most vigorous spokesman. Beginning in the 1820s, his defenses of poetry culminated in "The Hero as Poet" (1840) and "The Hero as Man of Letters" (1840), which became part of *Heroes, Hero-Worship, and the Heroic in History* (1841). Carlyle offered his contemporaries an apology for the poet as spiritual liberator in a world of materialists. "Have we not heard," he writes, apparently in rebuttal of Macaulay, "have we not heard gifted men complaining that poetry had passed away without return; that creative imagination consorted not with vigor of intellect, and that in the cold light of science there was no longer room for faith in things unseen?"[27]

At odds with Macaulay though he is, Carlyle comes closer than his rhetoric suggests. Like Macaulay both an energetic writer for periodicals and a professional historian, Carlyle acknowledges the public responsibilities of the poet and shares a sense of the poet's historical role. He merely sees the responsibilities and the role continuing. His defense of the heroic poet in fact begins with an argument that parallels Macaulay's while it illustrates the pervasiveness of historical schematizing in critical thought. In "The Hero as Poet" he has this to say:

> The hero as divinity, the hero as prophet, are productions of old ages; not to be repeated in the new. They presuppose a certain rudeness of conception, which the progress of mere scientific knowledge puts an end to. There needs to be, as it were, a world vacant, or almost vacant of scientific forms, if men in their loving wonder are to fancy their fellow man either a god or one speaking with the voice of god. Divinity and prophet are past. We are now to see our hero in the less ambitious, but also less questionable, character of poet; a character which does not pass. The poet is a heroic figure belonging to all ages.[28]

Carlyle shares with Macaulay the sense of history as phases or periods, and seems to concede the Peacock-Macaulay scheme as to the *progress* of society. But in public this is all he concedes. He deplores the worship of science and technology and denies the superannuation of poets. He uses the historical argument for an altogether different purpose.

How, then, does Carlyle defend the poet? Basically, his ideas are those of the German Romanticists and of Shelley, with whom he shares a historical enemy. He differs from Shelley in lumping poets with other heroes and in defending them with a kind of puritanical fervor. The poet is *seer*, man of *vision*, man of *truth*. In rebuttal of Benthamite felicific calculus—of a measurable general happiness—Carlyle says that the poet feeds "the life-*roots*. . .in a way that 'utilities' will not succeed in calculating" (99–100). Like Blake he feels that "our whole Metaphysics. . .from Locke's time downwards, has been physical; not a spiritual philosophy, but a material one."[29] Carlyle calls for and espouses, in Kitson-Clark's terms, "the importance of emotion" and "the importance of the human being who entertains the emotion." Against the poet's guilt-by-association with childhood, Carlyle—like Blake before him and Nietzsche a generation later—acknowledges the need to be "simple [and] open as a child" (11). Poets and prophets may resemble children, but in a world of stunted adults, naivety can become a necessary virtue.[30]

Carlyle's characteristic repetition and emphasis imply a kind of reification of words along with the deification of great poets. If words "ought not to harden into things for us" (103), his own use of words should have caused him disquiet. The man who claims that *The Divine Comedy* may prove "the most enduring thing that our Europe has yet made" (99) also proclaims as self-evident the virtues of *sincerity*, *earnestness*, *intensity*, and *truthfulness*. Carlyle's inflated claims and his "hardened" words make clear that the terms he finds for his hero-poet are terms of defense. They are also terms that reflect the preoccupations of his age and that show the adjustments Victorian critics were making to Romantic conceptions. What follows is a brief catalogue of favorite mid-century terms, most of which can be found in abundance in Carlyle.

SINCERITY

This puzzling word still haunts literary discussions. It is not a word that the English Romantics used much, although it occurs in Wordsworth's essay "Upon Epitaphs II" and is no doubt implicit in any rigorously expressive theory of literature. Patricia Ball and others have shown how "sincerity" came to imply both a necessary condition for art and a final test of its quality.[31] Scarcely any mid-century critic fails to invoke the word in a review or literary essay, especially in contexts which define the *seriousness* or *earnestness* of the writer. Since the criterion of sincerity clearly raises difficulties for writing that is not, say, meditative or expressive, we have perhaps one reason for the scarcity of good criticism of fiction (see chapter VII) and the inability of most writers to more than flirt with generic questions. Sincerity takes on a quasi-religious implication for Carlyle and his followers: it is "better than grace" and "sent from the infinite unknown with tidings to us" (46). Except that he too dismisses novels, it does not matter to Carlyle what the literary vehicle is so long as the message comes with earnest and righteous force. And though Carlyle's hyperbole is his own, his association of poets with prophets and his insistence on their higher powers are common to many of his followers. So much wretched literature of the middle years of the nineteenth century is justified by contemporary critics on the basis of its sincerity (witness the popularity of Bailey's *Festus*, the reception of Alexander Smith's "Spasmodic" verse, and, again, the aphoristic claptrap of Martin Tupper, which won for him a reputation as a sage). At the same time, critics tended to apologize for Thackeray's satire because satire involves irony, and irony involves duplicity. They enjoyed satire; they praised Thackeray as a writer without bitterness, whose criticisms were just or true. But they could not come to terms with satire as a literary mode. Even Thackeray himself needed to say that "under the mask satirical there walks about a sentimental gentleman who means not unkindly to any mortal person."[32]

The early Victorian elevation of the term sincerity approaches, as

Patricia Ball argues, a "reduction by apotheosis," since "the Romantic point about the artist's response to inner promptings has been inflated into a sign of any personal greatness."[33] An emphasis on sincerity may lead to reliance on the nonrational, even the anti-intellectual. "So elemental are most of these outpourings," wrote an 1850 reviewer of *In Memoriam*, "that the mere intellect scarcely furnishes any clue to their beauty and their reality."[34] Words like *elemental* occur with great frequency to writers who are occupied with their inner lives and who are looking to poets for articulation of their own longings. For the insistence on the elemental involves a recognition of shared experience, of fundamental "archetypes" (a word that occurs at mid-century), in a society that multiplies distinctions. Such an understanding of sincerity, instead of denying Romantic positions, recalls Wordsworth's equation between things and symbols and his hope that, in expressing himself, he spoke for all men.

At any rate, if Carlyle deludes himself about aesthetic questions and substitutes rhetoric for theory, he is advocating a position that he felt to be anything but reductive. What he and his followers failed to recognize was that the "apotheosis" of some poets implied the insincerity of most; hence a crippling approach to literature as either inspired scripture or so much rubbish. It was difficult for Carlyle's contemporaries to do justice to the bagatelle—as, for example, the "nonsense verse" that developed in the 1840s—but they had scarcely less trouble with the technical qualities of works they admired.

POWER

Whether mid-century critics drew the term *power* from De Quincey's famous distinction between "Literature of Knowledge and Literature of Power," or whether De Quincey himself (as was often the case) helped to popularize something already widely available, the word *power* had become almost as common as *sincerity* by the middle years of the century. Of course Wordsworth often uses the word, and like Shelley he seems to urge the power of the poet in rebuttal of utilitarian dismissals of poetry. Although by mid-century power may mean *energy*, it can also imply rhetorical effect, the control of the reader by the poet. Wordsworth's call (in 1815) for "a corresponding power" in the reader suggests the effect of the literary work as well as its energy or force. When Carlyle speaks of power, he equates the language and the effect of a literary work. Since

Carlyle thinks of history as the lives of great men, and since he thinks of such lives as exemplary, he can, ironically, conceive of literature in a utilitarian way, offering an idealized version of the individualism touted by his contemporaries and of the overwhelming mechanical forces that they were putting to industrial use. The power of the poet and the power of his work become measures of his worth in an age obsessed by new and unexpected force.[35]

NATURE

If, as John Stuart Mill wrote, "Nature, natural, and the group of words derived from them . . . have at all times filled a great place in the thoughts . . . of mankind,"[36] they filled an especially great space in the thoughts of Mill's contemporaries.

Probably no term occurs as often in mid-century literature as *nature*. David Copperfield as solitary wanderer in the Alps hears "great Nature" speak to him. Charles Mackay published an unremembered volume of poems entitled *Egeria: Or the Spirit of Nature* (1850), the preface of which is an elaborate self-apology decrying the want of earnestness in the age and urging practical and scientific people to seek pleasure in the beauties of nature. Charles Kingsley could write without fear of contradiction that Wordsworth's sense of the "dignity of nature" is "the root idea of the whole poetry of this generation."[37] I shall return to the applications of this word in a variety of contexts, but a few points might be raised briefly.

1. Neither critic nor artist in 1850 could avoid the invocation of nature as aesthetic norm. *The Germ*'s subtitle was "Thoughts towards Nature." Whether nature meant scenery, the order behind that scenery, a norm of temporal or causal events, the essential qualities of human beings, the evident workings of God, or whatever, the word was sure to occur.

2. As Kingsley suggested, most writers seemed to attribute the awareness of nature (as physical surroundings) to Wordsworth, and even critics who disliked Wordsworth, George Lewes for example, recognized his powers of description and his beneficent influence on men like Tennyson. *Nature*, like *sincerity* and *power*—words that Wordsworth also elevated—came down to Victorians as an acknowledged but largely unexamined legacy.

3. Carlyle again seems an intermediary. He speaks of literature as an "apocalypse of nature." "The seeing eye" of the poet "discloses the inner harmony of things; what nature meant, what musical idea nature

has wrapped-up in these often rough embodiments" (102). By partly *unconscious* powers, the poet perceives unity in nature; indeed, the poet's powers work analogously with those of nature itself, so that, for example, "Shakespeare's art is not artifice" (104).

4. A new voice, praised by diverse writers and cited with growing respect, rests his entire aesthetics on appeals to nature. John Ruskin, who owed much, as he admits, to both Wordsworth and Carlyle, defends Turner as the true interpreter of nature in *Modern Painters*, 1 and 2 (1843, 1846). Ruskin means that Turner has the greatest powers of observation *and* the greatest sense of aesthetic unity. Turner's strength is a happy combination of brilliant mimesis and original creativity. Ruskin is not only an apologist for the Pre-Raphaelite Brotherhood; he becomes for many writers the profound new spokesman for aesthetic principles.

5. Reverence for nature seems related both to new technical advances and to the use of new terminology. By the late forties it becomes common to hear of accurate portrayal of historical events as well as of natural scenery in terms of the daguerreotype. The work of Fox Talbot in England, and earlier of Daguerre, Niepce, and other pioneers of photography was at once emblematic of an age that worshiped and sentimentalized natural scenery and a further spur to such attitudes.

6. By only a small stretch of meanings what is *natural* can mean what is delineated most fully, is most complete in detail. This is the direction taken by the Pre-Raphaelites in painting; it is what Henry Reeve praises about the history written by Niebuhr and Ranke. Reeve speaks about Ranke's use of public records providing a narrative daguerreotype of human events. And the same apology can of course apply to fiction.[38]

TRUTH

It was perhaps the reluctant admission that the *truth* of art was not the direct *truth* of fact that pushed Carlyle away from literary study and into biography or other forms of historical writing. And clearly the emphasis on sincerity on the one hand and fidelity to impression on the other placed mid-century critics in a difficult situation. If poetry is (as Bryan Waller Procter argued) "a thing created by the mind,"[39] and if (as Ruskin said) the poet's and artist's job is to record nature with intensity and keenness, wherein lay the truth of art? Is expression itself a form of mimesis? Aubrey De Vere, whose essay on Landor I have already cited, says in an 1849 review of Henry Taylor's poems: "The opinion that a close observation of outward things is unworthy of poetry proceeds, not from too exalted a theory of Art, but from an unworthy estimate of Nature; as if the latter were something merely material, existed but for temporal purposes, and turned up by accident only its various products of good and evil." As for Carlyle, nature is something to be interpreted, something essentially *spiritual*, for which the poet find the key.

> It is from the union of Nature and the human Mind that Art as well as Science derives its origin and principle of growth. Accordingly, the most ingenious products of the imagination, unfecundated by nature, have always remained barren. Poetry drawn ultimately from experience flows forth in a rich and manly vein; for in its larger harmonies it reconciles all that belongs to our humanity.[40]

De Vere's review seems to sum up a generation of critical thinking and critical compromise. It lists various poetic truths necessary to the great poet: "Truth to Nature; Truth in fact; Truth in character; Moral Truth; Truth of Passion, of Style, of Generalization, of 'Keeping' (or Imagination)." Poetry for De Vere has "a moral origin, and . . . a human end." It works to the extent that it keeps in mind "the affinity of the beautiful and the true,–perceiving beauty itself to be but the outward manifestation of the highest truth which commeasures and reconciles the truth of idea and the truth of fact."[41] Ultimately, as for Carlyle, art is "not illusory."

De Vere's frequent references to Wordsworth and Ruskin (and, without acknowledgments, to Coleridge, Carlyle, and Keats) indicate how eclectic most critics of the time were. But De Vere, in spite of his unsystematic aesthetics, is a sensitive reader. He recognizes the inadequacies of periodical criticism, which creates "an irresponsible censorship." He speaks of his own age (in relation to the ever-recurrent "ruder times") as an age of "social uniformity." "Men are . . . cast in a mould." "It is not Individuality alone that is lost when the conventionalities of society [an "Industrial" society] overlay the humanities. Simplicity of character is likewise destroyed by a spurious self-consciousness."[42] De Vere, like George Lewes, feels that the literary climate has been determined by the social and physical. A "higher average" of morality, "the division of labor," "the shield of law" have made for a stable society, but also for "feeble" poetry. He calls for "originality, Robustness and energy," "as well as Individuality," and his appeal for the various forms of truth is at once an apology for poetry and an acknowledgment, like that of Carlyle and Lewes, of the poet as a necessary modern hero.

De Vere's essay raises one concluding point. Although his terms are exactly those that novelists and critics sympathetic to novelists use in contemporary discussion of fiction, De Vere simply excludes literature that is not poetry. In his as in most critical essays of the time there is the assumption that poetry subsumes other literary forms or at least sets their standards; but there is also, as I argue in chapter VII, a reluctance to see developments in fiction as related to those in poetry. It is not entirely true that the lyric poem becomes the poetic norm,[43] but assessments of contemporary works usually elaborate the virtues of epic and dramatic forms before commenting on the depths of feeling or the power and sincerity of the poet. Despite the numerous early Victorian attempts to define the nature of poetry (by Mill, Leigh Hunt, Thomas De Quincey, Newman), very few writers concern themselves with the attributes of fiction. George Lewes and David Masson are important exceptions, and both, as I shall try to show, tacitly recognize the related tendencies in contemporary poetry and fiction.[44]

Even Macaulay and Carlyle add nothing of importance to discussions of the novel (with the minor exception of Carlyle on *Wilhelm Meister*). We might have expected from either of these writers an account of the functions and ends of prose narrative, of historical romance or historical novels, or even of the intrinsically historical process within novels drawing on contemporary life. Carlyle could enjoy Dickens, and Macaulay, who praised Thackeray, was an avid reader of novels. Yet both men, despite their own novelistic techniques, shared with the bulk of their contemporaries a tendency to think of poetry as the literary standard. Carlyle, indeed, could use arguments like Macaulay's about the childishness of poets to dismiss novelists; at the same time he could speak of modern men-of-letters (presumably including the writers of fiction) as the principal heroes of the times.

I shall return to Carlyle's ambivalence, since it was, as usual, characteristic. But we can see in one brief example how Carlyle's readers shared his ambivalence. Tennyson confessed that he enjoyed the lightest of fiction, and he evidently thought of fiction as altogether different in nature as in quality from poetry. Yet Tennyson himself could say:

> The form of prose fiction is a vastly greater one, indeed it may be termed all-comprehensive, and admits of the introduction of lyric or epic verse, in all varieties, as well as the profoundest analysis of character and motive, and is susceptible of the highest range of eloquence and unrhythmical poetry, and whatever it may lose in metrical melody . . . it gains immeasurably in its other elements. All things considered, I am of the opinion that if a man were endowed with such faculties as Shakespeare's, they would be more freely and effectively exercised in prose fiction with its wider capacities than when crabbed, cabined, or confined in the trammels of verse.[45]

III

In Memoriam

The Uses of Dante and Wordsworth

1

> We can only conclude by repeating what we have said before, and what we trust the feeling of our readers, and of all who already know or may hereafter become acquainted with the work itself will justify, that it is the finest poem the world has seen for very many years. Its title has already become a household word among us. Its deep feeling, its wide sympathies, its exquisite pictures, its true religion, will soon be not less so. The sooner the better.—Anonymous review of *In Memoriam* in *Tait's Edinburgh Magazine* (1850)[1]

> It is now admitted by all qualified to give an opinion, that the influence of Wordsworth on the poetry of his age has been as beneficial as extensive.—Anonymous review, *Ainsworth's Magazine* (1850)[2]

For mid-nineteenth-century readers of poetry there were two poet-heroes: one died in 1850, the other succeeded him as Poet Laureate. Eighteen fifty was, without question, Tennyson's *annus mirabilis*.[3] In May he published *In Memoriam*; in June he married, finally, Emily Sellwood; in November he accepted the Laureateship. *In Memoriam* not only brought him acclaim, it gave him the combined critical and popular success that no poet had had since the days of Scott and Byron. Some readers thought that Elizabeth Browning ought to be Poet Laureate (a woman poet for the queen), and some thought that Leigh Hunt deserved the honor, among them Hunt himself. In terms of sheer popularity, Martin Tupper ranked as a candidate, and he found apologists even at Oxford. But as George Lewes shows in the William Bowles obituary, Tennyson was accepted as the poet of the times. Leigh Hunt himself admitted that, if the Laureateship were awarded to the best poet, Tennyson should have it.

Tennyson's fame may not have come especially slowly; relative to

Browning's, it came early and with ease, and by the mid-forties, Tennyson already had his Civil List Pension. Edgar Shannon, describing the growth of Tennyson's reputation, says: "The picture of him as a poet who slowly made his own way to popular acclaim in spite of persistent opposition from the press is exaggerated."[4] But it is true, nevertheless, that Tennyson received harsh early reviews and that these reviews mattered a great deal to him. His sensitivity to criticism caused him not to publish for several years, and even when he did publish, his poems were not commercially successful. Only in the mid-forties, in the years when Wordsworth acknowledged him as "the first of our living poets," did he win any large audience. By 1851, Edward Moxon, his publisher, had issued seven editions of *Poems* (1842); but for "five years following publication of the 1842 volume Moxon issued nothing of Tennyson save new editions."[5] Even *The Princess* had only limited success. Then came the "elegies." Moxon issued five thousand copies (a large edition) and had to issue four more editions within the following year. *In Memoriam* may not have established Tennyson's fame, but it initiated the flood of sales that greeted his later work.

Moxon, a friend as well as publisher of Tennyson, was also a friend and publisher of Wordsworth. He had persuaded Wordsworth to leave Longman in the mid-thirties, and despite some early setbacks, he had helped Wordsworth approximate his goal of a wide readership while giving him moderate commercial success. At the time of his death in 1850, Wordsworth was certainly more widely read than he had been in the 1830s. "In June, 1833 [by way of example], 1,600 of the 2,000 copies of the 1832 edition . . . had remained unsold."[6] Although critical response had been favorable in the thirties, and although Wordsworth's influence on a variety of writers was apparent, commercial popularity, like Tennyson's, came later, in the forties. When Moxon issued *The Prelude*, he printed two thousand copies, a sizable edition even for an established poet. He needed a second edition by 1851.

It is, then, worthwhile to remember that when *The Prelude* and *In Memoriam* were published—and they appeared within weeks of one another—Tennyson's fame was of relatively recent development, overlapping as well as succeeding Wordsworth's. If we tend to think of Wordsworth belonging to an earlier generation, his ideals of poetry were still of importance for mid-century writers, and his popularity was largely a phenomenon of early Victorian years. In this chapter I shall consider mid-century responses to Wordsworth and Tennyson in relation to that of a poet who had, in a sense, become another contemporary, if a less likely one. The respect that Tennyson and his contemporaries felt for Dante offers a way of reading *In Memoriam* and of understanding its mid-century acclaim.

2

> Could we conceive, not an Eolian harp, but a grand piano, played on by the swift fingers of the blast, it would give us some idea of the sweet, subtle, tender, powerful, and changeful moments of [Tennyson's] verse.—George Gilfillan, *Second Gallery of Literary Portraits* (1850)[7]

George Gilfillan's "Portrait" of Tennyson, with its unwitting parody of the traditional wind-harp—appropriate, no doubt, in the age of Franz Liszt—testifies to the mid-century hunger for critical assessments and to the interest in Tennyson. For Gilfillan, the grotesque auto-piano is an important metaphor. A man, in his own words, "of restlessness and uncertainty of spirit," he clearly looks to poetry for a new awakening. He wrote to a friend in the same months that he published the *Second Gallery*, "I want to [*sic*] my disparted and disentangled powers and feelings, now touching Christ and now Shelley, the one trumpet-blast of united purpose."[8] Forceful and technically brilliant as Tennyson is, he does not suffice. Indeed, his "changeful moments" reflect a sensibility too close, presumably, to Gilfillan's own. Gilfillan does not say where Tennyson's strengths come from, but he is sure of their limits. Writing in the months prior to Tennyson's becoming Poet Laureate, he predicts that Tennyson "is not likely ever to write anything which . . . can go directly to the heart of the nation." And he knows why. Tennyson is "a signal example of the intimate relationship which sometimes exists between original genius, and a shrinking, sensitive, and morbid nature."[9] Tennyson remains too private, too introspective, to become the national poet, the poet as hero. *In Memoriam* should, according to Gilfillan's arguments, have established Tennyson's permanent obscurity. Why did it have precisely the opposite effect?

Gilfillan's unacknowledged recognition that Tennyson spoke to his own private longings might have led him to realize that Tennyson could speak to the longings of others. His ambivalence is an ambivalence about Tennyson and about himself, but it is also an ambivalence about expressive theories of poetry and about the direction of poetry in his time. The assumption as to the exclusive qualities of the private and public world, of the demands of the man and the demands of the publishing writer, has entered critical discussions of Victorian writers since Gilfillan's time. To some extent it lingers today.

In *The Alien Vision* E. D. H. Johnson has isolated a conflict in Victorian times "between the public conscience of the man of letters . . . and the private conscience of the artist." Professor Johnson argues that the demands of public conscience turned writers "aside from their fields of special knowledge, to the end of making their theories more generally accessible. So Mill, Carlyle, Ruskin, Arnold, Morris, Huxley. . . ." But against the public spokesmen these same writers remained "solitary and isolated figures."[10] Johnson articulates what was manifestly a problem for Tennyson as well as for his critics. But the thesis itself raises certain questions: whether, for example, John Stuart Mill had a "private conscience" separable from that of the public spokesman; whether Carlyle was ever less than a profoundly mixed man, whose rhetoric continued to be aggressively private. Are Carlyle's *Latter-Day Pamphlets* more generally accessible than the early essays? Is Ruskin's *Praeterita* more accessible than *Modern Painters*? Even with poets, some of the same questions apply. No doubt Tennyson wanted to conform to Anglicanism when he pulled together the lyrics that became *In Memoriam*. Does this suggest a capacity for accommodation any more than it suggests Tennyson's intense need for faith? For Gilfillan was not far from the mark. We know that the public conscience was there and that Tennyson aspired to a less introspective poetry. He urged a symbolic reading of himself as speaker—along the lines of the *Divine Comedy*. But what this extremely reserved man published was evidently not a "generally accessible" document; it was the intimate record of his personal sufferings. Like Mrs. Browning, in *Sonnets from the Portuguese*, or Arnold in "Resignation"—indeed like so many mid-century writers: poets, essayists, novelists—he offered his readers an intensely personal rhetoric, and he elicited from readers the sort of contradictory response we can see in Gilfillan.

While Tennyson worked on the elegies that became *In Memoriam*, his friend Edward Fitzgerald wrote: "A. T. has near a volume of poems—elegiac—in memory of Arthur Hallam. Don't you [W. B. Donne] think the world wants other notes than elegiac now?"[11] If the world did want other notes, it welcomed those of Tennyson. Gilfillan's and Fitzgerald's objections to Tennyson, whom they both admired, are based on critical premises at odds with the literature of the time, but close to the expressed desires of the poets themselves. Matthew Arnold, more typical of the times than he could allow, was already rejecting the kind of poetry Tennyson wrote while approximating it himself. Arnold's call for a new classicism reflects a widespread tendency to think of contemporary poetry as altogether too expressive and therefore limited in its appeal. The alternative for Arnold was the "classical," just as for Browning it was the "objective" poet. Ruskin and others distinguished between Coleridge's polarities of fancy and imagination, supplanting the Coleridgean terms with "reflective" and "creative." So, for example, Gladstone on the poet Leopardi, who "is stronger in the reflective than in the perceptive, or the . . . more strictly creative powers."[12]

Ruskin, who respected Wordsworth and extolled memory, has this to say in *Modern Painters*, 3: "I admit two orders of poets, but no third; and by these orders I mean the Creative (Shakespeare, Homer, Dante), and the Reflective or Perceptive (Wordsworth, Keats, Tennyson)."[13] The examples of Homer and Shakespeare we might expect in any list at any time. In England, Dante as a model is a nineteenth-century re-discovery. Ruskin's chain of association moves from Dante as the third example of his creative faculty to Wordsworth as the first example of the reflective. The association might be arbitrary, but it would not have seemed so to many of Ruskin's contemporaries, who, while they often invoked Ruskin's poetic categories, still contrived to put Dante and Wordsworth together. My question here is how the unexpected marriage bears on a reading of *In Memoriam.*

We are not likely to think of Tennyson, any more than of Ruskin, as a neoclassicist, yet Tennyson shared the critical assumption of his contemporaries as to the two major classes of poets. "We must distinguish," he says, "Keats, Shelley, and Byron, from the sage poets of all, who are both great thinkers and great artists, like Aeschylus, Shakespeare, Dante, and Goethe."[14] Tennyson's insistence that the various poems in *In Memoriam* be read dramatically—so many "moods of sorrow as in a drama"[15]—suggests that he wanted to place his poem with those of "the sage poets," that he had gone beyond Keats and Shelley and Byron.

Here and elsewhere, Tennyson associates the highest creativity with Dante, who could be read "dramatically," but whose *Vita Nuova* and *Divina Commedia* are also highly personal. When Tennyson speaks of *In Memoriam* as "a kind of *Divina Commedia*, ending in happiness,"[16] his allusion is not, as Jerome Buckley says, merely "ponderous."[17] On the one hand it reflects Tennyson's artistic justification for a poem that he felt to require explanation, and on the other hand it is a further personal tribute to Arthur Hallam, for whom Dante was the greatest poet. Since Hallam himself associated Dante with Wordsworth, he serves as a link to the critics of *In Memoriam* as well as to Tennyson's own conception of his poem. Tennyson's appreciation of Dante stems from the time of his friendship with Arthur Hallam (beginning in the late twenties and extending to the time of Hallam's death in 1833), and it was Hallam who prompted him to read Dante, to learn Italian, and to see Dante as a poetic ideal. Hallam himself translated the *Vita Nuova.* He wrote a rebuttal of the *Disquisizione sullo spirito Antipapale* of Gabriele Rossetti, father of Dante Gabriel, Christina, and William Michael Rossetti and professor of Italian at King's College. Rossetti conceived of *The Divine Comedy* as "a gigantic cryptogram, conveying . . . an attack on the Papacy and all its works."[18] For Hallam, Dante played no such games: he was the consummate poet of Love, not a Protestant agent in disguise.

Hallam admired Wordsworth as the great modern poet, but in his 1831 review of Tennyson's early poems, he associates Tennyson with Keats and Shelley (as "Poets of Sensation") rather than with Wordsworth (the poet of "Reflection"). His argument, which anticipates the creative-reflective opposition, employs the same sort of historical scheme for poetry that we have seen in Macaulay and Carlyle. The age, Hallam says, is without harmony; versifiers abound, but "those different powers of Reflective, of Passionate Emotion, which in former times were intermingled . . . [are] now restrained within separate spheres of agency. . . . Hence the melancholy which so evidently characterizes the spirit of modern poetry; hence that return of the mind upon itself and the habit of seeking relief in idiosyncracies rather than community of interest. In the old times the poetic impulse went along with the general impulse of the nation." Hallam's inference from the state of the times is that "modern poetry in proportion to its depth and truth is likely to have little immediate authority over public opinion."[19] Here again (though twenty years before) we have Gilfillan's argument about the privacy of modern poetry and its inability to reach large audiences. Hallam defends Tennyson as a poet likely to find few readers, while thinking of Dante as the ideal public poet. The difference lies in the spirit of the age, for the age demands the muse.

Hallam's views reflect on *In Memoriam* in a number of ways. There is, first, the matter of subject. As Valerie Pitt writes, "The awareness of Dante which Tennyson gained from Hallam's studies gave him the *entrée* into what lies behind Dante, the whole corpus of a doctrine about love which the European tradition had taken over from Plato."[20] That corpus came to include both the New Testament and *The Divine Comedy*, in which "Love as Power" takes different but nonetheless essential forms. The immediate subject of *In Memoriam* is of course love of Hallam, and Hallam's death as it affects and directs "the melancholy which so evidently characterizes" this poem of Tennyson's above all others. Although Tennyson did not sit down to write a collection of elegiac lyrics called *In Memoriam*, the poems grew with a common theme and they pay a common tribute. And part of Tennyson's tribute is his sense of *In Memoriam*, in its final shape, as "a kind of *Divina Commedia.*" Tennyson would have thought of Dante as a personal link with Hallam. As the poet of exalted love, Dante would imply the poem's exploration of love and at the same time refer to the friend as master, to Hallam the literary and philosophical guide, Beatrice and Vergil in one.

The allusion to Dante also clarifies the mixing of "public" and "private" voices in *In Memoriam*. For in a sense, *In Memoriam* is both an illustration of Hallam's assessment of modern verse and a gesture—through "melancholy" and privacy—to the universal statement of a Dante. Behind Tennyson's comment is the realization of his own desire, not to accommodate, but to express "the general impulse of the nation" while writing poems that might seem to be "seeking relief in idiosyncracies." Like Hallam, Tennyson must have recognized the problem as crucial to his own poems and endemic to his times. We need only think of the preoccupation in mid-century poetry with personal-religious love: Elizabeth Browning's *Sonnets*, Meredith's *Modern Love*, and any of Coventry Patmore's poems about conjugal love are cases in point. The question for Tennyson was whether his introverted poems could achieve the voice of amplitude, the universal appeal of Dante. His trial version testifies that he shared Fitzgerald's and Gilfillan's doubts—doubts already articulated by Hallam twenty years before.

Tennyson's references—and they were private references—to *In Memoriam* as "kind of" *Divine Comedy* imply a tentative or hopeful comparison rather than a simple equation. We know from the poem "To Dante" (1865) that Tennyson did not rank himself with Dante:

> I wearing but the garland of a day.
> Cast at thy feet one flower that fades away.[21]

We might speculate that he thought of Dante not only as the poet of love but also as "the master craftsman," hoping that his readers would associate his "new" stanza with Dante's *terza rima*. And several reviewers were quick to make the connection. But whether or not Tennyson could have anticipated a favorable comparison, he could be sure of his readers' association of Dante with the highest creativity.

3

> Ere blasts from northern lands
> Had covered Italy with barren sands,
> A mightier Power she saw,
> Poet and Prophet.
> . . . .
> When Dante's strength arose
> Fraud met aghast the boldest of her foes.
>
> W. S. Landor, "Dante" (1850)[22]

Thanks in part to Henry Cary's pioneering translation, the first complete translation of *The Divine Comedy* into English, Dante had become common knowledge to literate Englishmen. In addition to Cary's translation (his blank verse *Inferno* was contemporaneous with Wordsworth's 1805 *Prelude*), there had been partial or entire translations by many hands, including the influential work of John A. Carlyle, brother of Thomas, in 1849. Patrick Bannerman, in 1850, published yet another translation of the *Paradiso*.[23]

Translations of Dante could not have appeared without some fairly constant demand, or without the publishers' sense that Dante had an English audience. And the appreciation for Dante was certainly there. The interest of Professor Rossetti's two sons in Dante led both William Michael and Dante Gabriel to attempt translations, and for several years Dante Gabriel Rossetti saw his life in terms of Dante's. The Pre-Raphaelite love for Dante suggests that their tastes were in fact shared tastes (see chapter IX). If, for example, we read a discussion of modern geological treatises (in the *Quarterly Review*) and find the author referring to prehistory and ancient history as "the *selva oscura* . . . of the poet,"[24] we can see that Tennyson might reasonably expect from his readers an awareness of Dante.

Apart from Cary's translation, the appreciation of Dante probably arose with Blake and Coleridge, Hazlitt and Shelley, who either imitated his verse or held him up as a model for imitation. Another unexpected impetus was Macaulay, who on this question agreed with Carlyle in finding Dante the supreme poet. But whereas Macaulay praises Dante for his lack of egotism (one of few qualities he shares with Milton), Carlyle emphasizes *The Divine Comedy* as Dante's "whole history." Macaulay also says that "*The Divine Comedy* is a personal narrative. Dante is the eye-witness and ear-witness of that which he relates."[25] Macaulay thinks, however, that Dante has transformed the self, or, in Ruskin's terms, "annihilated" the self. Carlyle's emphasis on the heroic character of the poet allows the sense that Dante has internalized the external world, so that, in poems like *The Divine Comedy*, "lie the soul of the whole past time." But, for Carlyle, Dante the man reaches beyond his age through what amounts to an assertion of self.

In the essays of the two historians we can see the opposing values of private and public, reflective and creative, albeit both Carlyle and Macaulay assume Dante's importance and both use comparable terms of praise. In 1850, shortly before Tennyson published *In Memoriam*, there appeared another essay on Dante, written by Richard Church, who became an important cleric in later years and wrote a seminal history of the Oxford Movement. Church's essay illustrates two things: how extensively Carlyle's literary judgments had come to be shared; and why Dante could mean so much for mid-century poets and their readers.

"Dante" appeared in the *Christian Remembrancer* for January. A long and sympathetic commentary, it is one of the most vigorous apologies for Dante written in England. Church assumes that "a strong personal character" is necessary for great poetry (the "egotistical sublime" rather than "the chamelion poet"), and, like Carlyle, he thinks that "history . . . is but a feeble exponent of the course of growth in a great mind."[26] This last remark, uttered at a time when Marx, Engels, and others were equating historic developments with impersonal forces, points to the importance for Church, as for Wordsworth and Carlyle before him, of aesthetic *power*. Because Wordsworth realized that, in a world dominated by Benthamite assumptions, poetry could be thought ephemeral, he recurs to the word *power* in a surprising number of contexts. So too does Carlyle; and so does Church. Church calls Dante "the man conscious of power." And power involves questions about the directions possible in literary history as well as about the personal attributes of poets. Dante, he argues, is the father of a long line of books, including *Pilgrim's Progress*, Rousseau's *Confessions*, Goethe's *Wilhelm Meister*, and Wordsworth's *Excursion*. Dante was first in this line for a number of reasons. To begin with, his "eye was free and open to nature in a degree new among poets." Dante also (and Church makes another nod to his times) restored "seriousness to literature."[27] More centrally, his personal power allowed the otherwise inconceivable, the incorporating of personal, trivial, even grotesque elements into the one sublime and "philosophical poem."[28] Thus *The Divine Comedy* "seems so abnormal, so lawless, so reckless of all ordinary proprieties and canons of feeling, taste, and composition" because "Dante is his own law."[29]

I have chosen points from Church's essay that echo Carlyle; and where he does echo Carlyle, Church might well be discussing not Dante but Wordsworth, whose *Excursion* he sees as Dante's literary offspring (*The Prelude* had yet to appear). "The course of growth in a great mind" describes Wordsworth's lifelong preoccupation, and Wordsworth spoke of his own life as "history." The "eye . . . open to nature" had come, for many mid-century readers, to mean Wordsworth's. I shall mention in a later chapter, and in relation to Dickens, Wordsworth's "matter-of-factness," as well as the question of the poet as law unto himself. The point here is that Church reads Dante's work in the way Wordsworth had thought of his own—as integrated autobiography. He finds for *The Divine Comedy* a characterizing phrase, "an epos of the soul."[30]

Now the word *epos* is new to nineteenth-century English, and Carlyle was one of its introducers. It was first used to designate simply "epic poetry" but was soon adapted to mean a series of events worthy of epic treatment. Since Dante's journey was understood as a type of autobiography, a connection between Dante and Wordsworth makes that much more sense. For the purpose of *The Prelude* was in part to test the poet's fitness and inspiration—the quality of his imagination—as he went on to address *The Recluse.* Wordsworth had made clear in the introduction to *The Excursion* (and in *The Prelude* itself) that his life was indeed worthy of epic treatment. Together with "soul," "epos" suggests the double quality of *The Prelude*, the poem addressing itself to elevated personal history and the poem defining the nature of being, since *The Prelude* is distinctly ontological as well as epistemological, philosophical as Coleridge recognized and, for Church's contemporaries, in ways comparable with *The Divine Comedy*.

Tennyson's allusions to Dante and Richard Church's conception of *The Divine Comedy* as "an epos of the soul" point to the conclusion that, however widely assumed or articulated, Ruskin's or Tennyson's distinction between creative and reflective in fact broke down in critical practice. The association of Tennyson with both Dante and Wordsworth raises, however, a further question, since if critics were describing Wordsworth and Dante in comparable terms, we might expect *The Prelude* to have received warm praise when it finally made its appearance. This question remained a problem for me as long as I accepted Herbert Lindenberger's assertion that, while *In Memoriam* was almost universally acclaimed, *The Prelude* fared badly with mid-century readers.[31] I have already mentioned that *The Prelude* sold relatively well, and that its publication almost coincided with the years of Wordsworth's greatest fame. Several further points obtain here.

It is true that certain established periodicals never reviewed *The Prelude*. It is also true that *The Prelude* described a world already half a century past. As an *Examiner* reviewer wrote, "Only those whose memory still carries them so far back can feel within them any reflex of that eager excitement, with which the news of battles fought and won or mail-coach copies of some new work of Scott or Byron, or the *Edinburgh Review* were looked for and received in those already old days."[32] It is possible, too, that Victorian readers sought a different quality of verse from that offered by Wordsworth:

> One wonders if *The Prelude* contained too much of the quiet, reflective quality of eighteenth-century meditative verse to move the mid-nineteenth-century reader with the assertiveness to which he had become accustomed by later Romantic poetry and the early Victorian novel. On the surface, certainly, many themes of *The Prelude* remained the central preoccupations of mid-century.[33]

Such an assessment of the changed climate for poetry may be right in general terms, but it is not right about the contemporary response to *The Prelude*, except insofar as *The Prelude* met with less ecstatic approval than *In Memoriam*.

In no review, says Lindenberger, was *The Prelude* "allowed to stand next to the greatest poems of the past, whereas Tennyson's poem was compared by various reviewers to *The Divine Comedy*, *Paradise Lost*, the sonnets of Petrarch, and, significantly, to *The Excursion*."[34] To illustrate his argument, Lindenberger cites a negative response of F. D. Maurice, the Christian Socialist. Maurice wrote to Charles Kingsley that *The Prelude* was "the dying utterance of the half-century we have just passed through, the expression—the English expression at least—of all that self-building process in which, according to their different schemes and principles, Byron, Goethe, Wordsworth, the Evangelicals . . . were all engaged."[35] Maurice's assessment is shrewd, except about the continuity of what he calls "the dying utterance." It is appropriate that he is writing to another Christian Socialist, a man who not only assumed the vitality of Wordsworth's method but who also wrote for *Fraser's* a strongly favorable review of *The Prelude*, in which he compared it to great poems of the past. "We doubt," writes Kingsley, "whether anything in the whole range of descriptive poetry, not excepting even *Manfred* and *Childe Harold*, surpasses [book 6 of *The Prelude*] in grandeur and truth."[36] In a later review of *In Memoriam* (also for *Fraser's*), Kingsley compares Tennyson with earlier poets, but he also compares his elegies with Wordsworth's "grand, posthumous work," which he feels to be the representative poem of his time.[37]

The Prelude was in fact not badly received. Its most damaging review came from George Lewes, who dismisses it as "an ambitious failure," uninteresting at that. But Lewes himself notes that "critics . . . have agreed to rhapsodize its glories." He acknowledges a review in the *Athenaeum* (actually his own) as the only other attack, and he laments what amounts to the unabated hero-worship by the Wordsworthians. In the *Athenaeum* review he says: "In as much as Nature appeals to all minds, and [Wordsworth's] diffuse egotism meets with responsive feelings, Wordsworth takes possession of us. There lies his strength. He is the greatest descriptive poet who ever lived." True, "as an autobiography [*The Prelude*] is meagre . . . ; as a philosophical survey . . . it fails in distinctness. . .," and it strays from the true subject of poetry, "the Human Soul."[38] But even in these condemnations, Lewes uses the same terms that Richard Church had used to attack what Church had praised. The point is that the terms are Wordsworth's own and—in this rare negative review—used a little unfairly against him. Other critics, like Kingsley, were content to see *The Prelude* as a fulfillment of their critical principles, and Lewes rightly says that the public response was largely favorable.

Furthermore, if contemporary reviewers wanted poetry of more technical brilliance and more brevity, their response to *The Prelude* (and to other long poems of the time) was odd. For when they found fault with *The Prelude*, they scarcely mentioned technical matters. George Brimley (in 1851) speaks, typically, of a certain "hardness in Wordsworth's nature towards the human world outside his own family," and, amid praise for Wordsworth's "permanent and elemental character," admits him to be without breadth.[39] Brimley mentions no technical failing. Lewes's reviews imply technical judgments, but Lewes wants to prove that Wordsworth fails as a philosopher, and that, contrary to Wordsworth's self-estimate, he has misunderstood the subject matter of poetry.

How, then, did Lewes and his contemporaries read *In Memoriam*? When they praised *In Memoriam*, they invariably praised it as an *epos of the soul*—that is, as a Wordsworthian type of poem, although with a great emphasis on its specifically Christian character. (The notorious attacks in the *Times* were lectures to Tennyson on the shape of his belief.) Kingsley spoke of *In Memoriam* as "the noblest Christian poem which England has produced for two centuries" and compared it with *Paradise Lost* and *The Divine Comedy*. Tennyson reminds Kingsley of "Dante of old." He reminds him even more of Wordsworth, who has a comparable religious quality, similar powers of description, and "a high idyllic faculty." Tennyson draws from Wordsworth the sense of "the dignity of nature," "the root idea of the whole poetry of this generation."[40] Kingsley seems to assume, then, that the qualities Tennyson owes to Wordsworth he also shares with Dante. Like many of his contemporaries, he has understood Dante in terms of Wordsworth's and Carlyle's aesthetics, interpreting Tennyson's personal and elegiac poems as though they fused traditions.

4

> The great resemblance between Dante and Wordsworth rather than any other of the English poets is that the work of each of these pretends to start from a definite and passionate personal experience.—Charles Williams, *The Figure of Beatrice*[41]

To appreciate that contemporary readers of *The Prelude* and *In Memoriam* could see parallels, or that, like Kingsley, they might associate Tennyson and Wordsworth with Dante, is not to say anything about real similarities and differences. Except for an occasional echo, Tennyson does not apparently imitate Dante, and there seems no more connection between the individual lyrics of *In Memoriam* and the cantos of *The Divine Comedy* than there is between the structures of the entire works. Tennyson's hope that the three Christmases and the final wedding might suggest Dante's work is only hope after all. Even the connection with *The Prelude* may seem arbitrary: Wordsworth's long, blank-verse paragraphs, his distinctly un-epigrammatic style, his open discussion of a range of autobiographical topics—these point to a different heir, perhaps, than Tennyson, although we know that in "Dora" Tennyson could out-Wordsworth Wordsworth.

Had I begun this discussion with a strictly stylistic analysis, I might have concluded that Tennyson's mid-century poetry is *normative*, that it employs a certain ratio of adjectives to verbs and nouns and is, in short, what we might take it to be: closely connected in its language to the poems of Arnold, Clough, and Browning—as well as to American poets of the time, like William Cullen Bryant, who had something of an English vogue. Josephine Miles shows that the "language of poetry" in the 1840s had shifted from that of an earlier generation. " 'Ballads' and 'Songs' came back into titles. In form, lines shortened and varied, adding odd short syllables. . . . Statements left off in mid-air, did not always draw conclusions, or by their downright literal intensity indicated that even more was being said."[42] These comments provide a clear sense of what we might call physical differences between *The Prelude* and *In Memoriam*: the *In Memoriam* stanza, not blank verse; elegies, not verse paragraphs; and a long poem composed of intense short lyrics—cells and oratories, as Wordsworth might have called them, rather than the whole Gothic church.

But if the physical differences are striking, what can be said about differences in diction between poems early in the century and those written toward 1850? Josephine Miles says that poets, on balance, "gave up *nature* and *power* for *light*, *night*, and *spirit*" as "the fulness of poetic statement lessened."[43] This is I think both true and misleading. Although the word *power* enters more into comments about poetry than into the poetry itself, references to nature in Tennyson, Arnold, Browning, and Clough seem to be as numerous as they are complex (see the following chapters). But even if we recognize a shift in mid-century poetry in the direction of fine "powers of discernment," or of "mysteries, silences, hints, and hesitations," we still have poets preserving "the classic human norm as Wordsworth wished," and using, moreover, a good part of a Wordsworthian vocabulary (*eye*, *heart*, *love*, *man*).[44] Much of the vocabulary deals with affection and friendship, much with the poet's relationship with physical nature. We might remember that Ruskin, a writer obsessed with nature, was soon to coin his phrase "pathetic fallacy," and also to illustrate the pathetic fallacy with a passage from Kingsley's 1850 novel, *Alton Locke*. Clearly, nature remained in the major vocabulary, and Wordsworth's own poetry continued to exemplify it, just as Wordsworth's "power" began to dominate the critical vocabulary assessing the poetry.

Again, differences between the poetic generations are both marked and important. And specific differences between *The Prelude* and *In Memoriam*—as D. G. James has shown—are themselves pronounced. Tennyson's preoccupation with metaphors of form reflects a hope for unified poetry, and Tennyson does progress in *In Memoriam* from a denigration of words—as inadequate in themselves or merely solace—to a sense of poetry as triumph. Still, Tennyson never has the overriding faith in the imagination that characterizes Wordsworth, and perhaps "the assimilation of nature to the mind, the reading of the spiritual in the language of sense, the erection of the visible into symbol, was hardly possible to Tennyson."[45]

What we can see in Tennyson and other poets at mid-century is a subtle shift toward limited, personal vision, toward more formal but more private verse, and toward a diminished sense of poetic possibilities. If we understand the shift in terms of poets moving—in Wordsworth's and Coleridge's terms—from imagination back to fancy, we are faced with an intriguing paradox. For Carlyle's apologies for poetry, so widely accepted by his contemporaries, presuppose the "fulness of poetic statement" and the explicit reading of nature in spiritual and symbolic ways. We can recognize, again, the stridency in Carlyle's polemics as a measure of the changes in poetry or of the fears for its future.

But we might go further. The mid-century emphasis on autobiography coincided, as I have suggested, with an emphasis on historiography. Indeed, the autobiographical impulse is intimately connected to historical understanding. As Karl Weintraub says, "The growing significance of autobiography is . . . a part of that great intellectual revolution marked by the emergence of the particular modern form of historical mindedness we call historism or historicism."[46] I shall come back in later chapters to this question. It bears here on Tennyson's sense of *In Memoriam* as re-creation of "the phases of our intercourse" as they recurred to memory. Tennyson writes with the consciousness of personal time contrasted with endless history. He writes, as Carlyle says Dante writes, with the specificity, the acuteness of vision, that characterizes the poetic language of his era and that merges with a new historicism.

Tennyson's feeling that *In Memoriam* reflects phases of his relationship with Hallam, while the development of the poem reflects phases of the poet's recovery, implies the intense moments of suffering we might associate with Dante's poetic journey and with Wordsworth's autobiographical "prelude." Building upon passionate experience, both *The Divine Comedy* and *The Prelude* begin with a large crisis in the spiritual and creative life of the poet, a crisis fusing personal despair with a conviction of widespread human failure. If this overstates Wordsworth's pessimism, it acknowledges his emotional complexity and his expression of what D. G. James calls "dereliction."[47] As James points out, Wordsworth shares the negative vision with Tennyson, who similarly lives with, while he tries to overcome, the awareness of dereliction. Wordsworth's dramatic ambivalence points back to the *selva oscura* of Dante and forward to the "dark street" of *In Memoriam*.

Carlyle, who thought of the writer's life as a pilgrimage through "the Waste of Time,"[48] cites the legendary comments of the people of Verona about Dante: "See, there is the man that was in hell." He also quotes Dante's line about the difficult path: "*Come è duro calle.*"[49] Like Dante's, Wordsworth's poetic journey involves the way through a personal hell toward moments of vision, in which past and present are redeemed. Hence, Tennyson's stanza

> So word by word, and line by line
> The dead man touched me from the past,
> And all at once it seemed at last
> The living soul was flashed on mine.[50]

may remind us either of Beatrice and the final light in *The Divine Comedy* or of Wordsworth's book 14, in which, at a moment of profound insight, "a light upon the turf/Fell like a flash."[51]

If Dante's journey is precise, deliberate, recorded with exactitude, and Wordsworth's is ambulatory and, to an extent, repetitive, Tennyson's is almost wholly metaphoric. No less than the others, however, he writes about a journey, and he makes the journey into a type of pilgrimage. His metaphors of light and dark, of haunting natural rhythms, of poetry and "form," are all essential to *In Memoriam*; but "the sad mechanic exercise" allows a slow progress to the paeon of joy and faith heralded in the "Prologue." The progress can be seen in two dominant metaphoric strains: the *path* and the *waste*. Tennyson's profound melancholy, which Hallam's death both elicits and identifies (and Hallam had pointed to Tennyson's melancholy years before he died), materializes in *In Memoriam* as it does in Browning's "Childe Roland" or Clough's *Dipsychus* as a vision of waste, of "dereliction," through which the poet must seek his path. The "waste places" in stanza 3 of *In Memoriam* represent a condition of mind that is reinforced by dark houses and the heaving deep and the barren branches and dreary west. And the "path by which we twain did go" of stanza 22 anticipates the reiterative paths, the long slow wanderings and pathways, the tracks and dreary ways to come.

Like Wordsworth's, Tennyson's are paths of retrospection, which regress as well as advance. Melpomene, muse of both elegy and tragedy, directs his steps, reminding him of lost happiness rather than of Dante's ineffable vision. But Melpomene may share her role with Mnemosyne, mother of the muses, and with Clio, muse of history. For the personal journey of the poet involves the assessment of the past not only for the poet but through him. Hallam's loss prompts the equation that Carlyle and Church see in Dante: the intensely aware poet making of his tortured journey the epitome of his age.

Title page from *Punch*

Crystal Palace
Western entrance

Crystal Palace
Interior of the transept as seen from the south entrance

Crystal Palace
Southern entrance to the transept

Crystal Palace
The transept from the north side

Thomas Carlyle
A medallion by Thomas Woolner

Alfred Tennyson
Portrait by Samuel Laurence

William Thackeray
A chaulk sketch by Samuel Laurence

Thackeray
"Editors of the Leader*"*

Thackeray
"The overburdened author"

Matthew Arnold
A photograph

Robert Browning
Portrait by D. G. Rossetti

Francis Newman
A photograph

John Newman
A portrait

John Ruskin
Portrait by George Richmond

IV

Dramatic Elegists

Arnold, Clough, and Browning at Mid-Century

1

> We believe it may safely be assumed that at no previous period has the public been more buzzed around by triviality and commonplace; but we hold firm, at the same time, that at none other has there been a greater or grander body of genius, or so honorable a display of well cultivated taste and talent. . . . if the fact be so, it will make itself known, and the poets of this day will assert themselves, and take their places.—William Rossetti, in a review of Clough for *The Germ*[1]

When Robert Browning published *Christmas-Eve and Easter-Day* (at Easter time, 1850), he was accused by some critics of invoking Momus, the spirit of satire. How, critics wondered, could he use a satiric mode for the most serious of themes? Could one even conceive of Christ speaking in a version of Hudibrastic doggerel? What sort of poem was Browning offering? He was, despite his dramatic voices, writing like Tennyson, under the inspiration of Melpomene. His work is retrospective and meditative, expressive of Browning's religious doubts and struggles to believe. Whether or nor Browning responded directly in this poem to the death of his mother in the previous year—at a time when he was unable to return to England to see her—the poem is a record of self-scrutiny and religious longing. Like *In Memoriam* it represents a turning point in the poet's career, a kind of preliminary move toward Browning-as-sage.

Arthur Hugh Clough did not publish his *Dipsychus* in 1850, though he wrote most of the poem in that year, and hence did not risk the kind of public criticism that Browning received for *Christmas-Eve*. His witty, Faustian dialogue treats ironically both the self-conscious Dipsychus and the Spirit (Mephistopheles) with whom he speaks. No doubt Clough, too, would have been criticized for want of seriousness by the public press. But like Browning and Matthew Arnold, who was always ready to find fault with his work, Clough expresses a sense of an isolated, dispossessed life, in which all questions have to be asked and few seem capable of answer.

If Clough's questions are overt and intellectualized, Matthew Arnold's tend to be covert and implied. But Arnold's poems are equally probing, introspective, elegiac. Along with Tennyson, Arnold and Browning and Clough may remind us that mid-century poetry so often records "solitary and unassimilated figures" writing of their "ways" and "journeys," their "paths" through darkness, their hope for assent, their struggles against ocean tides (the metaphors are common property, even hackneyed), in attempts to discover what Carl Jung was to speak of as "the self." Jung's notion of "the self," "our life's goal," not only echoes the language of mid-century poets, it seems almost a commentary on their works. In *Memories, Dreams, Reflections,* his reluctant autobiography, Jung speaks of his "buried life" in terms that English writers would have understood. "In the end the only events worth telling are those when the imperishable world irrupted into the transitory one. That is why I speak chiefly of inner experience, amongst which I include my dreams and visions."[2] I mention Jung (and will again) simply to suggest how nearly his speculations and his language approximate the implicit aim of mid-century poetry, which is preoccupied with dreams and visions—and volcanic eruptions—and which weighs an "unsatisfactory and transitory" against an "imperishable" world. Obviously Jung's heritage, no less than Browning's, Arnold's, or Clough's, is early nineteenth-century poetry. "The light of inner happenings" (another of Jung's phrases) recalls Wordsworth and Shelley. But Jung points to an important development, for while mid-century poets inherit Romantic methods, they seem shy of Romantic egotism and unsure about the value of their work. The expression of "inner experience," of *self*, comes with reluctance and pain.

2 MATTHEW ARNOLD

i

> My poems represent, on the whole, the main movement of mind of the last quarter of a century, and thus they will probably have their day as people become conscious to themselves of what that movement of mind is, and interested in the literary productions which reflect it. It might fairly be urged that I have less poetical sentiment than Tennyson, and less

> intellectual vigour and abundance than Browning; yet, . . . I am likely enough to have my turn, as they have had theirs.—Arnold, in an 1869 letter to his mother[3]

So far as I know, only one critic published articles on Arnold, Clough, and Browning in 1850, and he was a young man, editor of *The Germ*, who "was more or less expected to do the sort of work for which the other [Pre-Raphaelites] had little inclination—such especially as the regular reviewing of new poems."[4] William Michael Rossetti wrote reviews of Arnold's *The Strayed Reveller* (1849), Clough's *Bothie of Toper-na-fuosich* (1848), and Browning's *Christmas-Eve and Easter-Day* (1850). Rossetti prided himself on being an untypical reviewer; he pleaded for such qualities as thoroughness and sympathy, which he found wanting in established journals like *Blackwood's*. Thoroughness he lacks, but he is sympathetic. His interest in Arnold, Clough, and Browning reveals a sharp sense of their relative merit in a period of prolific versifying. Apart from Tennyson, these are the poets of the time who are best remembered and (with one exception) they are the only poets Rossetti chose to review.[5]

To begin his assessment of Arnold, Rossetti picks up a phrase from Carlyle: "If any one quality may be considered common to all living poets, it is that which we have heard aptly described as self-consciousness. . . . Every species of composition—the dramatic, the narrative, the lyric, the didactic, the descriptive—is imbued with this spirit; and the reader may calculate with almost equal certainty on becoming acquainted with the belief of a poet as of a theologian or a moralist."[6] This acute observation applies to all three of the poets Rossetti reviews—and to dozens he does not. Rossetti calls Arnold a lyric poet, technically brilliant, who has "little to learn." With surprising shrewdness, he guesses that there will be no great developments in Arnold's verse, partly because Arnold lacks "passion," partly—and relatedly—because, whatever the shape of Arnold's poems, "the reflective [mode is the] essential form of his thought." Rossetti also speculates that Arnold is "no longer young" (he was twenty-eight), a feeling oddly enough shared by Arnold himself, who often spoke of his wasted youth.[7] For Rossetti, then, Arnold is preeminently self-conscious, the representative poet of his generation. His sense of Arnold is close to the poet's immediate impatience with his work and close to his later estimate, when he said that, though lacking Tennyson's brilliance and Browning's energy, he represented the main movements of mind in his time.

Rossetti makes a further point that bears on Arnold's self-assessment. He says that the self-consciousness of modern poets means that "mere pretenders, in their desire to emulate the great [Tennyson primarily], feel themselves under a kind of obligation to assume opinions, vague, incongruous, or exaggerated; often not only not their own, but the direct reverse of their own." The tendency to assume opinions, which Arnold himself deplored, brings about much unreadable poetry. It has "on the other hand . . . created a new tie of interest between the author and his public."[8] Rossetti plays with the paradox that Gilfillan could not allow, that the more private the poetry the more popular it may become. And since self-consciousness is an aspect of modern fictional narrators as well as speakers in poems, Rossetti hints at a useful relationship between poets and novelists. I shall return to this later. For the moment I want to see how his reviews of Arnold, Clough, and Browning point to creative and moral dilemmas shared by the three poets—poets who in other ways or at other times may seem far apart.

ii

"The classical in art is what marches by intention with the cosmology of the age."—"Pursewarden," in Lawrence Durrell's *Balthazar*[9]

Just as Arnold the critic dominates English criticism in the 1860s and 1870s, so Arnold the poet offers a good index to the climate for poetry at mid-century. On the one hand, he embodies what Asa Briggs calls the intellectual aristocracy: an employee of Lord Lansdowne the Whig aristocrat, the son of a respected headmaster and historian, and soon to be one of Her Majesty's Inspectors of schools. On the other hand, Arnold was a tormented young man, torn in his love affairs, dissatisfied with his friendships, obsessed by thoughts of death, "self-conscious" to the point (in Carlyle's phrase) of "spiritual paralysis," and generally prey to what Charles Kingsley (in a review of *The Strayed Reveller*) described as a morbid and egocentric "self-culture."[10] Arnold in 1850 had already published *The Strayed Reveller*, a collection of poems that surprised even members of his family with its poignant self-scrutiny and that evidently disappointed Arnold himself. He may have known that his poetry was to be almost indelibly introspective, that it would approximate the elegiac beauty of Sénancour's *Obermann* more than the tragic strength of Sophocles. It was, perhaps, the elegiac quality of his poetry that most troubled Arnold.

Whether describing "The Sick King" or the Egyptian king Mycerinus, the strayed reveller or the scholar gipsy, or whether speaking in what is evidently his own voice to "Marguerite," he sounds again the "eternal note of sadness."

Arnold's meeting with "Marguerite," in 1848 and 1849, led him to write his haunting love poems. But his love for Marguerite, like Wordsworth's love for Lucy, or Tennyson's for Hallam, seems less a passion than a dirge for a passion that has been, with the emphasis on the "salt, estranging sea." In *In Memoriam* Tennyson eulogizes his dead friend and interrupted love; Arnold laments his lost love and dying life. Youth, energy, nature, passion: he weeps for them all. His best-known poem, "Dover Beach" (probably written 1851, though included in the 1867 collection), is a poignant statement of his sense of loss, with the small mitigation of a presumably sympathetic listener, she, that is, whom he calls to the window.

Whereas in his essays Arnold came to be thought unflappably witty and suave, in his poems he was seen from the outset to be another voice of modern despair. And so in sense he thought of himself. His 1853 Preface to *Poems* was as much self-criticism as a general indictment of the poetry of the age. The closest Arnold was to come to his prescribed ideals for poetry represented his furthest digression from his real talents. *Merope*, published in 1859 to "inaugurate" his tenure as Oxford Professor of Poetry, was to remain an experiment in classical tragedy. If *Empedocles on Etna* is a more successful poem, Arnold himself saw *Empedocles* as a "dialogue of the mind with itself," as an example of latter-day Romanticism. Arnold's explicit and public estimate of Romantic literature, introduced by the 1853 Preface, continues through several decades of critical writing. Already at mid-century he was thinking of the Romantics in terms of his own talents and of the literary climate in which he had to write.

Against Wordsworth and against the disposition of his contemporaries, who continued to revere Wordsworth, he responded with contempt to the notion that man can be "in harmony with nature," and while Wordsworth's twin ministries include fear along with beauty, his hope is always for some potential harmony, which is what he finds on the flanks of Snowdon or what he remembers as the redeeming quality in his past. The "received" Wordsworth of mid-century at any rate stressed the optimistic and descriptive poet rather than the poet of "dereliction," or of "Michael," who wrote a version of tragic pastoral. Implicitly, when Arnold later scoffs at the Wordsworthians and questions the power of

Wordsworth's long poems, he acknowledges more than the strength of diction in "Michael." "And never lifted up a single stone"—his literal touchstone—is a line from a poem in which hope is minimal and human loss immense.[11] Arnold's public assessment of Wordsworth belongs to a later time. His private assessment begins in letters to Clough and to his family at mid-century and also—with a difference—in his poems.

"Memorial Verses," published in *Fraser's Magazine*, is a tribute to Wordsworth, an elegy or dirge, written shortly after Wordsworth's death in April. Arnold considers Wordsworth in relation to two other giants, Goethe and Byron, who had died long before. Wordsworth had carried on, at once separate from new literary movements and influential in them. It is worth remembering how Arnold, who knew Wordsworth personally, and who knew himself to be influenced by Wordsworth, contrived this farewell poem:

> Goethe in Weimar sleeps, and Greece,
> Long since, saw Byron's struggle cease.
> But one such death remained to come;
> The last poetic voice is dumb—
> What shall be said o'er Wordsworth's tomb?[12]

Arnold thought of his poem as an elegy "in the grand style," a phrase which could suggest either high-flown and laudatory or merely formal and classical in manner. Edward Quillinan, Wordsworth's son-in-law (and editor of *Fraser's*), spoke of its as "*very* classical, or it would not be Matthew Arnold's." Quillinan called the poem "a triple epicede on your [Henry Crabb Robinson's] friends Wordsworth and Goethe, and on Byron who . . . is not tall enough for the other two."[13] In his excellent edition of Arnold's poems, Kenneth Allott points to Goethe's distinction between classic and romantic as bearing on Arnold's understanding of the three dead poets. To Eckermann, in 1829, Goethe had said: "I call the classic healthy and the romantic sickly. . . . Most modern productions are romantic, not because they are new, but because they are weak, morbid, and sickly; the antique is classic, not because it is old, but because it is strong, fresh, joyous and healthy."[14] The distinction makes sense for Arnold, but not quite for "Memorial Verses," in which Byron figures as an unaccountable thunderbolt, Goethe as the "Physician of the iron age" (whether diagnostic or healing), and Wordsworth as a kindly nurse:

> For never has such soothing voice
> Been to your shadowy world conveyed
> . . . .

> He spoke, and loosed our hearts in tears.
> He laid us as we lay at birth
> On the cool flowery lap of earth. . . .
>
> (*Poems*, 228)

Together with Goethe and Byron, Wordsworth represents an age in poetry, an age at once of profound importance and of limited usefulness. Although in "Memorial Verses" Arnold refers only to virtues in Wordsworth, his general estimate follows Goethe's: the classic is healthy, the romantic sickly. For if the elegy praises Wordsworth as the poet who can make us feel, "In Memory of the author of 'Obermann'" allows doubts. In this poem, "Wordsworth's eyes avert their ken/From half of human fate" (*Poems*, 132)—from half of human fate because of the very preoccupations that Arnold praises in the elegy. The dilemma seems to be that, while Wordsworth is the needed healing nurse, the comforter, the poet who lays us in the lap of nature, he is so at the expense of what we need equally much, the classical, the healthy-minded. And now that the greatest of English nature poets is dead, what are the possibilities for poetry? Where can it go?

In a letter to his sister Jane (Mrs. Forster), Arnold complained that Wordsworth represented a false direction in English poetry. "More and more I feel bent against the modern English habit (too much encouraged by Wordsworth) of using poetry as a channel for thinking aloud, instead of making anything."[15] The distinction is exactly the distinction he was to elaborate in the 1853 Preface: between the classically healthy and the romantically unhealthy, between action and meditation. When Arnold looked at the poetry of his contemporaries, he found it, as William Aytoun and Charles Kingsley found Arnold's own poetry, to be self-indulgent.

As evidence of self-indulgence, Arnold might have listed Charles Mackay (remembered for his share of the "labor and poor" contributions to the *Morning Chronicle*, and in fact a shrewd and observant journalist), who wrote an apology for his *Egeria; or the Spirit of Nature* (1850) in the form of an introduction: "An Inquiry into the Alleged Anti-Poetical Trends of the Present Age." While Arnold was complaining to Clough that the age was unpoetic, Mackay defended modern poetry, including of course his own, by asserting its moral utility and by invoking the Great Man theory of Carlyle. "Those who speak great truths from the fulness of heart . . . will never want listeners."[16] An instance of Mackay's own verse illustrates why Arnold might despair: "Thou sittest moping o'er ideal griefs:/A moony idiot were not worse than thou."[17]

Mackay's "Spirit of Nature" suggests again how widespread the appeal to nature was at mid-century, how universal its importance. Quite obviously Arnold is far more a nature poet than Mackay (or any dozen of his contemporaries), sensitive to natural forces, to details of flowers and mountains, to the qualities of place and season. He invokes nature as conspicuously as Mackay does, and he uses nature analogously as a norm of human behavior. But just as he rejects the Wordsworthian introversion, the poetic "thinking aloud," so too he rejects the Wordsworthians' semireligious faith in nature's healing powers. The poems, however, are not quite so clear as the theory. What we see in Arnold's poems is a rationalized but urgent sense of nature's destructiveness conflicting with an inherited acceptance of nature as both a real and a symbolic (if unattainable) unity. Two of Arnold's poems, "To Marguerite—Continued" and *Empedocles on Etna*, reflect his dominant metaphors of ocean and mountain and offer a way of seeing his early theory in terms of his poetic practice.[18]

iii

Alone!—
On this charred, blackened, melancholy waste,
Crowned by the awful peak, Etna's great mouth,
Round which the sullen vapour rolls—alone!

Empedocles on Etna
(*Poems*, 175)

Yes! in the sea of life enisled,
With echoing straits between us thrown,
Dotting the shoreless watery wild,
We mortal millions live *alone*.
The islands feel the enclasping flow,
And then their endless bounds they know.

"To Marguerite—Continued"
(*Poems*, 124)

In the first stanza of "To Marguerite—Continued"—a poem deserving a better title—Arnold glosses on the italicized word *alone*. Life, he says to the woman he loves, is a sea which separates us, diminishes us (as "mortal millions"), and leaves us not only *on* but also *as* islands in the "watery wild." All men are islands, but death tolls for each nonetheless. The sense of death comes from traditional associations of the sea with a "watery" wasteland, but Arnold stretches his metaphor. The "echoing straits have been "thrown" between us, so that we merely "dot" the sea of life. "The islands feel the enclasping flow," and know "their endless bounds." Kenneth Allott thinks that "'enclasping' . . . suggests an embrace rather than imprisonment" (*Poems*, 124), but the context, in spite of the expression of love, implies a willed control, a physical paralysis that is an emblem for the isolated mind. And "bounds" suggests something like Blake's manacles, with the difference that, for Blake, the manacles are "mind-forged." Arnold, like Hardy after him, seems to imply both an arbitrary fate and a fate directed by a less than generous will.

The second stanza posits, in language reminiscent of Keats's "Ode to a Nightingale," nature as deceiver. Then, led back in the third stanza from nightingales to perilous seas, Arnold distinguishes the longings for unity and wholeness which the metaphoric shores at once inspire and deny.

> But when the moon their hollows lights,
> And they are swept by balms of spring,
> And in their glens, on starry nights,
> The nightingales divinely sing;
> And lovely notes, from shore to shore,
> Across the sounds and channels pour—
>
> Oh! then a longing like despair
> Is to their farthest caverns sent;
> For surely once, they feel, we were
> Parts of a single continent!
> Now round us spreads the watery plain—
> Oh might our marges meet again!
>
> (*Poems*, 124–25)

The ebb and flow of emotion, explicit in the metaphor of the sea, allows the vision of starry nights and divinely singing birds, yet, as in "Dover Beach," the sweet night air (Keats's "fairy midnight") elicits the longing that it mocks. The nightingales *divinely* sing: they are of another order. If Arnold, like Keats, implies the temporary leap of poetry to bind island with island, he similarly recognizes that imagination brings to fuller consciousness the sense of incompleteness in our lives. At the heart of this poem—as of "Balder Dead" and "Sorhab and Rustum"—is a recognition of profound loss, and a loss which recalls vanished Edens (the "single continent" and "balms of spring"). Much that we attribute to post-World War I despondency is here: the spring which does not renew; the parts which are scattered by history and within the individual; the sea which reminds us of our separation.

> Who ordered, that their longing's fire
> Should be, as soon as kindled, cooled?
> Who renders vain their deep desire?—
> A God, a God their severance ruled!
> And bade betwixt their shores to be
> The unplumbed, salt, estranging sea.
>
> (*Poems*, 125)

Arnold wrote *Empedocles* during the same years as the Marguerite poems (and the Obermann poems, "The Forsaken Merman," "Resignation," "Tristram and Iseult," and "Memorial Verses"), in the years, that is, of his greatest poetic activity and his most profound discontent. He was only thirty when he wrote to Clough (in April 1852): "How life rushes away, and youth. One has dawdled and scrupled and fiddle-faddled—and it is all over."[19] *Empedocles* appeared in 1852, although Arnold had evidently finished it some time before. It represents in its renunciation, its despair, and the final suicide of its hero, all that Arnold felt about his lost youth and lost friendships, and all, ironically, that Arnold had come to distrust in his poetry. Already by 1853, when he prepared the preface to the *Poems* (most of which were culled from the two previous volumes), Arnold rejected *Empedocles*. By attacking the failure in his most substantial work, a work conspicuously missing from the volume, Arnold held up an ideal that had less to do with the poems that he included than with the drama he held back.

Why Arnold singled out *Empedocles*, which at least hinted at Greek tragedy and had for its hero a classical philosopher, we can only surmise. The poem certainly dealt with the "essentials" of the protagonist's life, and the protagonist emerged from "a long distant mythic time," stripped of "what was accidental and passing." In terms of Arnold's defense of Greek literature, his insistence on the importance of "the inner man," of the "whole" poem instead of "separate thoughts and images," of the "calm" and "clarity" associated with Greek tragedy (*Poems*, 591-92), *Empedocles* seems the one poem that approximated his ideals. But the problem with *Empedocles* is that, despite his final leap into the crater, the central character finds no significant action and therefore elicits no real "enjoyment."

> What then are the situations, from the representation of which, though accurate, no poetical enjoyment can be derived? They are those in which the suffering finds no vent in action; in which a continuous state of mental distress is prolonged, unrelieved by incident, hope, or resistance; in which there is everything

> to be endured, nothing to be done. In such situations there is inevitably something morbid, in the description of them something monotonous.
>
> (*Poems*, 592)

Although content to publish his unrelievedly sad lyrics in the 1853 collection, Arnold seems consciously to dismiss his favorite work. More than this, his renunciation of *Empedocles* points to the larger renunciation of his poetic energies, which, like his youth, he felt somehow to be "over."

> Away the dreams that but deceive
> And thou, sad guide, adieu!
> I go, fate drives me; but I leave
> Half of my life with you.
>
> (*Poems*, 135)

The lines from "Obermann" illustrate Arnold's sense of choice that is no choice, the necessary farewell to a world of imagination. His intuition, partly suspected by William Rossetti, did of course come true. When Browning persuaded Arnold to republish *Empedocles* in the 1867 *Poems*, it stood out as the central work among largely mid-century poems. And Arnold's inclusion of *Empedocles* anticipated his later acceptance of his poems on their own terms. The poet who can say, in the 1853 Preface, that the ideal poets are those who "do not talk of their mission, nor of interpreting their age," because "all this . . . is the mere delirium of vanity" (*Poems*, 605), can say in after years that his poems will live because they do reflect the times.

In *Empedocles* Arnold escaped the mere "externals" of the present, but he seems to have recognized immediately that his poem, despite its remoteness in setting and time, coincided with the spirit of his age. Although a number of critics (Arthur Clough among them) complained about the artificial classicism of *Empedocles*, the poem was precisely the type of poem they were calling for. The modern critic, says Arnold,

> not only permits a false practice; he absolutely prescribes false aims. "A true allegory of the state of one's own mind in a representative history," the poet is told, "is perhaps the highest thing that one can attempt in the way of poetry." And accordingly he attempts it. An allegory of the state of one's own mind, the highest problem of an art which imitates actions! No assuredly, it is not, it never can be so: no great poetical work has ever been produced with such an aim. *Faust* itself . . . , judged as a whole, and judged strictly as a poetical work, is defective.
>
> (*Poems*, 598–99)

In spite of his writing about an ancient philosopher in ancient times,

Arnold makes of Empedocles a Manfred or Faust. He may be able to define the nature of modern despair, but he is no more able than he regards either Byron or Goethe able to find for despair a correlative of action (except, perhaps, in suicide). He must write a dialogue of the mind with itself. In this sense, Arnold's classicism, like Yeats's masks, is a self-imposed alternative to his own and his epoch's subjective tendencies. His classicism is also an ideal he could not attain. What he could attain, he saw to represent either the poetic or the critical commonplaces of his age, and Arnold the young poet was no more generous about his age than Arnold the literary, social, and religious critic of the decades to come.

Arnold's impatience with these "damned times" and with his own almost mesmerized "consciousness of . . . difficulties" rarely led him, as a poet, to deal directly with the political or social events of his times; it did lead him to the religious and philosophical self-consciousness that Rossetti notices and to a consequent melancholy:

> Hither and thither spins
> The wind-borne, mirroring soul,
> A thousand glimpses wins,
> And never sees a whole; . . .
>
> (*Poems*, 159)

These lines from Act I of *Empedocles* point to another aspect of the *Zeitgeist*. Whereas a poet like Wordsworth uses mountain sublimity to signify his imaginative power to unite, Arnold responds more to the gloom than the glory. Mountain wastes like the watery wastes of "To Marguerite–Continued" call attention to lonely struggles in a ruptured world. Still, Empedocles' slow ascent of Etna, from idyllic woods to blackened waste, is not just a paradigm for lives without significant action. His final vision or understanding, though it coincides with suicide, reflects the poet's own longings for emotional and aesthetic wholeness.

I have mentioned Carl Jung's insistence on the importance of inner events stripped of ephemera and looked upon with reverence. While Arnold spoke in comparable terms, he could have served as an example for Jung of a modern man unable to use his symbols and therefore distraught in his psyche. Significantly, what Jung begins to discuss in our century, Arnold's contemporaries were already addressing in theirs. A good example might be Charles Bland Radcliffe, who published *Proteus, or Unity in Nature* (in 1850). Radcliffe says that he expects little favor "in a materialistic age like the present. The zeit-geist is decidedly against me." There is no question that Radcliffe was in a minority in Crystal Palace England, but there is also no question that his concerns were widely shared–and by more people than Arnold. Radcliffe uses Proteus, "an authentic symbol of nature," to suggest the breakdown of imaginative thought in his own age. We can no longer think mythically, according to Radcliffe, can no longer feel the "communion in all things." We insist on scientific accuracy and trivial detail; our fiction deals exclusively with unconnected things. What Radcliffe urges is an awakening of the heart and a lifting of "the veil under which the face of nature is hidden." Arnold seems close to Radcliffe. He points toward an "organic" unity by means of natural symbols, or what Radcliffe, in anticipation of Jung, calls "archetypal forms."[20] Whereas Arnold turns to classical genres and to "a long-distant mythic time" to avoid "the hopeless tangle of our age," Radcliffe turns directly to classical myth. But Arnold's poetic practice, his appeal to the metaphoric sea of life, is a gesture like Radcliffe's toward a symbolic vision:

> Oh, that I could glow like this mountain!
> Oh, that my heart bounded with the swell of the sea!
>
> (*Poems*, 188)

The sense of an elusive unity to which Empedocles here appeals provides in Arnold's poems a corollary longing for quiet, for stasis, for "calm," a word that recurs throughout the poems. Arnold's conception of tragedy, though it emphasizes action "to affect what is permanent in the human soul," probably led, as Rossetti suggested, to poems that fail in passion. Milton's "Calm of mind, all passion spent" comes close to Arnold's ideal for tragedy, but we rarely see the passion in his poems. He tells Clough that "the Indians distinguish between meditation or absorption and—knowledge,"[21] and leaves no doubt that his friend is too much the Western intellectual. If this is the choice within his own poems, however, then action can hardly belong. Empedocles' final meditation on the mountain is explicit rejection of the world below, the world of potential action, while the process of his awareness moves from useless knowledge to lonely absorption.

When Arnold says of modern literature that "the calm, the cheerfulness, the disinterested objectivity have disappeared," he acknowledges his own values—values that seem appropriate in his later public criticism. In the poems, calm suggests the state of mind that might result if "littleness united" were not invincible, if the speakers in the poems could realize the missing unity in their lives. Empedocles' tragedy at least points in the theoretical direction that Arnold advocates in the preface. *Empedocles* closes with this stanza:

> The day in his hotness,

The strife with the palm;
The night in her silence,
The stars in their calm.

(*Poems*, 194)

Calm for Arnold, as for Tennyson, whether in *Empedocles* or the elegiac lyrics of the same years, seems to be "if any calm, a calm despair."

Ah! calm me, restore me;
And dry up my tears
On thy high mountain-platforms,
Where morn first appears. . . .

(*Poems*, 120)

In "Quiet Work," probably written in 1848, Arnold says: "One lesson, Nature, let me learn of thee. . . ."

Of toil unsevered from tranquillity!
Of labour, that in lasting fruit outgrows
Far noisier schemes, accomplished in repose,
Too great for haste, too high for rivalry!

(*Poems*, 106)

Arnold's poetry is a search for calm or "absorption" or "tranquility" more than for a new classicism, if only because the dialogue of the mind with itself seems to preclude physical action. To put this another way, the self-consciousness of the speakers is analogous to their elegiac quality, and what they speak about, what they regret, seems always to be past. And though nature for Arnold, as for Charles Radcliffe, offers a potential alternative to the dull "grating roar" of contemporary life, its unity is less an ideal to be attained than a condition somehow lost.

3 ARTHUR CLOUGH

So I desisted, and have only poured forth a little to Clough, we too agreeing like two lambs in a world of wolves. I think you would have liked to see the correspondence.—Arnold to his sister Jane in 1848[22]

Dear Matt
Why the d——l I shd write to you he only knows who implanted the spirit of disinterested attention in the heart of the spaniel—Clough to Arnold in 1849[23]

i

That "unplumbed, salt, estranging sea," as haunting to Arthur Clough as to Tennyson and Arnold, points to the breakdown of friendship between Arnold and Clough. Nearly the same age (Clough was born in 1819, Arnold in 1822), raised almost as brothers at Rugby and at the Arnolds' home in the Lake District, the two young men benefited from the rigorous training and the intellectual pursuits of Thomas Arnold, a father in a sense to both. They had in common a love of classical literature, of historical theory, of Goethe, and of the two institutions, Rugby and Oxford. They certainly shared a dedication to poetry, thinking of themselves as poets and thinking of poetry in the highest terms. They may, indeed, have shared a love for Tennyson's *In Memoriam.*

Arnold's lifelong dissatisfaction with contemporary English literature extended to Tennyson but not apparently to *In Memoriam.* Kathleen Tillotson has called attention to Arthur Butler's fictionalized autobiography, *Three Friends* (1900), which includes a conversation between Arnold and Clough in 1850 (at Rugby). The report seems at once too hyberbolic to be accurate and, still, perhaps, too plausible to be ignored. Clough says:

> "A new book of poems, Mat. . . . just out. It marks an era."
> "Yours," said Arnold inquiringly, "yours, beloved?"
> "No! Something far higher! Something for the highest heaven! It is one of the immortals." And he handed him . . . a little brown volume, from which Arnold read eagerly. "In Memoriam A. H. H. No author! Who is A. H. H.?"
> "They say it is Arthur Hallam," replied the other, "and the author shines out in every line. It must be Tennyson. Read No. 56."[24]

Appropriately, Clough has picked out the one section from *In Memoriam* that has seemed to many readers expressive of Tennyson's deepest anguish—an anguish that parallels Clough's own in "Easter Day, Naples 1849." If we assume Butler's account to be accurate, moreover, it was about "Nature red in tooth and claw" and "life as futile, then, as frail" so that Arnold exclaimed: "Beautiful! Luminous! A new metre! A masterpiece! It must be Alfred." Beautiful and luminous the poem may be, but surely it represents Tennyson all too close in Arnold's terms to the spirit of the times? In section 56, Tennyson speaks directly to issues raised by Sir Charles Lyell's *Principles of Geology*:

> "So careful of the type?" but no.
> From scarpèd cliff and quarried stone
> She [nature] cries, "A thousand types are gone:
> I care for nothing, all shall go."
> . . . .
> O life as futile, then, as frail!
> O for thy voice to soothe and bless!
> What hope of answer, or redress?
> Behind the veil, behind the veil.[25]

If Arnold and Clough did respond favorably to Tennyson's lament for his lost friend, they might perhaps have seen its application to their own breaking friendship. They rarely could agree about literature, and, by 1850, they agreed about little else. Arnold's letters show a friendship deteriorated to the point of continual misunderstandings and renewed apologies. While we may know that friendships die, that people are separated and contrive to separate themselves, still the slow estrangement between Arnold and Clough seems particularly sad, as though Arnold willed the two apart, cutting off his friend for obscure reasons. "Thyrsis," the elegy for Clough, could in a sense have been written by the time the two friends read *In Memoriam.*

We have almost no correspondence from Clough to Arnold, but the letter quoted above (from June 1849) seems to express Clough's bewildered response to his friend: "Dear Matt/ Why the d--l I shd write to you he only knows who implanted the spirit of disinterested attention in the heart of the spaniel—"[26] Arnold's own letters are a mixture of reluctant affection (with terms of endearment similar to those recorded by Butler) and something that resembles cruelty. At one time he implies that Clough's letters are themselves unkind: "I think you are sometimes—with regard to *me* especially—a little cross and wilful."[27] Clough does elsewhere acknowledge his inability to "compliment," though to other friends his letters are usually full of affection.

Arnold's letters treat Clough almost as his later prose treats antagonists like Francis Newman and Frederic Harrison. After telling Clough that "many persons with far lower gifts than yours yet seem to find their natural mode of expression in poetry," he says: "I often think that even a slight gift of poetical expression which in a common person might have developed itself easily and naturally, is overlaid and crushed in a profound thinker."[28]

Arnold's frank and occasionally ruthless analyses of Clough's work seem to imply that what Arnold mistrusted in his own poems he hated in

Clough's. He is disturbed by Clough's preoccupation with the times, with the *Zeitgeist.* Clough ruins his art because of an inadequate sense of beauty, but his sense of beauty has been diminished by his cerebral activities. A poem like *The Bothie* is at once too topical and too intellectual. Moreover, Clough appears to think of his own emotions not only as important in themselves but as something to urge. "You succeed best," Arnold writes in 1849, "in the hymn, where man, his deepest personal feelings being in play, finds poetical expression as *man* only, not as artist:—but consider whether you attain the *beautiful*, and whether your product gives PLEASURE, not excites curiosity or reflection."[29] At a time, then, when both men were committing themselves to poetry—and writing at their most productive—Arnold tells Clough that he is no poet.

Although we have none of Clough's immediate responses to Arnold's poems, we do have his comments on the poetry of other people as well as his 1853 review of Arnold's *Strayed Reveller* and *Empedocles.* To William Allingham, who had just published his first volume of poems (in 1850), Clough writes what might have been a rebuttal of Arnold's positions. "Somehow," he says, "I fancy that a large experience and a decisiveness of character is [*sic*] necessary to attract the modern world to poetry." Allingham should forget his "short things" and "follow Chaucer and facts."[30] The letter suggests, perhaps, one of Clough's reasons for quitting Oxford: he may have sought a wider experience for his own poetry; it also points to Clough's respect for the Byronic inheritance that Arnold was already beginning to deplore.

In his discussion of Arnold's poems for the *North American Review* (written in America), Clough offered what must have seemed a crowning insult, although Arnold said that he was not offended. Clough compares his friend's work with that of Alexander Smith; while he praises Smith for his albeit "imperfect" "Life Drama," he complains about Arnold's "more than poetic dubiousness" in poems that offer a plaintive rejection of modern life in favor of a rarefied "self-culture." Tacitly, Clough follows the criticism of Kingsley, who invoked the memory of Thomas Arnold; and Clough's criticism may show the lasting influence of Thomas Arnold on his assumptions. Clough admits that Smith's poems are imperfect; but he distrusts Arnold's poems for their scholarly privacy while he seems to paraphrase Arnold himself. "There is a disposition [in "the present age"] to press too far the finer and subtler intellectual and moral susceptibilities; to insist upon following out, as they say, to their logical consequences, the notices of some single organ of the spiritual nature." Hence—and with Arnold and Smith in mind—we need poetry that lies "between the extremes of ascetic and timid self-culture, and of unquestioning, unhesitating confidence."[31]

Clough's conception of an ideal poetry leads him, like Tennyson, to think of the vigor and the popularity of fiction. Poetry has something to learn, not from the scholar's archives, but from Thackeray and Dickens. "There is no question," he says,

> that people much prefer Vanity Fair and Bleak House [to poetry]. Why so? Is it simply because we have grown prudent and prosaic, and should not welcome, as our fathers did, the Marmions and the Rokebys, the Childe Harolds, and the Corsairs? Or is it, that to be widely popular, to gain the ear of the multitudes, to shake the hearts of men, poetry should deal more than at present it usually does, with general wants, ordinary feelings, the obvious rather than the rare facts of human nature?[32]

Because of his self-culture, Arnold has cut himself off from the power of poetry: he too, presumably, should "follow Chaucer and facts."

Behind Clough's remarks may lie a certain animus, the result of years of odd treatment from his friend. On the other hand, Clough obviously differed with Arnold about the nature and the uses of poetry, and his allusion to Thackeray and Dickens helps to clarify both his sense of Arnold's poems and his ambitions for his own. Trained classicist and scholar though he was, Clough wanted for poetry something more than the role of cultural caretaker. He shared with Arnold a love of drama, as *Dipsychus* shows, and *Dipsychus* is a far more vigorous work than Arnold's classical *Merope*. But Clough also felt with Browning and William Rossetti that poetry must catch the energy of the age and "shake the hearts of men." If we recognize the academic pastoralism in both "The Scholar Gipsy" and *The Bothie*, and if we see some sort of parallel between Arnold's *Empedocles* (written 1849–52) and *Amours de Voyage* or "Easter Day" or *Dipsychus*, the two years before 1850 sent the two poets in different and irreconcilable ways. Although closer than they thought in what they were actually writing, they saw themselves as poles apart in what they wanted or what they chose to advocate.

ii

> Forgive me all this: but I am always prepared myself to give up the attempt, on conviction: and so, I know, are you: and I only urge you to reflect whether you are advancing. Reflect too, . . . how deeply *unpoetical* the age and all one's surroundings are. Not unprofound, not ungrand, not unmoving:—but *unpoetical*.—Arnold, in an 1849 letter to Clough[33]

I have mentioned in chapter II George Lewes's contemptuous response to those who complained that the age was "unpoetic": Lewes calls them inadequate poets who cannot win for themselves a wide audience and who therefore blame the times rather than their own talents. William Rossetti approaches the question in a different way. His predilection for poets who, in Arnold's terms, "excite curiosity or reflection," is evident in his review of Clough's *The Bothie of Tober-na-Vuolich* ("a somewhat singular title, to say the least"). "The sentence," he says, "of those who do not read is the best criticism of those who will not think."[34] Although Rossetti later castigates "those who do not read," in his defense of Clough as well as in his defense of Browning, he feels that great poetry attains the beautiful precisely because it can stimulate the mind. As the son of a Dante scholar and a student of Dante himself, Rossetti remembers the powerful mind informing *The Divine Comedy*.

But while Rossetti criticizes the pettiness of his own age and scoffs at shoddy writers along with lazy readers, he thinks of his age in a vigorously optimistic way. "At no other time," he says, "has there been a greater or grander body of genius, or so honorable a display of well-cultivated taste and talent."[35] For Rossetti and the other Pre-Raphaelites—apparent idolators of things medieval and of values at odds with those of their contemporaries—the mid-nineteenth century was in fact a time of promise and achievement. It was only unpoetical to the extent that tired aesthetics dominated contemporary taste.

Rossetti later dismissed his review of Clough, calling it "somewhat ponderous."[36] But if the writer of this and the other three reviews for *The Germ* was still young, unpracticed, and given to quoting pages of text, he shows a genuine understanding of Clough's poems. Against the views of Arnold, which he could not have known, he praises the "peculiar modernness" of Clough, his "recognition of every-day fact," and his "willingness to believe it as capable of poetry as that which, but for having once been fact, would not now be tradition."[37] As a Pre-Raphaelite, Rossetti welcomed the specificity in Clough's poems, just as he praised it in Dante and Wordsworth, and he associated fact with "truth to Nature," the Pre-Raphaelite call-to-arms.

Rossetti's admiration for Clough anticipates his response to Browning. He understands the great poets of his time as achieving a kind of "completeness," by which he means a full "elaboration" of "character and incident" and a wide range of stylistic innovation. We might expect from the Pre-Raphaelites special allegiance to Tennyson or to Patmore, who was friend to both Tennyson and the Brotherhood. But William Rossetti's own long poem of the time, *Mrs. Holmes Grey*, is a "realistic" narrative about a woman who abandons herself to an uninterested lover and dies, with the story recounted by a double first-person (story within a story) and by newspaper accounts.[38] Rossetti was attempting what he admired in Browning and Clough.

In Rossetti's eyes, Clough achieves a kind of inclusive art akin to Browning's, by which the completeness of the novel is grafted on an accommodating poetic form. Clough's experiment, like some of Browning, reflects a new sense of poetry that is seen at once as narrative, dramatic, even epistolary, as well as lyric. Clough's "fearless and unembarrassed" poetry presumably—though Rossetti does not make the point—contrasts with Arnold's which is reserved in vocabulary and wholly introspective in mood.[39] Clough's modernity is not, as Arnold would have it, a rejection of beauty, but rather a courageous approach to beauty through "everyday fact."

iii

> My dear Mr. Clough
> I have been reading the Bothy all the morning and am charmed with it. I have never been there but I think it must be like Scotland—Scotland hexametrically laid out that is . . . and it seems to me to give one the proper Idyllic feeling which is ½ sensual and ½ spiritual I take it. . . . Your description of the sky and the landscape—and that figure of the young fellow bathing shapely with shining limbs and the blue sky for background—are delightful to me. . . . I have been going over some of the same ground (of youth) in this present number of Pendennis; which I fear will be considered rather warm by the puritans: but I think you'll understand it—that is if you care for such trivialities, or take the trouble to look under the stream of the story.—Thackeray in November 1848[40]

Between 1848, when he published *The Bothie*, and 1850, when he wrote most of *Dipsychus*, Clough had undergone the major crisis of his life. His hero, Philip Hewson, in *The Bothie*, finds a beautiful young woman during his long vacation in the Scottish Highlands, marries her, and sets off with a few tools for a pastoral life in Australia. Clough himself flirted with the idea of Australia, but from a self-imposed necessity, and without the mitigation of a lovely wife. Unable any longer to subscribe to the Thirty-Nine Articles of the church, he resigned his Oxford tutorship and fellowship in 1848, searched for a time for new employment, and finally—with the help of young Walter Bagehot—found a post at University Hall, a nonsectarian institution associated with the University of London. He was soon to lose even this post, and it was some years before he secured his final employment with the Education Office.

Giving up the Oxford posts would have been for most academicians next to impossible. Clough not only cut his relationship with the center of academic studies, he also lost friends, social status, and a very comfortable income. And he made his decision in the face of advice from his superiors, who urged him to think longer, to be patient. Clough's resignation had several consequences. He was, for example, no longer able to marry, and the fact that he was thirty and unmarried troubled him. His new penury gave temporary relief to his religious conscience, though the reasons for his resignation meant that old supporters would now no longer recommend him, but the scruples that led to his resignation soon returned. The line "Christ is not risen!" from "Easter Day, Naples" recurs in *Dipsychus*, and from doubts about Anglican dogma, Clough seems to have moved on to doubts about the existence of God at all. The lines

> The good are weak, the wicked strong;
> And O my God, how long, how long?
> Dong, there is no God; dong![41]

may not reflect a confirmed atheism, but in their odd cacophany and in the repetition of "Dong, there is no God," Clough expresses a profound sense of religious alienation.

The term *alienation* is appropriate. I have mentioned Asa Briggs's statement that mid-century intellectuals were neither "rootless nor rebellious," but rather "stable and assured," because they had "enough property to buy leisure and independence."[42] A number of writers might come to mind to contradict Briggs's estimate, but Clough seems particularly apposite. In Evelyn Greenberger's words:

> Economic alternatives for the man without capital were few. In a world without an open civil service, large corporations, nonsectarian education, modern sophisticated communications media, or almost any of the other economic apparatus by which our own largely unreligious intelligentsia now supports itself, a man with Clough's record was nearly unemployable. . . . Almost no one could support himself and a family on literary work: a "literary man" was almost inevitably one with a private income or a rich wife. A man who left his profession to make a career of literary hack work might find himself barely able to survive even as a scribe, like David Masson's acquaintance, John Christie.[43]

While Ms. Greenberger herself forgets to mention that many writers managed well as men-of-letters, making handsome incomes, or moving, like the author of *Vanity Fair*, in the social circles of their choice, she is right about Arthur Clough. He was not a fluent writer, and he would never be a glib one. Writing purely for money would have been as difficult for him as holding a fellowship purely for money. And though it was possible for him to find a civil service position, Clough could not—like John Stuart Mill, Thomas Love Peacock, William Allingham, Anthony Trollope, or even Matthew Arnold—quietly divorce his work from his life. This, more than the wholesale lack of opportunity, probably accounts for his sense of alienation.

Clough was a complex man, for whom private struggles would remain private, except to a few friends and, when he did finally marry, to his wife Blanche. The man who mocked the public commandments of his age also subscribed to a sense of duty—witness his service to his wife's friend Florence Nightingale in years to come—and lived by an almost stoical code. But it is not unfair to Clough to think of "Easter Day I" as an expression of deep and unanswered religious misgivings and of *Dipsychus* as an ironical and witty but nonetheless disillusioned utterance about modern life as well as about Clough's own shattered career.[44] For Clough, as for Francis Newman, whose *The Soul* he reviewed in 1850 (see the following chapter), religious doubts serve as means to self-awareness, becoming tenor and vehicle in what Clough calls "communing" "with my secret self."

From the good humor and happy conclusion of *The Bothie* through the unfulfilled loves of *Amours de Voyage* and the skepticism of "Easter Day" and "Epi-Strauss-ion" to the personal confrontations of *Dipsychus* lies a long and difficult emotional journey. *The Bothie* was written in England while Clough still held his Oxford post; *Amours de Voyage*, "Easter Day," and *Dipsychus* were all written in Italy (like Browning's *Christmas-Eve and Easter-Day*) and set there too. *Amours* describes in loose epistolary verse the tentative and unconsummated relationship of Claude (Clough?) and Mary Trevellyn, English travelers, who not only do not sail happily for Australia and a new life, they never even come together to confess their reluctant love. Mary writes to her friend Miss Roper at the poem's conclusion:

> You have heard nothing; of course, I know you can have heard nothing.
> Ah, well, more than once I have broken my purpose, and sometimes,
> Only too often, have looked for the little lake-steamer to bring him.
> But it is only fancy,—I do not really expect it.
> Oh, and you see I know so exactly how he would take it:
> Finding the chances prevail against the meeting again, he would banish
> Forthwith every thought of the poor little possible hope, which
> I myself could not help, perhaps, thinking only too much of;

> He would resign himself, and go. I see it exactly.
> So I also submit, although in a different manner.
> Can you not really come? We go very shortly to England.
>
> (*Poems*, 133)

In its account of Claude's *Weltschmerz* and in its arbitrary division into cantos, *Amours* recalls *Childe Harold*, which Clough invokes for self-parody in *Dipsychus*; in its emphasis on diminished *hope* and on the possibility of *nothing*, in its acquiescent and partly self-understanding characters, who calmly dissect their own lives, *Amours* anticipates the muted and brittle conversational worlds of T. S. Eliot's later plays. The word *submit*, though Clough may understand it in various ways, carries with it a double sense of accepting the world as we find it and accepting a religious burden—a burden all the heavier for being so incompatible with the everyday world. This, as I take it, is at the heart of *Dipsychus*, a work in which Clough barely allows a story and altogether dispenses with epistolary forms. A story may imply an ordered life; letters, even to distant friends, imply a compassionate listener. In *Dipsychus* "I with my secret self held communing of my own." The result is one of the most powerful mid-century poems and—in spite of its lack of narrative context—one of the most available to modern readers. Clough's "communing" is an experiment with various interior voices, each of which toys with fragments of truth. The poem is at once a witty dialogue with the self and what might be called a dramatic elegy.

iv

> What is it to be a poet? It is to have one's personal life, one's actuality, in categories entirely different from the poetical productions, that is, to relate one's self to the ideal only in imagination, so that one's own personal way of living is more or less satire upon the poetical or upon one's self.—Søren Kierkegaard, in January 1849[45]

Arnold complained to Clough that his poems succeeded best as hymns, because Clough, overwhelmingly sincere and unable to leave religious problems unresolved, used his art for ulterior purposes. Arnold's own concern with the *Zeitgeist*, which later manifested itself in his exploratory assessments of nineteenth-century culture, may have been masked by classical settings or by self-imposed poetic limits, yet the man who bemoaned the unpoetic condition of his age is the man preoccupied with his age. As Rossetti noticed, moreover, the poetry of both Arnold and Clough deals with fundamentally religious questions. In recent years, critics have deplored Clough's reputation as "the poet of doubt," and in the sense that such a tag reduces a poet or falsely limits him, its rejection is understandable. Rossetti is nevertheless right in seeing Clough and his contemporaries as chronically unable to leave religious topics alone.

The quotation from Kierkegaard's journals about the nature of a poet helps, I think, to put *Dipsychus* in perspective. We are not inclined, perhaps, to think of Kierkegaard, precursor of existentialism, profound religious thinker, and Danish priest, in relation to an English poet like Clough.[46] Yet Kierkegaard's life (1813–1855) parallels Clough's (1819–1861) in some interesting ways. Apart from the fact that both died at about the same age, that they wrote autobiographically, that they were private men who often chose not to publish what they had written, that they were hostile to their established churches and punished themselves by their actions toward those churches—apart from all this, they were preoccupied with their sense of themselves as poets, and as poets necessarily divided by the times. The problem of living in "a world of worldliness"[47] with the possibility that "Christ has not risen" or that "God is dead" meant for both men "all the sufferings of inwardness" (the phrase is Kierkegaard's). A poet for Clough as for Kierkegaard seems to be "an unhappy man who conceals deep torments in his heart, but whose lips are so formed that when a groan or shriek streams out over them it sounds like beautiful music."[48] Arnold thought this untrue of Clough, but, as Rossetti knew, Clough's sense of music was simply different from Arnold's; hence again his criticism of Arnold in the 1853 review, his feeling that Arnold's quest for the beautiful involved self-indulgence.

And yet there recurs in Clough's poems, just as in Arnold's, a conflict between selves: between the self of imagination and the self of ordinary existence, "so that," again in Kierkegaard's words, "one's personal way of living is more or less satire upon the poetical . . . self."[49] I can think of no better comment on Clough's life at mid-century and Clough's sense of his life as expressed in *Dipsychus* than the following passage from Kierkegaard:

> Contemplating my personal life, am I a Christian. . .? or is not this personal existence of mine a mere poet-existence, though with a trait of daimonia? The logical thing to do would be to venture on so prodigious a scale and bring upon myself such misfortune that I should then be in a situation to become really a Christian. But have I a right to do it dramatically, so that the Christianity of the whole land is involved in the game? Is there not something of desperation in all this. . .? Perhaps, for perhaps it might turn out that I do not become a Christian.[50]

Dipsychus records an extremity of intellectual and emotional strain, after the fact as it were of Clough's own prodigious "venture," and with a kind of desperation. The speaker picks up from "Easter Day" the line "Christ is not risen," and contemplates it after a year's delay. "Easter Day" and *Amours* may have reflected imaginary circumstances, but both are set in Italian cities and at a time of revolutionary activity—*Amours* parallels Clough's letters from abroad about Mazzini and the Italian patriots and the French attack on Rome (1849). Clough sets *Dipsychus* in Venice, the city that had long been a symbol for decadence. Like Thomas Mann's later Aschenbach in *Death in Venice*, Dipsychus is a northerner, reduced emotionally, and at some sort of crisis in his life. He is intoxicated by the city; he fights against a long suppressed sexuality; he is haunted by vague longings; he encounters his own "daimonia." And if the general time of the poem is vague, Clough's allusions are not. The "Spirit" says for example:

> The Doge's palace though, from hence,
> In spite of Ruskin's d--d pretence,
> The tide now level with the quay,
> Is certainly a thing to see.
>
> (*Poems*, 244)

While Clough wrote *Dipsychus*, Ruskin, of course, was at work on *Stones of Venice*.

Clough's dialogue is with the Spirit, and the Spirit is an articulate and witty "Spirit of the Times," a voice who is himself the *Zeitgeist*. He is also the voices of sensuality, of skepticism, of self-satire. In terms of Dipsychus's aspirations, he is "*der Geist der stets verneint*," Goethe's negating spirit from *Faust*. Clough's Spirit anticipates those seedy middle-class Mephistos in Dostoyevski, Gide, and Mann, the disreputable tempters, close to the unacknowledged side of the somewhat dubious modern Faust. Dipsychus, according to Walter Houghton, should not be confused with the Spirit; the Spirit is a separate character with whom the divided spirit of Dipsychus speaks. While recognizing a parallel between Clough's character and Arnold's Empedocles, Houghton suggests that Dipsychus is simply an intellectual in disarray, another Claude, who confronts a separate being. For "apart from the verbal difficulty . . . requiring 'the two-natured' man to talk with his other nature, the text leaves no doubt, I think, that Clough meant Dipsychus himself to be two-psychied."[51] Houghton cites the lines

> To thine own self be true, the wise man says.

> Are then my fears myself? O double self!
> And I untrue to both.
>
> (*Poems*, 275)

to argue that Dipsychus could hardly be untrue to the Spirit and must therefore refer to a polarity within himself.

It may be that Clough intended his divided hero to be speaking with a wholly separate character, and it may be, too, that in a poem he never entirely finished or polished, he left certain inconsistencies. But Dipsychus could, as a matter of fact, be untrue to what the Spirit represents in the sense that he would lack the courage to act, that he could not perform in the world of "actuality," however sordid he might find it. Like Empedocles, he is a poet made aware finally of his own capacities. An indication that Dipsychus does speak with a dramatized version of himself can be seen in the way that the Spirit enters the poem. In Scene I, Dipsychus muses about the year past and quotes his own (Clough's) "Christ is not risen." The Spirit (as Kierkegaard's "satire upon the poetical self") quotes in turn, then says: "Oh indeed! /Wasn't aware that was your creed." Dipsychus takes no apparent notice, and the two voices speak across each other through the entire scene, with Dipsychus finally saying, "Ah, heaven, too true, at Venice/Christ is not risen either" (*Poems*, 220). In the next scene, Dipsychus says:

> What is this persecuting voice that haunts me?
> What? Whence? of whom? How am I to detect?
> Myself or not myself? My own bad thoughts,
> Or some external agency at work,
> To lead me who knows whither?
>
> (*Poems*, 222)

The Spirit is an external agency to the extent that he is dramatized; and in conversation with him, Dipsychus will push and be pushed to extremities of opinion. Clough, however, insists on our seeing the intimate connection between the troubled poet and the mocking spirit:

> Whate're I think, he adds his comments to;
> Which yet not interrupts me.

"Not interrupts" because somehow expected or anticipated. In the same passage he says:

> I have scarce spoken yet to this strange follower
> Whom I picked up—ye great gods, tell me where!
> And yet he seems new come. I commune with myself.
>
> (*Poems*, 265)

In fact, Clough seems purposely to hedge on the nature of his two psyches, since he wants the extraordinary state of Dipsychus's mind to remain enigmatic. In the humorous epilogue to the poem, in which Dipsychus (now Clough himself) tries to clarify the poem for his friendly but obtuse uncle, he says:

> "You see, dear sir, the thing which it is attempted to represent is the conflict between the tender conscience and the world. Now, the over-tender conscience will, of course, exaggerate the wickedness of the world; and the Spirit in my poem may be merely the hypothesis or subjective imagination, formed—"
>
> "Oh, . . . for goodness' sake, my dear boy," interrupted my uncle, "don't go into the theory of it. If you're wrong in it, it makes bad worse; if you're right, you may be a critic, but you can't be a poet. And then you know very well I don't understand all those new words."
>
> (*Poems*, 292)

Dipsychus's uncle may be intended for the baffled reader whom Clough anticipates for his poem, or he may be yet a further self, another voice of self-parody in a work that continually undercuts its speaker.

> The Devil! we've had enough of you,
> Quote us a little Wordsworth, do!
>
> (*Poems*, 246)

The uncle's lethargy and the Spirit's impatience raise another (and here a final) point about Clough's poem. Dipsychus does occasionally quote Wordsworth, or at least echo him. His apostrophe to the

> great Alps,
> That wrapping round your head in solemn clouds
> Seem sternly to sweep past our vanities. . . .
>
> (*Poems*, 223)

recalls, however, that Dipsychus wanders through Venice rather than the Alps and that he refers to physical nature in a largely symbolic way. In this poem as in *The Bothie* he is conscious of the archetypal Garden of Adam and Eve, an intellectualized garden, which, as the Spirit in another context says, "has a strong Strauss-smell about it." Dipsychus is an intellectual with the knowledge of things but with a rationalizing mind that robs the life of things. For Dipsychus-Clough as for Empedocles-Arnold, nature itself will not suffice.

If nature serves as an intellectualized alternative instead of a "healer" in *Dipsychus*, then Clough shares with the Arnold of "Obermann" the sense of Wordsworth as a somewhat ineffectual nurse. My question is whether, in that case, Goethe is Clough's diagnostic physician? In the first drafts of *Dipsychus* Clough referred to his speakers as Faustulus and Mephisto. His "Prologue," a brief conversation between Dipsychus and his uncle, who hopes the poem will be "in good plain verse," is not set, quite obviously, in heaven. But it serves, like Goethe's "Prologue" to poke fun at what follows. Goethe's Mephistopheles consciously practices his conversational art with God, and he makes light of his interview: *"Es ist gar hübsch von einem grossen Herrn/So menschlich mit dem Teufel selbst zu sprechen."*[52] Clough altered the names Faustulus and Mephisto to Dipsychus and the Spirit, no doubt to make his indebtedness to Goethe's *Faust* less obvious. But whether or not Clough models his protagonist or his protagonist's struggles on *Faust*, he certainly meant his reader to see affinities and to bear *Faust* in mind.

Just as Tennyson could assume his reader's awareness of Dante, Clough could assume his reader's awareness of Goethe. Mid-century reviews remind us of an 1850 translation of Eckermann's *Conversations*, of a Henry Bohn edition of Goethe's plays, and of several reissues of letters and other works. The page of George Lewes's *Leader* (and Lewes was soon to publish his *Life of Goethe*) are full of references to Goethe. Lewes even calls Thackeray "a mocking Mephistopheles," with a Goethe sitting at his elbow.[53] Lewes was a student of Goethe, but his respect for Goethe, his sense of Goethe as the great spirit of the age, was not uncommon. Many of Lewes's contemporaries had followed Teufelsdröck's admonition to put away their Byron and to read their Goethe.

So Goethe was very much in the air. And he was in Clough's mind as he wrote the third major poem of his own Italian journey. How far should we push the parallels? Evelyn Greenberger argues against comparison with *Faust*: "Those who see in *Dipsychus* only another Faust have not looked deep enough. Indeed, the implicit criticism here of Faust's willingness to learn at the expense of another human spirit is both clear and profoundly important."[54] While it may be true that Clough inverts the moral positions of *Faust*, so that his Mephisto becomes more sympathetic than the character he tempts, in fact neither the Spirit nor Dipsychus is entirely wrong or right throughout the poem. Clough admires action, yet action, like self-denial, can never absolutely be linked with moral good. By presenting a psychological and moral vision of more complexity than Goethe's, Clough approximates—as I have suggested—the rhetorical and moral antitheses of Kierkegaard, who is similarly concerned with the attractions and the effects of renunciation. To say this is not, however, to dismiss parallels with *Faust.* It would make more sense to argue that Clough parodies Goethe, just as he parodies Byron and himself, to call attention to similarities as well as differences. Clough's obscure woman is no Gretchen, but she is an object of lust, and lust in *Dipsychus* as in *Faust* is both a physical and an intellectual passion. Dipsychus lacks Faust's energy; his "yearning sensibilities of soul" lend themselves to a terrible inertia; hence, perhaps, the contrast between Goethe's dramatic structure and Clough's sequence of scenes, each of which echoes and sometimes repeats the others. "Alas, how quietly/Out of our better into our worse selves . . ." (*Poems*, 233)—like the lines "Christ is not risen," or "Dong, there is no God"—recurs. The sense is not of a rejuvenating memory as in Wordsworth, but of a haunting memory, and the Spirit reminds Dipsychus of his own troubling thoughts as well as of the world of action and success. Dipsychus does not so much have a soul to sell as a soul that he must partly lose.

The affinities with Faust nevertheless remain. Clough's overly intellectual hero has come to a crisis. If he reminds us, with his passivity and his repetitions, of Eliot's Prufrock—

> Ah, pretty thing—well, well—. Yet should I go?
> Alas, I cannot say. What should I do?
>
> (*Poems*, 224)

he has the self-understanding, the physical appetite, and the need for some emotional or spiritual breakthrough of Faust.

Apart from Dipsychus himself, Clough leaves no doubt that the shapes of his dialogue look back to Goethe. The well-meaning uncle's plea for "good plain verse" may be answered in a poem that is more complete and more colloquial than Rossetti found *The Bothie* to be. But in *Dipsychus* Clough experiments with a variety of forms from rolling blank verse to fragments from songs to epigrammatic couplets to rhyming monologues. Even more than Browning, Clough is testing the limits of poetic rhythms and experimenting with poetic vocabulary. From one point of view he is using dramatic monologue in a way that anticipates Pound and Eliot in the early years of the twentieth century; from another point of view he is developing the dramatic voices of the Romantics, just as Melville, in *Moby Dick*, was soon to do in prose. In either case, the process is an "escape from personality," or—as Harriet Martineau described her own mid-century crisis—an escape from "the prison of the self" in an experimental poetic drama.[55]

4 ROBERT BROWNING

> The correct theory is precisely an aspect of the conception of art as intuition or lyrical intuition. Inasmuch as every work of art expresses a state of mind, and inasmuch as a state of mind is individual and always new, intuition implies infinite intuitions, which it is impossible to fit into a set of pigeon holes for genres, unless the set itself is composed, too, of infinite pigeon holes, and, thus, no longer pigeon holes for genres, but for intuitions.–Benedetto Croce, *Guide to Aesthetics*[56]

i

William Rossetti's final review for *The Germ* addressed itself to the poet who seemed to the Pre-Raphaelites "the modern giant," but who caused great difficulties for mid-Victorian readers. Most critics of Browning acknowledged his "genius" while deploring his "grotesque" and "obscure" style. A typical critic was the Scottish author and physician David Moir, who presented a series of lectures to characterize the poetry of the first half century. Moir argues that Browning, however gifted, "has utterly mistaken singularity for originality." Similarly Elizabeth Barrett Browning, despite "a high, peculiar, and speculative genius," has become "more and more inverted and involved."[57] Whether Moir thinks that Robert influenced Elizabeth, or whether–as seems likely from his comments on Tennyson and others–he merely thinks both poets reflective of dangerous tendencies, he approves of neither.

Moir understands criticism to be a matter of historical assessment. Can Elizabeth Browning return to her strengths, leaving the "dark November day" for the sunshine of poetry to come? Will Tennyson ever fulfill his promise? How does Wordsworth stand now? His attempts to rank and to judge indicate that Moir shares with social and historical writers a desire to estimate his own age and a readiness to understand the age in terms of historical movement. He does not, as Taine was soon to do, explain the poetry by the character of the nation and by the times; but he sees a parallel. As a Scot, he is interested in the development of national literatures. And while, unlike some of the cruder Utilitarians, he assumes no necessary connection between social and literary "progress," he does assume that the morbidity of his own era will be supplanted by health and light. I cite Moir because his desire to make historical distinctions is analogous to Browning's own, in the essay on Shelley, and because, in his assumptions and his readiness to judge, he represents critical tendencies that the young Rossetti categorically rejects.

Rossetti's approach to literature is similarly historical, and he may relapse into clichés about earnestness and sincerity. He is, however, far more sophisticated. He assumes that, in the face of "genius," the critic's first responsibility is a sympathetic *diffidence.* "Of all poets, there is none more than Robert Browning, in approaching whom diffidence is necessary." The principle of diffidence defines "the critic's function," which is "to interpret rather than judge, to state facts, and to suggest considerations; not to lay down dogmas."[58] What is remarkable in the brief review of *Christmas-Eve and Easter-Day*—apart from the fact that Rossetti never speaks directly about the work at hand—is his accounting for Browning's "extravagance" and "grotesqueness" of style. Rossetti scoffs at the insularity of his countrymen, who "'can't read Sordello.'" They fail to understand that "style is not stationary, or, in the *concrete,* matter of principle: style is, firstly, national; next chronological; and lastly individual."[59] Since poetic styles must change, the sort of criticisms made by Moir are senseless, for it is at once futile to advocate the mannerisms of earlier writers and irresponsible to attack poets whose stylistic manner is new. We might appreciate that, as a Pre-Raphaelite, Rossetti would be concerned with style, but it is testimony to his and to his colleagues' generosity that they could appreciate a poet as different from their own apparent ideals as Browning.

Rossetti acknowledges that singularity is no virtue in itself. He simply says it may be required. Browning is evidently unconventional; the question is whether his manner is appropriate for his conceptions, and Rossetti feels there can be little doubt.

> To those who yet insist: "Why cannot I read Sordello?" we can only answer: —Admitted a leading idea, not only metaphysical but subtle and complicated to the highest degree; how work out this idea, unless through the finest intricacy of shades of mental development? . . . Admitted an intense aching consideration of thought; how be self-consistent, unless uttering words condensed to the limits of language?—And let us last say: Read Sordello again. Surely, if you do not understand him, the fact tells two ways.[60]

Rossetti's defense of the poet, his desire "to explain and justify the state of feeling in which we enter on the consideration of a new poem by Robert Browning," is a strong apology for Browning's "difficulties." It comes close, moreover, to Browning's own feelings about his poetry. If the "leading ideas" in Browning are "the emanation(s) of the poet's most secret soul," then Rossetti has understood precisely what Browning himself came to see as the heart of his poetry. For a later (1863) edition of *Sordello*, Browning was to write to Milsand, the French writer, by way of preface.

> Dear Friend,—Let the next poem be introduced by your name. . . . I wrote it twenty-five years ago for only a few. . . . My own faults of expression were many; but with care for a man or a book such would be surmounted, and without it what avails the faultlessness of either? I blame nobody, least of all myself, who did my best then and since. . . . The historical decoration was purposely of no more importance than a background requires; and my stress lay on the incidents in the development of a soul: little else is worth study. I, at least, always thought so—you, with many known and unknown to me, think so—others may one day think so; and whether my attempt remain for them or not, I trust, though away and past it, to continue ever yours, R. B.[61]

Browning may well have forgotten, as Robert Langbaum suggests, "that the Romantic poets had thought so, that even Arnold, who disagreed, could hardly help but write poetry as though he too thought so, and that the enormous popularity of the 'spasmodic' poets gave evidence that by mid-century almost everyone thought so."[62] It is more likely that Browning was entirely aware of poetic tendencies in his age and of complementary poetic theories—as his own distinction between "objective" and "subjective" would indicate. But to say that expressive theories of art were pervasive at mid-century is not to say that they were accepted without reluctance (the antithesis of creative and reflective makes this clear) or that Browning himself was understood to be an expressive poet. The letter to Milsand—a public declaration—suggests that Browning wanted his contemporaries to see the representative qualities of his poetry (much as Arnold asserted the representative qualities of his poetry in later years), his use of dramatic forms toward lyric ends.

The rival energies of objective and subjective, dramatic and personal, bear on Elizabeth Barrett Browning's relation to *Christmas-Eve and Easter-Day* and on the ways this odd but pivotal work continues to be read. When the poem was announced, a *Leader* reviewer (probably Lewes) said: "Browning's new poem . . . excites peculiar expectations partly because it is his first publication since his marriage; and we may anticipate tracing the influence upon his impressionable mind of a remarkable woman; and partly because it is understood to be an elaborate defense of Christianity."[63] By and large, the poem has always been thought of in the terms suggested here: a reflection of Elizabeth Barrett Browning's influence and a defense (however awkward) of Christianity. What the reviewer evidently would not have known is that Elizabeth Browning had long tried to persuade Browning to write about religion (his "soul") and also to write in his own voice.

Elizabeth urged Browning "to speak for himself, 'out of that personality which God made, & with the voice He turned into such power & sweetness of speech.'"[64] *Power* seems accurate; *sweetness* implies a quality distinctly unlike Browning's but close to her own talents. And a problem with Elizabeth Browning's poems at this time (in *Sonnets from the Portuguese*) was that they spoke perhaps too much of personality and of private emotion. Robert Browning later referred to "the strange, heavy crown, that wreath of Sonnets." "'Heavy,' perhaps," as William Irvine and Park Honan write, "because they seemed too personal to be made public and yet were too good to be kept private. Of course the argument of merit prevailed. The sequence was included in the 1850 edition of Elizabeth's poems."[65] The intimacy of the poems, which yoked together love for Robert Browning with love of God, no doubt prompted David Moir to call Elizabeth Barrett the "reflex" of Alfred Tennyson, who also memorialized his love with a sequence of sonnet-like lyrics.

If Elizabeth urged Robert to write out of himself, she was at the time concerned about his not writing at all. Since their marriage (in 1846) he had written little. "What am I to say about Robert's idleness and mine? I scold him about it in the most anti-conjugal manner."[66] A few months after this report of scolding, Browning was hard at work on *Christmas-Eve and Easter-Day*. Whether that "remarkable woman" determined its subject or urged its manner, the poem reflects interests of both poets, and it comes as close as almost any of Browning's works to unmediated poetic statement.

But did Browning, indeed could Browning, write directly "out of that personality which God made"? J. Hillis Miller argues that Browning "is a multivocal personality, and there is no way in which he can accede to Elizabeth Barrett's repeated request that, having written so much dramatically, he should now speak in his own person." In point of fact, "he cannot throw off the mask, for there is nothing behind it, or nothing but a face that is all faces at once."[67] Professor Miller's sense of Browning struggling with "the formlessness prior to all form," with the "chaos" of life, each poem a temporary "crystallization leading to discovery of its inadequacy," accounts well for the constant projections of "internal dialogue" in Browning and for the "breathless haste of his language." Yet Miller himself seems to argue that Browning *must* write out of himself, and in ways, moreover, that Elizabeth Browning had specifically in mind. He speaks about Browning's sympathetic relativism, his acceptance of "the great crowd of grotesques and idealists," who manage to express "the consciousness of Browning himself."[68] Elizabeth's own terms are not too different:

> But you . . . you have the superabundant mental life and individuality which admits of shifting a personality and speaking the truth still. *That* is the highest faculty, the strongest and rarest, which exercises itself in Art,—we are all agreed there is none so great faculty as the dramatic. Several times you have hinted to me that I made you careless for the drama, and it has puzzled me to fancy how it could be, when I understand myself so clearly both the difficulty and the glory of dramatic art. Yet I am conscious of wishing you to take the other crown besides—[69]

The terribly high expectations for Browning's art point to ambitions that Browning shared with contemporaries like Arnold and that he probably drew from Shelley. At a time when he had trouble writing, however, his own ambitions and the reminder and articulation of them by his wife must have been daunting. What Elizabeth wanted of Browning and what he expected of himself is an art beyond poetry as such, which nonetheless subsumes great poetic force. Browning's long interest in the Swiss alchemist Paracelsus, about whom he had written an early work, characterizes his ambitions, for Paracelsus seeks more than the mere changing of base metals into gold. He represents for Browning "the transmutation of his own mortal clay into angelic brilliance."[70] The Promethean longing in Paracelsus could explain why Browning was to admire Arnold's more or less contemporary *Empedocles*, since Empedocles for Arnold has as much of the alchemist about him as the Promethean figure.

Paracelsus may also remind us again of Carl Jung's later infatuation with alchemy, which Jung equates with profound psychic processes. The transformation of mortal clay begins for Jung in self-understanding. He draws parallels between his own ideals and the alchemists' codes of behavior, between the rigor of their intellectual and moral discipline, and the shape of his own professional life. His work, Jung said, is inseparable from his life, which necessitates a constant assessment of himself as "patient," a constant investigation of psyche or soul.[71] Such, I think, was the way Browning thought of his own poetic life, and how Elizabeth wanted him to feel. For Browning as for Jung, "Soul [is] the unsounded sea";[72] it is Arnold's "unplumbed" sea, emblem of the buried life, and of Carlyle's great "unconscious." His preoccupation with the demands of the soul shows Browning, like his own Paracelsus, leaning toward alchemy, looking, in the twistings and windings of his language, to express the inexpressible, attempting some sort of self-transformation through and in spite of words.

> What is left for us, save, in growth
> Of soul, to rise up, far past both,
> From the gift looking to the giver,

And from the cistern to the river,
And from the finite to infinity,
And from man's dust to God's divinity?

(*Poems*, 406)

To read *Christmas-Eve and Easter-Day* in a biographical context may have the sanction of Browning's later letter to Milsand. Ironically, at the time when he seemed to be following his wife's suggestion and attempting "the other crown," he deplored the kind of biographical gossip associated with Shelley and implied that for his own type of poetry biography was superfluous. It may generally be for Browning; certainly he shared Jung's impatience with biography, and asked people to read his work, perhaps thinking of himself as his work: "R. B. a poem." Yet it does help to remember that *Christmas-Eve and Easter-Day* is Browning's only published book between the last of *Bells and Pomegranates* (1846) and *Men and Women* (1855), that, like Arnold's *Empedocles* and Clough's *Dipsychus*, it coincides with a time of crisis in Browning's life, and that it seems to bear some relation, not only to Elizabeth's urging, but also to Arthur Clough's example. The Brownings may have met Clough in Italy in 1849. They were definitely reading Clough's "Easter Day" and "Epi-Strauss-ion," along with Arnold's *Strayed Reveller*. Elizabeth praised Arnold and Clough, but she found neither "poetic." And when *Christmas-Eve and Easter-Day* was finished, she evidently found it too intellectual. Thus, while she persuaded Browning to a poem like *Christmas-Eve*, she seemed to have reservations akin to Arnold's about the result.

Arnold accused Clough of excelling at hymns. In a sense, his own "Stanzas from the Grande Chartreuse" or "Dover Beach" might be hymns, hymns without hope on the order of Clough's "Easter Day." So, too, Browning's mid-century poem. Like Arnold and Clough, he is preoccupied with the spiritual climate of the age. By 1850 he probably knew David Friedrich Strauss's *Life of Jesus* (as translated by George Eliot in the year the Brownings married), and he was concerned about the Catholic revival, which soon culminated in the restoration in England of the Catholic sees. As the later "Bishop Blougram's Apology" illustrates, Browning kept an eye on the careers of Catholic leaders such as Wiseman (appointed cardinal in 1850), John Newman, and Henry Manning. *Christmas-Eve and Easter-Day* weighs the appeal of Rome and the speculations of a Strauss-like professor against the inherited principles of English dissent, Browning's unlikely *via media.* But behind the external forms of religion and religious doubt lie Browning's personal exploration, his "particular expression," in Croce's terms, "of a particular personality."

ii

> As a page out of the history of a life, the poetic confession of a troubled soul, *Christmas-Eve* has a significance and a value peculiarly its own. . . . Since Butler, no English poet has exhibited the same daring propensity and facility in rhyming. If the verse is sometimes rugged it is but the better exponent of the thought Realism in Art has Truth as an aim, Ugliness as a pitfall.—George Lewes (?) in a *Leader* review[73]

The *Leader* review of *Christmas-Eve and Easter-Day* raises further questions about Browning's mid-century work and about its relation to the poems of Arnold and Clough. Lewes—if Lewes was the reviewer—uses the word *realism*, with a meaning he himself is credited with introducing into English, but uses it at this early time in a way he assumes will be understood, and applies it to poetry rather than to fiction. Like Rossetti, he recognizes the risk of *ugliness* in a work that seeks accuracy and completeness. Style, instead of a pretty ornament of the thought, is integral with the thought. "In the bold and artful mingling of the ludicrous with the intensely serious [Browning] reminds us of Carlyle. His style is swayed by the subject." His choice of subject, his honest treatment of the subject, and his disregard for his reader's expectations allow Browning a radically new version of modern literary directions: "the poetic confession of a troubled soul."[74]

The reviews by Lewes and Rossetti both make virtues out of perceived faults. Both are apologies for a work that has, from the outset, seemed to need apology. "It does not strike us," wrote the *Spectator* reviewer, "that Mr. Browning has at all advanced himself by this new poem."[75] And for the *Athenaeum*: "Our complaint against Mr. Browning is—that while dealing with the highest themes of imagination . . . , he has recklessly impaired the dignity of his purpose."[76] Such an opinion of *Christmas-Eve and Easter-Day* has lingered ever since. If critics mention the work at all, it is to dismiss it as an aberration, or an interlude between better things, or as a work of "conscience" rather than imagination, interesting only in what it tells us about Browning's ideas.[77] Even a sympathetic reader like William Clyde De Vane can say that "in spite of many splendid passages . . . ," Browning's mid-century work "was not significant for its day, and is even less so for ours."[78]

Christmas-Eve and Easter-Day has certainly avoided popularity. It sold only about two hundred copies when first published, and it is not now anthologized. But whether or not it is significant for our age, it proved significant for its own. Browning's poem crept into people's consciousness because—apart from its artistic innovation—it seemed to express so much. A contemporary reviewer for the *English Review* recognized in the poem not only a difficult theme that required a difficult treatment but an achievement that paralleled Tennyson's. Like *In Memoriam,* it was destined to live. We can see how it did live by thinking of *Tess of the d'Urbervilles,* in which Hardy, while echoing Arnold on "the ache of modernism," quotes a few lines from *Easter-Day.*

> you indeed opine
> That the Eternal and Divine
> Did, eighteen centuries ago,
> In very truth. . .
>
> (*Poems*, 411)[79]

For Hardy as for many nineteenth-century readers, Browning's poem characterized the dilemmas of men and women for whom Christian faith had become most questionable when it seemed most needed. It summed up a generation of writers whose poems—as William Rossetti pointed out—unavoidably expressed their religious beliefs. Yet Browning was both representative and defiant. Unlike poets such as Philip Bailey, who published *The Angel World* in 1850—a vague and formless lyric version of Milton's account of heaven—Browning offered no glib assurances. Contemporary reviewers saw an appropriate parallel between Browning's poem and Butler's *Sir Hudibras* (a poem frequently mentioned at the time, though apparently at odds with the practice of most poets), and Browning's language certainly suggests Donne's, with its crabbed syntax and exclamatory rhetoric.

Despite the qualities that offended Browning's contemporaries, what we see in, say, Tennyson's poem of tentative and hard-fought affirmation, or in Clough's arguments with the Spirit, or in Arnold's laments about "the sea of faith" is manifest in Browning's twin poems about the difficulties facing a believer:

> How hard it is to really be
> A Christian, and in vacancy
> I pour this story!
>
> (*Poems*, 412)

Is the vacancy a world no longer invested by spirit, or is it a world in which the speaker cannot be heard? At any rate, *Christmas-Eve and Easter-Day* is a kind of diary, or confession, as assessment of the poet as well as of his faith.

Browning's religious background in English dissent, which Elizabeth

Barrett Browning delighted to find paralleling her own background, becomes the point of departure and involves the tentative resolution in *Christmas-Day*, which begins in a dissenting chapel and returns, after a series of dream visions, back to the chapel. Readers of the poem have often objected to two of the visions, one of Saint Peter's in Rome, the other of a lecture by a "higher critic" in Göttingen, as illustrating Browning at his least sympathetic, and indeed at his most thoughtless in depicting other men's beliefs. His vision of "papist" Rome may reflect a common English prejudice of the time, but the speaker says:

> I see the error; but above
> The scope of error, see the love—
>
> (*Poems*, 402)

He seems more impatient with the "exhausted air-bell of the Critic," who seeks to find a Christ among historic fragments, myth and meaning having vanished in his sad, "over freighted" academic mind. But here, too, the speaker feels a "sympathetic spasm," and he makes his judgment by leaving the lecture hall, just as (in a dream) he has left the dissenting chapel. The point is that the fetid, hostile chapel, with its ranting preacher, seems hardly better than the "raree-show of Peter's successor, /Or the laboratory of the Professor!" (*Poems*, 408). The choice is evidently made with reluctance and with uncertainty, none of the options really sufficing, and all coming in for satire. *Christmas-Eve* anticipates in its unsatisfactory resolution the opening lines of *Easter-Day*—

> How very hard it is to be
> A Christian! Hard for you and me,—
>
> (*Poems*, 409)

which recur like Clough's "Christ is not risen" as a refrain.

The scrutiny of the different ceremonies and the contrast they make with the vision of Christ—

> All at once I looked up with terror.
> He was there—
>
> (*Poems*, 401)

point to the obvious conclusion that Browning is "tracking his way through doubts and fears" rather than establishing the rights of a particular sect or of the higher criticism. The poem is confessional and should remind us of the essentially inward, individual, and self-conscious nature of Christianity itself, and of the self-probings of Christian apologists, such as Augustine, Dante, or Bunyan.[80] The evangelical movements of the eighteenth and nineteenth centuries, with their Puritan source and puritanical fervor, dwelled on the inner light, which we associate with the Gospels ("Let your light so shine. . .") and with the metaphoric patterns in poets as diverse as Wordsworth and Shelley. At a time when many men and women found it "hard to be a Christian," the self-exploration implicit in Romantic literature was likely to coincide with specific assessments of faith and doubt.

iii

> Then is the imperative call for the appearance of another sort of poet, who shall at once replace this rumination of food swallowed long ago, by a supply of the fresh and living swathe; getting at new substance by breaking up the assumed wholes into parts of independent and unclassed value, careless of the unknown laws for recombining them. . . .—Browning, "An Essay on Percy Bysshe Shelley"[81]

In his essay on Shelley (published in 1852), Browning attempted to refine the contemporary distinctions between creative and reflective, classical and romantic, or what he himself accepted as subjective and objective poets. Browning's oppositions, like Tennyson's and Arnold's, involve the recognition of differences between the generations of Wordsworth and Shelley and the writers of mid-century, and Browning implicitly agrees with Arnold about the subjective quality of early nineteenth-century poetry while sharing some of Arnold's ambivalence. If by this time he thought of Wordsworth as the lost leader, he could praise Shelley as the poet of "the self-sufficing central light." "The objective poet . . . chooses to deal with the doings of men, . . . while the subjective poet, whose study has been himself, appealing through himself to the absolute Divine mind, prefers to dwell upon those external scenic appearances which strike out most abundantly and uninterruptedly his inner light and power, selects the silence of the earth and sea in which he can best hear the beating of his individual heart."[82] Browning appears to categorize Shelley as a subjective poet and to elevate the subjective over the objective; but he attributes to Shelley the self-sufficient qualities of the objective poet and assumes the complementary values of both poetic categories.

Where, then, would Browning place Browning? Apparently he thinks of himself as an objective poet, a necessary voice for the new times, who stands apart from the romantic-subjective hangers-on from a previous generation.[83] But the essay may, with regards *Christmas-Eve and Easter-Day*, allow another reading. Browning wrote it as introduction to Edward Moxon's publication of spurious Shelley letters, the year after *Christmas-Eve.* If we imagine, along with the praise for Shelley, a specific defense of his recent poem as well as a general defense of "objective " monologues, we can see Browning pointing to his own peculiar mixture of personal and impersonal, objective and subjective, in an experimental poem that had not found wide acceptance. Praise of Shelley's diversity reflects on his own. And a poem full of solitary visions and religious questioning is also a poem about Browning as subjective poet "appealing through himself to the Divine mind."

The first part of the poem, *Christmas-Eve*, is a narrative, in certain ways a Shelleyan narrative, in which an Alastor figure pursues his own interior visions while finding correspondences for them in fully realized physical settings.[84] True, the description of the chapel sounds more like the satirical Shelley than the Shelley of *Epipsychidion*, but the multicolored rainbow suggests Shelley of the inner light:

> suddenly
> The rain and wind ceased, and the sky
> Received at once the full fruition
> Of the moon's consummate apparition.
> The black cloud-barricade was riven,
> Ruined beneath her feet, and driven
> Deep in the West. . .
>
> (*Poems*, 400)

The account of a lonely and lost wanderer meeting with representative manifestations of his thinking recalls *Alastor*, but it suggests also Arnold and Clough and their sense of man alone. "Alone! I am left alone once more."

The second part, *Easter-Day*, also comes close to Arnold and Clough; it is a dialogue of the mind with itself. But as a break with the personal narrative of *Christmas-Eve*, *Easter-Day* reads like the dramatic lyrics that Browning was already making famous. At least two speakers converse in the crabbed, at times "obscure," way that Lewes and Rossetti argued to be necessary. Browning seems, on the other hand, to force the realization that his voices in *Easter-Day* are close to the voice in *Christmas-Eve*, since one of the speakers in the second part refers to "our friend," the narrator of the first part. The voices themselves in *Easter-Day* are not distinguishable in the way of the voices of *Dramatic Lyrics* or *Men and Women*. The distinctive feature of Browning's usual monologues is a lonely speaker, pushed by some interior monomania to an ironic confession of unacknowledged guilt. *Easter-Day* anticipates the fuller characters of *The Ring and the Book*, without setting the speakers apart or separating them from one another. Though at first the speeches are contrasted, one with, one without quotation marks, the confusion of voices seems as intended as it is real.

> Did you say this, or I?—Oh, you!
> Then, what, my friend?—(thus I pursue our
> parley). . .
>
> (*Poems*, 411)

The implication is that one mind might have made any of the comments, since the debate—as in Clough's *Dipsychus*—is not between eccentrics, but between similar people, even between the two sides, or among the several sides, of another divided but sympathetic consciousness.

When George Lewes described Browning's achievements in *Christmas-eve and Easter-Day*, he called the poem "a page out of the history of a life."[85] He meant, perhaps, something akin to what Browning meant in the dedicatory letter to Milsand and what Benedetto Croce, in a general statement about the nature of poetry, had in mind when he was to speak of art as the particular expression of a particular personality, of dramatized "intuition."[86] One assumption behind such remarks is the essentially expressive (Croce speaks of the lyric) nature of poetry, which for Browning as for Tennyson and Wordsworth is at the same time epistemological. *Christmas-Eve and Easter-Day* is about knowing rather than about knowledge, and about knowing in terms of renewed perceptions. "The world," as Browning says, "is not to be learned and thrown aside, but reverted to and relearned."[87]

To think of Browning's entire career, from *Pauline* through the dramas, the "dramatic lyrics" and monologues, to *The Ring and the Book*, may tempt us to put aside *Christmas-Eve* as an exceptional "page out of the history of a life." And rarely is Browning so openly confessional or so directly concerned with "how it strikes a contemporary." Yet, even when he sets his poems in a remote past, Browning's historic interest lies precisely in the shifting moods and feelings of his subjects. "England's most distinguished historicist" speculates about past and present worlds with the sympathetic imagination of a man who has abandoned absolute judgments and who risks the apparent chaos of matter-of-fact.[88]

Browning's historicism is, then, related to both Rossetti's hope for "completeness" and his recognition of "self-consciousness." Completeness in a poet meant using a poetic vehicle with the potential effect of fiction, risking a breach of ordinary decorum in poem that fuses public and private, that filters diverse experience through personal consciousness. *Christmas-Eve and Easter-Day* is in these terms both a useful clue to Browning's art and a representative work that reaches beyond its apparent genre. To recall Richard Church's description of Dante, Browning's "epos of the soul" is "reckless of all ordinary proprieties and canons of feeling" because Browning aims at a comprehensive art. I shall return to questions of historicism and self-consciousness in the following chapters. Here I want only to emphasize that Browning's interests, like Clough's, imply some of the same experiments in mid-century poetry that we can see in the fiction of the time.

V

Phases of the Soul

The Newman Brothers

1

What a man's or nation's available religion at any time is, may sometimes, especially if he abound in Bishops, Gorham Controversies, and richly endowed Churches and Church-practices, be difficult to say.—Thomas Carlyle, *Latter-Day Pamphlets* (1850)[1]

In wading through the recent arguments of counsel on baptismal regeneration and prevenient grace, we could not help asking ourselves—How will all this whole scheme of doctrine look when gazed at from an historic distance. . . ?"—J. S. Mill, "The Church of England" (1850)[2]

"Phases of the Soul" is a conflation of two titles, both of mid-century works by Francis W. Newman: *The Soul, Her Sorrows and Aspirations* (1849) and *Phases of Faith; or Passages from the History of My Creed* (1850). Newman's titles characterize the religious preoccupations of the day as much as his own concerns, and Newman, though soon to be eclipsed by the brother he distrusted, won a limited but genuine fame as "lecturer, scholar, and influential critic of society and religion."[3] George Eliot (still Marian Evans) spoke of Newman as "our blessed St. Francis";[4] George Lewes described *Phases of Faith* as a great and seminal work (see below). Eliot's praise implies the importance for both herself and her future husband of Newman the man. She later shrugged off Newman's thinking as quaint and inadequate, but at first she saw in Newman a laudable pioneer: a worthy successor to David Strauss, and a man who had been brave enough to write a book that she had "long wished to see written."[5] George Eliot's praise is exceptional, but her awareness of Newman is not. Whereas Browning found little acknowledgment for his mid-century religious work, Newman won praise and notoriety, *The Soul* and *Phases of Faith* stirring up as much interest as the tracts of John Henry Newman had stirred up a decade before.[6]

If Newman's *The Soul* tries to define (with Coleridge's terms) the elements of divinity in men and to characterize the "Infinite Personality" of God, *Phases of Faith* draws together two heavily used words of the time to indicate that Newman's own life is a more or less paradigmatic vehicle in a common search for belief. An "honest doubter," as Basil Willey calls him,[7] Newman wrote *Phases* in an autobiographical mode in order to indicate the relation of a representative man—a finite personality—to a God whom Newman found unavailable through Anglican dogma. His book lacks the novelistic force and the full sense of an emergent self that we find in Gosse's later *Father and Son*, but Newman writes with a comparable self-deprecation and economy. He details the problems of faith for a man unafraid to ask questions.

Both the Newman brothers faced religious perplexities, struggled with self-doubts, and came to record their personal histories as though they were of use to their countrymen. But, almost uncannily, the two men moved in contrary directions, possibly seeing their own ways according to the darkness they associated with the other. While John rejected the religious liberalism of his day and found, in 1845, surety in Rome, Francis came increasingly to reject any dogma and any church authority. John respected his younger brother, but with a grudging acknowledgment of his "independent mind." In the *Apologia pro Vita Sua* (1864) he records that he and Francis had returned to England in 1833 on the very same day, John from Italy ("I have a work to do in England"),[8] Francis from an ill-fated mission in the Near East. Since he has emphasized the significance both of his need to return and of the impending historical events (in fact, the Oxford Movement), and since he knows what Francis has in the meantime thought and published, he evidently calls attention to the physical gulf between them, which is in no way lessened by their coincidental proximity. Similarly Francis, accounting for his years at Oxford, describes his brother's development so as to point out how utterly unlike the two have become. Each distrusts, each is hurt by the other; each seems prodded toward an extreme clarification of his own position. Rarely have two brothers moved so far apart. Even after John Henry Newman died, Francis could not resist what most readers still consider the unkind and petty comments in *Contributions to the Early History of the Late Cardinal Newman* (1891).[9]

At mid-century the Newman brothers represented extremes of religious differences—and difficulties—facing their countrymen. How urgent religious issues were for ordinary men and women of the time would be difficult to say with any certainty, since evidence like the Census of 1851 suggests a blurry picture.[10] But we can guess from the religious topics treated in periodicals and from the large number of periodicals representing religious positions that in one way or another religion was on people's minds. We have seen the preoccupation with faith in Tennyson, Clough, Browning, and other poets, and will see it again in a different guise in Charles Kingsley (chapter VIII). A work of Kingsley's friend James Anthony Froude, *Nemesis of Faith* (1848), had seriously offended academicians, just as *Essays and Studies* was to disturb them a decade later, and Froude's book was publicly burned at Oxford.

A lucid and seminal discussion of religious issues, which attacks any theological and emotional extremes, is John Stuart Mill's "The Church of England," published in the *Westminster* (1850), the year before George Eliot became its editor. Mill's position is perhaps predictable, given his and the *Westminster*'s Utilitarian assumptions. But that Mill would concern himself with the church, that he would try to find for it what amounts to a Broad Church justification, implies the importance of both doctrinal and social aspects of faith to the age. In his recommendations, Mill anticipates the latitudinarian positions of Matthew Arnold (in *Literature and Dogma* and *St. Paul and Protestantism*), although Arnold at this time is writing about the ebbing "sea of faith," while Mill is finding for the church a role as social mediator and public servant. Arnold's response to Mill is clear in his remark to Clough: "How short could Mill write Job?"[11]

Mill may be sympathetic to the "alienation" of men and women who are "above the faith they profess," but his concern is with the institution rather than with the individual. He wants to demonstrate the general "blight of unreality" caused by a church that has "worn itself out," and which "gives no adequate voice to the faith and piety of the present day."[12] By defining the church as "the product of compromise," he accepts neither the personal and skeptical course of Francis Newman nor the road toward authority and dogma of John Henry Newman. Mill feels that the church must, if it is to survive, assert again its open welcome as "a system of pacified discrepancies."[13]

Behind Mill's essay, and of course behind the writings of the Newman brothers, lie at least two decades of religious controversy, including the High Church movement associated with the Tractarians (especially Newman and Keble), the Broad Church movement associated with Thomas Arnold (to whom Francis Newman turned for guidance), and the claims for something more than religious tolerance by Roman Catholics on the one hand and various groups of Dissenters on the other. Mill seems to have written his essay, however, in specific response to what came to be known as the Gorham Controversy. Gorham was an elderly Anglican clergyman with evangelical leanings. Because he denied the doctrine of Baptismal Regeneration, the bishop of Exeter (Phillpotts) refused him a benefice. Gorham appealed his case and finally won, when the Judicial Committee of the Privy Council decided, in Mill's terms, that the church must have "provision for variety." Unfortunately, to many thinkers, a lay authority had no right to enter theological debate, let alone to demand any sort of provision. Although the case might seem slight enough in itself, it involved issues of establishment and of church authority that the Tractarians had raised in the thirties. To read contemporary reports (like the *Greville Memoirs*) is to see how much energy the Gorham Case released, how much it interrupted political routines. A flutter of conversions followed the controversy, of which the best known was Henry Manning's. Manning, after attending worship with Gladstone, said to his friend: "Come with me." Gladstone could not and did not. But he wrote about Manning's conversion: "I do indeed feel the loss of Manning. . . . Nothing like it can ever happen to me again."[14] Kingsley might mock those who went over to Rome, including and above all John Henry Newman, but the conversions were signs of religious turmoil that involved Kingsley himself.

The Gorham Case occupied people in the spring. In the fall, there arose what seemed an even more serious issue. Pope Pius IX restored the Catholic hierarchy in England and appointed Nicholas Wiseman cardinal. Wiseman's notorious letter "Out of the Flaminian Gate" offended many Englishmen, including the prime minister, Lord John Russell, who saw Wiseman's gleeful announcement as an insult if not a threat to the country.[15] It is in the context of anti-Catholic sentiment that John Henry Newman's writings have to be read. Before turning to Newman's "Christ upon the Waters" and *Certain Difficulties Felt by Anglicans*, I want first to look at Francis Newman's *Phases of Faith*, a book that prefigures John Henry Newman's *Apologia* and that seems to embody a generation of religious insecurity.

2

> English book reading habits were essentially serious. . . . of the 45,000 books listed by the *London Catalogue* as published between 1816 and

> 1851, 10,300 were works on divinity. Sermons were bought, and presumably read. Newman's *Tract 90* (of controversial interest to be sure) sold 12,000 copies before it finally went out of print in 1846. . . . In a list of 117 new books noted in the *Athenaeum* on October 23, 1841, thirty-nine were on religious subjects, eleven were poetry, ten medical, thirteen travel, and only sixteen were novels.—John Dodds, *The Age of Paradox*[16]

Like *The Prelude* and *David Copperfield*, *Phases of Faith* is a work about education. It is also a retrospective work, which treats, from the perspective of a mature narrator, the "progress" of the author's religious growth. "The progress of his *creed* is his sole subject." Newman recognizes that *Phases* "is perhaps an egotistical book; egotistical certainly in its form, yet not in its purport or essence." Egotistical in form, not in essence. Why, then, run the risk of being called egotistical? Newman raises several points. He says that he does indeed want to show that he had "*no choice*" in arriving at his conclusions and hence he admits his defense against those "unjustly alienated" from him. "But the argument before the writer is something immensely greater than a personal one. So it happens, that to vindicate himself is to establish a mighty truth."[17] His truth approximates the distinction made in our time by Paul Tillich between *Faith* (which is internal, is true "fidelity" "to God and Righteousness") and *Belief* (which is "intellectual" and "dogmatic"). Newman is sure that a personal narrative in "historical form" will interest his reader, although he carefully disclaims autobiographical intent, even the intent to give a full "mental history." He spares us in Copperfield's words "all the weary phases . . . through which I passed." Yet in a sense he does give a full history. His book like John Stuart Mill's is an autobiography, which is limited by choice, but also by temperament. Mill includes in *his* autobiography what he too calls "phases" of his intellectual development. Newman includes phases of a life seen as spiritual quest.

To read *Phases of Faith*, to encounter what U. C. Knoepflmacher calls the "centripetal I," which "appropriates for itself all those elements from the outside world pertinent to its growth,"[18] is to enter the world of a sophisticated innocent. Newman relentlessly examines Anglicanism, Unitarianism, Evangelicalism, and Catholicism—in addition to the Bible itself—as each of these dominates a period of his life; but he also approaches experience as if he were a Citizen of the World for whom any custom or belief will finally prove alien. Newman's tools of criticism may seem crude, and they lacked the sophistication, for example, of the higher critics, whom Newman says he did not know. Since German criticism of the Bible had been available to other linguists for decades, and since Newman refers to Strauss and fellow scholars for authority, Newman apparently means that his early doubting was independent of the Germans. Still, his oddly reverential, literal approach to experience would probably have remained the same regardless of such readings. John Henry Newman spoke of Francis's independent mind needing to "unravel the web of self-sufficient inquiry,"[19] of a kind of intellectual doggedness, which reflected personality, not training. Francis's either/or thinking and his desire for definable certainties lead him into troughs of bathos as well as into moments of lonely insight.

Yet there is in *Phases of Faith* a quiet heroism that parallels John Henry Newman's. Whatever the results, Francis lives by his conclusions. The implications of modern science, particularly the work of geologists like Lyell, mean for Francis inescapable decisions: "Thus at length," he says of one point in his career, "it appeared, that I must choose between two courses. I must either blind my moral sentiment, my powers of criticism, and my scientific knowledge (such as they were) in order to accept the Scripture entire; OR I must encounter the problem . . . of adjusting the relative claims of human knowledge and divine revelation" (69–70).

Such a writer is not "egotistical" in the sense of being self-congratulatory or self-important; he is egotistical in his self-exploration. And so he had to be. Newman thinks of faith as private, as the effect of an active and morally engaged mind coming to terms with the obstacles posed to religion by his age. He believes that truth "can in no other way so well enter the heart, as when it comes embodied in an individual case" (iv). This comment, which might apply to Browning's *Christmas-Eve* or to any retrospective chapter of *David Copperfield*, indicates that Newman is necessarily more confessional than his "mental history" disclaimer allows. It raises a further question about his intellectual "unraveling."

An empirical and personal approach to truth does not make Newman a novelist, but it may point to new directions for fiction taken by Dickens and other novelists of the time (see the two following chapters) and to the dilemma faced by mid-century writers between collective as opposed to personal or individual theories of mind. J. D. Morell, in his *Philosophical Tendencies of the Age* (1848) had described the main intellectual problem of his generation in terms of the conflict between *individualism* and *collectivism*. For Morell, collectivism meant primarily forms of science, particularly social science like Comte's Positivism, which Morell already isolates as the most powerful of collective theories. Opposing collectivism is individualism, which Morell thinks of at once as the political activism of

Sheffield and Manchester industrialists and as the dominant attitude toward truth emerging in his time. He feels that individualists are rejecting authority, tradition, accepted beliefs, while trying to base their ethics upon private ideals. Morell himself curses both houses and wants a Mill-like compromise. But other writers, including Charles Radcliffe, were thinking of a different answer, by which personal exploration might lead to universal truth. I have mentioned Radcliffe and will turn to him again. A related thinker is Robert Mackay, who published *The Progress of the Intellect* in 1850.

Ostensibly a study of ancient religions, Mackay's book is directed at various tendencies in the thought of his own age. Mackay believes, for example, that modern fiction is too matter-of-fact (a question I take up in the following chapters), but also, and more importantly, that it reflects a society in which there is no sense of poetry. Implicitly, Mackay accuses a radical individualist like Newman of lacking imagination. He shares with Newman a distrust of dogma, deplores the falling back "upon a worship of form," but he also finds fault with "fallacies of perverted ingenuity." Our faculties must "work in unison," and we cannot separate mind from emotion.[20] The fact that we do separate marks us as unimaginative, disjointed people, who can no longer think "mythically." It would not be too unfair to Francis Newman to see him in Mackay's terms as obsessed by intellectual ingenuity. What complicates such criticism is Newman's insistent emotions: his weeping, like Tennyson's, for the infant in the night, and his appeal, like Dickens's, to "the heart" as final arbiter.

"My heart was ready to break," he says at one point; "I wished for a woman's soul, that I might weep in floods." His book describes his "great transition," his progressive isolation from other people, his "alienation," until he can accept what amounts to a newly "disciplined heart," the comfort of a wiser and sadder man. He describes his dark night, when friends have deserted or foresworn him, and before he finds Agnes in the form of renewed faith: "Now I am alone in the world: I can trust no one" (36–37).

In company with Copperfield and John Stuart Mill, Newman seems to describe his lonely progress in terms of fathers. He says at one point, "I had begun to think that the old writers called *Fathers* deserved but a small fraction of the reverence which is awarded to them" (15). The comment is apt in an account of a personal and theoretical search for *the* father. Interestingly, the individuals Newman singles out for detailed attention all serve as "a father, or indeed as an elder brother," who invariably both disappoint and hurt. John Henry Newman offers a good example of Francis's almost repetitive patterns of relationships with older figures.

> One person there was at Oxford, who might have seemed my natural adviser: his name, character, and religious peculiarities have been so made public property, that I need not shrink to name him:—I mean my elder brother, the Rev. John Henry Newman. As a warm-hearted and generous brother, who exercised towards me paternal cares, I esteemed him and felt a deep gratitude; as a man of various culture and peculiar genius, I admired and was proud of him; but my doctrinal religion impeded my loving him as much as he deserved, and even justified my feeling some distrust of him. He never showed any strong attraction towards those whom I regarded as spiritual persons: on the contrary, I thought him stiff and cold towards them. Moreover, soon after his ordination, he had startled and distressed me by adopting the doctrine of Baptismal Regeneration; and in rapid succession worked out views which I regarded as full-blown "Popery." I speak of the years 1823–6: it is strange to think that twenty years more had to pass before he learnt the place to which his doctrines belonged. (7)

The difficulty with John Henry Newman epitomizes Francis's entire struggle with authority. His brother, like the Irish clergyman, the Calvinistic leaders, the "unitarian gentlemen," and several others whom Francis meets, serves much like the Thirty-Nine Articles and finally the Bible itself as an obstacle to true faith. And the true faith, for Francis Newman, involves the right "path" toward a private spiritual morality. As with most autobiographers, Newman has arrived at a certain self-understanding when he begins his narrative. His understanding is that "Faith is a moral art," that "Morality is the end, Spirituality is the means" (93). *Phases of Faith* is thus a record of Francis Newman's coming of age. If his sense of the private religious experience recalls Clough and Browning, or Kirkegaard, another contemporary, his emphasis on right behavior and the effect of faith again suggests the retrospective self-assessment of David Copperfield, who similarly turns alienation into psychic integrity.

3

> "I see [the truth] . . . in that man who, driven fatally by the remorseless logic of his creed, gives up everything, friends, fame, dearest ties, closest vanities, the respect of an army of churchmen, the recognised position of a leader, and passes over, truth-impelled, to the enemy, in whose ranks he is ready to serve henceforth as a nameless private soldier:—I see the truth in that man, as I do in his brother, whose logic drives him to quite a different conclusion, and who, after having passed a life in vain endeavours to reconcile an irreconcilable book, flings it at last down in despair, and declares, with tearful eyes, and hands up to Heaven, his revolt and recantation."—W. M. Thackeray, *Pendennis*[21]

Thackeray's easy-going Pendennis, finding it difficult to take sides on any question, reflects the ideological confusions shared by his author and anathematized by Carlyle or by the Newman brothers themselves. "Driven," no less than Francis, by his own "remorseless logic," John Henry Newman had undergone his conversion, had entered the Roman Catholic priesthood, and, with his work in the Birmingham Oratory, had accepted the possibility that he might be the nameless soldier anticipated by Pendennis. But Newman's writings tell of neither self-abasement nor simple obedience. While still years away from the autobiography by which he is best remembered, his writing at mid-century already springs from religious controversy and meets opposition out of hard-won personal assurance. How personal Newman's writing had become we know from the fictionalized portrait of Charles Reding in *Loss and Gain*, the novel of 1848 which describes a young man's intellectual and spiritual journey toward the Roman Church. The sermon "Christ Upon the Waters" and the lectures *On Certain Difficulties Felt by Anglicans in Submitting to the Catholic Church* restate the arguments of *Loss and Gain* and point to the self-estimate elaborated in the *Apologia*.

Eighteen fifty was an important year for English Catholics. *The Rambler: A Catholic Journal and Review* (which Newman was to edit) spoke in January of "Hopes and Fears for 1850," anticipating "the coming conflict between the Church and her foes."[22] The pope's restitution of the Catholic sees and Wiseman's announcement brought out the enemies but also pointed to divisions among English Catholics. Newman's "Christ upon the Waters" is a discussion of the new situation facing Catholics, the new problems, the new challenges. It is an analysis of Newman's own "Hopes and Fears" in light of English religious history and of the English character as Newman sees it.

Essentially, Newman thinks of the English along the lines he sketches in the *Apologia*, except that here English honesty is a gruff hostility, English fairness an illusion, English independence of thought a myth perpetrated by the press, which itself forms the hodgepodge of judgments held by most Englishmen. One might have argued, as Kingsley was to argue, that Newman tailored his remarks to fit both audience and argument, or that his estimate of his countrymen changed conveniently. But in fact the situation for Catholics was anything but comfortable. If by the 1860s Newman could receive a fair hearing for his *Apologia*, he had reason for pessimism when he wrote "Christ upon the Waters." Carlyle's final "Latter-Day Pamphlet" was, for example, an attack on "Jesuitism" and seemed a general indictment of Roman Catholics.

> I hear much also of "obedience," how that and the kindred virtues are prescribed and exemplified by Jesuitism; the truth of which, and the merit of which, far be it for me to deny. Obedience, a virtue universally forgotten in these days, will have to become universally known again. Obedience is good, and indispensable: but if it be obedience to what is wrong and false,—good Heavens, there is no name for such a depth of human cowardice and calamity; spurned everlastingly by the gods. Loyalty? Will you be loyal to Beelzebub? Will you "make a covenant with Death and Hell?"[23]

If untypically irate, Carlyle's diatribe was typical in its sentiments. Moreover, his essay appeared in August, before the pope's reinstitution of the English sees and before Wiseman's offending announcement.

"Christ upon the Waters" was a sermon addressed to Catholics; *On Certain Difficulties Felt by Anglicans* was a series of lectures Newman delivered to his unconverted countrymen, also in 1850, but before the reestablishment of the Catholic hierarchy. In the lectures Newman attacks the English Church more than the English character. He argues that Anglicanism is an untenable *via media*, a shoddy compromise. The English Church is essentially identical with the state and has neither "personal nor integral quality." "The [Roman] Catholic Church, and she alone, is proof against Erastianism."[24] Newman's position is that the people of the Oxford Movement ("the Apostolical Party of twenty years ago") can no longer be true to the Church of England, because the church has shifted, has betrayed Tractarian ideals. Hence, the individual must move toward the constancy of the mother church. Newman's views are of course elaborated in the *Apologia*: they need not be repeated here. What interests me is Newman's sense of personal *development* (to borrow one of his own favorite words). He thinks of the believer as joining the church "to encounter, and to beat back the spirit of the age." To be true to the spirit of the church, one cannot "remain still." Thus, here, as in the *Apologia*, Newman conceives of a personal struggle away from the incertitudes of Anglicanism and the evils of Erastianism toward the sanctuary of inherited dogma.

Newman's address to the men and women frustrated by the Anglican Church involves a kind of double history. The *Rambler* aptly pointed to Newman's "singular and unusual pains to saturate his mind in the wisdom of the past . . . ,"[25] understanding that Newman imposes on his subjects a sense of historical order. Unlike *Loss and Gain* and *Phases of Faith*, *Certain Difficulties* provides no chronological exposition, no approach to its subject through personal or biographical development. But Newman reaches constantly for historical parallels on the one hand and for autobiographical evidence on the other. Conscious of his "power" (60) and using himself as example, he too speaks out of a centripetal "I":

> Now, as I have no desire to imitate a line of conduct which I cannot approve, I will not follow [my opponents] in leaving the question unsettled: I will not content myself with insisting merely upon the external view of the subject, which is against them, leaving them in possession of that argument from the inward evidences of grace, on which they especially rely. I have no intention at all of evading their position,—I mean to attack it. I feel intimately what is true in it, and I feel where it halts. . . . (59)

Newman sounds here much like his brother, with whom he shares an urgent and apparently egotistical rhetoric. Although rejecting out of hand the topics that disturb Francis—"the science of criticism, the disinternment of antiquities, the unrolling of manuscripts, the interpretation of inscriptions" (124)—Newman worries about another order of questions, equally compelling. Both Francis and John need to deliver themselves of a personally achieved "truth" for the benefit of potential followers and for the embarrassment of hostile opponents. Both practice a confessional rhetoric that reveals, if not their evangelical background, at least their evangelical intent. Yet John, with his scathing attacks on the Evangelical Establishment, is the more evangelical. Why else a challenging series of lectures in a country increasingly hostile to popery? Why, that is, a personal apology with a call to conversion when the very arguments proposed admit the small likelihood of conversion?[26] True, he says he addresses the few, the remnant, who have sympathized with the Oxford Movement. The beckoning from the far shore comes, however, with fervor and intensity.

Newman's ingrained confessional tendency, apparent in his habit of polishing and preserving letters, keeping a journal, writing (in *Loss and Gain*) a novel drawn from his own sufferings, is, as Thomas Vargish has shown, related to "the Evangelical emphasis upon self-examination."[27] It is also a sign of Newman's close ties with the fiction and the poetry of his age. Confessional literature, as Tennyson and Browning illustrate, was not limited to religious documents as such. Arthur Clough recognized that Wordsworth's poetry offered a version of lay, spiritual autobiography, inverting and extending a confessional mode that comes down from earlier English writers and that—to go beyond Clough—perhaps substitutes imagination for faith in its central discussions.[28] We might think of John Newman affected by Wordsworth, and by Keble's writings on Wordsworth, assessing his soul for his chosen work, which is the work of a writer as well as a priest. But the zeal in his writings, the preoccupation with faith, the use of an emblematic self for purposes of religious discovery—these suggest both a link *through* Wordsworth to seventeenth-century confessors such as Fox, Donne, and Bunyan and a shared obsession with the poets of his own day.

4

> Our age, amidst its many forms of skepticism and worldliness, is ill at ease; and . . . exhibits an irrepressible yearning . . . after something more settled and satisfactory than it has found.—Robert Vaughan, *The Age and Christianity* (1849)

Robert Vaughan, as the editor of the conservative *Quarterly Review*, would seem to have little in common with either of the Newman brothers, whose "irrepressible yearnings" took them, from Vaughan's point of view, in equally dangerous, if antithetical, directions. But Vaughan's metaphors are indicative. They are, in fact, similar to those of the Newmans and similar to those of Tennyson, Browning, Clough, and Arnold. "My object," he says, "is to demonstrate to bewildered and weary wanderers, that the old path is, after all, the true one." Without the "old path," "existence is a wide sea overspread with cloud, and storm, and darkness."[29] (An older, disillusioned John Ruskin was to characterize what he saw as evil and destructive forces as "The Storm Cloud of the Nineteenth Century.")

If in their differing ways the Newman brothers reject Robert Vaughan's appeal to tread "the footprints of our [English] sires," both—like Bunyan and Dante before them—think of the religious struggle as a journey. John Henry Newman wants "to remove difficulties from the path" of potential converts (v); he also thinks of the religious journey in terms of storms at sea: we are all on perilous waters awaiting the advent of Christ. "Christ upon the Waters" sustains the traditional metaphors of ships and sea in its commentary on mid-century religion and culture. Of course, as the reference to the New Testament makes clear, such metaphors are as old as Christianity itself. What I want to suggest is simply that writers of exclusively religious works—whether Robert Vaughan or John Henry Newman—rely upon the same metaphoric patterns as poets and novelists of the time, in part because they are concerned with the same questions. It is surely no accident that John Henry Newman's play on shipwreck should echo or be echoed in any number of melodramatic novels of the time—including *David Copperfield* with its climactic storm scene. After the death of Ham and Steerforth, David Copperfield is forced in upon himself; he, too, sees the darkness about him, becomes aware of his loneliness and suffering. Similarly, "the sea of faith" in "Dover Beach" with the description of barren shingles tossed upon the shore and—in the second "Marguerite" poem—the shores themselves separated by subtly hostile forces (geological as well as theological?) are characteristic of the age.

George Saintsbury pointed out (in the 1908 Oxford edition of Thackeray's novels) that Arnold's metaphors of sea and islands and separation may have come from Thackeray's *Pendennis*. "Matthew Arnold . . . did not think Thackeray a great writer yet Mr. Arnold's finest poem by far, the second *Isolation*, is simply an extension of a phrase in an early chapter of *Pendennis*."[30] In chapter 16, "Which Concludes the First Part of This History," Thackeray speculates about human isolation in a way that reflects on his narrative methods and his relationship with his readers as well as on the life that he imagines for his characters.

> Thus oh friendly readers, we see how every man in the world has his own private griefs and business. . . . How lonely we are in the world! How selfish and secret, everybody! . . . O philosophic reader, answer and say,—Do you tell [your wife] all? Ah, sir—a distinct universe walks about under your hat and mine—all things in nature are different to each—the woman we look at has not the same features, the dish we eat from has not the same taste to one and the other—you and I are but a pair of infinite isolations, with some fellow-islands more or less near to us.[31]

Arnold may well have borrowed his phrasing from Thackeray's novel:

> Yes! in the sea of life enisled,
> With echoing straits between us thrown,
> Dotting the shoreless water wild,
> We mortal millions live alone.
>
> (*Poems*, 124)

But Arnold shares the sense of isolation, the metaphoric patterns, and the exclamatory rhetoric with Newman, Browning, and Tennyson, as well as with Thackeray. The common feeling of isolation, of anxiety—to use a modern term—expresses itself as a rupture in nature and with nature, at a time when religious surety was often seen in terms of harmony with nature. And Arnold is not alone in mocking the glib command to live in harmony with nature. A letter to the *Leader*, a paper priding itself on its liberal and humanitarian positions, defends Malthus and attacks "sentimentalists" in a reply to the *Leader*'s views: "The fact is, though sentimentalists are apt to forget it, that Nature is no sentimentalist—she is, on the contrary, rigidly stern—nay, often, according to the morbid sensibility of civilization, unjust and cruel."[32] Here, nature is seen as historical necessity, as movement, divided from human consciousness.

One response to this negative view of nature is a recurrent and perhaps "sentimental" pastoralism in the fiction of the time, including Thackeray's (see the following chapters). The response of poets, as I have tried to show, is altogether ambivalent. Arnold sometimes finds "calm" in the natural world he loves; Browning takes pleasure in the energies of natural forces; and Tennyson seeks to resolve his antithetical feelings. All imply a hope for a state of nature less hostile than that which is "red in tooth and claw." Like Francis Newman they are sensitive to the findings of science but are unwilling to accept a mechanical view of the universe. Presumably none of these writers knew the works of Karl Marx (who now lived in England), but Marx had in part spoken to their dilemma. In 1844, he had written: "Every alienation of man from himself and from Nature appears in the relation which he postulates between other men and himself and Nature. Thus religious alienation is necessarily exemplified in the relation between laity and priest, or . . . between the laity and a mediator."[33] Without trying to define Marx's terms, let me just suggest that the pervading sense of isolation, in the Newman brothers and in poets who were their contemporaries, clearly does imply (1) a break with benevolent theories of nature, (2) a sense of division, both within the man himself and between him and his society, and (3) a fundamental change in the possibilities for religious life. William Rossetti's conviction that self-consciousness in poets has manifested itself in religious preoccupations not only parallels Marx's train of thought—which moves from a recognition of a loss of self and divorce from nature to a necessary application in religion—it seems historically accurate. Both Newman brothers are working on assumptions close to those of Rossetti and Marx. But whereas the older brother sees the spirit of the times demanding a vigorous priesthood and Catholic dogma, the younger brother remains explorer rather than priest, emphasizing the need for protestant conscience. *The Soul*, again, asks how man's spiritual "organ" itself mediates between this world and God's.

5

What a crisis for religion at large is this period of the world's history.—
W. E. Gladstone in a letter from Germany (1846)[34]

John Henry Newman had told his brother that, once started, his critical inquiries would not be stopped. And it was Francis's ruthless scrutinies that won him so much ill-will. Entire volumes were written to denounce his writings, and from the Evangelical periodicals especially, he found bitter opposition. His systematic questioning (again, his oddly *innocent* questioning) of the Bible naturally invited doubts as to whether he could ever have been a Christian. As usual, Newman seems not to have anticipated harsh criticism, perhaps because he was, unlike his brother, never really seeking recruits. He lashed out at Henry Rogers, whose *The Eclipse of Faith*, an attack on *The Soul* and *Phases*, itself went into ten editions within the following ten years. The controversy surrounding Newman's works made a great stir; more importantly, as A. W. Benn writes, it served to polarize opinion: "For years to come the great issue between reason and faith almost resolved itself into a personal controversy between Francis Newman and the Evangelical party."[35]

Newman found defenders, conspicuously in James Martineau (though even his defenders were hard pressed when Newman began to doubt Christ himself).[36] Among the stoutest defenders was George Lewes, who devoted several articles in the *Leader* to a clarification and apology for *Phases of Faith*. Lewes thought of Newman as ideally combining "piety and learning." *Phases*, despite the "discreet silence" of the Quarterlies "is destined . . . to exercise a powerful influence on our religious literature." Returning in later reviews to *Phases*, Lewes speaks of it as "more than a striking book—it is a great action." It is "the story of a mind."[37] Implicitly, Lewes defends the book in terms of the characteristics of poetry of the day; what he praises in Newman is exactly what he praises in Browning—and what he finds absent in Wordsworth. In his review of *The Prelude*, Lewes calls Wordsworth deficient in his understanding of the true subject of poetry, "the Human Soul." Newman's profound "history of the conflicts of a deeply religious mind" is, then, important literature as well as religious testimony.

If Lewes overstates Newman's strengths, he is fairer than Matthew Arnold about what are genuine virtues. When Francis Newman's *Phases* first appeared, Arnold dismissed it as a contemptible and reductive book: Newman "bepaws the religious sentiment so much that he quite effaces it to me."[38] Arnold's anger at this book anticipates and helps to explain his later anger at Newman's translation of the *Iliad*, which seemed to Arnold to represent all of England's cultural difficulties massed together for ill-effect. Arnold thought of Newman as a dangerous and representative man, a kind of brilliant John Bull, if that were possible, whose immoderate learning and inadequate culture combine to defeat sweetness and light. As Lionel Trilling says, the apostle of culture can hardly be expected to have appreciated a humorless, pendantic, and unpoetic professor of Latin from London University.[39] Still, Arnold tended to be unfair to most of his contemporaries, and he was unfair to Newman.

The "beast" who wrote *Phases of Faith* indulges in the sort of critical arithmetic that offended Arnold in another biblical scholar, Bishop Colenso, but Newman also anticipates Arnold's own religious writings of the decades to come: in his medium, he searches for the buried life, the efficacy of hope; and he tries, honestly and intelligently, to make the case for a "being-not-ourselves," while stressing the importance of "Righteousness."

It is intriguing that Arnold, so quick to dismiss Francis, should be so sympathetic toward John Henry Newman. One can understand his delight in Newman's "urbanity."[40] Even more, perhaps, one can see a connection between Newman's Catholic "remnant" and the later apostles of culture, for Arnold shared with Newman a respect for certain kinds of authority. He deplored the making public, or popular, private doubts about religion, even though his own sense of the Anglican faith was to remain as hazy as critics (including Francis Newman) complained. Theological debate was not for the masses. Hence, Arnold could share with John Henry Newman the contempt for periodicals of his day, which "teach the multitude of men what to think and what to say," and which perform a dangerous pedagogical role: "And thus it is," Newman says, "in this age, every one is, intellectually, a sort of absolute king, though his realm is confined to himself and his family. [The Englishman] . . . is in his own way the creature of circumstances; he is bent on action, but as to opinion he takes what comes, only he bargains not to be teased or troubled about it."[41] Newman's contempt for the chaos of English intellectual and spiritual life clearly parallels Arnold's, and Arnold acknowledges Newman as teacher. Some of the later writings in *Culture and Anarchy* or *Friendship's Garland* might have grown specifically out of Newman's censure, as, for example, the historical survey of English decline in "Christ upon the Waters," which leads Newman to the passage I have quoted.

Consider Arnold's famous comment in "My Countrymen" (1864), in which the metaphors themselves seem to continue Newman's argument:

> As often as I consider how history is a series of waves, coming gradually to a head and then breaking, and that, as the successive waves come up, our nation is seen at the top of this wave . . . , I ask myself, counting all the waves which

have come up with England on top of them: when that great wave which is now mounting has come up, will she be at the top of it?[42]

Apart from what are evident influences of affinities, Arnold was in fact no Catholic and, for that matter, no friend even to Anglican dogma; and his reactions to the Newman brothers remain somehow imbalanced, if not inverted. Was it because Francis lacked humor or subtlety, because he failed in urbanity, that Arnold continued to think ill of him? Was it his manner or his matter? Did Arnold think of him, as he thought of Clough, failing in a sense of beauty?

In a letter of 1848, while admitting that Clough's poems "are not suited to me at present," Arnold laughingly relates Arthur Stanley's judgment that Francis Newman is "offensive," if harmlessly so, "being insane." Arnold here comes as close to unreserved praise of Clough's poems as he ever does—and in terms appropriate for Newman as well as his friend:

The good feature in all your poems is the sincerity that is evident in them: which always produces a powerful effect on the reader—and which most people . . . lose totally when they sit down to write. The spectacle of a writer striving evidently to get breast to breast with reality is always full of instruction and very invigorating—and here I always feel you have the advantage of me.[43]

How far apart Arnold and Clough had grown by 1850 can be seen in their responses to Newman. Arnold's earlier praise of Clough's poems sounds rather like Clough's own praise of Newman. For in the year in which Arnold dismissed Newman as an "hass," Clough was writing a favourable review of *The Soul* (not published, however, in his lifetime). Clough is skeptical about some of Newman's arguments in proof of divinity, and he sees Newman as an example of "over-irritated" conscience in an age too worried about sin. But he offsets what might be self-criticism as much as criticism of Newman with high praise:

The appearance of this book is a novelty, and may be thought an epoch, we do not say in literature, but in a more weighty matter[,] religious writing. For the first time since we know not what remote period mercy and truth are met together in the world of publication, religion and knowledge have kissed each other. He whom our fathers would have called a Methodist is also what our contemporaries entitle a rationalist: one well known to be rich in historical and philological lore and great in critical acumen is found also possessed of those stories of devout experience which delight the readers of pious biography, proves himself also powerful in those searchings of spirit and delicate self-introspections which are the shibboleth to the tender conscience.

. . . Mr. Newman . . . is sincere with himself and outspoken with others.[44]

Clough's commentary on Newman (which gets in manner increasingly Carlylean) finds virtues in *The Soul* that Arnold finds grudgingly in Clough's poems—and that George Lewes praises in *Phases of Faith.* The association points again to the importance of "the soul" and of the writer's "sincere self" in apparently unlike works, and to the community of themes and assumptions shared by writers otherwise as far apart as Francis Newman, John Henry Newman, Arthur Clough, Robert Browning, and Matthew Arnold. Hence, Newman's largely forgotten "mental history" offers ways of reading a generation of poets, including those, like Arnold, who found Newman contemptible.

VI

"The Lamp of Memory"

Wordsworth and Dickens

1

> But in speaking of this passion, at first slightly artificial, though later deeply felt, which I had for Ruskin's thought, I have to call memory to my aid. . . . It is only when certain periods of our life have gone forever, when, even at such times we feel power and liberty have been given to us, we realise that the gates of the past are forever bolted; it is when we find it impossible to put ourselves back, even for a moment, into the state of mind which for so long was our daily companion; it is then only, that we refuse to believe that these things have gone irrecoverably.—Marcel Proust, "John Ruskin"[1]

> I cannot at the same time do homage to power and pettiness—to the truth of consummate science, and the mannerism of undisciplined imagination.—John Ruskin, *Modern Painters*[2]

When Marcel Proust, most eloquent of apologists for memory, praised Ruskin as his mentor, he referred at times to *Stones of Venice, Modern Painters*, and the autobiography, *Praeterita.* Proust also appreciated *The Seven Lamps of Architecture* (1849), which prompted him, soon after Ruskin's death, to search for a tiny figure among the "superhuman army" of carvings in Rouen Cathedral. Ruskin's illustration of the figure, typical of his lifelong devotions, signified to Proust, the man "for whom there was no death, no anonymous infinity of matter, no forgetfulness."[3] In his homage to Ruskin's powers, Proust does not mention from *Seven Lamps* the chapter "The Lamp of Memory," in which Ruskin uses personal memory to illustrate the importance of memory, his recollection somehow unfolding the principles to be urged. But in both its methods and its preoccupations, Ruskin's "Lamp of Memory" anticipates Proust. It also serves as introduction to Wordsworth's *The Prelude* and Dickens's *David*

Copperfield. With all their obvious differences, the two works are related to the confessional intimacy of Ruskin's criticism and to Ruskin's sense of the purposes of art. Both rely on a "lamp of memory," a way of imagining that is at once retrospective and self-assertive; and both (like "The Lamp of Memory") offer analogous scenes in Swiss mountains. Before turning to these scenes, we might glance at Ruskin's chapter, which epitomizes mid-century interest in memory, just as it points to the obsession with memory in a writer like Proust.

Ruskin begins his chapter by recalling a personal experience:

> Among the hours of his life to which the writer looks back with peculiar gratitude, as having been marked by more than ordinary fulness of joy or clearness of teaching, is one passed, now some years ago, near the time of sunset, among the broken masses of pine forest which skirt the course of the Ain, . . . in the Jura. It is a spot which has all the solemnity, with none of the savageness, of the Alps; where there is a sense of a great power beginning to be manifested in the earth, and of a deep and majestic concord in the rise of the long low lines of piny hills; the first utterance of those mighty mountain symphonies, soon to be more loudly lifted and wildly broken along the battlements of the Alps. But their strength is as yet restrained; and the far-reaching ridges of pastoral mountain succeed each other, like the long and sighing swell which moves over quiet waters from some far-off stormy sea.[4]

The scene and its recreation seem self-consciously Wordsworthian: the "sense of a great power," "those mighty mountain symphonies," the "far-reaching ridges of pastoral mountain" succeeding each other, the analogy of "some far-off stormy sea," all clearly echo Wordsworth. The passage also recalls a favorite Wordsworthian process, since personal recollection of a scene leads to emotions felt at the time and felt later with incremental effect. Having established the pastoral beauty of the Jura, Ruskin moves from thoughts of joy to thoughts of despondence:

> But the writer well remembers the sudden blankness and chill which were cast upon [the scene of a river] when he endeavored, in order more strictly to arrive at the sources of its impressiveness, to imagine it, for a moment, a scene in some aboriginal forest of the New Continent. The flowers in an instant lost their light, the river its music; the hills became oppressively desolate; a heaviness in the boughs of the darkened forest showed how much of their former power had been dependent upon a life which was not theirs, how much of the glory of the imperishable or continually renewed creation is reflected from things more precious in their memories than it, in its renewing. Those ever springing flowers and ever flowing streams had been dyed by the deep colors of human endurance, valor, and virtue.[5]

The remembrance of emotion felt in that distant springtime leads Ruskin to a principle of memory in art. The moment of insight, precipitated by a shift of mood, by the intrusion of a new train of thought, allows a revelation that is both intuitive and incontrovertible: that the "sacred influence" of civilization endows nature with some of its beauty, just as it conditions the artist to appreciate its beauty. Without civilization, nature is potentially ugly as well as cruel; it allows the wastelands that Ruskin dreaded as did Tennyson, Carlyle, Browning, Arnold. To prevent the wastelands Ruskin—like T. S. Eliot after him—urges a sense of reverence, of tradition, as antidote to the ugly vision he imagines. His lamp of memory, therefore, sustains in two ways: it renews the individual in his recollections, and it illumines the values of both nature and civilization.

Memory has perhaps a further role. Ruskin wrote at a time when theorists about art often mentioned "the unconscious," implying by the term the depths of the individual soul and the common inheritance shared by all. By way of example, Charles Radcliffe's *Proteus; or the Unity of Nature* discourses on the interrelationship of created things, the organic unity of man with man and man with nature, and Radcliffe's comments on memory draw from Coleridge and Plato to show the existence of a higher "reason" and what amounts to a collective unconscious. For Radcliffe as for Ruskin, personal memory stimulates another order of memory, and in Radcliffe's opinion such memory is indivisible from imagination. If imagination reflects the highest reason, and if imagination cannot function without memory (which gives us a sense of identity, of "I am"), then it is not absurd to say that "the history of memory is substantially the history of the imagination also, any difference being no greater than that which is produced in one and the same song by altering the key and words."[6] Ruskin's position seems to be substantially the same as Radcliffe's. Both men present arguments that might be used to rebut Ruskin's own distinction between creative and reflective, except that Ruskin never goes so far as Radcliffe in equating memory absolutely with imagination.[7] He does, however, come close in "The Lamp of Memory." Since to forget is to lose everything, the artist functions (as Ruskin does in his chapter) to recall "the deep colors of human endurance" along with all that is beautiful and otherwise lost. "There are," Ruskin says, "but two strong conquerors of the forgetfulness of men, Poetry and Architecture."[8] The forms of each are the forms of nature, which the artist learns to perceive.

Ruskin elsewhere praises in Turner the facility to remember and record such details as the reflected sunlight on a river softening the shade of overhanging foliage; he himself is proud of the accuracy of his studies of cathedrals, studies which involve a rigorously exercised memory, and for which, in early years, he appreciated the service of the daguerreotype. "The Lamp of Memory" chapter illustrates how Ruskin's mind—like Wordsworth's before him—moves from one remembered detail to another, as though each had been committed to its place in the writer's mind. The emphasis on memory training as well as the association of specific objects with identifiable thoughts or emotions may recall the use of traditional mnemonic devices, even perhaps the "artificial memory," which, as Frances Yates has shown, dates as far back as the poet Simonides and had a full history at least through the Renaissance.[9]

Artificial memory was a process of forced retention that linked things to be remembered with objects "placed" in the mind by a spatial formula. The formula might involve a building, a theater, a street, or a journey. What mattered was the progression within the remembered landscape, since each (well-lighted) place could hold the object or idea to be remembered. The artificial memory was a learning device with rhetorical purposes. It would serve the lawyer or politician, whose memory might seem boundless. Now Quintilian's ability to recite a list of several hundred names (heard once) in reverse order was remarkable, but it would seem at first glance to have more to do with Gladstone's parliamentary speeches than with Ruskin's enumeration of remembered experiences in the Jura. There are, nevertheless, some useful parallels. Ruskin's training of the eye, his emphasis on accuracy, his catalogue of mountain gloom and glory, suggest an analogous form of mnemonic process—with overlapping ends. Ruskin's emphasis on the truth of personal utterance, developing as it does from accurate memory, involves a rhetorical purpose, since the artist or critic uses his own remembered emotion to persuade and to move his audience.

I mention the artificial memory only to suggest analogies. Like most of his countrymen (Coleridge was an exception),[10] Ruskin was probably unaware of the tradition of the artificial memory, yet he lived at a time when memory was emphasized in educational theory, when politicians—again, like Gladstone—used trained memories to great effect, and when a large amount of literature employed devices of memory in ways comparable with his own. Wordsworth's "Tintern Abbey" could almost serve as an illustration of how the artificial memory works, the enumerated objects of the Wye scene prompting certain remembered emotions while the scene as a whole evokes a complete retrospective vision.

The association of retrospective literature with artificial memory may help to suggest not the survival of a mnemonic art (though that would be worth pursuing) but the widespread emphasis on memory as imagination.

Whatever the historical reasons for the nineteenth-century emphasis on memory—whether an increased interest in history, the acceptance of associationist theories of psychology, or the effect of certain literary tendencies themselves—it developed paradoxically along with such expressive theories of art as Ruskin's *reflective* and *creative* categories. Thus in Wordsworth's famous line, poetry is the "spontaneous" overflow of powerful feeling "recollected" in tranquillity. The relation of the poet to his remembered emotions is, of course, central to Tennyson, Arnold, and Browning, as well as Wordsworth. It is just as central to David Copperfield's personal narrative, which, while it approximates Ruskin's theory, seems indebted to Wordsworth's practice.

2

> The salvation of reality is its obstinate, irreducible, matter-of-fact entities, which are limited to be no other than themselves. . . . Nature poetry, of the romantic revolution, was a protest against the exclusion of value from the essence of matter-of-fact.—Alfred North Whitehead, *Science and the Modern World*[11]

The importance of memory to *David Copperfield* can be seen in the simple recurrence of the word. Phrases like "caverns of memory," "prismatic hues of memory," and "depths of memory" come easily in this retrospective novel. David's narrative calls attention to several "Retrospects," chapters in which his present emotions mingle with the remembered emotions of certain important episodes, and David, like the Wordsworth of "Tintern Abbey," hears and sees again his former self, while speculating about the gulf of time that has elapsed. He thinks, too, of a larger gulf of time, speaking of the "shore where forgotten things will reappear" without the help of autobiography. So much of the book turns on the act of remembering: Mr. Dick's never-to-be-finished Memorial veers off at every effort into a different historical past than the one which Mr. Dick would like. Mr. Omer, the undertaker, who recurs at various times in the narrative, has a memory as short as his breath. Aunt Betsey tells her nephew that "it is vain to recall the past unless it has some bearing upon the present."[12] David not only remembers, he is aware of his remembering, and he recognizes that his ways of remembering bear directly on his present mood and on his stature as a writer. He knows, for example, that aspects of his mind will "unconsciously develop" (135), implying, as

Charles Radcliffe did, the unity of conscious and unconscious, as of memory and imagination.

David also makes fun of memory. When he works toward his temporary employment as Parliamentary reporter, he learns the hieroglyphics of stenography:

> I bought an approved scheme of the noble art and mystery of stenography (which cost me ten and sixpence), and plunged into a sea of perplexity that brought me, in a few weeks, to the confines of distraction. The changes that were rung upon dots . . . ; the unaccountable consequences that resulted from marks like flies' legs; the tremendous effects of a curve in the wrong place; not only troubled my waking hours, but reappeared before me in my sleep. (418)

The process reminds David of some "Egyptian Temple" peopled by odd characters, and though the account is humorous, the labor itself is "almost heartbreaking." However absurd, the stenography must be mastered. David implies that such tasks—specifically here an act of "artificial memory"—allow the unconscious developments and the ordered remembering and understanding of his life. Instead of recording absurd Parliamentary speeches for newspapers, he will, as a beginning novelist, record the elements of his own past for the readers of fiction.

The grotesque Egyptian Temple and David's general preoccupation with memory raise a question pertinent to both *David Copperfield* and *The Prelude*. When *The Prelude* first appeared, G. H. Lewes criticized Wordsworth's autobiographical poem as self-indulgent and cluttered. Despite its fine description, it allowed trivia; in focusing on the poet's petty self it deflected too often from an account of "the human soul." Macaulay (who also disliked *Copperfield*) brushed aside *The Prelude* as so much "twaddle," his comment echoing the earlier and gentler criticism of Coleridge, who complained of Wordsworth's "matter-of-factness."[13]

But what is matter-of-factness? For Wordsworth's early critics and for some reviewers of *The Prelude* it implied irrelevant materials and the trivial account of trivial lives. For Coleridge it meant rather an indiscriminate manner and an occasional failure of judgment. Of course Coleridge's admiration for Wordsworth far exceeded his sense of Wordsworth's deficiencies, and his praise of Wordsworth as philosophical poet acknowledges that, in spite of his faults, he has the capacity for an almost biblical prophecy. Wordsworth, like the Old Testament writers, sees the life within objects and thus unites disparate things by imaginative power. For Coleridge even the charge of matter-of-factness is mitigated. Elsewhere, he praises Dante *for* his matter-of-factness, acknowledging the relationship between the highest imaginative vision and the eye-on-the-object account in Dante's poetic journey.[14]

When Carlyle and Richard Church extolled Dante's powers they acknowledged, in the manner of Coleridge, an imagination which could transform trifles. If, to the "mean eye all things are trivial,"[15] it is the power of the poet rather than the range or variety of subject matter that determines the quality of a work of art. This is Ruskin's sense behind *discipline*, and it helps to explain some of the mid-century responses to Wordsworth discussed earlier.

But if one grants the possible virtues of matter-of-factness, Coleridge and Ruskin would have discriminated between a poet like Wordsworth and even the greatest writer of fiction. Such a discrimination pervades mid-century criticism of the novel—and for good reason. The assumption of contemporary reviewers is that, because of the exigencies of serial publication, matter-of-factness is a necessary failing in the best of fiction. Poetry tends to the *ideal*, fiction to the *real* (the term *realism*, attributed to G. H. Lewes, grows out of a common distinction.) The *real*, though it could be associated with truth in discussing history, usually implies *light* literature, the *ideal* implies poetry; in Ruskin's words the one remains *undisciplined*, the other allows "the truth of consummate science."

But what of Dickens's art in *David Copperfield*? Interestingly, when David Masson reviewed *Copperfield* and *Pendennis*, he contrasted the two novels in terms of *real* and *ideal*, arguing that Dickens's "ideal" imagination peopled his world with characters never before seen on land or sea.[16] If this seems paradoxical in a novel of retrospection, it implies Masson's conviction that *David Copperfield* is more than a loose aggregate of "parts" and that it may well work on the lines of disciplined art. The word *undisciplined* recurs throughout *David Copperfield* as a measure of the progress of David's emotional maturity.[17] Like Wordsworth's in *The Prelude*, David's retrospective account records the disciplining of the self, and, in less explicit ways, records the disciplining of the imagination. Dickens's novel asks, in Ruskin's terms, how pettiness can become power, how trivia can be made to matter. These concerns of the novel are, much of the time, in the consciousness of the speaker himself, who seems in the story of his own life to test the limits of inconsequence. At a time when he recalls the remorse and suffering attendant on Dora's death, David says that "trifles make the sum of life" (586). In any Dickens novel they do. In *David Copperfield*, trifles accrue around the central character, who relates his own history, and whose narrative is packed with apparent trifles. Without trying to justify all Dickens's digressions and indulgences,

I would argue that his matter-of-factness (in tone as in substance) is analogous to that of Wordsworth before him. Out of what Macaulay called the "dull, flat, prosaic twaddle" of *The Prelude* emerges the disciplined imagination of the poet; out of David's own protracted narrative emerges a pattern of art that is more than the sum of the trifles of its parts.

How closely Dickens's conception of art approximates Wordsworth's remains to be shown. First, let me say that I am not arguing the necessary influence of Wordsworth on Dickens any more than I would argue that Dickens knows and applies Ruskin's aesthetical theories. The novelist we associate with teeming city life and the poet who has been linked, from the outset, with the English Lakes seem on the face of it to have little in common. We know, moreover, that Dickens in these mid-century years became increasingly influenced by Carlyle, who taught him another sort of lesson. For Carlyle, something was profoundly wrong, not only with specific institutions but with middle-class civilization itself. In contrast to Marx and Engels, who anticipated a social cataclysm, Carlyle urged a revolutionary change of heart, a conversion from nay-saying to an everlasting yea. The process was to work through individuals who would undergo a sort of conversion, one perhaps no more definite than that celebrated in *Sartor Resartus*. Gradually, Carlyle came to see the impetus for rebirth as either manifest in the hero or initiated by the hero, and the hero might be—in modern times very likely would be—a poet or man-of-letters.

Although *David Copperfield* would be one of the last of Dickens's works that we would associate with profound disquiet or revolutionary energy, the novel seems to reflect Carlyle's preoccupation with change of heart, with journeys toward a new self, and with the nature of a man-of-letters. Probably echoing Carlyle, the opening sentence of *David Copperfield* introduces the indirect question: "Whether I shall turn out to be the hero of my own life. . ." (9). Implicit in the question are further questions: What is a modern hero? Can there be a middle-class hero? An industrious and hard-working hero? A hero who plays it safe? A hero whose life is embroiled in trifles? Dickens keeps the questions in his reader's mind by proposing a succession of heroes. He introduces the false heroics of Steerforth and the genuine if humble heroics of Mr. Peggotty and Traddles. Finally, however, he leaves no doubt that David has earned his title to hero, if only because the lives of his friends have become a part of his own creative memory, his "written memory," the autobiographical novel itself.

If Carlyle's notion of the hero as man-of-letters gave impetus to David's pattern of growing up and to the emphasis on change of heart in the man of letters, Carlyle himself reflected assumptions that had developed earlier in the century and that, in his singular prose, he interpreted for Dickens's generation. Many inherited assumptions, including the idea of the individual as both normative and exceptional, could be found in Wordsworth, in poems that were second nature for most educated Englishmen.

Dickens's contemporaries often accused him (not improperly) of a vigorous illiteracy. But like Tennyson, Browning, and Arnold, Dickens knew his Wordsworth. Who did not? At mid-century, Thomas Shaw called Dickens the most popular modern novelist, Wordsworth the best known poet. "Who has not read 'The Fountain,' 'Matthew,' and 'We Are Seven?'"[18] Dickens often quotes Wordsworth, especially the "Immortality Ode" and *Lyrical Ballads.* He calls "We Are Seven" one of the great poems in the language.[19] I can find no mention of Dickens praising *The Prelude*, but in *Household Narrative* (the monthly supplement to *Household Words*), for July 1850, there appeared a review of *The Prelude*, which had just been published. Though brief and scanty of detail, the review is generally favorable. If not written by Dickens himself (and concerning itself with Wordsworth's Cambridge education, it probably was not), it must have been approved by him, because as editor he was a scrupulously careful overseer.[20]

What interests me here is the apparent relationship between Wordsworth's growth of a poet's mind and Dickens's hero as man-of-letters. The relationship may best be seen in a particular correspondence—Dickens's chapter 58, "Absence," and Wordsworth's book 6, which had been published separately in 1845 as "Vacation in France." Like Ruskin's "Lamp of Memory," both episodes involve a moment of recognition in Swiss mountains with a consequent insight into nature and into art.

3

> He, if any novelist, surely was the heir of the Wordsworthian romantic tradition, and especially in what concerned memory, dreams, childhood influence.—Angus Wilson, "Dickens on Children and Childhood"[21]

After what seems to be the dramatic climax of *David Copperfield*, the storm scene at Yarmouth (prompted perhaps by a great spring storm in 1850),[22] with the resulting deaths of Steerforth and Ham, Dickens attempts something new. In a sense, he reserves the psychological climax for a later scene. And he isolates David from all of his friends and associates.

The novelist who was advocating emigration writes a chapter "The Emigrants," in which David sees the Micawbers, Mr. Peggotty, and Little Em'ly sail for Australia. At this point in the novel, David is still blind to much in himself, although the enormity of his loss of Dora and his friends has left him chastened and thoughtful. Having watched the emigrant ship slip down the Thames, he himself decides to leave England, to endure what he calls his "long and gloomy night," "haunted by the ghosts of many hopes," as dark in spirit as the Kentish Hills are in fact, when he looks—as Conrad's Marlow was to look—across the reaches of the Thames. The horizon over the river is an emblem of his despair as he faces "the ruined blank and waste" of his own dark horizon (620). His choice for exile is Europe.

Dickens arranges for David both a conventional period of loneliness and wandering and a particular moment of understanding—a moment far from the dramatic incidents associated with sea, though a moment he later links with the sea. Instead of recording his usual flood of "trifles," David now becomes circumspect in his accounts, self-deprecating in his personal narrative, yet far more intimate and self-revelatory than he has been in some time. Prior to the scene in the Alps, he quickly dispenses with two years of his life, while he makes, in Carlyle's terms, his "dark pilgrimage through the Waste of Time."[23]

The young man who goes abroad carries his "accumulated sadness" with him, a sadness from which he has "no hope of ever issuing again." If we know, because Dickens has not been light in his hints, that David will recover and will marry Agnes, he does not yet know. Here the knowledge that we have of his character and the knowledge of the retrospective narrator make the dramatic irony somewhat creaky. We simply wait for the narrator to allow David's moment of recognition. What seems especially unconvincing is the nature of David's suffering, which grows out of the events that will insure his claiming of Agnes and which extends over the two eventless years. With his hard work and his need for success, David is no young Werther or Childe Harold. He describes himself as the lost and wandering hero, but he is closer, perhaps, to John Stuart Mill, whose own emotional crisis looms large in the *Autobiography*. Mill learns, at a time when the Utilitarian philosophy of his father and of Bentham will no longer sustain him, the value of poetry and of solitude. The *Autobiography* was still to be written in 1850, but Mill had said, in *Principles of Political Economy* (1848): "Solitude . . . is essential to any depth of meditation or of character; and solitude in the presence of natural beauty and grandeur, is the cradle of thoughts and aspirations which are not only good for the individual, but what society could ill do without."[24] In the *Autobiography*, Mill's suddenly overwhelming sense of solitude leads him to Wordsworth's poetry; in this passage he discovers what David Copperfield apparently discovers, which is Wordsworth's example.

"I was in Switzerland," David writes. "I came, one evening before sunset, down into a valley, where I was to rest" (621).[25] In the course of his descent he experiences an awakening similar to Wordsworth's, when Wordsworth crosses the Alps, witness to mountain grandeur, to the "types and symbols of eternity."[26]

The scenes are similar, not of course identical. In the first place, men of different backgrounds and temperaments are involved, the one as close as possible to the poet's remembered self, the other a fictionalized projection. David's sorrow may be comparable to Wordsworth's, but Wordsworth's profound melancholy lies in other sections of *The Prelude*, not in book 6. David, listless, preoccupied, "brooding," climbs into the Alps. He resembles Wordsworth in the first stanzas of the *Immortality Ode*, or Coleridge in *Dejection*, who sees not feels how beautiful things are. Wordsworth, as he approaches the Simplon, has "hopes that [point] to the clouds." Apart from the further observation that David's experience is atypical and Wordsworth's one of a series of recurrent visions, there are the more mundane differences. Wordsworth travels with a friend (whom to be sure he conveniently ignores); he is still on his voyage out, crossing the Simplon from Switzerland to Italy. David has crossed back from Italy to Switzerland (probably over the Simplon, as Dickens recounts in *Pictures from Italy*, 1846), slowly and unknowingly on his way home. He has already left the main way over the pass and is now in the "by-ways of the mountains."

So much for differences. Similarities are more striking. The scenes follow parallel disclaimers: "It is not in my power to retrace . . . all the weary phases . . . through which I passed," says Copperfield. Wordsworth writes: "'Tis not my present purpose to retrace/That variegated journey step by step." Each uses a traditional storyteller's gambit: "One evening . . ." and "One incident . . ." introduce the specific accounts. David mentions again his "undisciplined heart," Wordsworth speaks of his "unripe state/of intellect and heart." Both travelers describe themselves as *pilgrims*; both describe as dreamlike their mental states prior to the experience in the mountains. Both descend after the event, after the turmoil and energy associated with mountain sublimity to a quiet valley, pastoral in character. But what of the sublimity, the mountain grandeur and its responsive life in the mind of the observer? In each case, interestingly, it is after the actual crossing, after the physical heights are behind, that realization comes. It appears to come in retrospect even during the experience itself. The greatness of the physical world endures, but, as Ruskin says, it needs the interpreting mind, needs to kindle sensual experience of human hopes with the sympathetic power of the imagination. Wordsworth pauses during his account to discuss "Imagination–here the Power so called/Through sad incompetence of human speech," and he relates imagination to things eternal. "Our destiny is with infinitude, and only there; with hope it is, hope that can never die." After the association of sublimity with imagination Wordsworth continues the narrative of descent. He recognizes in "woods decaying, never to be decayed," in "Winds thwarting winds," "Characters of the great Apocalypse,/The types and symbols of Eternity." So, too, in the footsteps of the poet, David, still insensitive to their power, crosses the mountains. In the course of his descent "some long unwonted sense of beauty and tranquillity, some softening influence . . . moved faintly in my breast . . .," and when he arrives in the pastoral valley, "great Nature spoke to me; and soothed me to lay down my weary head upon the grass, and weep, as I had not wept yet, since Dora died." He is, in short, ready for hope, ready for Agnes, who symbolizes his newly disciplined heart and gives it a definite purpose. More than this, Agnes represents his newly disciplined imagination. Throughout the episode, Agnes remains for David his beloved sister, his Dorothy, who points to things forgotten or unachieved. Her "sisterly affection" "inspires" him "to resume my pen; to work."

> I worked early and late, patiently and hard. I wrote a story, with a purpose growing, not remotely, out of my experience, and sent it to Traddles, and he arranged for its publication very advantageously for me; and the tidings of my growing reputation began to reach me from travellers whom I encountered by chance. After some rest and change, I fell to work, in my old ardent way, on a new fancy, which took strong possession of me. As I advanced in the execution of this task, I felt it more and more, and roused my utmost energies to do it well.

He can now seek "out Nature, [which is] never sought in vain." Enabled finally to admit his more than brotherly affection for Agnes, he is also able in his "written memory," his autobiography, to deal with his change of heart, so that while he confesses "the most secret current of [his] mind," he may also "cancel the mistaken past." The moment in the Alps, the moment of sublimity, may be brief, but it is sufficient. His autobiographical story (a forerunner of the autobiography he now writes, but also closely analogous to it, since the energy for the autobiography presumably comes from remembrance of the Alpine scene and its effect) sells well, brings a certain fame, and anticipates his financial and social success. Whereas Wordsworth emphasizes the power inherent in the Alpine scene and speaks of imagination as the poet's reciprocating power, David (or Dickens) uses the scene as a sign of conversion and moves on to thoughts of hard work and social success. "Ah! I see!" as Aunt Betsey puts it. "Ambition, love of approbation, sympathy, and much more, I suppose?" (655). Wordsworth himself domesticates sublimity. He, too, comes down from the mountain. He applies his private insight to an understanding of "eternity," but also remembers Dorothy, "sister of my soul," and Coleridge, who serves throughout as his "fit audience though few." These two provide sympathy and approbation and spur on his ambition to thoughts of *The Recluse.* It is to his sister and friend that he turns after the illumination on Mt. Snowdon.

No less for David than for Wordsworth, the mountain episode allows a release of energies along with a cessation of pain. Solitude, as Mill argues, cooperates with natural scenery to stimulate the mind. But neither Wordsworth nor David Copperfield forgets the sadness and desolation in the world. Toward the close of his autobiography, in the chapter "A Light Shines on My Way," a chapter in which we might expect hope and joy to appear almost unchallenged, David allows himself a brief retrospect. "It was," he says,

> a cold harsh, winter day. There had been snow some hours before; and it lay, not deep, but hard-frozen on the ground. Out at sea, beyond my window, the wind blew ruggedly from the north. I had been thinking of it, sweeping over those mountain wastes of snow in Switzerland, then inaccessible to any human foot; and had been speculating which was the lonelier, those solitary regions, or a deserted ocean. (654)

Here in recollection the scene in the mountains takes on the wasteland quality of Ruskin's Jura and connects with the Yarmouth storm scene and the other references to the ocean as divider. Solitude may be necessary for self-awareness, and solitude in natural scenery may be exquisitely beautiful as well as exhilarating, but solitude is also close to loneliness. "Inaccessible to any human foot" suggests Ruskin's impression of a landscape untouched by civilization, and, like Ruskin, David learns the value of civilization. Whether the implications of this for his "stories" are that only the first of them will be autobiographical, the rest social and depicting the lives of others, would be hard to say. Certainly David Copperfield is Dickens's last attempt to scrutinize his own childhood. Esther Summerson will tell her story in *Bleak House*, and Pip will tell his in *Great Expectations*. But Esther's life is a part of a vast anatomy of mid-century civilization; and Pip is an ironical character, whose sufferings are not specifically those of Charles Dickens.[27]

4

> He [Wordsworth] has, moreover, done more than any poet of his age to break down . . . the conventional barriers that, in our disordered social state, divide rich and poor into two hostile nations.—George Brimley, "Wordsworth" (1851)[28]

David's experience in the Alps prompts further questions about the novel and about its relationship to Wordsworth. When "Great Nature" speaks to him, David testifies to something closely resembling a "spot of time"; and the association of a particular moment with a particular place, the compounding of past and present memories, works as fully in *David Copperfield* as it does in *The Prelude*. If Wordsworth emphasizes the renovating effect of moments of insight, David emphasizes something more akin to Joyce's epiphanies, in which trivial events may work as fully as sublime moments to illuminate the writer. But, as they do for Wordsworth, David's events or patterns of events seem to recur. When he begins his wanderings in Europe, he repeats a boyhood episode, becoming, like so many of his acquaintances, an "orfling" once again. His child wife has died just as his child mother has died before. His isolation, his adult return to the orphan days of childhood, indicate that Dickens wants David to suffer remorse and loneliness, to undergo a trial analogous to his trials as a boy, when, disheartened by life in the bottle factory, he has run off to find Aunt Betsey. That childhood sequence—with its actual stripping of David's possessions and clothes—concludes with David lying comfortably in bed in the house at Dover, shortly to be revenged on the Murdstones and to meet with Agnes.

> I remember how I thought of all the solitary places under the night sky where I had slept, and how I prayed that I never might be houseless any more, and never might forget the houseless. I remember how I seemed to float, then, down the melancholy glory of that track upon the sea, away into the world of dreams. (158)

To return again to Dover, and again to find Agnes, David leaves London as a young man: not houseless now, but homeless, the sufferings of his manhood more intense than those of his childhood because more fully comprehended.

Like Wordsworth before him, Dickens is clearly obsessed with childhood.[29] When Wordsworth finds himself at one with nature's sublimity, he finds, in a sense, an adult equivalent for "spots of time," a counterpart for the unmediated responsiveness of the child, whether that responsiveness means fear or joy or something—as in *Nutting*—dramatically in between. In this way the child *is* father to the man, as a structural as well as psychological principle. Wordsworth emphasizes the distinction between the responses of the child and those of the adult: with maturity come interceding forces, not necessarily bad, but necessarily mitigating. Age begets the attenuation of sensibility. Only in the Alps or on the broad back of Snowdon does Wordsworth seem able to re-create the intensity of earlier vision, to find that "tap-root" to childhood.[30] *David Copperfield* offers a comparable re-creation of childhood (drawn in part from Dickens's own life) along with rhythmic recurrences that suggest the spots of time.

While the scene in the Alps is exceptional for David, it serves as reminder how often the narrative emphasizes scenes of nature (especially rivers and the sea) as a means to establish the lives of characters. After her attempted suicide, the prostitute Martha likens herself to the Thames, which begins in purity and ends in corruption and pollution. But it is also down the river that Martha, Em'ly, and Mr. Peggotty sail for their renewal in Australia and it is the river that prompts David to his own exile.

Possibly, as G. K. Chesterton and others have insisted, the best part of *David Copperfield* is its opening sections,[31] in which David grows up, missing ironies and unable to understand cruelties, though as sharp in his observations as Brooks of Sheffield who fails to grasp Mr. Murdstone's joke with friends. The vividness of David's re-creation in the early chapters is unarguable: the window scenes in the Rookery, Murdstone's impossible sums, Mr. Peggotty's boat, overwhelming black dogs, and so on. The reason for the greater vividness in the early scenes reflects an old truth about the workings of memory. The anonymous author of *Ad Herrenium* (ca. 85 B.C.), a tract on artificial memory, wrote as follows:

> Now nature herself teaches us what we should do. When we see in every day life things that are petty, ordinary, and banal, we generally fail to remember them, because the mind is not being stirred by anything novel or marvellous. But if we see or hear something exceptionally base, dishonourable, unusual, great, unbelievable, or ridiculous, that we are likely to remember for a long

time. Accordingly, things immediate to our eye or ear we commonly forget; incidents of our childhood we often remember best.[32]

The child's perceptions transform the banal into the extraordinary; and David like Dickens or like any retrospective writer—Wordsworth, Proust, Joyce, Faulkner—remembers best the "incidents of our childhood." Susanne Langer distinguishes between the "flashback memory" associated with childhood and the "biographical memory" of later years.[33] The more recent past recurs, oddly enough, with less intensity than earlier days, perhaps because of the increased consciousness with which it is first experienced. The "banal" is a function of experience, which alters perception as well as the memory of perception.

If this is self-evident, of memory in general and of *David Copperfield*, it is something that Dickens uses with effect. The result of David's retrospection is a developing intimacy of narrative. Yet as he grows up, Dickens allows him to retract from the central actions of the story and to realize the nature of his earlier self-centeredness. His "abundant recompense," like Wordsworth's, is a kind of emotional equipoise between the energy of childhood and the understanding of maturity. A sign of the shift in David's consciousness is the arrangement of the various chapter titles. In the first ten numbers of the novel (thirty-one chapters), David begins twenty chapters with "I" or "My," and several other chapters include phrases such as "I form a great resolution" and "My Aunt makes up her mind about me." In the last nine numbers (thirty-three chapters), he begins only three titles with "I." While he remains at the center of the story as a recording mind, reporting both what happens to him and what he observes, his interests become wider and his self-preoccupations fewer. Ironically, his extremely private experience in the Alps teaches him about his art as well as about his life. In fact, for Dickens as for Wordsworth, the two are scarcely distinguishable, although Wordsworth emphasizes the details of his imaginative growth, David the details of his social growth.

If we think again of Coleridge's matter-of-factness charge, we may recall that Coleridge shared to some extent the wonder of his contemporaries about Wordsworth's preoccupation with ordinary men and women, and that Coleridge found it hard to approve Wordsworth's indiscriminate praise of rustic speech and manners. Wordsworth's infatuation with rustics is of course related to his interest in children and childhood vision. He tries to show, in works as different as *Lyrical Ballads* and *The Excursion*, that apparent eccentrics are often humorous because they have the powers and limitations of children along with the infirmities of age or circumstance. But the humor is always close to tragedy. In *Michael*, the old shepherd's history is "the first of those domestic tales that spake to me of shepherds," and Michael's life has become Wordsworth's own remembered narrative, gaining importance in the elegiac mind of the poet. In his Wordsworthian experience, David Copperfield learns a distinctly Wordsworthian lesson about people.

The Alpine episode, giving David energy and courage once again, unites him, in Proust's terms, with his "former self," but also with his former friends. As a man David makes few if any friends: he merely rediscovers the "friends of his youth," though with the sad loss of some and with the joy of rediscovery muted by the recurrent note of elegy.

Like Wordsworth's, Dickens's protagonists are the world's innocents. And *Copperfield* is conspicuously a novel about innocence and about the fate of innocence in an unimaginative world. Shortly before David meets Steerforth again (in chapter 19) and before he leads Steerforth, inadvertently, to the seduction of Em'ly, he finds himself witness to what he thinks the wrongdoing of Mrs. Strong. He says of his experience:

> I cannot say what an impression this made upon me, or how impossible I found it, when I thought of her afterwards, to separate her from this look, and remember her face in its innocent loveliness again. It haunted me when I got home. I seemed to have left the Doctor's roof with a dark cloud hovering on it. The reverence that I had for his grey head was mingled with commiseration for his faith in those who were treacherous to him, and with resentment against those who injured him. . . . I had no pleasure in thinking, any more, of the grave old broad-leaved aloe-trees which remained shut up in themselves a hundred years together, and of the trim smooth grass-plot, and the stone urns, and the Doctor's walk, and the congenial sound of the Cathedral bell hovering above them all. It was as if the tranquil sanctuary of my boyhood had been sacked before my face, and its peace and honour given to the winds. (221)

The fact that David is mistaken, that Mrs. Strong is quite worthy of trust, or that the mischief lies elsewhere, is not the point. What matters is David's profound sense of innocence lost: Em'ly's, Martha's, his own. When he takes the coach away from Canterbury the day after his false recognition, he speaks of "a distrust with myself," and of losing his "Box-seat" as "the first fall I had in life" (222). Here the minor humiliation of the boy turns into humor the sense of loss in the previous scene and anticipates the "greater losses" yet to come. One of the lessons he learns is his need for people and specifically his need for people whose careers run less smoothly than his own. He learns that Mr. Peggotty and Ham are real gentlemen, whereas Steerforth, in spite of his virtues, is an aristocratic sham (though Steerforth's face after death recalls to David the innocence of childhood). He learns that Traddles is the salt of the earth. Aunt Betsey he has already come to respect as well as love, and if Aunt Betsey seems less eccentric toward the close of the novel than she does when applying her nose to the window of the Rookery, she, like the other eccentrics, has also been mellowed by David's understanding. Mr. Dick and Dr. Strong, eccentrics in their own separate ways, come to love one another, and David learns to respect them both.

George Orwell, who speaks of Dickens as a Cockney depicting the lives of London parasites, argues that Dickens's characters represent neither farmers nor workers. If they represent the poor, in G. K. Chesterton's view, that poor is never clearly understood, because its condition is not understood. Dickens's sympathies are with the "shabby genteel."[34] Contemporary reviewers of *Copperfield* and *Pendennis* essentially agreed with Orwell's estimate, at least in finding Thackeray the more "realistic" in his portrayals. But they recognized what Orwell has trouble recognizing, that Dickens's characters have little to do with the actual world of men and women. They are, indeed, conspicuously set apart as "orflings" and outsiders, as though revealing society from its frontiers. Whatever Dickens's view of progress and however topical his references, he was interested in characters who would not otherwise exist in literature and who were purposely indeterminate in their status or class. His experiments of course follow those of Walter Scott, who depicted unprepossessing men and women (see the following chapters), but they also parallel Wordsworth's in *Lyrical Ballads*. Dickens's people are to the city, perhaps, what Wordsworth's are to the country.

Two of David's acquaintances serve to illustrate the stature of the socially unprepossessing for Dickens. Mr. Peggotty is a fisherman; Mr. Micawber a genteel, if hard-working, ne'er-do-well, until his metamorphosis in Australia. Dickens admires Mr. Peggotty's allegiance to Ham and Em'ly, his help for Martha, and his constancy to friends or purpose. But Dickens also uses Mr. Peggotty to suggest a quality of his own narrative. When recording a conversation with Mr. Peggotty (in chapter 51), David says:

> He saw everything he related. It passed before him, as he spoke, so vividly, that, in the intensity of his earnestness, he presented what he described to me, with greater distinctness than I can express. I can hardly believe, writing now long afterwards, but that I was actually present in these scenes; they are impressed upon me with such an astonishing air of fidelity. (553)

Mr. Peggotty is, in Wordsworth's terms, one of those silent poets, someone with sympathies and the eyes of a poet, though nothing of a writer. But the matter of seeing what one describes is also the way that David tells much of his own story. David says for example (in chapter 45):

> The gentleness of the Doctor's manner and surprise, the dignity that mingled with the supplicating attitude of his wife, the amiable concern of Mr. Dick, and the earnestness with which my aunt said to herself, "*That* man mad!" (triumphantly expressive of the misery from which she saved him)—I see and hear, rather than remember, as I write about it. (502)

Implicitly, David suggests that his frequent shifts to present tense, to a kind of "concrete memory,"[35] his emphasis on making his reader *see*, are testimony to the "fidelity" of Mr. Peggotty.

Mr. Micawber is yet more central to David's story. In contrast to Mr. Peggotty, he is a man without a memory, at least without a memory for suffering. If Mr. Omer's memory is as short as his breath, Mr. Micawber's is as brief as his moods. Some things, however, he does not forget. Young David wonders why Micawber calls him the "friend of his youth," since Micawber is of course a grown man when he takes home the bottle factory operative to his precarious household. But Micawber is right. He has the naivety of perpetual youth and, in the ways of the world, is no less a boy than David himself. His imagination is untrammeled, his vision unspoiled. Such a man can suddenly prosper, because he is always able to begin again. Micawber speaks of "the prismatic hues of memory" (535), which implies the varieties of imaginative vision involved in retrospection. The past like the present and future must be seen in shifting lights, and the mood of recollection alters momentarily.

Micawber's prismatic hues bear directly on the shape of David's autobiography. His unlikely recurrences suggest the aptness of the improbable in an imaginary world. How *can* someone "turn up" in so many situations? Micawber obviously means much to David himself, partly because of his kindness, partly because of his helplessness, partly because, whatever the odds against him, Micawber looks forward and upward as Agnes herself does. Micawber also seems to serve as a recurrent sign to David of the state of his growing up. Before each of the four "Retrospects" (so called) in the narrative David has been discussing Micawber or has heard from him again. Three times, Micawber's inimitable letters precede the Retrospect; once, Micawber's conversation. Micawber prompts the self-estimate of the narrator. His abundant energy (a quality David loses and finds again in the Alps), his good-will, optimism, shifts of mood—his own prismatic character—live in David's mind as Wordsworth's eccentrics live in his.

To put the significance of Dickens's eccentric characters in other terms, and to return to David Copperfield's initial question as to the hero of his novel, we might say that Dickens, like Wordsworth, experiments with the potential stature of what Northrop Frye calls "low mimetic" characters,[36] characters who would usually be humorous, and who in Wordsworth are at times inadvertently humorous ("Betty Foy, idiot mother of an idiot boy") and in Dickens intentionally humorous, but who nevertheless have for both writers great strengths and virtues and who educate the writer himself. The leech-gatherer and the old Cumberland beggar live at the periphery of society, though in "the eye of nature." Ruth and Lucy Gray's tragedies gain power for being "unknown." Michael is a tragic character whose class or place of birth augments instead of detracts from the dignity of his life. So, too, Mr. Peggotty and Ham. So, in an entirely different and nontragic way, Mr. Dick and Mr. Micawber. These are people simple in spirit, generous in love, odd in speech. They are the ordinary and unspoiled characters of Wordsworth's ballads.

David Copperfield is, in many respects, as unprepossessing as the characters he depicts. His slow acknowledgment of their virtues, which runs parallel to his relationship with Agnes, and which culminates in the recognition in the Alps, is perhaps the main reason he becomes the hero of his own novel. Although David shuns Mealy Potatoes and the other employees in the bottle factory (an experience too close, no doubt, to Dickens's own in the blacking factory),[37] his origins are not especially illustrious, and his story is partly one of social rise. Conscious of success and eager to prove himself, David is capable of smugness, even of snobbishness, but in the course of his long retrospect he learns that growing up demands both self-awareness and generosity of spirit. David, unlike Wordsworth, may not be especially acute in his introspection. He may have trouble—with Martha, Em'ly, and Steerforth—coming to terms with lost innocence. Yet his book is no less his account, his reckoning, his own narrative justification for his improbable success, his self-judging in a world of apparently fixed but largely hazy values.

David's values would probably be similar to those categorized by Ruskin in *Seven Lamps*: Sacrifice, Truth, Power, Beauty, Life, Obedience (along with Marriage, Home, Generosity). Such values matter a great deal, but they reflect aspiration more than realization. They exist for both writers as a function of vigorous perception and of sympathetic memory. The creative memory, "the tap-root to childhood," allows an understanding of self through time and a means to understanding the lives and deaths of others. It tends to restore a sense of lost identity within the multitudinous and matter-of-fact adult world, although its achievement is as delicate as David's nightmares of waste suggest.

By emphasizing the Alpine episode and the loneliness of David's second exile, Dickens seems to share Ruskin's perception of a Wordsworthian truth: "There is a singular sense," Ruskin writes, "in which the child may peculiarly be said to be father of the man. In many arts and attainments the first and last stages of progress, the infancy and the consummation, have many features in common."[38] Ruskin anticipates here his own remarkable *Praeterita*; he also adds to our sense of the importance of Wordsworth to David Copperfield. Memory serves David, the man-of-letters, to make his pilgrimage through "the Waste of Time," to accommodate his adult life by imaginative remembering and by the acknowledging of human suffering. This is what Ruskin's "Lamp of Memory" epitomizes, and it is what *Copperfield* and *The Prelude* evidently share—differ as they may in genre, origin, and intended audience.

Charles Dickens
An 1849 photograph

"The River" from *David Copperfield*

Title page from *David Copperfield*

Ruskin
"Chamouni: View from the Hotel de L'Union"

J. M. W. Turner
"Yarmouth Sands"

Title page from *Pendennis*

Hill and Adamson
"The McCandlish Children," *a calotype*

Charlotte Brontë
A portrait by George Richmond

Charles Kingsley
An 1851 portrait

George Cruikshank
An illustration from Frank Fairlegh

Richard Doyle
Drawing for The King of the Golden River

D. G. Rossetti
Portrait by Holman Hunt

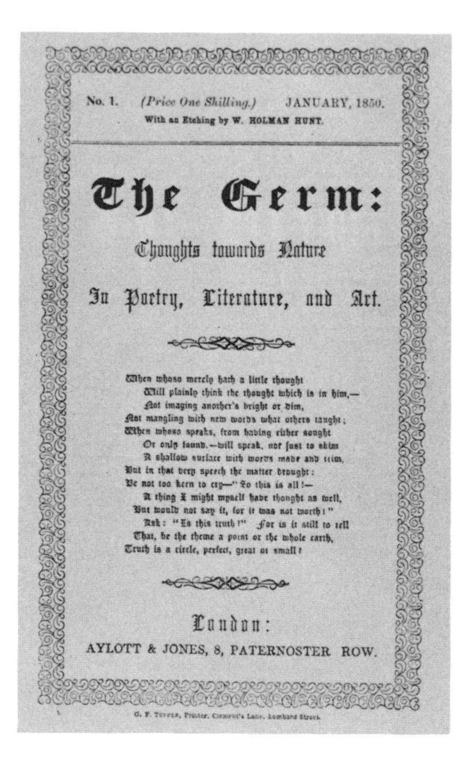

No. 1. *(Price One Shilling.)* JANUARY, 1850.
With an Etching by W. HOLMAN HUNT.

The Germ:

Thoughts towards Nature

In Poetry, Literature, and Art.

When whoso merely hath a little thought
Will plainly think the thought which is in him,—
Not imaging another's bright or dim,
Not mangling with new words what others taught;
When whoso speaks, from having either sought
Or only found,—will speak, not just to skim
A shallow surface with words made and trim,
But in that very speech the matter brought:
Be not too keen to cry—"So this is all!—
A thing I might myself have thought as well,
But would not say it, for it was not worth!"
Ask: "Is this truth?" For is it still to tell
That, be the theme a point or the whole earth,
Truth is a circle, perfect, great or small?

London:
AYLOTT & JONES, 8, PATERNOSTER ROW.

G. F. Tupper, Printer, Clement's Lane, Lombard Street.

Title page from *The Germ*

Monthly Supplement to "*HOUSEHOLD WORDS*," *Conducted by CHARLES DICKENS.*

THE

HOUSEHOLD NARRATIVE

OF CURRENT EVENTS.

1850.] FROM THE 30TH MARCH TO THE 26TH APRIL.* [PRICE 2*d*.

THE THREE KINGDOMS.

ENGLISHMEN are said to begin whatever they have to say, by talking about the weather. As the weather has a very material influence on the condition and prospects of the "Three Kingdoms," in the changing month of April, we need offer no apology for availing ourselves of an Englishman's privilege in commencing our account of it.

For, in Spring, as we all know, the first indications of good or bad harvests present themselves. Upon these, a vast deal nationally depends,—prosperity or depression; wealth or want; employment or idleness; mercantile activity, or commercial stagnation. In politics, also, "our agricultural prospects" have their influence. A bad harvest surrounds the minister with accumulating difficulties, while a good one smooths many away. It is said of an ex-premier, who has been at the head of affairs more than once, that when called upon to deliberate on taking office, he is guided less by the aspect of what is called "the political horizon," than by the state of the barometer. He calculates that if there be a reasonable chance of excellent crops, there is a corresponding probability of the people being good-humoured. It is astonishing how a man's mind clears up with the weather; and how it darkens (on such subjects as the Income Tax, and other trifles of that nature) with the sky.

Happily, the month's accounts from almost every part of the country give hope of an abundant season. A dry seed-time was followed by an unusually cold and nipping frost during March, which, though retarding vegetation, kept it from peering above ground to be bitten and blighted. April was ushered in with storms, the disastrous effects of which on shipping we have to record,—but the genial weather which followed, was only interrupted by heavy showers, much required for irrigation after the long drought. An unusual amount of electricity discharged itself on two occasions in severe thunderstorms. Upon the whole, vegetation promises unusually well. And, as things run on smoothly with the human, as with the equine race, when it can command abundance of corn, we are happy in the prospect before us.

Plenty, however, so advantageous to the buyer, is, according to protectionist theories, a bane to the seller. Indeed, it is so, unless means of production are multiplied by skill, energy, and industry, in an inverse ratio to the diminution of prices. It has yet to be seen, whether the downward tendencies in the price of farm produce will be met by the farmer so as to decrease "the agricultural difficulty" which still exists.

The emigration movement has not slumbered, and is making head vigorously, as the season advances. Vast numbers of persons have recently departed from Ireland, chiefly to the United States. The public, at length awakened to a sense of the vast magnitude of the subject, and to its immeasurable benefits,—both to those who go abroad, and to those who remain at home,—are beginning to bestir themselves out of doors. Attention is universally directed to our great Australian colonies, but it rests with the public, still, to enforce upon the Government and Legislature the necessity of a careful, comprehensive, liberal scheme of popular emigration, and of a system of regulations for the health, comfort, and happiness of emigrants. There is no question of importance to the community, which is not included in this question. Its vital interest to every man who has the least care for the welfare of his country, and the progress of his race, cannot be exaggerated.

The lamentable intellectual wants of a vast proportion of the humbler classes have occasioned during the month much solicitude and discussion. These are due chiefly to Mr. Fox, member for Oldham, whose educational Bill—to extend the means of instruction to all sects and classes—has excited much wholesome and energetic agitation throughout the more *thinking* districts of the country; by which we mean the districts where men think, and act. It is striking, but discouraging, to note the contrast between the manner in which such comprehensive educational projects as that of Mr. Fox are met by the practical men of action in the manufacturing districts, and by the passive theorists of the House of Commons. But, in the manufacturing districts, they know the danger, and the monstrous ignorance and degradation lying at the base of all society; and in the House of Commons they do not,—yet. The party-walls of that building are extremely thick, and keep out a great deal of social knowledge.

Our record of party politics presents features of vicissitude, and therefore of interest. April has been (as Francis Moore, physician, might have predicted, if he had foreseen it,) a disastrous month in the ministerial calendar. In the first week of the meeting of parliament after the Easter holidays, the Cabinet had to endure, in the House of Commons, three defeats,—two positive, and one comparative; and, shortly after, a fourth. On a motion, having for its object improvement in the status and accommodation of Assistant-Surgeons on board her Majesty's ships, ministers were placed in a minority equal to eight votes. On the measure for extending the jurisdiction of County Courts, to which they were not disposed to agree, they voted with a minority, which numbered 67 against 144 votes. These were the positive defeats; the comparative one arose out of a motion to abolish the window tax. Against this the Cabinet made some effort, but its supporters only mustered in sufficient strength to afford a majority of three. Their last disaster was in a committee on the New Stamp Duties Bill.

* It will be remembered by the readers of the preliminary announcement of this Supplement, that it is intended that numbers of the "Household Narrative of Current Events" for the months of January, February, and March, shall be published, at convenient intervals in time to complete the volume for the year. This is the explanation of the first page of the present number being page 73.

First page of *The Household Narrative*

VII

Men of Letters as Hacks and Heroes

1

> The prevailing literary form, or type, of the present age, is undoubtedly the novel—the narrative picture of manners; just as the epic is the natural literary form of the heroic or traditional period.—Thomas Shaw, *Outlines of English Literature* (1849)[1]

Contemporary reviewers of *David Copperfield* did not compare it with *The Prelude*. A given reviewer might have been interested in both works, thought of them in comparable ways, and written separate reviews of each, in which he used interchangeable terms. But lines were drawn. Basically, critics considered poetry and fiction to belong in two distinct compartments; they gave poetry one sort of review, fiction another. David Masson, who was soon to establish a reputation as a critic of fiction, and who published an influential essay on Wordsworth (in 1850), ignores Wordsworth in his review of *Copperfield* because *Copperfield* belongs with *Pendennis*:

> Thackeray and Dickens, Dickens and Thackeray—the two names now almost necessarily go together. It is some years since Mr. Thackeray, whose reputation as an author had until then, we believe, been of somewhat limited extent, suddenly appeared in the field of literature already so successfully occupied by Mr. Dickens. . . . From the printing-house of the same publishers they have simultaneously during the last few years, sent forth their monthly installments of amusing fiction—Dickens his "Dombey" and his "Copperfield," and Thackeray his "Vanity Fair" and his "Pendennis." Hence the public has learned to think of them in indissoluble connection as friendly competitors for the prize of light literature.[2]

As a friend of Thackeray, Masson would be inclined to place him first in the pairing, but the pairing itself, the comparison between Dickens and Thackeray, reflects the interest of Masson's contemporaries.

Masson went on to write an acute discussion of narrative techniques, characterization, and the respective novelistic worlds of Dickens and Thackeray, both of whom he very much admired. He thinks of them nevertheless in an oddly patronizing way. Here, after all, is "light" literature intended for amusement and determined in part by public demand. Less patronizing than Masson but even more ambivalent is an anonymous writer for the *Prospective Review* (in 1851), who begins his article on *Copperfield* and *Pendennis* by saying that, because of serial publication, the novels of Dickens and Thackeray are necessarily formless, and while one attribute of art is the overcoming of difficulty, there can be no way to overcome the restrictions faced by the two novelists: "The serial tale . . . is probably the lowest artistic form yet invented; that, namely, which affords the greatest excuse for unlimited departures from dignity, propriety, consistency, completeness, and proportion. . . . With whatever success men of genius may be able to turn this form to their highest purpose, they cannot make it a high form of art, nor can their works in that kind ever stand in the first class of the products of the imagination."[3]

These comments by a reviewer sensitive to the achievements of both Dickens and Thackeray illustrate a widespread assumption about the inferiority of the novel. If Dickens and Thackeray cannot make the novel a first-class imaginary work, then no one can. "Consistency, completeness, and proportion," terms that would have suited Stephen Dedalus's aesthetics, imply a type of literary work that is almost antithetical to the loose baggy fictional monsters of the nineteenth century (with those of Jane Austen and perhaps a few other authors excepted). "Dignity" and "propriety" suggest a social aspect of the criticism; at least they raise the issue (discussed in the previous chapter) as to the kinds of characters and the range of materials appropriate in literary art. The reviewer assumes a decorum that comes directly from eighteenth-century theories of art, theories scarcely friendly to the practitioners of fiction because drawn from essentially artistocratic notions as to the subjects, the kinds, and the readers of literature. But even if we construe "completeness and proportion" in a Coleridgean sense, still, an understanding of literature predicated on poetry lumps all fiction in a bothersome category of the unorganic, the unformed, and the unarguably second-rate.

In Coleridge's time there was, no doubt, good reason for such a judgment. By and large, fiction was written for commerical or polemical reasons, rarely getting the care given to poetry and rarely thought of, even by the novelists themselves, as serious literature. By mid-century, certain things had changed. Sir Walter Scott had won a modicum of respect along with enormous popularity for the novel, and Jane Austen had convinced some readers that novels might indeed aspire to artistic unity. More recently, Disraeli, Mrs. Gaskell, and "Charlotte Elizabeth" had used the novel for political or moral ends, raising sympathies and pleading cases, but tempering propaganda by the introduction of articulate and intelligent characters. And then, by the late 1840s, the Brontë sisters had offered their radically passionate—and provincial—books to the reading public.

The public itself, increasingly large and influential, had already recognized in Dickens and Thackeray the two outstanding fiction writers of the age, agreeing tacitly with Dr. Johnson that the great writer subverts the genre that he uses, creating of it something valuable as well as new. Possibly because the public was so large and influential, it prompted critics like the *Prospective* reviewer to make their negative assessments. They could see the glut of books published, the insatiable need, or at least demand, for entertainment, and they knew that, as in earlier years, most novels were written by hacks for people who wanted simply to be amused.

When we look back to the fiction of the middle years of the nineteenth-century, we remember the Brontës, Mrs. Gaskell, Kingsley, Disraeli, and Borrow, along with Dickens and Thackeray. We forget the vast armada of novels appearing in penny magazines, or even in reputable publications. G. W. M. Reynolds, who published the *Political Instructor* (1849–50), was in the middle of his long career at mid-century, writing popular favorites like *The Mysteries of the Court of London*, the first volumes of which appeared in 1849. Mayne Reid began his amazing career in 1850 with *The Rifle Rangers*, a story set in Mexico, which is simply a catalogue of extraordinary adventures told in a careless first-person account. Among others, Lamartine admired the book, which won for Reid almost instant success. By the turn of the century, his works had sold over a million volumes.[4] Another nineteenth-century favorite also appeared in 1850. Thomas Prest's *String of Pearls*, the story of "the Demon Barber" who kills his clients and passes them on to a co-conspirator to be made into meat pies, became one of the most famous fictional melodramas, though the novel as novel is repetitious, sentimental, and almost interminable. Prest's literary failings are understandable: he had published five dozen books in the previous ten years. Charles Lever's picaresque *Con. Creagan:*

The Irish Gil Blas reminds us of another prolific writer of the time, and Lever's books, if largely forgotten today, are more than a step above Prest's *Fatherless Fanny; or the Mysterious Orphan*, "embellished with the most splendid engravings," and *Ela the Outcast, or the Gypsy Girl of Rosemary Dell.* The range of fiction at mid-century was enormous, in quality as in kind, and reviewers of Dickens or Thackeray seem to have kept *Ela the Outcast* and her innumerable cousins in mind whenever they addressed themselves to *Copperfield* and *Pendennis*.

An obvious question, however, is why the glut of bad poems in the middle years of the century affected reviewers in an altogether different way from the glut of fiction. Just as critics assumed the "low" stature of fiction and the moribund state of the drama, so they also acknowledged a great deal of second-rate verse. Looking back on his mid-century years, William Bell Scott writes in his autobiography that they were poor years for poetry.[5] If he forgets Tennyson, Browning, Rossetti, Arnold, Meredith, and Clough, he recalls a common enough complaint about the deluge of versifiers. This was indeed a time of prolific versifying, a time when a surprising number of people were able to write with a certain fluency and able, too, to get their works published.[6] Bailey's Faustian *Festus* won an incredible popularity after its publication (in 1839), surely because his competition was not too great. And if we except Browning, who was unpopular still; Tennyson, whose great fame began with *In Memoriam,* and Wordsworth, as representative of an earlier generation, the 1830s and 1840s might have seemed inauspicious to contemporary readers.

Nevertheless, critics could admire *Festus* or Sidney Dobell's *The Roman* (1850) while acknowledging its faults. When they discussed fiction, they worked at a critical disadvantage, accepting the long relegation of fiction to a second-class position. A bad poem was a bad poem, whereas a bad novel illustrated once again that novels were an inferior literary type. Neither history, epic, tragedy, comedy, lyric, nor satire, the novel might combine all, but this was identifiable as none. At mid-century, it remained a bastard form. Divisions of literature (in magazines, for example) continued to follow not only classical or neoclassical categories but also the values associated with those categories. The fact that poets were not producing epics or classical dramas or Horatian satires, or that such works, if written at all, were not read, may have prompted critics to new understandings of poetry, but it seemed to have little effect on their estimate of new directions in fiction.

To say that critics were reluctant to acknowledge a vigorous and modern genre on its own terms is not, however, to say that they saw no merit in it.

Masson's review of Thackeray and Dickens testifies to his admiration just as it shows his reservations. Like many of his colleagues, Masson is simply ambivalent. When the *Prospective* reviewer draws parallels between the theater in Shakespeare's time and serial publication in his own time, arguing the common nineteenth-century idea that the age demands the muse, his conclusion is that contemporary novelists cannot overcome the liabilities imposed by periodical publishing, although Shakespeare achieved his greatness precisely because he could overcome the liabilities of the theater. This is a shrewd enough assessment of the problems and pitfalls of serial publication, which most novelists of the time themselves admitted, and which caused Trollope, in the coming years, to insist on finishing a book before it began to appear. Thackeray's illness during the writing of *Pendennis* and Dickens's startled recognition, while he was writing *Copperfield*, that someone next to him was trying to buy a number he had yet to write indicate the hazards of piecemeal composition. But while the reviewer deplores such composition and regrets its effect on both writer and reader, he finds for Thackeray and Dickens surprisingly high praise. Having listed their faults, he goes on to say that they are, after all, the characteristic writers of their generation. In a "chaotic" and "unquiet" time, fiction represents the "indigenous epic and genius of our country."[7] And once more his opinion is typical. Earlier I have quoted Tennyson and Clough in praise of fiction. Here again is a forgotten writer, Thomas Shaw: "The prevailing literary form, or type, of the present age is undoubtedly the novel—the narrative picture of manners; just as the epic is the natural literary form of the heroic or traditional period."[8] For these as for other mid-century critics, novels are at once cheap entertainment and indigenous epic, light literature and accurate recorder, the victims of impossible publishing circumstances and the voice for millions. They are the representative works, spawned by the age, potentially powerful as well as rich—and, withal, manifestly lacking in art.

2

"I long to unburden my memory."—Eliot Warburton, *Reginald Hastings* (1850)[9]

Some of the ambivalence about the novel came, then, from its broadly public and at times shoddy role as entertainer, some from its inherited classification as low art. But just as the debunking of the novel continued at mid-century, so too did the confusion as to what the novel is and what it can do. From the outset, the novel was associated with the *new*, with the formless, the sprawling, the chaotic, and this holds whether we think of the novel originating with Defoe, or with Rabelais, or whether we look back to classical sources in Petronius. What seems ironical about so many mid-century discussions of fiction is the hackneyed assumption that the genre itself is new. Wordsworth's blank-verse epic about his own life might cause George Lewes to shudder, but Lewes does not ascribe the faults of *The Prelude* to its novelty. Conceiving of literature as the "reflex" of the age, he can join the widespread praise for Tennyson and stand almost alone in his praise for Browning. He knows that Browning risks ugliness with his audacious verse, and he is wise enough to see a comparable risk in Charlotte Brontë's *Jane Eyre*. But though many of Lewes's contemporaries came to share his assumptions about *realism*, they wanted ugliness neither in poetry nor fiction. The more Dickens assessed the failings of his society in years to come, the more his readers would call for "entertainment," as if Dickens had somehow overstepped his privileges. While assuming a lack of precedent or authority for an art form that seemed to be new, critics were nevertheless distrustful about the new directions that the art form took.[10]

Along with confusions about novels and novelty, mid-century critics accepted a lingering misconception as to the subject matter of fiction. They assumed like John Stuart Mill the distinction between the inner world of poetry and the outer world of fiction, and though there were critics who realized the inappropriateness of the division, it remained for most a stumbling block. Even a sensitive reader like Aubrey De Vere, who could recognize the need for poetry to observe "outward things" and to infuse mere things with symbolic life (see the "Poetics" chapter), failed to see that fiction might learn from poetry. Novelists themselves were ahead of their critics. Charlotte Brontë knew that she was speaking of a world that took possession of her from the inside. No less than poets of the time (whose work she generally deplored), she realized that her source of strength was an unconscious force, her subject an interior life. Similarly, a few years later, George Meredith speaks of the essential subject of fiction as "internal history," because self-knowledge is the end of novelistic no less than of poetic composition.[11]

Meredith points ahead to more sophisticated theories of fiction that we might associate with George Eliot or Henry James. Like Brontë, Meredith assumes a connection between fiction and poetry, proposing what is really an expressive theory of the novel—and an alternative to misunderstandings of his day. We have this further paradox in mid-century writings about fiction, for the common distinction between the inner and "ideal" subject of poetry and the outer and "natural" subject of fiction contrasts with the workings of the literature itself and with two of its evident traditions.

In *The Rise of the Novel*, Ian Watt describes *Moll Flanders* in terms I have used for *The Prelude* and *David Copperfield*. He says, for example, that Defoe's "total subordination of the plot to the pattern of autobiographical memoir is as defiant as assertion of the primary of individual experience in the novel as Descartes' *cogito ergo sum* was in philosophy."[12] Moreover, the primacy of individual experience is a conception understood by English empirical philosophers as a function of memory. To Locke, "the individual was in touch with his own continuing identity through memory of his own past thoughts and actions."[13] Self-awareness has, in other words, been a recurrent subject in the English novel, inasmuch as the consciousness of time and of personal identity in time elicits both the "unburdening" and the exploration of memory.

If we borrow one or two of Watt's arguments about the early novel, we might find them even more useful applied to a later literature. For his understanding of fiction in its double capacity of realistic narrative and self-exploration seems at least as appropriate for the novel in the age of Brontë and Dickens as for the novel in the age of Defoe or Sterne. The very terms we rely on for description—*realism*, for instance—are mid-nineteenth-century terms, which reflect both new and renewed directions in fiction.

A "pattern of autobiographical memoir" aptly describes *Moll Flanders, Pamela*, or *Tristram Shandy*, but it is especially pertinent for *David Copperfield* or *Jane Eyre*, in which the narrator indentifies a *pattern* in the "phases" of his or her life, and interprets the shape of the book according to the disciplining of emotions.[14] Here the recollections of a centripetal "I" (see chapter V) equate self-discipline with plot and bend heterogeneous experiences to the autobiographical perception. Behind the autobiographical energy lies a profound shift in apprehensions about mimesis and truth.

I wonder, to approach this in another way, how many eighteenth-century confessing narrators truly grow in awareness, truly match in their complexity the complexity of the narrative itself? Pamela's self-understanding is minimal throughout her story. Neither she nor Robinson Crusoe, nor Roderick Random, nor even Tristram Shandy, changes significantly in the course of time. Clarissa, who best illustrates Ian Watt's argument, is perhaps an exception in her century. In the middle of the nineteenth century, David

Copperfield becomes the rule. At least part of the reason for the flood of autobiographical fiction is, as I have suggested in the previous chapter, the example of the Romantic poets, who explore the particular in terms of the author's own memory, and hence present the fullest literary equivalent for the *cogito ergo sum*. Dickens has the experiments of Wordsworth and of Carlyle behind him, and he shares with Browning a sense of the intensity of his art which recalls an earlier generation of poets.

But while mid-century novelists are aware of Romantic poets, they do not, any more than their critics, point to them as models. (Kingsley, as I shall show in the following chapter, is an exception.) Thackeray, who was to lecture on the English humorists in 1851, pays constant homage to Fielding, turning like so many of his colleagues to eighteenth-century forerunners. David Copperfield's reading, like his author's, emphasizes Smollett, Fielding, Goldsmith, and Defoe among English writers, although Dickens thought Defoe lacking in "tenderness." When Bulwer-Lytton at mid-century attempts an autobiographical narrative, he borrows from his immediate contemporaries, but he also invokes Sterne, introducing outlandish names, chapters that go nowhere, hobbyhorse-like uncles and scholarly fathers, and calling attention in his preface to the "extremely slight" plot and the experimental nature of his novel as a whole.[15] George Borrow time and again asserts his own eccentricity along with the novelty of *Lavengro* (his book began as autobiography and turned into a magnificent hodgepodge, an "anatomy," told in the first person), and like Wilkie Collins and other contemporaries, he still refers to the archetypal book about man alone: Defoe's *Robinson Crusoe*. Maybe with Defoe's novel in mind, several mid-century novelists—and nonfictional writers like Newman—introduce shipwrecks, which disturb normal relationships, alter perceptions, and, as in *David Copperfield*, result in death for some characters while isolating others as though they were young orphans.

Whether or not writers turned specifically to Defoe or to Sterne, certain characteristics of *Robinson Crusoe* and *Tristram Shandy* seem to occur in mid-century fiction. Melville's *Moby Dick*, though American and still a year away from publication (and unfavorable English reviews), nicely combines Sterne's amorphous narrative with Defoe's sense of a new Adam, offering a first-person exploration of time and human isolation—as well as of seas and ships and large whales. There is nothing in English literature of the time like Melville's novels, but there is a related preoccupation with the materials of Defoe and Sterne and with the possibilities of an expanding art. As Melville and Dickens, Bulwer and the Brontës, Thackeray and Borrow, indicate, a central quality of that art is the radical emphasis on self-discovery. Autobiographical fiction is at mid-century the characteristic fiction. While it drew from eighteenth-century predecessors, it depicts, not man alone, but individual men and women alone, sharing the "introverted vision,"[16] the self-discovery through memory, with poets in the tradition of Wordsworth.

To a limited extent the emphasis on self-discovery is recognized by mid-century critics, though without significant application. The *Prospective* reviewer of *Copperfield* and *Pendennis* agrees with Patmore and De Vere, Carlyle and William Rossetti, about a prevailing "self-consciousness":

> Perhaps the chief reason why we call so many of the works of imagination produced in the present day "unhealthy," is the self-consciousness of the beings which they depict. The books called moral, and those called immoral, are alike occupied with the actions, thoughts, and sensations of men and women, who are striving, not to act out their inmost selves, but to determine, throughout the details of action, what their inmost selves would really be about.[17]

One assumption behind this statement is that shared by Matthew Arnold and Eneas Sweetland Dallas—the two men of the early fifties who come closest to proposing a coherent literary theory—as to the problems inherent in fundamentally expressive works and the need for "action," in a traditional dramatic sense. Neither Arnold nor Dallas, however, really addresses himself to fiction, and what we see in most of their contemporary critics is a floundering based on the prejudices they shared. Arnold admired and later cited *David Copperfield*; he was "moved" by Mrs. Gaskell's *The Moorland Cottage* (1850);[18] and later he did write on Tolstoi; but by and large he seems to have read fiction as though it had no connection with genuine literature.

3

> It is scarcely decorous . . . to speak at all, even where we speak impersonally. But—as thoughts are frozen and utterance benumbed, unless the speaker stand in some true relation with his audience—it may be pardonable to imagine that a friend, though not the closest friend, is listening to our talk; and then, a native reserve being thawed by this genial consciousness, we may prate of the circumstances that lie around us, and even of ourself, but still keep the inmost Me behind its veil. To this extent and within these limits, an author may be autobiographical, without violating either the reader's rights or his own.—Nathaniel Hawthorne, "The Custom House" (1850)[19]

Like his countryman Melville, Hawthorne indicates that "the autobiographical impulse" (his own phrase) was as active in America as in England. The rambling "Custom House" introduction to *The Scarlet Letter* bears an apparently slight relation to the work that follows, since Hester Prynne's story belongs to a distant historical time and is told by third-person narrator. But Hawthorne, essentially proferring a contract to his readers, places the narrative that follows in the context of his own historical understanding, while acknowledging a compulsion to confess.

Few English prefaces of the time are so explicit as Hawthorne's. To read them is not to get such an immediate sense of self-expression as the dominant fictional interest, as though writers turned in concert to a new purpose. Pertinent as he is, Hawthorne may remind us that the autobiographical interest is neither limited to England nor of spontaneous flourishing. Much of what I am describing began in earlier years. *Wuthering Heights* and *Jane Eyre*, though reissued in 1850, and recognized by Lewes and others as of great importance, had appeared in 1847. James Hogg had published the tortured *Confessions of a Justified Sinner* twenty years before. And Godwin's *Caleb Williams*, a story of haunting self-scrutiny, belongs to the last decade of the eighteenth century. George Borrow's echo of Goethe's *Dichtung und Wahrheit* at the beginning of *Lavengro*[20] or Kingsley's invocation of *Sartor Resartus* in *Alton Locke* show novelists responding to influences that had been available for a long time. A change is marked at mid-century, but it is not monolithic, and it obviously does not occur exclusively in the year 1850.

Aspects of the change are clear in a number of mid-century prefaces, albeit acknowledged in different ways. More than anything else, novelists were interested in defending the *truth* of their narratives, along with the sincerity of their motives. The word *truth* has always been a thorn to writers and to literary theorists since the time of Plato's *Ion*. It has been a particular thorn for writers of fiction. Fielding wants to establish the truth of his portrayals, and though his truth is a generic truth, it is as central as the ironic appeal in Lucian's "True History" or in the innumerable assertions of personally realized truth in nineteenth-century literature. I have mentioned Macaulay's theories about the inutility of traditional literary forms in times of a matured civilization and Macaulay's inference that scientific prose is the appropriate literature for his age. This is, again, close to Carlyle's position at mid-century, at least with regards the novel. It was said of Carlyle that he admonished novelists to write history and biography and poets, including his friend Tennyson, to write prose. In the essay "Diderot" (1833) Carlyle had speculated that novelists

> must, in a new generation, gradually do one of two things: either retire into nurseries, and work for children, minors and semi-fatuous persons of both sexes; or else, what were far better, sweep their Novel-fabric into the dust-cart, and betake them with such faculty as they have to understand and record what is true,—of which, surely, there is, and will forever be, a whole Infinitude unknown to us, of importance to us! Poetry, it will be more and more come to be understood, is nothing but higher Knowledge; and the only genuine Romance (for grown persons) Reality.[21]

Kathleen Tillotson, in quoting this passage from Carlyle, says that "novelists knew better than to accept such advice and threats," though they may have been "put on their mettle." But if, "after Carlyle, the rift between the 'prophetic' and the merely entertaining novel widens,"[22] novelists were perhaps responding to his criticism. Of course novelists were hardly likely to give up their source of livelihood because of his opinions, and on this as on so many topics, Carlyle both reflects and stimulates current ideas. His impatience with the novel might simply have been the traditional and widely shared distrust of imaginative literature, charged with Carlyle's own rhetoric. Yet looked at another way, his admonition in the "Diderot" essay introduces a kind of hope for fiction, so long as writers of fiction contrive to supplant their fictions with truth. To remind ourselves that fiction is art and that art is artifice has really little to do with what mid-century novelists told themselves and their readers in justification of their work. Sharing an ambivalence or a confusion similar to Carlyle's own, they may after all have followed his advice. Only the rare writer at mid-century—like Ruskin in his preface to *The King of the Golden River*—admits that his work is intended for "amusement"; and Ruskin's disclaimer points out his sense of the novel as "light" literature, which he contrasts implicitly but absolutely with serious art and with his own other writings. One might say that Ruskin, like Marryat and Charlotte Yonge, is taking Carlyle literally—and writing for children. By 1850, when *King of the Golden River* appeared, Marryat had, toward the end of his life, published *Children of the New Forest* (1847), and Charlotte Yonge, who was planning her children's magazine, *Monthly Packet*, had already written *Kenneth*, her first romance for children.[23]

No doubt Carlyle's facetious recommendation to "work for children" had little to do with the rapidly increasing numbers of children's magazines and stories, of which the mid-Victorians were masters. Still, a writer like Kingsley, who considered himself a disciple of Carlyle, could think of a work like *Water Babies* as prophetic, just as he could think of a novel like *Yeast* as true. Many writers of children's books were unwilling to categorize their work merely as entertainment. Nor, for that matter, were writers of cheap adult fiction necessarily happy to be entertainers; and if Carlyle created a rift between prophetic and entertaining books, the entertainers could at least claim to be prophets. Thus lesser novelists at times invoke truth to suggest the object lesson of the book. In *The Maniac Father*, Thomas Prest says that his book describes "the miseries which a dereliction from the path of virtue is sure to entail." The actual melodramatic and exploitive quality of the novel is clear in almost any sentence: "With feelings of exultation the profligate and unprincipled Baresford quitted that fair girl whom he was seeking to make the victim of his secret and disgusting passions."[24] *The Maniac Father* points again to the flood of cheap fiction published at the time and to the obvious fact that much of this fiction had as little to do with self-awareness as it had with "the path of virtue." The appeal to moral value is a gesture we might properly associate with statements about literature in early and mid-Victorian England—remembering, however, that "the path of virtue" was not as yet quite so equatable with prudishness as it later became and that it was not invoked so often as we might assume.

The widespread assertion of truth suggests that the authors of *The Maniac Father, The Rifle Rangers*, and *The Old Oak Chest* share an ambition for their fiction with the authors of *Copperfield* and *Pendennis*. Thackeray's preface to *Pendennis* cleverly manipulates the author's acknowledged showmanship into a defense of the authenticity of his fiction. He says that "if this kind of composition, of which the two years' product is now laid before the public, fail in art, as it constantly does and must, it at least has the advantage of a certain truth and honesty, which a work more elaborate might lose."[25] Thackeray is acknowledging the validity of contemporary criticism about fiction, accepting even artistic failure as a consequence of the novel's serial publication and of its desired effect. Although *Pendennis* is not autobiographical in method (it *is* autobiographical in content), Thackeray sees his book as confessional. He identifies precisely what Kaye and other reviewers notice about the workings of his novels and their relationship with the public. The novel is, for Thackeray, "a sort of confidential talk between the writer and the reader, which must often be dull, must often flag. . . . The perpetual speaker must . . . lay bare his own weaknesses, vanities, peculiarities." Self-consciousness then seems for Thackeray something to be aimed for, since the confessing and reminiscing mind of the narrator becomes the necessary mediator between the subject and the involved reader. Thackeray sees his method as "natural." It cannot be direct or formally precise, because truth itself is neither. Yet it "strives to tell the truth."[26]

Dickens points to some of the same ends in his brief preface to *David Copperfield.* Reluctantly finishing his "favorite child," and sending off his characters, as David sends off Micawber, Peggotty, and Little Em'ly, Dickens assures his readers that "no one can ever believe this Narrative, in the reading, more than I have believed it in the writing."[27] The story comes out of himself and, presumably, works on the reader to the extent of the novelist's own emotional involvement. I shall return to this question shortly. Here let me add that Thackeray's and Dickens's assertion of truth is the Carlylean truth of *sincerity.* And sincerity for most mid-Victorian novelists is thought to complement that other Carlylean truth, *reality.*

If we think of mid-century novelists aiming at the truth of reality on the one hand and the truth of sincerity on the other, we can appreciate tendencies in their fictions which are, while not necessarily contradictory, at least potentially so. Carlyle's implied categories may be subsumed under the general word *truth*, but they reflect mimetic assumptions about fiction as reality and expressive assumptions about art as sincerity, to both of which the mid-nineteenth-century novelist often makes his appeal. We can understand the two assumptions best, perhaps, by looking at the contemporary interest in history and in painting. Shifts in the uses and understanding of history indicate the applications of words such as *manners*, while analogies with painting raise questions about *nature* and therefore about the subjects as well as the techniques of the new fiction.

Even granting the humor in a title like *The Personal History, Adventures, Experience, & Observation of David Copperfield the Younger, Of Blunderstone Rookery (Which He never meant to be Published on any Account)*, or *The History of Pendennis, His Fortunes and Misfortunes, His Friends and His Greatest Enemy*, we can acknowledge an emphasis on detail, on inclusiveness, on some equivalent for "history," the principal word in both Dickens's and Thackeray's titles. We might construe history ironically, as comic history, but the irony in these two titles does not quite obscure the justification of fictional truth as history that characterizes so many novels of the time. As Fielding's "History" of Tom Jones suggests, the justification is not new to mid-century fiction; the emphasis may be.

The example of Sir Walter Scott is still in the minds of mid-century writers, who come at the tail end of the vogue for "costume novels," but who are interested in several of Scott's historical precedents. G. P. R.

James, a workhorse of a novelist—he had written thirty novels within the previous decade—prefaces *The Old Oak Chest* (of 1850) with an invitation to remember the model of Scott. James looks back sixty years, cites the example of *Waverley*, and pointedly remarks the parallels between 1789 and 1849 (when thoughts of revolution were still in his readers' minds), while discussing the changes that have occurred in this most eventful period of human history.[28] Once the narrative begins, however, James's historicism seems at best a gentle nostalgia for the time of the narrator's own youth. Anthony Trollope, publishing his third work of fiction in 1850, assumes a comparable time perspective in *La Vendée*, a staunchly antirevolutionary study of upper-class life in western France during the revolutionary period. These books, like Harrison Ainsworth's *Lancashire Witches* (1848), are costume novels, offering detailed pictorial accounts of a past era, usually with a conservative or reactionary political intent. Michael Sadleir calls Trollope's work "a queer, unreadable lump of anti-revolutionary propaganda."[29]

Whatever their attitude toward revolution and other social and political upheavals, mid-century novelists accepted historians' roles. Wilkie Collins's first work of fiction, *Antonina; or the Fall of Rome: A Romance of the Fifth Century* (1850) mixes Goths and Gibbon with patricians and defenseless heroines in a long account about the sacking of Rome. Collins flaunts his historical accuracy in his preface, citing historians, weighing historical evidence, and defending what he calls "proper notes," in support of characters who are "the practical exponents of the spirit of the age."[30] Although the story is set centuries earlier, Collins boasts about "the appearance of verisimilitude" in a book that he labels romance. As the phrase *spirit of the age* suggests, he sees himself working as a historian, though with greater impact because of the powers of his imagination.

So, too, Eliot Warburton, who tells the story of *Reginald Hastings; or a Tale of the Troubles in 164–*. Warburton does not use the term *daguerreotype*, which Henry Reeve adopted to describe the historical method of Leopold von Ranke, but he assumes with Reeve the fundamental importance of "the discovery of Old Manuscripts." Manuscripts embody "the frank and manly, yet tender spirit" of lives otherwise lost to our understanding, and Warburton thinks that sympathetic identification with his hero can thus bridge the years. "For the passions. . .are unchangeable by time."[31] Writing about the English revolutionary period, he allows his hero "Confessions" from prison, turning his story into autobiography.

Warburton's insistence that "passions are unchangeable by time" offers an apology for historical fiction while indicating the new directions of that fiction. *Reginald Hastings* is set in the 1640s, *La Vendée* in the 1790s, and historical studies of this sort not only continue to be written at mid-century, they have continued to be written ever since. Nevertheless, the great popularity of such works was waning, and the novels like *Copperfield* and *Pendennis* that critics and other readers thought characteristic of the times are histories of another order. Trollope records in his *Autobiography* an interview with a publisher who remembers *La Vendée*: "I hope [your new book] is not historical, Mr. Trollope? Whatever you do, don't be historical; your historical novel is not worth a damn."[32] For Trollope, as for Collins after *Antonina*, the new emphasis is to be on a different kind of historicism, on what Bulwer (in the preface to *The Caxtons*) calls "domestic manners."[33]

Yet whether novelists address themselves to a remote or recent era, they are writing, in their own terms, a version of history, and Warburton's defense of historical fiction raises questions as appropriate for the past of *Copperfield* and *Pendennis* as for that of *Reginald Hastings*. Warburton knows that the authenticity of his story is dependent on both a believable picture of Hastings's times and on the psychology of the character himself, the storyteller, whose perspective may be different from the author's or from that of the dispassionate historian. Warburton recognizes that "one fault (or merit, as the case may be) of an Autobiography, is, that it necessarily leaves its chief moral deductions to the reader."[34] Implicit here is an important awareness. For in spite of the political messages in novels like *La Vendée*, Warburton identifies a major development in the fiction of his time. His historicism—like Thackeray's and like Browning's, which I have touched on earlier—is essentially a method of sympathetic narrative, interested in cause and event, and committed to the notion of an unchanging "human nature," but desirous of illustrating human nature in the private thoughts of a particular individual. The effect *is* to leave moral deductions to the reader, who, for this reason too, becomes an active participant in mid-century fiction.

4

> Many of our best artists are now employing Photography with the greatest advantage in their studies, with a camera . . . the lover of Nature is enabled to select his subject, and by a delay of a few minutes only to carry off a transcript.—Robert Hunt in the *Art Journal* (1850)[35]

The concern with historical truth coincided not merely with an interest in "Old Manuscripts," or historical evidence but also with graphic accuracy and with a widespread interest in verisimilitude. The 1840s were active years for experiments in photography, with Fox Talbot and other Englishmen competing with French pioneers like Daguerre and Blanquart-Evrard.[36] In *The Thirty Years' Peace*, Harriet Martineau speaks of photography as a way of preserving invaluable evidence for posterity,[37] and photographers were soon, in the Crimea, to record their first war. Most photographers (witness Hill and Adamson in Scotland) seem, however, to have been particularly interested in portraits on the one hand and landscape on the other. Early photographic essays of the Alps indicate how the "sun paintings" were used to record the beauties of nature. Fox Talbot called his 1844 book on photography *The Pencil of Nature*. Ruskin admitted to an interest in the daguerreotype, though he later recanted; and the paintings of the Pre-Raphaelites probably owe something to the new cameras.[38] Holman Hunt's overwhelmingly detailed painting *The Scapegoat* shows Hunt, like a number of contemporary photographers, performing a kind of pilgrimage to the Near East, from which he brought home his photographic record.

Possibly the Pre-Raphaelite interest in bright color has as its origin the desire to outdo the various browns of the early photographers as much as the browns of the Royal Academy. At any rate, photographic accuracy, however labeled, is something that we can see appreciated in historical studies, in social reports (such as Mayhew's), in painting, and of course in photographs themselves. We can see the same appreciation in contemporary fiction, although, interestingly enough, most novelists equated the "realist" tendency with painting or with lithographic rather than with photographic art. Mayne Reid speaks typically of having "drawn [his book] from nature."[39] The novelist Lady Chatterton, as if to define her own stylistic peculiarities, asserts that she has "followed nature, instead of proceeding on the supposed principles of art."[40] The common appeal of the times to nature may take, in fiction, the direction indicated by Harriet Martineau toward a general accuracy, or it may take a more personal and subjective direction, with an altogether different emphasis. The problem is epistemological as well as aesthetic, and it represents a basic division in mid-nineteenth-century theories of the mind.

R. H. Horne's *The Poor Artist; or Seven Eye Sights and One Object* (1850) is a short, allegorical piece of fiction about a struggling artist trying to "deal with external nature." The painter learns various lessons from animals and insects in the woods, among them the need to preserve "the memory of any new object."[41] His painting of a bright, gold coin for various animals results in a work called *The Private Experience of an Artist*, and the painting, which illustrates the tyranny of the eye and the privacy of knowing, leads the artist back through sympathetic realization to civilization, success and marriage. Horne's work is untypically short and untypically like a fairy tale, but Horne's interest in the vision of artists and the importance of perceiving nature are both common preoccupations with his fellow novelists. The moral of Ruskin's fairy tale *The King of the Golden River* also rests on sympathy and on respect for the bounty and beauty of the natural world.

I have mentioned earlier Ruskin's difficulties when he confuses the Coleridgean "I am" of the imagination with a view of art that seems otherwise impossibly mimetic and the related thinking of Charles Radcliffe and Robert Mackay. Radcliffe's *Proteus* insists on the minute observation of nature in order to assert "the unity of nature," and Radcliffe urges what amounts to a symbolic reading of the external world. Similarly Mackay, in *The Progress of Intellect*, reminds his countrymen of their lack of a visionary quality, all too evident in their inability to think mythically. Any civilization, he says, "is imperfect and comparative." "A man is never perfectly sane, or perfectly matured. In every stage he shows more or less of that tendency to self-delusion most conspicuous in the earliest recollections of his race."[42] What Mackay urges is a renewed sense of wonder, an appreciation of the unseen, in a jaded civilization. As for Horne and Ruskin and Radcliffe, he finds an ambiguous but necessary restorative in nature. Nature does not, for any of these men, supplant religion, but it is thought of in largely religious terms: it must be witnessed, interpreted, studied with a "disciplined" and sympathetic eye. In a society rapidly becoming mechanized while it mechanized the thinking of its people, nature seemed to offer both a means to self-awareness and possible escape.[43]

When Kingsley's Alton Locke leaves London for Cambridge, his first journey outside of London, the English countryside comes to him as a revelation, a commentary on his own life and on the life of those condemned forever in Jacob's Island and other London slums. Even the epitome of slums, the places where criminals and outcasts and the unspeakably poor were packed together, had the ironic title rookeries, an indication of how far they were from the pure English countryside. Dickens in his *Household Words* tells about accompanying policemen to the rookeries, suggesting that most Englishmen would not indeed believe in their existence. And yet, "fidelity to nature" could be invoked when an author described such places. Truth of observation, verisimilitude, and accuracy applied to squalid lives as well as to the beauties of the countryside, the two directions part of a single equation. The emphasis on country beauty was in part a pastoral gesture, a reaction against the ugliness of Manchester, Birmingham, or London itself. David Copperfield returns to London after living in the Alps and after hearing "great Nature" to find the city covered in its winter blanket of fog and smoke and cold. In *Pendennis*, Thackeray follows his master Fielding in equating certain virtues not only with the country as opposed to the city (although his London is not that of Dickens) but also with country people.

One of the best examples of implied pastoralism is Mrs. Gaskell's *Lizzie Leigh* (published in *Household Words* in 1850), which contrasts the austere but honest life in the country with the evils of the city, to which Lizzie Leigh goes, happily to be saved from prostitution at the last moment. Mrs. Gaskell's *Mary Barton* (1848) begins with some of the Barton family and other operatives on the edge of Manchester, close to the beauties of nature that are such a small part of their difficult lives. And *The Moorland Cottage*, published as a Christmas book in 1850, uses pastoral conventions as well as settings. The conventions, however, are Wordsworth's. The narrator sets this book in the Lake District and begins with an invitation taken from *Michael*: "If you take the turn to the left. . .you will come to the wooden bridge over the brook; keep along the field-path, which mounts higher and higher, and. . .you will be in a breezy upland field. . . . Look!"[44]

Even Frances Trollope, prolific writer, like her son, of novels of manners, introduces a bit of pastoralism into her mid-century book. *Petticoat Government* (1850) describes the courtship of Judith Maitland, who, after minor difficulties with her maiden aunts (she is wealthy, like Thackeray's Blanche, but also wholesome and orphaned, like Laura), and a relationship with an inappropriate baronet, finally marries the relatively impecunious Charles Worthington. Trollope's new comedy ending, which is still a parody of the silver-fork ending, is apparent, yet Trollope includes in this novel two further nods to the times. Worthington is a painter, "a poor artist," who bests the wealthy aristocrat, but more important, he takes his bride, not to a house in London, but to a retreat somewhere in the mountains near Cortina D'Ampezzo. The narrator tells of a friend who has been stranded on his journey out of Italy and who meets the young couple:

> Every step seemed to disclose some new charm, for charm there was even in the black gorges that sometimes opened almost beneath their feet; and in the strange variety of light and shade there was a charm too—and in the wide-spreading distance there, and in the close leafy covert here, none of it could be passed by

> without pausing. But at last this enchanting path seemed to end, for it came to a turn so sudden, as to show nothing beyond it but a vast mass of perpendicular rock.[45]

Predictably, the turn leads to "a smiling lawn" and to domestic happiness, where artist and wife and child will live happily ever after, except for their equally happy winters in Rome.

While the artist is relatively insignificant in *Petticoat Government*, he shows Frances Trollope aware of a new sort of protagonist, an articulate, educated, and sensitive man—a forerunner of George Eliot's Ladislaw, who is similarly the unfavored suitor in the eyes of the heroine's family. Trollope is also aware, despite her satire on the "English tourist," of natural beauty. This gentle comedy of manners concludes with a lesson on the virtues of isolation and the importance of natural scenery.

The picture of "manners," which novelists as well as critics assume as a primary responsibility of the literature, involves a further aspect of "truth to nature." In *Lavengro*, George Borrow mocks an English historical painter (intended possibly for Benjamin Haydon), who clothes a country mayor in Roman costume and poses him before an imaginary Roman arch. Borrow's satire on historical painting may also be a commentary on the pomp and trappings of historical fiction, which forgets the romance in English life along with the beauty of English scenery. For a painterly model of English scenery, Borrow suggests Crome, his contemporary. For the painterly model of characterization, he turns back to Hogarth, just as Smollett and Fielding had done before him. Yet he does not want caricature. He thinks of Hogarth as the honest English painter, he who will paint the red nose and the large paunch, but who—like the best novelists—will also record all that he sees without the falsities of convention.

In an apparently contradictory way, Wilkie Collins (son of a painter, whose biography he had recently written) defends his narrative about the fall of Rome in terms of its fidelity to nature, and, no less than Borrow, shows his awareness of painting techniques:

> . . . it was thought that the different passages in the story might be most forcibly contrasted with one another, that each scene, while it preserved its separate interest to the mind of the reader, might most clearly appear to be combining to form one complete whole; that, in the painter's phrase, the "effects" might thus be best "massed," and the "lights and shadows" most harmoniously "balanced" and "discriminated."[46]

So far as anything of Hogarth is here, it is his theoretical "line of beauty," although the narrative as scenes, separate but united, might suggest

Hogarth's progress paintings. What is interesting in Collins's description is his assumption that a narrative must move from compelling scene to compelling scene, even if it is not a serial publication. Like Thackeray, Collins will not allow that this makes for failure in art; on the contrary, he introduces the parallels with painting to give authority to what he calls his narrative "system." He was in years to come to accept something akin to Borrow's thinking, in that the defense of *Antonina* seems to fit a novel like *The Woman in White* (1860) better than the epic narrative of the fall of Rome. In taking his materials from English scenes and middle-class people, Collins in his later novels illustrates Borrow's view that what interests most is that closest to home.

The obsession with nature and with accuracy of description coincides, then, with the mid-century trend toward a more recent historical past. Bulwer's appeal "to common household affections" characterizes the time and the setting of his novel as much as its values, and Bulwer, in this as in so much else, offers a good indication about the interests of his fellow novelists. *David Copperfield, Pendennis, The Moorland Cottage,* and in its way *Lavengro*, all insist on the centrality of "household affections" and all deal with a version of manners, asking how people live their lives—lives which, like Thackeray's characterization of his narrative—"must often be dull, must often flag."

But the emphasis on "manners" in mid-century fiction can be misleading. In the first place, as Kathleen Tillotson has pointed out, novelists of the late 1840s may be describing the habits and social relationships of people, but they are not describing the habits of their immediate contemporaries.[47] They are far more interested in a somewhat earlier generation, the years of the author's youth, before the advent of railways or in the early years of the railways. (Collins's next book, a record of his 1850 walking tour in Cornwall, was called *Rambles beyond Railways.*) In *Pendennis*, the railway is just making its way into the countryside where Pen and Laura grow up, and this critical moment in the lives of individuals as in the development of communities remains as important in later years to George Eliot and to Thomas Hardy (in *Tess of the d'Urbervilles*, for example) as to Dickens and Thackeray. *Middlemarch* is a typical novel in this respect. By the 1860s, the portrayal of near-contemporary manners—manners divided from the reader by a generation—has become the norm. But the relation of *Middlemarch* to mid-century fiction qualifies still further the emphasis on manners.

Like mid-century novelists before her, George Eliot compares her work with that of the Flemish painters (not, significantly, with Hogarth), whose honest and accurate depictions of a middle-class society, along with a sensitive appreciation of country landscape, provide a model for the novelist. Almost without an English rival, *Middlemarch* describes the march of middle-class men and women in the Midlands toward the middle years of the century. Yet the emphasis on the ordinary in George Eliot's novel usually sets off the extraordinary in her characters. George Eliot was of course aware of her husband George Lewes's speculations about fiction, including his theories of *realism*, and she was probably aware of the conflicting tendencies in his assessment of the functions of the novel.

In an 1850 review of Charlotte Brontë's *Shirley* (for which Lewes repeats much from his earlier review of *Jane Eyre*) he speaks of the Brontë novels as though they were types for George Eliot's fiction. Not only does he discuss the role of women writers, finding them the best observers of everyday life, he sees Charlotte Brontë as an important force in contemporary fiction. Charlotte Brontë is "graphic" and "powerful," perhaps unmatched in her "pictorial" sense. "The aspects of external nature [in *Jane Eyre*] were painted . . . to your *soul* as well as to your eye, by a pencil dipped into the soul's experience for its colours." Lewes asserts that "Art . . . deals with broad principles of human nature, not with idiosyncracies," but his sense of the power in *Jane Eyre* comes from a recognition of its intensely personal expression of "reality. From out of the depths of a sorrowing experience, here was a voice speaking to the experience of thousands."[48]

If we remember Lewes's definition of poetry as the account of the human soul, we can see that, without quite saying so, he reads *Jane Eyre* as though it were an "epos of the soul," suggestive of "broad principles," but immersed in "individual experience." And though *Middlemarch* is a provincial novel of an altogether different sort, George Eliot expresses a comparable interest in individual experience and in the "singular" and idiosyncratic. Dorothea, while living in a calmer world than Charlotte Brontë's Jane, is important to her author as an illustration of modern heroism, specifically sainthood. In spite of its panoramic vision, *Middlemarch* concentrates on the aberrants, on the Dorotheas, the Lydgates, the Bulstrodes, the Ladislaws. Looked at in this way, George Eliot's world, like Charlotte Brontë's, is a world of eccentrics. What Charlotte Brontë offers in *Jane Eyre* is a study of an ordinary girl (as Jane keeps reminding us) who is yet courageous and independent. She serves as a type, not only for George Eliot's characters in the decades to come, but also for a host of mid-century works, works which, like *David Copperfield*, read at times like essays on the nature of modern heroism.

When reissuing *Jane Eyre* (in 1850), along with the novels of her now dead sisters, Charlotte Brontë tried again (unsuccessfully) to find a publisher for *The Professor.* She wrote in her preface:

> I said to myself that my hero should work his way through life as I had seen real living men work theirs—that he should never get a shilling he had not earned—that no sudden turns should lift him in a moment to wealth or high station . . . that he should not even marry a beautiful girl or a lady of rank. As Adam's son he should share Adam's doom, and drain throughout his life a mixed and moderate cup of enjoyment.[49]

This could serve at once as a reaffirmation of principles in eighteenth-century fiction and as an epigraph for the new fiction of the time. In *Frank Fairlegh* (1850), Francis Smedley boasts about the dubious stature of his "hero." Frank's "shortcomings doubtless evince a lamentable contrast to the perfection of the steroetyped novel hero; but as it has never been my good fortune to meet with that faultless monster, a perfectly consistent man, or woman, I prefer describing character as I find it."[50] If Smedley had remembered *Jane Eyre*, or looked at *Copperfield* and *Pendennis*, he would have admitted to setting up a straw man. For the new heroes are, like Jane Eyre, obviously flawed characters, usually from less than the highest ranks of society (usually, indeed, like Pendennis, of lower-middle-class background), and they are held up by their authors as "real" alternatives to the heroes of romance or the heroes of silver fork novels. In the same year as *Frank Fairlegh*, Dickens's hero wonders if he will turn out to be the hero of his own book, and Thackeray is saying, categorically, that Pendennis is no hero at all. Thackeray is also telling his readers to look at their own lives and to find heroism there—if they can.

If the hero or heroine in mid-century fiction is "in eclipse"—to use Mario Praz's phrase[51]—we might expect novels of social interaction rather than novels about the emotions and experiences of isolated individuals. To some extent this is true of *Pendennis*, in which the hero meets a great number of people from a range of social classes. Even *Copperfield* can be read as a great panorama, in which David is merely a recording personality. And yet the emphasis on manners, like the emphasis on broad historical trends, seems less important to most of the novels of the time than what Lewes calls the "reality" of one voice "speaking to the experience of thousands." Novelists who insist on the unheroic attributes of their characters are simultaneously preoccupied with the nature of the hero and the limited possibilities for heroic action. There may not be, as in *Middlemarch*, direct allusions to saints' lives or to epic possibilities, but there are explicit questions about the role of modern heroes in works that are likely to be both large and ironic. If these are questions that have lurked behind fictional narratives from the time of *Don Quixote*, with its parody of romance, they are particularly appropriate for fiction about ordinary lower- or middle-class lives, the more so when the characters are articulate and intelligent.[52] Despite their intelligence, such characters are not privileged, and they know they are not privileged; they are aware of life as "a mixed and moderate cup of enjoyment at its best."

Preoccupation with heroes reflects, as I have suggested earlier, Carlyle's hope for modern heroes, and if Carlyle himself found most fiction sordidly lacking in heroism, a type of his modern hero materializes in the novel. At mid-century, the sensitive and articulate characters who often tell their own lives (and are therefore implicitly writers, like Jane Eyre) are also sometimes men of letters. Like George Lewes's own struggling poet in *Ranthorpe* (1847), they are "poor artists," often lonely and orphaned or at least independent, and they must succeed, in spite of their sensitivities and sufferings, as literary hacks.

The career of Pendennis is the stumbling career of a man who, without great talent, energy, or discrimination, can work as a literary hack and finally establish a modest reputation in London's vast publishing empire. Thackeray is scornful about the publishers, editors, and the other writers whom Pendennis encounters, and the early readers of the novel had good reason for taking Thackeray's satire as indictment of what reviewers and other writers are proudly calling the literary profession. Thackeray's own feelings, as I noted in the introduction, are ambivalent about the status of writers, and he comes in part to regret the extremes of his criticism. But the criticism is there and legitimately there. Oddly enough, young men growing up at mid-century will look back on *Pendennis* as a proud defense of journalists and of periodical literature in general. Edmund Yates, in *Recollections and Experiences*, recalls Thackeray's novel as the turning point in his professional life: "I was encouraged to hope that I might succeed, perhaps more than anything else, by reading the career of *Pendennis*. . . . There is no prose story in our English language . . . which affects me as much as *Pendennis*."[53]

Thackeray's is the most detailed of contemporary descriptions of the publishing world, but Kingsley's *Alton Locke* (see chapter VIII), Borrow's *Lavengro*, and Dickens's *David Copperfield* are all narratives about future men-of-letters making their way and (with *Pendennis* excepted) telling their own stories. When R. H. Horne, in a novel that combines characters and dialogue out of Peacock with the polemics of Kingsley, prefaces *The Dreamer and the Worker* (1851), he says that his book though comparable with Kingsley's "claims for the literary man, and public teacher [embodied in the character Archer], a due recognition of his order."[54] Implicit here, as perhaps in the other novels about novelists, is a defense of the literary man as a necessary "dreamer" or outsider—as the "self-conscious" recorder of his own life, and as the apparently ordinary voice who can "speak for thousands."

5

> In his constant communication with the reader, the writer is forced into frankness of expression, and to speak out his own mind and feelings as they urge him.—Thackeray, Preface to *Pendennis*[55]

We come back, then, somewhat deviously, to the questions raised by mid-century reviewers or implicit in their judgments. "The serial tale," dismissed by many reviewers as lacking consistency, completeness, and proportion, while praised—often within the same article—as the indigenous modern epic, was, as Thomas Shaw said, the "prevailing literary form of the age." The prejudice against "light" literature was also a measure of both its self-consciousness and its popularity, a word used commonly for either approbation or censure. At a time when the reading public bought large numbers of sermons, scientific treatises, as well as histories, the word *popular* could have strange applications. The Dean in Kingsley's *Alton Locke* may be partly a satiric figure, but when he tells young Alton that works like John Locke's *Essay Concerning Human Understanding* are popular, he represents a common desire to separate widely known or available works from the erudite or scientific. Whatever else novels accomplished, they cut across privilege and class, for they were read by men and women of all classes, including people like Arnold, who thought, with Kingsley's Dean, in terms of a cultural elite.

In such a literary climate, it is not surprising that Carlyle and Macaulay might dismiss genuinely popular works of imagination, knowing that serious literature would be read and that fiction, to a great extent, catered to the uneducated, the unthinking, and the "semi-fatuous persons of both sexes." Only a rare critic like George Lewes at mid-century discusses fiction as though it should be taken seriously. Lewes's review of *Shirley*, which attempts to place Brontë's novels in a great tradition of English fiction, addresses such questions as fictional "reality," the novelist's "artistic fusion," "power," and "discipline." Again, Lewes's comments on

Charlotte Brontë anticipate his later conversations with Marian Evans, who, as George Eliot, fully embodies his critical principles while she exploits mid-century fictional developments. But even Lewes, though he uses the same critical standards to judge Charlotte Brontë as he does to judge Wordsworth, does not make the association between new tendencies in poetry, which he, like most critics, ascribes to Wordsworth. The contemporary recognition of "self-consciousness" as a hallmark of the literature seems to be made about both fiction and poetry separately—without the inference that the exploration of personality, the experiments with versions of autobiography, and the reliance in memory are attributes equally of the novels and the poems of the age. But since self-consciousness is itself often deplored in poetry, it is in any case hardly likely to improve the status of fiction. As light literature, condemned to formlessness, novels still receive the skimpiest of estimates from most reviewers, even when the reviewers admit that novels have tremendous influence, that they can cut across class lines, and that, because of their inclusiveness, they should be looked at as equivalents for epic.

Against the prejudices of reviewers, and against the traditional prejudices against imaginative literature, writers of fiction tend to justify their works in the terms of their critics, although always with the awareness that the public would decide their fate. Hence Thackeray admits to his failing in art, but, like so many of his colleagues, claims that what he loses in art he gains in both sincerity and reality. The emphasis on the truth of narratives, as I have indicated, often takes the form of justification as history, and writers like G. P. R. James point to the still revered model of Walter Scott, while Wilkie Collins and Eliot Warburton claim accuracy of fact along with the authority of manuscripts or the analogy of painting. Ironically, the parallels drawn with history more or less coincide (as Collins and Trollope indicate) with the demise of the costume novel and the increased emphasis on a recent past.

With the shift to a recent past comes a defense of the novel as the picture of *manners*, a word invoked as often as *history* or *nature*. What I have tried to suggest, however, is that the "realistic" tendency (and Lewes uses the term *realist* in discussion of *Jane Eyre*), apparent in references to Hogarth and to Flemish painters, as well as to history and to the recording of manners, in fact implies what Mayne Reid calls "depicting any new phase in life and manners." The new is the singular for Reid, as it is in different but analogous ways for George Borrow, Bulwer-Lytton, the Brontës, and even Dickens, who, according to David Masson and other reviewers, draws a picture of a social world that bore small resemblance to an England they knew. The singular character becomes, moreover, not only the center of works as diverse as *Petticoat Government* and *Lavengro* and *Jane Eyre*, he (or she) becomes in many cases the narrator of his (or her) own story. Thus the self-consciousness complained about by the *Prospective Review* writer and other readers of Carlyle is really a necessary function of literary works with a new, if unacknowledged, intent. "Moral deductions," in Warburton's words, are left in mid-century novels "to the Reader," who participates in the workings of the books. *Truth*, therefore, for many of these novelists, as for Wordsworth before them and for Browning their contemporary, is the truth of personal experience, of reminiscence, of a relative historicism, which meets with corresponding sympathy in the mind of the reader.[56] For the reader is invited time and again (as in *Pendennis*) to compare his own memories, his own self-estimate, with those of the narrator.

Finally, the potentially contradictory assumption about accurate history and honest treatment of "Adam's sons" on the one hand and the preoccupation with heroes on the other hand lead in many novels to a protagonist who is "ordinary," who is not a hero, or who doesn't know if he will become a hero in the course of the narrative. This self-conscious figure turns out, often enough—and really for the first time in English fiction—to be a man-of-letters.

VIII

Polemics

Charles Kingsley and Alton Locke

1

> Jeremiah is my favorite book now. It has taught me more than tongue can tell. But I am much disheartened, and am minded to speak no more words in this name [Parson Lot]. Yet all these bullyings teach one, correct one, warn one, show one that God is not leaving one to go One's own way. "Christ reigns," quoth Luther.—Kingsley in a December 1850 letter to F. D. Maurice.[1]

Charles Kingsley was a sort of mid-century Jeremiah, lashing out at his own Church of England, imploring workers to choose Christ, demanding that the aristocrats and middle classes change their ways, seeing himself as a necessary prophet. The letter to his "Master," F. D. Maurice, written after failure of the *Christian Socialist* magazine (to which he contributed as Parson Lot), shows Kingsley at his open, honest, self-doubting best. This man who scorned Newman's *The Soul* and who feared the "higher criticism" of men like Strauss could urge his underprivileged countrymen to accept the teachings of Christ while himself admitting that the Old Testament figures meant most to him. Parson Lot, not Paul; Jeremiah, not Luke. And the choice is not random. The New Testament for Kingsley described a millennial world, a world of socialism, and Kingsley joined J. M. Ludlow and Maurice in equating Christianity with socialism. But socialism was for Englishmen, men who could learn to love their work and know their place. The clergymen who was to dismiss Irish peasants as so much dirt and African tribesmen as slightly elevated apes was also the man who thought, almost in spite of himself, of a revenging God and of a chosen race. Kingsley's famous announcement: "I am a Chartist" was a courageous admission to a group of working men. But Kingsley's whole sentence was: "I am a parson and a Chartist—Church of England I mean."[2]

In 1850 the parson, rector of Eversley, was thirty-one years old. He had published *The Saint's Tragedy*, his anti-Catholic, anti-ascetic play based on Elizabeth of Hungary (and in its original, incomplete version, his wedding present for Fanny, his wife). As "Parson Lot" he had written his polemics in *Politics for the People* and was to write again soon for the *Christian Socialist.* He had published *Yeast*, his polemical novel, in *Fraser's* (1848). And he had turned to reviewing, also for *Fraser's*, publishing a long series of commentaries on various writers and topics of his day. I have mentioned his praise of *In Memoriam* as the greatest Christian poem in centuries and his advice to Matthew Arnold to emulate the self-discipline and robustness of Thomas Arnold. Kingsley also wrote lyric poems, essays on land reform, and social tracts. In 1850 he published "Cheap Clothes and Nasty," which he said he drew for from his experiences in Chelsea, but which clearly owes much, as his notes suggest, to Mayhew's *London Labour and London Poor* articles in the *Morning Chronicle*, articles that shocked more people than Kingsley into outraged polemics.

A related piece of writing in 1850 was *Alton Locke*, perhaps one of the oddest literary documents of nineteenth-century England. Before turning to Kingsley's novel, subtitled *Tailor and Poet*, I want first to glance at Kingsley's other activities as a Christian Socialist and missionary clergyman.

2

> A new idea has gone abroad into the world. That Socialism, the latest born of the forces now at work in modern society, and Christianity, the eldest born of those forces, are in their nature not hostile, but akin to each other.—J. M. Ludlow, in *The Christian Socialist*, November 1850[3]

Kingsley's fame has come to rest on what he would have thought an accidental aspect of his career. Not his Cambridge professorship, his work at Eversley, his efforts for social reform, his defense of Christianity, his literary labors—not these, but rather his attacks on John Henry Newman are remembered. The attacks did him little service, if only because his antagonist was the subtler man, and they eclipse what is perhaps the most important feature of Kingsley's life. For although contemporaries praised Kingsley as a potentially great poet or as the novelist of his day, he was manifestly neither. But there is no question, as G. M. Young writes, that Kingsley's varied activities, his controversial positions, his often inconsistent attitudes, as well as his exchanges with Newman, make him a useful index to the times.

> In dealing with a past age [Young writes] we constantly need a central man to refer to, and naturally he will not be one of its greatest men in the eyes of later generations. Kingsley is very nearly the central man of that period of swift change which sets in soon after 1845 and was consummated about twenty years later.

Young sees the age as committed to both "liberation and conservatism." He says that "the triumphant *bourgeoisie* of 1830 was looking rather small in 1850: the gentry, who, in 1846, seemed to be down and out for ever, were in fact just entering their golden age. There was a great deal of day-dreaming in it all."[4] What Young construes from his picture of mid-century England is a nation in need of Benthamite policies and Tory governers—enlightened authority, in short. He thinks of the combination as England's secret, sees the secret established at mid-century, and finds Kingsley to be its embodiment and spokesman. And indeed Kingsley's affection for aristocrats (he was later to tutor the Prince of Wales), if not for Tories, and his affection for workers seem to illustrate the direction of much contemporary thought. So, too, Kingsley's Broad Church philosophy, his virulent antipopery sentiments, his "muscular Christianity,"which for Young suggest the historical development of a church that had become somewhat more active in its social responsibilities and that had lived through almost a generation of Tractarian challenges. By 1850, Newman had long ago abdicated in favor of Rome, and the High Church movement "had been re-absorbed with the main stream of religious tendency."[5]

This common view of mid-century England is of a nation making a reasonable compromise toward "equipoise" and "equanimity" after suffering through social and religious upheavals; and certainly mid-century Englishmen, looking with delight on improved harvests, and shrugging off the Chartists—who a scant two years earlier had made them fearful of property and life—tended to assess their situation in optimistic terms. What I would question in such an estimate is the sense—not shared by Kingsley—that problems were solved. Problems of religion were perhaps never to be solved, whatever the abated energy of the Oxford Movement. Even the Census of 1851 showed poor church attendance, particularly among the poor. As for problems of social inequality, they have endured with at least as much tenacity as any Benthamite-Tory working alliance. But even if we agree with general assessments about an "age of equipoise," it is still hard to see Kingsley, the young Kingsley, the man at mid-century, fitting very well as its embodiment. A man of passion, of anger, of powerful loves and powerful prejudices, he serves as an index to the times. But he is hardly typical of the times. Perhaps he is central because he is involved in so much, but he is also an outsider, the self-styled Jeremiah, a voice of angry conscience, who won the praise of a later generation, to be sure, but who, as the author of *Yeast* or "Cheap Clothes and Nasty," seemed to the establishment he loved more of a hostile force than the comforting herald of compromise.

Looking back on his association with Kingsley, Thomas Hughes (fellow Christian Socialist and later author of *Tom Brown's Schooldays*) spoke of Kingsley's social-religious mission in this way:

> I have often thought that [at mid-century] his very sensitiveness drove him to say things more broadly and incisively, because he was speaking as it were somewhat against the grain, and knew that the line he was taking would be misunderstood, and would displease and alarm those with whom he had most sympathy. For he was by nature and education an aristocrat.[6]

No doubt Hughes wanted to make Kingsley seem less radical than he had been, but he also isolates an important quality. For Kingsley was, as Hughes suggests, both a reluctant prophet and a prophet with mixed sympathies. His vigorous Anglicanism and his social causes share with his writings an odd pattern of commitment and retreat. Even when he worked at a novel, for example, he wrote a few pages at a time, then withdrew from his study, created a few more pages in his mind, returned to his writing, and so on. He was at once preoccupied with the job to be done and unable to work without interrupting himself. And his method of writing offers a pattern for his life. Whether at Cambridge or Eversley or London, he worked feverishly hard for a certain time, then apparently collapsed, as though his entire energy had gone into the task at hand. When he quoted Byron (in a letter to his mother), saying that he was the sort of person who became middle-aged when young and who died early, because he would burn himself out—he uses the same quotation in *Alton Locke*—he was accurate in his prediction and apparently right about the reason. To understand Kingsley, we need to remember his profound reluctance along with his compulsive desire to serve. His driving energy had as its counterpart an obvious frailty and weakness: physical and mental breakdowns occurred with almost predictable frequency. The effect of his temperament on his writing, which is usually polemical writing, is a chronic overstatement and a total lack of sympathy for his opponent, although he himself, often enough, had expressed views similar to those of his opponents or had felt what they had felt. We can see how this works in terms of his religious development and of his response to the Newman brothers, neither of whom he admired.

Kingsley's father was an Anglican clergyman, and Kingsley grew up—in the Fens, in Cornwall, in London—aware of the church and of its role and responsibilities. He did not approve of his father's clerical methods, and he became increasingly lonely and ill at ease at home. When he went to Cambridge, he found himself an unbeliever. His slow return to faith resulted largely from his relationship with Frances Grenfell, with whom a long and at first unacknowledged courtship matured into a discovery and later an acclamation of belief. When he met her, Fanny had more or less committed herself to becoming a nun. Kingsley felt compelled, while showing her the evils of physical abstinence, also to find his own ironclad belief. In spite of her family's opposition, of repeated separations, and of their personal differences, they did at last marry. And they seem, with interludes, to have lived well together. The relationship has nevertheless its odd side. Kingsley's passionate attraction to Fanny coincided with his own flirtation not only with asceticism but also with the church he publicly flayed, the Church of Rome. "There is no middle course. Either deism, or the highest and most monarchial system of Catholicism."[7] Although he chose neither, his statement shows an understanding of the position consistently held by John Henry Newman, the position that led Newman and Manning and their followers into the Church of Rome.

Kingsley's religious struggles during his courtship also took a form that seems at the furthest remove from his public, and indeed from most of his private, remarks. "I once formed a strange project," he wrote to Fanny. "I would have travelled to a monastery in France, gone barefoot into the chapel at matins (midnight), and there confessed every sin of my whole life before the monks and offered my naked body to be scourged by them."[8] Even while campaigning for sexuality and sensuousness against Fanny's waning asceticism, Kingsley could admit his terrible fear of his sexuality, his need for confession and for penance. Often, when separated from his fiancée, he imposed on them both a harsh course of self-denial, urging Fanny's continued fasting, which came at the expense of her health. All the while he worked on his *Elizabeth of Hungary*, his story, with his own drawings, of a woman perverted by asceticism, whose life he found terrible, though obviously compelling.

No less than Francis or John Henry Newman, Kingsley underwent a religious conversion, in his case a Carlylean shift from naysaying to a very loud yea. But whereas John Henry Newman's acceptance of Rome followed years of self-doubting and theological inquiry, Kingsley's conversion coincided with his winning of Fanny and his choice of a profession. No sooner had he devoted himself "to the religion I have scorned, making the debauchee a preacher of purity and holiness," than he chose his father's calling and decided to become a clergyman.[9] I am not questioning his motives, although clearly his calling fitted nicely with an almost self-willed conversion and with his winning of his wife. I am saying that his sense of himself as a potential theologian and his often foolish attacks on Newman cast doubt on his self-understanding. For on the one hand Kingsley could at certain moments see the essential line of Newman's arguments and could advocate a kind of asceticism or bodily mortification that would have made Newman seem the English voice of common sense, and on the other hand he could dismiss the whole of Newman's struggles—along with Newman himself—in a satirical comment: "How silently Newman has glided over *to his own place*! No doubt more will follow—which will do them little harm—& us much good."[10] This was a private remark. In his first review for *Fraser's* (in 1848), Kingsley wrote with no less a Calvinistic glee:

> Among [the German] converts it cannot name a first-rate man. . . .So it is with our own late conversions. Have we lost a single *second*-rate man even? One, indeed, we have lost, *first*-rate in *talents*, at least; but has not he by his later writings given the very strongest proof, that to become a Romish priest is to lose, *ipso facto*, whatever moral or intellectual life he might previously have had? . . . Above all, in all their authors, converts or indigenous, is there not the same fearful want *of straightforward truth*, that "Jesuitry," which the mob may dread as a subtle poison, but which the philosopher considers as the deepest and surest system of moribund weakness?[11]

Which is the philosopher's voice here and which the mob's?

In his campaign for Fanny's love and his own belief, Kingsley approximated another aspect of Roman Catholicism that mid-century Englishmen theoretically deplored. Clearly he treated Fanny both as a woman to be saved from celibacy and as a symbol of his highest aspirations. If he reminded her that the woman was the weaker vessel, in the manner of Ruskin's later "Queens' Gardens" essay, he could argue from at least two opposing points of view. Like John Stuart Mill, he became a feminist in part because of his admiration for the woman he loved, and at mid-century he worked in the movement for women's higher education, arguing—again as Mill did—that women were at least the equal of men in most pursuits. Whereas Mill turned Harriet Taylor into a paragon of learning and sense, however, Kingsley conceived of Fanny as a type of Beatrice:

> I feel that in the tumult and grossness by which I am surrounded my mind is seldom, very seldom, in a tone capable of approaching the subject [religion] as it ought to be approached, and of coming pure and calm into your pure and calm presence. I feel that I am insulting you when I sit down reeking with the fumes of the world's frivolities and vices to talk to you. . . .I have, however, I assure you, struggled to alter lately and this alteration has been remarked with pleasure by some and with sneers by others. "Kingsley," they say, "is not half so reckless as he used to be." You are to me a middle point between earthly and ethereal morality. I begin to love good for your sake. At length I will be able to love it for God's sake.

He began this letter of confession with "My dearest Lady."[12]

Whatever Kingsley's acknowledged or unacknowledged leanings toward Catholicism, his assessment of the Roman Church and of Newman as its principal English exponent was always contemptuous. One is tempted to think of his often gratuitous attacks along the lines of his attacks on the "feminine" qualities of men he disliked. Browning he thought effeminate; Arnold, too. Conversely, his favorite term of praise was "manly." Since Kingsley's own acquaintances often spoke of *his* effeminacy, his preoccupation with "manliness," like his hatred of Catholicism, reflects less on the objects of his scrutiny than upon his own character. Yet he could be honest about his affection for men, if not about his own effeminacy of manner. He told Fanny that, were she a man (he is defending his friendship with Charles Mansfield), "we should have been like David and Jonathan."[13] His praise of the beauty of the male body is much like that of D. H. Lawrence: he calls a keeper on a trout stream "a river god in velveteen."[14] The point is that Kingsley's passions and hatreds tumbled over one another, causing him agonies of doubt. When he had arrived at a belief or a social conviction, he seemed instantly to have no understanding, either of his own ambivalence or of opposing points of view. Like Carlyle, he found no room for tolerance.

There is little record of Kingsley's relationship with Francis Newman, although we know that he visited Newman shortly after Newman published *Phases of Faith*. Apparently, the two shared a great deal, especially the sense that John Henry Newman's road to Rome approximated the road to hell. Both resented in the future cardinal the quiet self-scrutiny, the evident indecision, the acquiescence in choosing a foreign and authoritarian church. Both shared, temperamentally, a ferocious high seriousness, at least to the extent that they were rarely seen to laugh. Yet Kingsley did laugh at Newman's *The Soul*. After an embarrassing episode in London, when a clergyman who had invited him to offer the sermon actually denounced him for his views, Kingsley was speaking with several Christian

Socialists at the house of F. D. Maurice. Someone mentioned Newman's *The Soul*, and Kingsley, who stammered, said: "Oh, yes! the s-s-s-soul and her stomach-aches!"[15] If he had read Newman's book, he should have realized that Newman was trying to sort out precisely the dilemma that he himself had articulated at Cambridge: How does one find belief between the extremes of unbelief or deism and the authoritarian theism of the Church of Rome?

In *The Soul* as in *Phases of Faith*, Newman wants to establish religious sanction for right conduct, although *The Soul* emphasizes the problem of faith rather than its social implications as such. Kingsley's impatience, which may have reflected his mood more than his considered opinion, has to do with his notion of the uses of religion, of religion's fight for social reforms. Newman's appreciation of "romantic scenery," his conviction that right actions follow strong convictions, his precise assessment of what had been Kingsley's own predicament–these could easily be overlooked by a reader who saw his mission as changing men and women, bringing the news of Christ and the news of socialism.

By 1850, Kingsley's association with Maurice and Ludlow had already resulted in the short-lived *Politics for the People*. Joined by Charles Mansfield, Thomas Hughes, and other men committed to social reform, the Christian Socialists wanted to prompt the Anglican Church toward social responsibilities and to show poor people why they needed a socialism tempered by Christianity. The origins of Christian Socialism go back, as Robert Martin says, to "Samuel Taylor Coleridge, whose work *On the Constitution of Church and State*, 1830, with its assumption of the social ethic implicit in Christianity, had influenced Maurice's thinking when he was studying at Oxford. . . . To Maurice, Ludlow, and Kingsley, their own theological position, roughly that of what came to be known as the Broad Church movement, seemed the only one capable of carrying out Coleridge's ideas."[16] Martin thinks of the social philosophy of the Christian Socialists as having derived from the French Socialists and from Robert Owen, whose New Lanark had been a pioneer manufacturing community. The connection with Owen makes good sense, because of the paternalism inherent in the group's attitudes: they themselves worried about the absence of working class people in the movement. The call for association and for equitable distribution and for what resembles, at times, a labor theory of value could, however, have come from a variety of sources. Socialism at mid-century was, in the words of Marx and Engels, a "specter" across Europe. It was a central issue in England as well. Periodicals like the *Leader* were self-acclaimed organs of socialism no less than the *Christian Socialist* itself.

One can find in the pages of the *Leader* acknowledgment of the new Communist periodical *The Red Republican*, notices of Socialist movements on the continent, defenses of articles on socialism in the *British Quarterly Review*, and praise of such contemporary assessments of the poor as Mayhew's articles in the *Morning Chronicle* and Joseph Kay's pioneering survey of British and European educational systems. Whether contemporaries took the evidence presented to them and, like Carlyle, began making grim forecasts, or whether, like George Lewes, they assumed the need for reforms, they had available a battery of incisive surveys and a large number of interpretive prophets. One of the cant words of the time indicates a yet further direction in contemporary social thought. Herbert Spencer's *Social Statics* uses *statics* to imply the empirical, scientific nature of the social inquiry that Spencer shared with men as diverse as Comte, Engels, and Carlyle. Similarly John Stores Smith, a clergyman like Kingsley, in his *Social Aspects* (1850) discusses what he considers the driving forces in his society, speaking of "the Decay of Nations" of "the Social and Domestic Tendencies of the Age." He is intent on isolating the energies and the characteristics of his age, though he cares most about its degeneracy and Pharisaism. But while wholly opposed to Spencer on matters of progress, national destiny, and various other features of "the modern Phasis," he shares the tendency to sociological methods.[17]

Socialism and communism (in this first great age of *isms*) are in one aspect polemical extensions of the insatiable search for statistics and what is probably its corollary, the need for explanatory social theories. If all this coincided with an almost universal clamor in favor of individual rights and liberties, the reason is not hard to find. For the acceptance of great historical forces like evolution or progress carries with it the implication of the individual's frailty. Hence a writer like Lewes can embrace the social meliorism of a variety of Socialist thinkers while praising the excessive individuality of Carlyle and defining poetry (after Carlyle) as the history of a single human soul.

Kingsley's conception of socialism reflects the anger of Carlyle at England's blindness to social ills; it reflects the widespread sense—shared by Marx and Engels—that historical forces were creating a new order and that, in a time of great change, it was necessary to define the conditions of change and to act with conviction. Whereas Marx and Engels posit a vast historical reordering of class and wealth and urge their readers—with the sanction of historical necessity—to claim what the future promises, Kingsley thinks in terms of reformable institutions. He berates his middle-class contemporaries for their blindness and ridicules their folly. He shows that the diseases of the poor are the diseases of the rich, since the disgraceful buyers of "slop" tailoring are contaminated by the illnesses of the poor tailors themselves. But Kingsley's arguments center on local issues, on how people live. He details, after Mayhew, the prices paid for clothing, the moneys extracted by the "sweaters," or middlemen, the wages received by the tailors, the conditions of the tailors' lives. "And now comes the question—What is to be done with these poor tailors, to the number of between fifteen and twenty thousand? Their condition, as it stands, is simply one of ever-increasing darkness and despair. The system which is ruining them is daily spreading, deepening."

He also makes specific suggestions to his readers about where to shop or what not to buy.

> What can be done?
>
> First—this can be done. That no man who calls himself a Christian—no man who calls himself a man—shall ever disgrace himself by dealing at any show-shop or slop-shop. It is easy enough to know them. The ticketed garments, the imprudent puffs, the trumpery decorations, proclaim them,—every one knows them at first sight. He who pretends not to do so is simply either a fool or a liar. Let no man enter them—they are the temples of Moloch—their thresholds are rank with human blood.[18]

Kingsley's polemic has general application to working-class conditions in other trades and in other places, yet it flies at a particular target in the hope of redressing a particular ill. This would be true, of course, of writers like Dickens or Mrs. Gaskell or Disraeli. Because all assume the essential permanence of the system itself, they may be limited to attacking what a Marxist would call the symptoms of the disease. Kingsley, oddly enough, is especially limited. He may call himself a Socialist and he may, he does, cry out for public conscience and social reform. His ideal, however, is far even from the implied classless society in Dickens's novels. He wants workers to remember that they are workers and ought to remain workers, since those above workers have a rightful place as well as their unfulfilled responsibilities.

When Kingsley told those assembled workers that he was "a parson, and a Chartist," he defined his own relation to the movement for reform. In fact, he did not have a very high opinion of the People's Charter: "*My only quarrel with the Charter,*" he said, "*is that it does not go far enough in reform.* I want to see you *free*, but I do not see that what you ask for will give you what you want. I think you have fallen into just the same mistake as the rich, of whom you complain—the very mistake which has been our curse and our nightmare. I mean the mistake of fancying that *legislative* reform is *social* reform, or that men's hearts can be changed by an Act of Parliament." The implications of this point to a revolutionary plan far in advance of the Chartists, and Kingsley does say, "The French cry of 'organization of labor' is worth a thousand [charters]."[19] What he actually wants for workers is something similar to what the Chartists want and differs only in a few specifics. Kingsley *is* a Chartist, a man with limited and potentially realizable goals, who uses "the French cry" to give urgency to his message.

> We are teaching [the workers] to become Christians by teaching them gradually that true socialism, true liberty, brotherhood, and true equality (not the carnal dead level equality of the Communist, but the spiritual equality of the church idea, which gives every man an equal chance of developing and using God's gifts . . .) is to be found in loyalty and obedience to Christ.[20]

Such principles, from the Revolution of 1789 rather than from that of 1848, mean for Kingsley definite social objectives:

> We must touch the workman at all his points of interest. First and foremost at association—but also at political rights, as grounded both on the Christian ideal of the Church, and on the historic facts of the Anglo-Saxon race. Then national education, sanitary and dwelling house reform, the free sale of land, and corresponding reform of the land laws, moral improvement of the family relation, public places of recreation (on which point I am very earnest), and I think a set of hints from history, and sayings of great men. . . .[21]

In the first of these passages, Kingsley calls for a change of heart among the workers made possible, as it turns out, by the ruling classes, who do the *teaching* and who bring the message of Christ. And Kingsley rarely writes his polemics without putting the main paternal burden for reform on clergymen. In the second passage, he has left the world of Carlyle for that of Disraeli. An implied and necessary change of heart of the governing classes must, he says, "touch the workman at all his points of interest." True, some of the announced goals are vague at best and some are perhaps whimsical. Where Marx scoffs at the bourgeois marriage contract as a sign of slavery and injustice, Kingsley calls for its reinvigoration. His theory of "political rights," grounded alike on Christianity and Anglo-Saxon history reflects the widespread contemporary interest in theories of race (at least two books about the subject appeared in 1850 alone)[22] and Kingsley's own pet theory about the "feminine" qualities of the Anglo-Saxons that need fertilizing by the "masculine" Nordic peoples. But whatever his general theories about "this . . . puling, quill-driving, soft-handed age," he returns consistently to hopes for workingmen's association and cooperation, to specific questions of sanitary reform, to the need for "public places of recreation (on which point I am very earnest)," to matters that could and would be handled by "legislative reform."

After a few years of vigorous social work, work which, along with his duties at Eversley and his almost continuous literary work, caused his recurrent breakdowns, Kingsley ended his role as Parson Lot. He became again Canon Charles Kingsley and Professor Kingsley, assuming the history professorship at Cambridge, and it was to the undergraduates at Cambridge that Kingsley directed his final preface to *Alton Locke*. But then, in spite of the Parson Lot letters to the workers, Kingsley's real message had always been to those he thought remiss in their duties. He agreed with Matthew Arnold about the need to educate the middle class, because he assumed that the hierarchy of classes would endure. In this respect he was more a prophet than Marx.

It is easy to find inconsistencies and inadequacies in Kingsley's arguments and to wonder—when, for example, he lashes out at John Henry Newman—what intellectual center there was to his life. The religious thinker could forget his own past while bemoaning the course of his opponent's life; he could dismiss celibacy while imposing it upon himself and his wife (for the entire first month of their marriage). He could articulate arguments like those of *The Soul* and dismiss Francis Newman's book as the symptom of stomach ache. As a social thinker, he could argue the inadequacies of the People's Charter and tender a somewhat watered program himself. As Parson Lot, he envisaged himself writing tracts on the model of the Tractarians, whose beliefs and methods he deplored equally. He could argue the responsibility of the local clergyman and seek, with his colleagues, to wage a war for reform in the streets of the Great Wen.

And then, surely before they had won, Kingsley was no longer fighting. He defended *Alton Locke* in the preface to the Cambridge undergraduates, and he was happy to see it reissued, but he no longer spoke as Jeremiah, capable of this earlier outrage and scorn:

> Sweet competition! Heavenly maid!—Nowadays hymned alike by penny-a-liners and philosophers as the ground of all society. . . . Man eating man, eaten by man, in every variety of degree and method! Why does not some enthusiastic political economist write an epic on "The Consecration of Cannibalism"?[23]

The writer who excoriates Cambridge in *Alton Locke* says in the 1860s:

> I have received at Cambridge a courtesy and kindness from my elders, a cordial welcome from my co-equals and an earnest attention from the undergraduates with whom I have come in contact, which would bind me in honor to say nothing

> publicly against my University, even if I had aught to say. But I have naught. I see at Cambridge nothing which does not gain my respect.[24]

To think of Kingsley, as a lost leader, ready to forget both his own anger and the reasons for the anger, nevertheless, would be misleading. The inconsistencies in his thinking are, in the first place, endemic and temperamental. Not only could he not continue as the self-proclaimed tribune of the people, he really did not want the role in the first place. While he accepted the consequences of his polemics, he always suffered from adversity and took pains to explain to almost anyone why he wrote what he had to write. Conversely, he felt uncomfortable among "restless and eccentric persons," and even in the company of vegetarians and men with beards. When he admitted to "the love of praise," he had in mind the love of "all men," but he also made a distinction between "the esteem of good men, and the blessings of the poor." He honored "public opinion," thinking of it as a sort of honest English jury (along the lines of Newman in the *Apologia*), and he confessed to wanting its approval.[25]

So there are obvious reasons for Kingsley's short-lived role as the prophet without honor. He needed honor—and precisely within his own country. It is also true that Kingsley's efforts on behalf of the poor had their effect. Frederic Harrison could look back on Kingsley's work and say:

> Of that small band [of social novelists] Charles Kingsley was the most outspoken, and most eloquent and assuredly the most effective. When we remember how widely this vague initiative has spread and developed, when we read *Alton Locke* and *Yeast* again and note how much practically has been done in the last forty years to redress the abuses against which the books uttered the first burning protest, we may form an estimate of all that the present generation of Englishmen owes to Kingsley.[26]

After 1848, when Kingsley's work with Maurice and the Christian Socialists began, conditions did slowly change. In 1848 most political commentators could say with Kingsley, "Look at France, and see." By the mid-fifties, the energy for reform seemed to have waned; by the early 1860s, the date of Kingsley's last preface to *Alton Locke*, even a moderate reform bill like that of 1867 seemed a distant prospect, although Kingsley pointed out to his readers that the spirit for reform would certainly return again. Kingsley did not reform England single-handedly, but he was an important voice and he could see—because of trade unionism, cooperative societies, and so forth—that conditions had changed. As a respected professor, Kingsley would have found it hard, after the mid-fifties, to speak again like the author of *Alton Locke*.

He was no longer the same man, his world no longer the same world.

3

> Never let it be forgotten that every human being bears in himself that indelible something which belongs equally to the whole species as well as that particular modification of it which individualizes him.—S. T. Coleridge, *The Friend*[27]

Kingsley had suffered during the writing of his first novel, *Yeast*, both because of the effort necessary to meet monthly deadlines (the novel appeared serially in *Fraser's* in 1848) and because the message of the book worried Parker, its publisher, and offended readers. Its publication followed the rejection of Kingsley for a Cambridge position, the result of his association with Christian Socialism and its brief-lived magazine, *Politics for the People*. Knowing that his polemics could hurt him, Kingsley went ahead to write a novel attacking landlords, Roman Catholicism, the Irish, and celibacy, while it urged the rights of the rural poor. He obviously thought of *Yeast* in the way that Disraeli thought of his fiction.

Disraeli wrote in the preface to the fifth edition of *Coningsby* (1849): "It was not originally the intention of the writer to adopt the form of fiction as the instrument to scatter his suggestions, but, after reflection, he resolved to avail himself of a method which, in the temper of the times, offered the best chance for influencing opinion."[28] Disraeli's terms suggest Kingsley's: the scattering of suggestions, like seeds, implies the same assumption about the societal need for change and growth. Whether Disraeli quite expresses Kingsley's early ambivalence about the novel, he shared the common view of the novel as a literary form of dubious stature yet of powerful impact. For Disraeli, novels like *Sybil* and *Coningsby* were useful extensions of politics; for Kingsley, *Yeast* and *Alton Locke* were useful extensions of the Sunday sermon. *Yeast* is a novel of 1848, the year that many Englishmen considered with dread, because it showed them the instability of political institutions, and Kingsley wanted his readers to heed and remember.

Some of the technical problems of *Yeast* grow out of its polemical intent and are implicit in the title itself. The novel assesses, as Kingsley puts it, the social and intellectual "ferment" of the age. "These papers have been, from beginning to end, as in name, so in nature, Yeast—an honest sample of the questions, which, good or bad, are fermenting in the minds of the young."[29] *Papers* and *sample* point to the discursive quality of the novel, about which the author himself was well aware.

Yeast describes, in the words of the subtitle, "The Thoughts, Sayings and Doings of Lancelot Smith, Gentleman." Smith's education has not prepared him to use his sympathies or to deal with moral questions. For his Carlylean change of heart, Kingsley provides him with a Carlylean figure, Barnakill, "The Prophet," and with an ideal woman, Argemone. Drawing like Dickens on *Past and Present*, Kingsley lets Argemone die, as Dickens's Esther Summerson nearly dies, because she has been serving the poor and the ill; her typhus, like Esther's smallpox, symbolizes the revenge of the poor on the rich, since Argemone's father has refused to accept his responsibility for the poor on his estate. As for Lancelot, he engages in political and philosophical conversations with Tregarva, a gamekeeper, then in the manner of David Copperfield, Arthur Pendennis, and so many other fictional heroes, he goes penniless to London. His money has disappeared in a bank crash, and he must accept menial employment. In London he meets Barnakill, begins his moral education, and prepares himself for his change of heart. Unfortunately, Argemone's death precludes a happy ending.

After reading a part of *Yeast* in manuscript, J. M. Ludlow wrote to Kingsley: "There is little awkwardness now & then in the putting together, but for the depth, & breadth & wit, & fun, & thought, & feeling, & interest, it holds as much of all this as a first-rate three-volume novel of the day. It is easy for you to become the greatest novelist of the age." Ludlow urges his friend to try to make the novel "if possible, ten times pleasanter, thoughtfuller, truer than before," because Kingsley as Christian Socialist must "shew to all the world what a great Xtian work a novel can be, written by a great Xtian man." This would seem to imply that Ludlow approved of Kingsley's fiction and felt that it had, or could have, unprecedented importance as applied Christianity. Oddly enough, he concludes by imploring his friend to stop: "Write never tale more till you are sixty."[30] Whether the suggestion reflected his unacknowledged prejudice against the novel or his secret dislike of *Yeast* itself, or whether, as Robert Martin suggests, it reflected his sense that Kingsley should concentrate on poetry, Ludlow anticipated Kingsley's own feeling when he came to finish the novel. He would, he said, stop writing fiction. He had "no more to say."[31]

Kingsley's resolution waned as his energy returned. He was soon talking of two more novels, making *Yeast* part of a trilogy, and imagining perhaps some sort of resurrection for his dead heroine, along with continued adventures for his hero. When Ludlow and other friends joined Fanny in arguing against the trilogy, Kingsley gave up the idea. His next novel, not to be written for almost two years, was to be, though a thematic continuation of *Yeast*, another kind of story with an altogether different kind of hero. *Alton Locke* is just as tendentious as *Yeast*, but it is more coherent, held together by the reminiscing mind of its narrator, who essentially confesses his story to "aristocratic readers." In making Alton a poet, Kingsley gives him a retrospective awareness; in making him poor, he gives a legitimate grievance to his complaints.

Alton Locke is an attempt to show Kingley's social philosophy from the point of view of a working-class boy. As a reader of Thackeray, Kingsley may have remembered Thackeray's hope for a novelist from the mine or the mill, or he may have known George Lewes's example of a working-class poet in *Ranthorpe*. In any event, he wanted his novel to herald what the Chartists themselves were calling for, a distinctively working-class literature. Thomas Cooper, "the Cockney Poet" on whom Kingsley probably based Alton Locke, wrote "To the Young Men of the Working Classes":

> It now becomes a matter of the highest necessity . . . to create a literature of your own. Your own prose, your own poetry . . . would put you all more fully in possession of each other's thoughts and thus give you a higher respect for each other, and a clearer perception of what you can do when united.[32]

In spite of the narrative guise, contemporary reviewers immediately recognized *Alton Locke* as the work of someone from the upper classes. The author's evident preoccupation with attitudes of the privileged, his use of Alton as an object lesson, his love of literary allusions—all these betrayed the hand of someone creating Alton rather than editing his posthumous autobiography. Still, Kingsley's narrative of an intelligent and finally luckless "artisan" is not only a sympathetic portrait of a plausible character; it reflects also a sharp sense of the character's world, of the social ills and insuperable obstacles facing a talented working-class boy. *Alton Locke* culminates the works of social protest of the 1840s—*Mary Barton, Sybil, Jane Eyre* (in one of its facets), and Kingsley's own *Yeast*—while it seems as a form to unite Dickens's *David Copperfield* with Carlyle's *Sartor Resartus*. With a large, Carlylean pun, Kingsley invokes the Philosophy of Clothes, since Alton becomes, in metaphor and in fact, a tailor-re-tailored.

Like "Mark Rutherford," Edmund Gosse, and so many other nineteenth-century autobiographers, Alton Locke grows up in a dissenting household, which offers him stern Calvinism, rigorous discipline, and very little affection. His mother, like David Copperfield's, is a widow, who contains within herself the relentless intolerance of the Murdstones. Her acquaintances are largely hypocritical denouncers of "bad doctrine," for whom any disagreement serves as reminder "of the narrow way of discriminating grace."[33] Alton grows up with a sense of inexplicable sin, and just as David bites Murdstone in his first gesture of independence, so Alton writes poetry and reads "pagan" literature, questioning the narrowness of his mother's advisers and finally rejecting his mother's religion. He too is orphaned before his mother dies, although in his case his mother banishes him from her own house. Since he is, as he calls himself, a "Cockney among Cockneys" (1:131), he need not come to London. He is of London. But he joins David and Oliver Twist and other orphans in the fiction of his time and finds himself in brutalizing circumstances. His inferno (a comparison he likes) is work as a tailor. Kingsley allows him descriptions that could have been transcribed from "Cheap Clothes and Nasty," but he also allows him moral outbursts that Dickens carefully keeps out of the narrative of David's early sorrows:

> I owe . . . an apology to my readers for introducing all this ribaldry [he has quoted in the manner of "Cheap Clothes" a group of tailors]. God knows, it is as little to my taste as it can be to theirs, but the thing exists; and those who live, if not by, yet still beside such a state of things, ought to know what the men are like to whose labor, ay, life blood, they owe their luxuries. They are "their brothers' keepers," let them deny it as they will. (1:162)

In addition to quoting scripture with a social purpose, Alton refers directly to contemporaries, though the ostensible time of the narrative predates the circumstances he discusses. He alludes, for instance, to "a few master tailors, who have built workshops fit for human beings." "Among them I may, and will, whether they like it or not, make honorable mention of Mr. Willis, of St. James's Street, and Mr. Stultz, of Bond Street" (1:163).

Just as Kingsley, without writing *romans à clef* as such, drew on people he knew for the portraits he made, so he also thought of his novelistic world more literally than did Dickens. Dickens may be equally topical. He has his factories, law courts, model prisons. David Copperfield goes to London, travels to Yarmouth, visits the Alps. The young boy's trek to Dover, like Alton Locke's escape to Cambridge, follows a recognizable road out of London and deals with places that his readers might themselves know. But Dickens uses his background as though it has become a part of David's life, whereas Kingsley reminds his reader that the "real" world exists, that it has its problems, that it needs reform. The effect is, like that of a morally charged picaresque novel, or of a philosophical and ambulatory novel of the eighteenth century, a continual mixing of the author's direct commentary (or the narrator's, since they do not always coincide) with the workings of Alton's memory. The resulting ironies are not the dramatic ironies of Dickens who allows his younger self only partly to understand what the older narrator fully understands in retrospect.

One possible reason for the lack of continuing irony and for its corollary the sometimes static quality of the various scenes is Kingsley's method of writing fiction. He composed his important scenes first, often writing a passage from late in the novel along with an early passage. He said at one time that he had "done [Alton's] conversion at the end, and today his becoming a poet towards the beginning,"[34] The effect was likely to be a series of set pieces, introduced or commented about in passages lacking the energy or even care of the primary scenes.

If we remember that Kingsley thought of the novel as an instrument of social justice, we might note additionally that he thought of his own novels as "true." He wrote to Ludlow in explanation of *Yeast* that his "tale of the country" acccurately depicted the problems of rural England: "I shall be very hard on the landlords—because they deserve it; but I will promise *to invent nothing*."[35] The comment indicates a further aesthetic handicap with which Kingsley worked when he applied himself to fiction. For while he lets Alton Locke appeal to high-born or privileged readers to acknowledge the *truth* of his narrative, Alton dismisses fiction as such, scoffing repeatedly at "mere novels." To some extent traditional to fiction, the ploy also reflects Kingsley's ambivalence about rhetorical indirections. When the Christian Socialists launched their *Politics for the People*, Kingsley and his colleagues had intended their writing as an antidote to the tracts of Newman and the Oxford Movement. *Yeast* and *Alton Locke* have similar purposes. In spite of the fictional method, Kingsley simply cannot write without some pamphleteering purpose working its way into the narrative.

Nevertheless, *Alton Locke* is not "a mere" tract. The narrator may at time be too dense and at other times too shrewd in his own retrospective account. He does a great deal of unnecessary explaining. But he is a character with genuine consciousness. Kingsley creates in Alton a self-educated and somewhat eccentric young man, but also a speaker who understands his readers and who tells a story that is both dramatic, or full of conflict, and diverse, as reminiscence alternates with reflection, biographical incident with historical or literary speculation.

Alton as a boy meets the Scot Sandy Mackaye, "the prophet" in this novel, the voice of Carlyle. Mackaye fosters Alton's interest in literature and he comes to be a kind of father. He introduces Alton to scenes of terrible poverty and suffering—scenes reminiscent in subject and in method of Mrs. Gaskell's *Mary Barton*, which Kingsley admired—where young girls are condemned to prostitution and where the sick die both hungry and cold. These, he says, are the proper subjects for Alton's poetry. Alton does not explain why he quotes Carlyle so often, but Mackaye is the main reason. However, prophet as he is, Mackaye also has his failings. Alton finds that Crosswaithe, a fellow worker and like Mackaye committed to The Cause, to Chartism, disagrees wholly with Mackaye about methods and goals, because he thinks of Mackaye as a tacit defender of existing institutions. Alton is caught between the two, just as he is caught between their combined world and the world of his mother, whose assumption is that whatever we do, the damned are damned and the saved are saved. So Kingsley makes Alton's life a series of choices or decisions, each following a "phase" of his life and each leading, with heavy foreshadowing, to the pathetic and lonely exile of the older narrator.

Alton's exile illustrates the irreconcilable aims of his life and his foolish, if understandable, choice of the wrong woman. Dickens allows David to marry Dora *and* to get Agnes, who has been admonished by the dying childwife to replace her. Alton meets Lillian, a woman above him in social station, for whom he abandons his fiery, working-class poetry, and about whom he is deceived. She marries Alton's wealthy and hypocritical cousin, a man who, when he becomes a clergyman, dies from wearing a piece of clothing contaminated by a diseased tailor. Kingsley may be arguing that Alton Locke should know his place and should work for his brothers, but he offers him real choices and he insists that those choices have lasting consequences. Thus Alton leaves London to visit Cambridge, becomes infatuated again by Lillian, whom he had first met in a London art gallery; he gradually compromises his role as poet of the people, until he rejects his new life and becomes a fervent Chartist. Chartism leads to involvement in a rural uprising, and the involvement results in a prison term. Alton's "conversion" follows a further stage of suffering, but it does not end the suffering. He finds no easy or unmerited reward.

Both Dickens and Kingsley share with Carlyle the sense of life as a difficult journey and the related preoccupation with heroes. Alton meets false heroes (missionaries who are arrogant hypocrites, scholars who are fools), and, like David Copperfield, he comes to the slow recognition of himself as a kind of hero. Dickens's indebtedness to Carlyle is tacit. Kingsley lets

Alton cite Carlyle. Sandy Mackaye tells him: "Ye're an unaccredited hero . . . , as Thomas Carlyle has it" (1:279). He is an unaccredited hero, not because he serves the Chartist cause, or suffers poverty and incarceration, but because he overcomes or endures adversity and undergoes a change of heart. Alton mentions Goethe's and Carlyle's "Wertherism" as something to live through. He passes a stage that he calls, if not the Everlasting No, then the "worship of negation." He learns Kingsley's lessons of patriotism and the rights of man along with a vaguer lesson, imparted by the saintlike sister of Lillian, about sacrifice, social responsibility, and the Anglican Church. His final conversion, neither defiant nor self-assertive, is a change of heart analogous to that urged by Carlyle, but it involves a humility and repentance, a rebirth that suggests the New Testament. "Repentance," as M. Scheler says, "forms the driving power of that miraculous process which the Gospels call the rebirth of a new man out of the old Adam, the acquiring of a new heart."[36] Rebirth follows a radical shift of purpose, which alters the past, as it does the future, allowing Alton the double vision of his earlier self. From a representative Cockney he has become the confessing type of a rejuvenated Christianity. He is doubly the unacknowledged hero.

Like David Copperfield, Alton also learns to understand his unconscious desires (and "unconscious" is a favorite word with Kingsley, too) as he orders his reminiscences. His narrative includes a dream sequence that complements Alton's sense of inadequacy with his vision of himself as an eclectic creature in evolutionary process. Even in the dream, Alton's response to frightening natural states merges with a pastoralism that recurs throughout the novel (see chapter VII). Alton sees himself as

> a vast sleepy mass [with "elephantine limbs" and a "little meek rabbit's head"]. . . . Intense and new was the animal delight, to plant my hinder claws at some tree-foot, deep into the black rotting vegetable-mould which steamed rich gases up wherever it was pierced, and clasp my huge arms round the stem of some palm or tree-fern; and then slowly bring my enormous weight and muscle to bear upon it, till the stem bent like a withe, and the lacked bark cracked, and the fibres groaned and shrieked, and the roots sprung up out of the soil; and then, with a slow circular wrench, the whole tree was twisted bodily out of the ground, and the maddening tension of my muscles suddenly relaxed, and I sank sleepily down on the turf, to browse upon the crisp tart foliage, and fall asleep in the glare of sunshine which streamed through the new gap in the green forest roof. (2:265–66)

The effect of the dream is to put his change of heart in a vast historical context, to imply the profound forces working on his mind apart from the circumstances of his daily life.

Like David Copperfield, Alton is a writer, but he is a far more critical writer, aware of his own art, of the purposes of his poems, and of aesthetic theory. He is aware that he lives "in these days of Dutch painting and Boz." Dickens as Boz is the Dickens who can depict the busy and full life of urban England, providing an account of his characters and their settings as had never previously been seen. Alton pays his own debt to such writing. Here is a description of his room as a boy that might recall passages in *Oliver Twist* or *Mary Barton* or *Jane Eyre*:

> I recollect it well, in the little dingy, foul, reeking, twelve foot square back-yard, where huge smoky party-walls shut out every breath of air and almost all the light of heaven, I had climbed up between the waterbutt and the angle of the wall for the purpose of fishing out of the dirty fluid which lay there, crusted with soot and alive with insects, to be renewed only three times in the seven days, some of the great larvae and kicking monsters which made up a large item in my list of wonders: all of a sudden the horror of the place came over me; those grim prison-walls above, with their canopy of lurid smoke; the dreary, sloppy, broken pavement; the horrible stench of the stagnant cesspools; the utter want of form, color, life, in the whole place, crushed me down. (1:144)

This has, as contemporary reviewers might have said, the verisimilitude of the daguerreotype.

Alton ends his first chapter by saying that his "next chapter is, perhaps, full enough of mere dramatic interest (and whose life is not, were it but truly written?) to amuse merely as a novel." He tells his readers to laugh at him if they will, but he also addresses an ideal reader, a reader who will understand the nature of his art and the reasons why it is not simply "Dutch painting"; "Those to whom the struggles of every, even the meanest, human being are scenes of an awful drama, every incident of which is to be noted with reverent interest, will not find [his recollections] void of meaning" (1:151). Alton's own story is "awful drama," the actions of a trapped human being, whose life will only be understood by those who can read with adequate sympathy. While technically different, the conception of the novel anticipates Ignazio Silone's *Fontamara*, in which the narrator is a kind of collective, saddened voice of an impoverished village.

Throughout his autobiography, Alton records his reading of poets as diverse as Byron, Shakespeare, and Macaulay. He moves away from an early infatuation with Byron to a love of Milton and the classics; he knows and cites the Old Testament; and he theorizes about the condition of poetry in his own time, understanding it in terms of the author himself, who lectured at Queen's College, London, about developments in English literature, and who urged the young women in his audience to read their contemporaries. Alton does not quote his own poems, but he sees them in context. "I always knew," he writes, in another pastoral passage,

> there was something beautiful, wonderful, sublime, in those flowery dykes of Battersea Fields; in the long gravelly sweeps of that lone tidal shore; and here was a man who had put them into words for me! This is what I call democratic art—the revelation of the poetry which lies in common things. And surely all the age is tending in that direction: in Landseer and his dogs—in Fielding and his downs, with a host of noble fellow-artists—and in all authors who have really seized the nation's mind, from Crabbe and Burns and Wordsworth to Hood and Dickens, the great tide sets ever onward, outward, towards that which is common to the many, not that which is exclusive to the few. (1:264)

So Alton recognizes that Dickens's art is more than clever description, that is related to his own narrative and to the work of Crabbe, Burns, Hood, and Wordsworth, all of whom write about "common things." Except for Dickens, Alton cites no other novelists. He himself is supposed to be a poet, and his readings would have tended to poetry, yet Dickens enters the list along with the author of *Peter Grimes*, the author of *Song of the Shirt*, and the author of *Lyrical Ballads*. In his defense of "democratic art," Alton implicitly argues (along the lines I suggested in a previous chapter) that Dickens's fiction attempts in its medium what Wordsworth had attempted in his, sharing with Wordsworth's verse the assumption that ordinary men and women are, though "low" to the advocates of "aristocratic" art, no less capable of tragic emotions and geniune stature. Alton wants to distinguish his own account from the cheap working-class fiction of the time—the "mere novels" or the penny dreadfuls—and to find its justification in the analogy with poetry.

Along with the poets of the older generation (Hood excepted), he places Dickens in the company of another "democratic" writer:

> Then, in a happy day, I fell on Alfred Tennyson's poetry, and found there, astonished and delighted, the embodiment of thoughts about the earth around me which I had concealed, because I fancied them peculiar to myself. . . . What endeared Tennyson especially to me, the workingman, was, as I afterwards discovered, the altogether democratic tendency of his poems. True, all great poets are by their office democrats; seers of man only as man; singers of the joys, the sorrows, the aspirations common to all humanity; but in Alfred Tennyson there is an element especially democratic, truly levelling; not his political opinions, about which I know nothing, and care less, but his handling of the trivial everyday sights and sounds of nature. (1:263)

A final literary model (apart from the Bible and Milton) is again Carlyle, whose *French Revolution*, "that great prose poem [is] the single epic of modern days" (1:262). Whatever Carlyle's ranting against democracy and whatever his bitterness at mid-century, he represented for Kingsley and his narrator the voice of prophecy. His works became, in their sympathy and insight, prose poems, equivalents of Wordsworth's verse and spiritual impetus behind novels like *Alton Locke*. Unfortunately for Kingsley, the prophet himself–always honest and rarely generous in these years–responded unfavorably to the work that he had helped to engender: "While welcoming a new explosion of red hot shot against the Devil's Dung-heat," Carlyle wrote to Kingsley, "I must admit your book is definable as crude. The impression is of a fervid creation left half chaotic."[37]

Carlyle's criticism of *Alton Locke* is certainly not inaccurate, and as a description of another book, it might have heralded a deserved obscurity. *Alton Locke* remained for a long time largely forgotten, but–as the appearance of several recent editions suggest–it has won some belated recognition in our time.[38] One reason for the attention is worth a concluding note here.

Kingsley's definition of social and scientific crisis raises issues that surface today in Marxist assessments of literature. By way of example, his lower-class hero, gifted with partial self-understanding and punished by a society that makes him an outcast, offers an apt illustration of William Empson's theory of "proletarian pastoral" (though Kingsley himself was not lower class, nor his pastoral tendencies untypical of various kinds of nineteenth-century literature).[39] Kingsley articulates the sense of *waste* in his protagonist's life; he equates Alton with the social upheavals of his age, setting him against middle-class virtues and assumptions; and he creates in Alton a psychic battle between social activism and pastoral escape.

Similarly, *Alton Locke* could figure in the survey that Georg Lukács makes of the middling hero in nineteenth-century historical fiction.[40] If I have emphasized the models that Kingsley himself emphasizes, Wordsworth and Tennyson, one might argue as persuasively the model of Walter Scott. Lukács describes Scott as the great impetus behind a century of historical fiction, accounting for Scott's strength in his sympathetic recreation of the conditions of earlier times: how it felt as an ordinary citizen to live in a particular era. This is very much Kingsley's aim, though compounded by his mixing of present and recent past, by his recognition of class upheavals, and by his irrepressible desire to educate. I have mentioned Silone's Marxist novel *Fontamara*. Kingsley's interests are also allied to those of Russian social realists of the twentieth century—for whom conflicting demands of *truth* also present difficulties. More directly, *Alton Locke* anticipates the self-conscious sociology of the Goncourts' *Germinie Lacerteux* (1864) and the novels of Bennett, Gissing, and Dreiser.

IX

The Germ

Aesthetic Manifesto

1

> "The Germ" No. *1*, came out on or about January *1, 1850.* The number of copies printed was *700.* Something like 200 were sold, in about equal proportions by the publishers, and by ourselves among acquaintances and well-wishers. This was not encouraging, so we reduced the issue of No. *2* to *500* copies. It sold less well than No. *1.* . . . Had we been left to our own resources, we must now have dropped the magazine. But the printing firm—or Mr. George I. F. Tupper as representing it—came forward, and undertook to try the chance of two numbers more. The title was altered . . . to "Art and Poetry, being Thoughts towards Nature, conducted principally by Artists". . . . Some small amount of advertising was done. . . . All efforts proved useless. People would not buy "The Germ," and would scarcely consent to know of its existence. So the magazine breathed its last, and its obsequies were conducted in the strictest privacy.—William Michael Rossetti in 1899[1]

Looking back over half a century to his association with *The Germ*, William Michael Rossetti could still smile at the hapless magazine and at the group of friends and acquaintances, "artists" and non-artists, who had, in the second year of their Pre-Raphaelite Brotherhood, followed Dante Gabriel Rossetti's suggestion and launched their artistic manifesto. By the end of the century, a continued interest in the Pre-Raphaelites warranted William Rossetti's republishing of *The Germ.* Low sales and short life notwithstanding, the prototype of so many "little magazines" to follow had served, first, to express the views of the Rossettis and friends, and, second, to record their views for later and more receptive generations.

In December of 1849, when the Pre-Raphaelites were debating the relative merits of such titles as "The Harbinger," "First Thoughts," "The

Sower," "The Truth Seeker," "The Acorn," "The Seed," and "The Scroll"–finally voting by six to four in favor of "The Germ"–Charles Dickens was also considering titles for a new magazine. Some of his possibilities included "The Robin," "Mankind," "Charles Dickens," "The Microscope," "The Household Guest," "The Household Face," and several others–among them "Everything." At last, *Household Words* found Dickens's approval.[2] The contrast between the organic metaphors of seeds and germs and the qualities implied by "Household Voice" and "Mankind," and by "Household Words" itself, points to the differences between the Pre-Raphaelites' manifesto and Dickens's magazine for the millions. For the one "conducted by artists," a modest issue of five hundred proved too optimistic by far; for the other, "conducted by Charles Dickens," forty thousand sales per week was soon a reality. As he wrote in his "A Preliminary Word" to the first issue of *Household Words*, Dickens wanted his magazine "to live in the Household affections, and to be numbered among the Household thoughts of our readers." He confidently expected *Household Words* to enter the hearts of untold readers, readers who would otherwise not constitute a predictable audience, but who might share certain hopes and sentiments. "In this summer-dawn of time," he writes, his magazine will introduce "the stirring world around us, the knowledge of many social wonders, good and evil," but with the editor's promise that the spirit of the magazine will be "no utilitarian spirit." Society must, after all, "tenderly cherish that light of Fancy which is inherent in the human breast."[3]

Unlike the Rossettis and their friends, Dickens had earlier experience with magazines, and if, in his usual way, he debated long about a proper title, he knew exactly what he wanted to publish, and for whom. He had behind him the editorship of *Bentley's Miscellany* (in the late thirties) and the editorship of the *Daily News* (in 1846). In addition to assessing his public, he carefully picked his writers, all of whom were to publish anonymously in the magazine "Conducted by Charles Dickens," but who included in their numbers Harriet Martineau, Elizabeth Gaskell, Wilkie Collins, Mrs. Lynn Linton, Henry Morley, R. H. Horne, William Blanchard Jerrold, and George Augustus Sala. Occasional contributors were George Meredith, Geraldine Jewsbury, Walter Savage Landor, Albert Smith, and Edmund Yates. Even Elizabeth Barrett Browning contributed –and so did Coventry Patmore, who wrote several poems and an essay for *The Germ.*[4] The combination of skillful editing (Dickens was assisted by William Henry Wills, his subeditor) and well-written material insured for *Household Words* its almost incredible popularity. And Dickens was able to maintain its popularity until 1859, when, by a brilliant sleight-of-hand, he assumed total financial command of the magazine and guided it into another phase of success as *All the Year Round.*

The reasons for the commercial success of *Household Words*, if not for the commercial failure of *The Germ*, probably lie in Dickens's uncanny assessment of his potential audience. He wanted to please a large audience and was ready to cater to its tastes—which, no doubt, he largely shared. His inexpensive, weekly magazine epitomized a broad popularizing of periodical literature that developed through the century and that reflected a growing reading public. Walter Graham speaks of *Household Words* in terms of the various penny and half-penny magazines, appearing for the first time between 1800 and 1850, which appealed to new readers among the working classes.[5] But Graham implies that Dickens aimed primarily at a lower-class audience. What he wanted was a weekly package for anyone's pleasant opening.

The contents of the first number of *Household Words* (30 March 1850) show how Dickens managed his material and how much he could pack into a magazine of less than twenty-five pages. In addition to his own "A Preliminary Word," he included an installment of Mrs. Gaskell's *Lizzie Leigh*, an article coauthored by himself and Wills on the Post Office, a poem by Leigh Hunt, an article (by himself) on theaters for the poor, a historical anecdote by George Hogarth, a poem by William Allingham (who was a friend of the Pre-Raphaelites, but who no doubt preferred to be paid for his writing), a selection of emigrant letters (selected by Dickens and Mrs. Chisholm), an article "Milking in Australia" by Samuel and John Sidney, and a final unidentified piece entitled "Metal in Sea-Water."[6] Except for the poetry and the story by Mrs. Gaskell, here clearly was no literary or artistic publication.

Dickens knew that a popular magazine needed fiction (like Mrs. Gaskell's) and topical essays (like his own) that would be both timely and readable. Implicitly, he rejected the format of the old quarterlies without offering a weekly newspaper, like Lewes's and Thornton Hunt's *Leader*, or like the *Athenaeum* and *Spectator.* (Dickens did introduce the *Household Narrative* later in the spring; it was a news supplement to *Household Words.*) He was also careful to avoid a conspicuously political bias—like that of George Hayley in *The Red Republican* (1850) or that of Kingsley and his friends in *The Christian Socialist*. It is true that he admitted social purpose behind *Household Words*. In a letter to Mrs. Gaskell, herself a reformative novelist, he described his "new cheap weekly journal of general literature," the purpose of which "is the raising up of those that are down, and the general improvement of our social condition."[7] But if social commentary was to play an important part in *Household Words*, it was not to dominate. Dickens sought, and achieved, a genuine *magazine*, a mixed publication that avoided the political bias of *Blackwood's*, the diffuseness of *Ainsworth's*, the satire of *Fraser's*, or the frivolity of *Punch*.

Dante Gabriel Rossetti was as important to the founding of *The Germ* as Dickens was to the founding of *Household Words*. Rossetti had persuaded his friends, in 1848, to form a Brotherhood. Now he persuaded them to publish a magazine. His enthusiasm for *The Germ* seems to have been as casual as his sense of the Brotherhood itself, which he increased (to the amazement of Hunt and Millais) at a whim. His extending the Brotherhood and his compulsion to confess the meaning of its initials, which the group had decided to keep secret, were gestures of a showman who wanted publicity. Yet just as Rossetti was to teach drawing and painting to working-class men, apparently with great skill and generosity, so he wanted to share the enthusiasms of the Brotherhood with a wider, public audience. *The Germ* would explain his views while showing his wares. The only Pre-Raphaelite who began as poet as well as artist, Rossetti prodded Thomas Woolner and William Rossetti to write poetry, George Stephens and Ford Madox Brown (not officially a PRB) to write prose, and he appointed his brother to do the editing, soliciting, and general managing of the magazine. He was happy to contribute to *The Germ*, but, unlike the editor of *Household Words*, he had little interest in the daily routines.

So the editing of *The Germ* devolved on William Michael Rossetti, who was twenty-one years old, and whose notions of editing can only have been minimal. No "artist" himself, he was drafted to do reviews as well as editorial work. To use his own words again, he was "more or less expected to do the sort of work for which other 'proprietors' had little inclination—such especially as the regular reviewing of new poems."[8] Although Rossetti later dismissed his four reviews as unimportant or immature (having in the meantime done half a century of reviewing), they showed a sense of new directions. In a time of much "triviality and commonplace," Rossetti picked out poems by Arnold, Clough, and Browning. He shared the Pre-Raphaelite respect for Browning, whom, with Tennyson, he saw as the great poetic spirit of his time. His discussion of Arnold's self-conscious, elegiac style identifies Arnold's poetry as the characteristic poetry of the age (see chapter IV). Holding "the inventor" above "the commentator" in a spirit of diffidence (a principle he may have taken from Coleridge), Rossetti applied what he believed, seeking out the best in the works he reviewed and relating their characteristics to what he saw as the main creative forces of the times.

As for the magazine itself, that, too, reflected thoughtful editing. It was almost uniformly serious, and sometimes ponderous, but Rossetti had to work with what was available, and he evidently did not have a large choice of contributions. Nonetheless, his offerings were impressive. Contents for the second number of *The Germ* (actually the final number of *The Germ* as such) looked like this:

> The Child Jesus [a poem] : By James Collinson
> A Pause of Thought [poem] : by Ellen Alleyn [Christina Rossetti]
> The Purpose and Tendency of Early Italian Art: by John Seward [F. G. Stephens]
> Song: by Ellen Alleyn
> Morning Sleep [poem] : by Wm. B. Scott
> Sonnet: by Calder Caldwell
> Stars and Moon [poem] : by Coventry Patmore
> On the Mechanism of a Historical Picture: by F. Madox Brown
> A Testimony [poem] : by Ellen Alleyn
> O When and Where [poem] : by Thomas Woolner
> Fancies at Leisure [poems] : by Wm. M. Rossetti
> The Sight Beyond [poems] : by Walter H. Deverell
> The Blessed Damozel: by Dante G. Rossetti
> Reviews: "The Strayed Reveller, and other Poems": by Wm. M. Rossetti[9]

In its length (a little less than fifty pages) and its range of contents, the second number was typical of *The Germ*'s offerings.

In contrast to *Household Words, The Germ* was manifestly literary and aesthetic in emphasis, publishing poetry rather than fiction, essays on art rather than "domestic" discussions. Other numbers included Coventry Patmore's analysis of the witches' role in *Macbeth* (a shrewd essay largely ignored by Shakespeare critics), John Orchard's "Dialogue on Art," Dante Gabriel Rossetti's "My Sister's Sleep" and "Sonnets for Pictures," along with "Hand and Soul," and it was for *The Germ* that Rossetti wrote "St. Agnes of Intercession," with the original and fitting mid-century title "An Autopsychology." Holman Hunt and Ford Madox Brown provided etchings.

The contents of the magazine suggest that, in spite of its polemical inception, *The Germ* was not entirely polemical in character. Rossetti's principle of "diffidence" may have reflected the tacit principles of the group, or the magazine may itself have followed the example of its young editor, presenting viewpoints without laboring them, or—to put this another way—addressing aesthetic instead of political or religious issues, but addressing these with moderation. William Rossetti's later paraphrase of his brother's *Hand and Soul* expresses what seem to have been his editorial aims:

> The design [of Rossetti's intended etching for the imaginary biography] showed Chiaro dell' Erma in the act of painting his embodied Soul. Though the form of this tale is that of romantic metaphor, its substance is a very serious manifesto of art-dogma. It amounts to saying, The only satisfactory works of art are those which exhibit the very soul of the artist. To work for fame or self-display is a failure, and to work for direct moral proselytizing is a failure; but to paint that which your own perceptions and emotions urge you to paint promises to be a success for yourself, and hence a benefit to the mass of beholders. This was the core of the "Praeraphaelite" creed; with the adjunct . . . that the artist cannot attain to adequate self-expression save through a stern study and realization of natural appearances.[10]

However cavalier the members of the Brotherhood may have been toward a medium that was not their own, or not their main interest, they created a magazine that reflected their views and was at the same time diverse and exploratory. The hope of reaching a "mass of beholders" may only have proven possible, and that to a limited extent, for Millais, Hunt, and Rossetti as painters, but the little magazine provided the Brotherhood with a timely, if short-lived outlet.

While the public response to *The Germ* was meager, it received some favorable and sympathetic attention. If nothing else, it secured William Rossetti's career, since he was soon hired as an art critic for the *Spectator*. Several magazines praised *The Germ*. One reviewer invoked the common complaint about the *material* tendencies of the age, protesting that *The Germ* was "too good for the time." In a later review the same critic spoke of Orchard's "Dialogue on Art" as "a paper which the *Edinburgh Review* in its best days might have been proud to possess."[11] Similarly complimentary was a writer for the *Guardian*:

> Here, at last, we have a *school*, ignorant it may be, conceited possibly, as yet with but vague and unrealised objects, but working together with a common purpose, according to certain admitted principles, and looking to one another for help and sympathy. This is new in England, and we are very anxious it should have a fair trial. Its aim, moreover, however imperfectly attained as yet, is high and pure. . . . A school of artists who attempt to bring back the popular taste to the severe draperies and pure form of early art are at least deserving of encouragement. Success in their attempt would be a national blessing.[12]

Praise of this sort, though of no help to *The Germ*, must have been gratifying to the Brotherhood, and a welcome change from the more common hostility issuing from the press. *The Times* deplored a "morbid infatuation which sacrifices truth, beauty and genuine feeling to mere eccentricity."[13] And the *Athenaeum*, which was soon to hire George Stephens as an art critic, scoffed at the work of "artists who" are "intellectual without belonging to the better order of intellect," and who have set up a clearly deformed "Art Idol."[14] Among the most vocal of detractors was Charles Dickens.

In an article for *Household Words*, "Old Lamps for New Ones" (15 June 1850), Dickens offered a satirical sketch of Pre-Raphaelite aims. "You will have the goodness to discharge from your minds all post-Raphael ideas, all religious aspirations, etc. . . . for the lowest depths of what is mean, odious, repulsive, and revolting." He proposes analogous brotherhoods to the PRB, such as "The Pre-Newtonian Brotherhood," the Pre-Gower and Chaucer Brotherhood," and he speculates about "promising students connected with the Royal College of Surgeons" holding "a meeting, to protest against the circulation of the blood." The article includes among its heavy jokes a nasty attack on John Millais's *Christ in the House of His Parents* (known as *The Carpenter's Shop* and exhibited by the Academy in 1850) that is a pure piece of Philistinism. The painting presents, Dickens says, "a kneeling woman so horrible in her ugliness that (supposing it were possible for any human creature to exist for a moment with that dislocated throat) she would stand out from the rest of her company as a monster in the vilest cabaret in France or the lowest gin shop in England." In sum, "Whenever it is possible to express ugliness of feature, limb, or attitude, you have it expressed."[15]

Dickens's appeal in this article is to an easy, know-nothing smugness. With no attempt either to look at Millais's painting or to understand the aims of the Pre-Raphaelites generally, he dismisses all as "mean, odious, repulsive, and revolting," terms clearly aimed at the artists as much as at their work. Millais, if he read the article, must have wondered why people looking at his paintings were seized with a desire to attack him; why, instead of taking pleasure, they took offense. He may have been irritated, too, at the catch-all denunciation, since he alone of the Brotherhood had affiliations with the Royal Academy—was soon, indeed, to become a member—while he had strong doubts about the judgments and eccentricities of several of his Pre-Raphaelite brethren. Millais had known that the name "Pre-Raphaelite" might cause laughter; he was disappointed when Dante Gabriel Rossetti confessed the meaning of PRB to a friend and hence made it public. For all his impatience with academicians, Millais was no Bohemian. (His later elopement with Effie Ruskin was to be handled with all possible proprieties, and Millais, after associating with the Pre-Raphaelites, was soon to seek his friends in different circles. His new friends were to include Anthony Trollope, John Leech, and, ironically, Charles Dickens himself, who grew to admire both Millais and Hunt in years to come.)[16] "Art wants you home," wrote Millais to Holman Hunt in 1855. "It is impossible to fight single-handed, and the R. A. is too great a consideration to lose sight of, with all its position, with the public wealth and ability to help good art."[17] Here speaks, for good or ill, a member of the establishment. He can hardly have relished Dickens's attack.

Apart from its inappropriateness for Millais, Dickens's indictment of *The Carpenter's Shop* reveals some odd misconceptions. Why, for example, would he think of Millais "discharging" "all religious aspirations" in the portrait (a kind of conversation piece, set in Joseph's workshop) of Christ, Mary, and Joseph? Did he, in spite of his own occasional impatience with the Royal Academy, subscribe to conventional opinion as to the proprieties for representing religious subjects? Apparently so. Yet Millais, while untraditional, and perhaps radically mimetic, was if nothing else devout. Was Dickens's attack based, perhaps, on the mistaken understanding that the Pre-Raphaelites were not only "art-Catholics" but Roman Catholics as well? He may have resented what he took to be an alien iconography in the painting, just as later critics resented the inexplicable literalism of Hunt's *Scapegoat*, simply because he lacked the sympathy to look. Had he known Millais's aspirations, he would have recognized an intensely religious and moral intent and a conception of art that was anything but "mean."

With the sympathy that he later found, Dickens might have seen in the oddly vivid and evidently disturbing pictures of the Pre-Raphaelites a medium comparable to his own. Contemporary reviewers sometimes accused Dickens of excessively detailed narrative, while they wondered about his odd gift for what they called "idealization." I have mentioned David Masson's review of *Pendennis* and *David Copperfield* in which Masson praised Dickens for his ability to "daguerreotype the interior of a hut," but in which he also contrasted Dickens with the more "real" Thackeray. Dickens's "fictions are hyberbolic." His characters "are real only thus far, that they are transcendental renderings of certain hints furnished by nature."[18] By a simple extension of such arguments, a reviewer of *Bleak House* actually called Dickens a Pre-Raphaelite, attacking his ugly vision as Dickens had attacked the vision of Millais.[19]

Dickens may not have recognized the idealization in Millais's work (though Ruskin and others did), but it was obviously there. Along with it went the commitment to mimetic accuracy. William Bell Scott later wrote about the Pre-Raphaelites that the impetus behind them was photography[20]—the challenge of the new medium, which demanded new skills, and which made the work of the Academy seem dreary and uninventive. I shall return to this question. My point here is that, if the sort of loose analogies I have suggested were likely to escape the unsympathetic viewer of the Academy exhibit in 1850, still Dickens's attack on the Pre-Raphaelites disregarded much that he implicitly shared with that odd assortment of artists and friends of artists who called themselves the PRB.

Perhaps Dickens never read *The Germ*. If he had, he would have encountered ideas and a vocabulary not far from his own. The Pre-Raphaelites' urgent advocacy of "Nature" often seems vague in intent and ambiguous in application. What does the phrase "Thoughts towards Nature" really mean? The writers for *The Germ* are, however, no vaguer than many of their contemporaries, including Dickens, who pay tribute to nature as a self-evident value and aesthetic standard. "Great Nature" is a phrase from *Copperfield* that the Pre-Raphaelites would have admired and understood. True, they themselves often invoked nature in relation to fourteenth-century artists, and they may have seemed, to outsiders, to have been at best quaint and at worst foolishly regressive. But the writers for *The Germ* always qualified their medievalism, emphasizing its application for their own times and referring to early masters to clarify modern aims. "If we have entered upon a new age," George Stephens writes in "The Purpose and Tendency of Early Italian Art," "a new cycle of man, of which there are many signs, let us have it unstained by this vice of sensuality of mind."[21] To argue the shared Pre-Raphaelite ideal of spiritual and aesthetic health (an ideal they shared with Kingsley, who despised them), Stephens relies on another of Dickens's favorite words. He speaks of the necessity of a "pure heart"; and his context makes clear that "pure heart" might just as well carry Dickens's tag of "disciplined heart." No less than Dickens in *Copperfield* the Pre-Raphaelites associate emotional readiness with mature expression—and they share a high regard for the "new cycle of man" in this "new age."

Here again is William Rossetti in his review of Clough:

> We believe it may safely be assumed that at no previous period has the public been more buzzed around by triviality and common-place; but we hold firm, at the same time, that at none other has there been a greater or grander body of genius, or so honorable a display of well-cultivated taste and talent.[22]

And Stephens, in "Modern Giants," says: "Yes! there are giants on the earth in these days; but it is their great bulk, and the nearness of our view which prevents us from perceiving their grandeur. . . . we lose the brightness of things of our own time in consequence of their proximity."[23] The argument here seems to echo that of Ruskin on Turner, for Ruskin also wanted his countrymen to learn how to see and to appreciate modern greatness. Stephens is defending Browning rather than Turner, but he addresses similarly the critical blindness of his contemporaries. He is not saying that poetry is dead or genius flown, nor is he bemoaning the death of Pan. Like Dickens he insists on something like "this summer-dawn of time"; he simply sees the sun rising from a different angle.

I have dwelled on Pre-Raphaelite parallels with Dickens because of the Dickens attack and because of the historical overlaps of *Household Words* and *The Germ*. Dickens's splenetic response and his later change of heart also serve to introduce the underlying qualities of the Pre-Raphaelites and the nature of their aesthetics as expressed in *The Germ*.

2

> The movement to which they gave their name was one of the most important and interesting in the whole history of 19th century art, but it was not, as often claimed for it, a revolution.—John Steegman, *Victorian Taste*[24]

Perhaps to a man like Dickens the irritating quality in the Pre-Raphaelites was their apparent single-mindedness, their devotion to a self-asserted "high art," which came with all the effrontery of youth. Coventry Patmore's comment on Thomas Woolner's poems, that they seemed "a trifle too much in earnest,"[25] fits the public proclamations of the Brotherhood generally. When George Stephens quotes Lessing to the effect that "the destinies of a nation depend on its young men between nineteen and twenty-five years of age," he leaves no doubt that he has in mind a particular group of young men. At the same time he boasts about the difficulty of their chosen "path" by raising an analogy with religious martyrdom. *"No Cross, No Crown"* qualifies the nature of the path while implying the fundamental struggle faced by "artists" of all times.[26] However sincere the invitation to share its ideals, the Brotherhood made clear that it was exclusive by necessity and that the necessity resulted from its awareness of the historical separation of creative youth from a smothering and conventional society.

When John Steegman speaks of the Pre-Raphaelite Brotherhood as "one of the most important and interesting" movements of the century, but "not, as often claimed for it, a revolution," he touches on the urgency behind the PRB and the implications of its protest. If, however, "the Pre-Raphaelite movement . . . was in deliberate revolt . . . ,"[27] it was in its intent a revolutionary movement, although it clearly engendered no revolution. *The Germ* is an apt emblem of the Brotherhood's lack of popular success. Yet Steegman's main reason for thinking of the movement as important rather than revolutionary lies not so much in its limited impact as in its second-hand thinking. Its ideals, far from being new, were rooted in nineteenth-century taste. Here we have a more interesting question.

In painting techniques the Pre-Raphaelites had been anticipated by the German Nazarenes, among them Cornelius, who prided themselves on accuracy of detail, on adhering to Pre-Raphael techniques, and on living morally upright lives. They had been anticipated in England by Fuseli and Stothard (specifically in Stothard's painting of the Canterbury pilgrims), by Turner (as interpreted by Ruskin), and by other painters, including William Dyce, who was in turn to be influenced by the Pre-Raphaelites (in a painting like *Pegwell Bay*), and by Ford Madox Brown. Dyce and Brown had known the work of the Nazarenes and learned something from their techniques. Brown himself wrote an article "On the Mechanism of a Historical Picture" for *The Germ* and he associated with the Brotherhood, though he was not technically a member.

Apart from painting techniques, the Pre-Raphaelites shared a great deal with their mid-century contemporaries—painters, poets, even the general public. Young men of "nineteen to twenty-five" often enough absorb what others have said and done before, making the hackneyed peculiarly their own. A sense of the times as hypocritical, uninspired, and morally bankrupt was, as Carlyle, Kingsley, Mayhew, and Ruskin show, a commonplace. *Fraser's* in 1850 carried a series of articles called "The Age of Veneering" (a name Dickens later picks up in *Our Mutual Friend*). Such criticism might, as with the Pre-Raphaelites themselves, complement a hope for progress, but it was widespread. So, too, the insistence on the importance of nature, which was so common and so broadly applied as to be a cliché. Yet the Pre-Raphaelites pledged themselves to honor nature as though they had themselves invented the word.

We can address the question of the Pre-Raphaelites' representative qualities by glancing at their appeal to nature and at their "medievalism," ideals which they contrived to pull together. In an obvious sense, the Brotherhood's reverence for the early Italian masters was wholly arbitrary—no more than the result of perusing a group of prints and deciding that they would serve nicely as models. Ruskin called the prints "execrable," and whatever their quality, they can hardly have provided the

Brotherhood with much information. To read *The Germ* or the *Pre-Raphaelite Journal* is to see, moreover, how limited the medieval interest was among the group. William Rossetti tells in the *Journal* how the group joked about having a door-knocker inscribed with PRB, which would signify "Please Ring the Bell" to the uninitiated. He has, otherwise, little to say about medieval art. He tells a great deal about conversations with Coventry Patmore, reports about Patmore's views on Tennyson and Browning, and Tennyson's on Clough, and he refers often enough to his brother's interest in Dante. His concern with literary figures—particularly those in his own time—might reflect his personal involvements rather than report the conversations of the entire group. Yet the famous "List of Immortals," drawn up by D. G. Rossetti and Holman Hunt (in 1848) presents a surprisingly broad—not to say strange—assortment of people. According to Hunt's account, the list included (with asterisks for emphasis):

Jesus Christ****
The Author of Job***
Isaiah
Homer**
Pheidias
Early Gothic Architects
Cavalier Pugliesi
Dante**
Boccaccio*
Rienzi
Ghiberti
Chaucer**
Fra Angelico*
Leonardo da Vinci**
Spenser
Hogarth
Flaxman
Hilton
Goethe**
Kosciusko
Byron
Wordsworth
Keats**
Shelley**
Haydon
Cervantes
Joan of Arc
Mrs. Browning*
Patmore*
Raphael*
Michael Angelo
Early English Balladists
Giovanni Bellini
Giorgioni
Titian
Tintoretto
Poussin
Alfred**
Shakespeare***
Milton
Cromwell
Hampden
Bacon
Newton
Landor**
Thackeray**
Poe
Hood
Longfellow*
Emerson
Washington**
Leigh Hunt
Author of *Stories after Nature**
Wilkie
Columbus
Browning**
Tennyson*[28]

One reason why the early masters fared poorly in this seriocomic list is perhaps simple. In spite of the public interest in Gothic architecture, the ignorance about medieval painting was widespread. Ruskin, in his 1851 pamphlet *Pre-Raphaelitism*—an odd and tangential apology for Hunt and Millais—summed up the situation perfectly. "Few English people," he wrote, have "ever seen a picture of early Italian Masters." Not many such paintings existed in public repositories (since the National Gallery's holdings remained slight: Charles Eastlake was to remedy this in time) and not many galleries were open to the public. If English people had seen pictures by the Italian painters, says Ruskin,

> they would have known that the Pre-Raphaelite pictures are just as superior to the early Italian in skill of manipulation, power of drawing, and knowledge of effect, as inferior in grace of design; and that in a word, there is not a shadow of resemblance between the two styles. The Pre-Raphaelites imitate no pictures: they paint from nature only.[29]

Whether or not we accept Ruskin's judgments, his point about the ignorance of English connoisseurs and his implication about the Pre-Raphaelites' own ignorance are well taken. Ruskin might have mentioned that the Pre-Raphaelites' medieval indebtedness seems to have been limited to the Rossettis, whose interest centered on Dante. D. G. Rossetti's "Dante in Exile" and his translation of the *Vita Nuova* belong to these years, and Rossetti's preoccupation with Dante (seen in his treatment of Lizzie Siddal, in the setting and tone of "The Blessed Damozel," and elsewhere) may have determined the choice of medieval models in painting. One might even expect in *The Germ* a literary manifesto equivalent to the "medievalism" in painting. But there is no such thing. Two of *The Germ*'s four etchings and one of its major articles (though by Patmore, rather than by a Pre-Raphaelite as such) were drawn from or about Shakespeare. The literary tastes expressed in the *Journal* as in *The Germ* (as the "List of Immortals" suggests) were inclusive rather than exclusive—and no more medieval than Ruskin allows Hunt's and Millais's paintings to be.

The hostility to the Pre-Raphaelites among men like Dickens probably reflected a wide dislike, if not a profound distrust, of things medieval. Within a month, however, of Dickens's attack in *Household Words*, James Collinson resigned from the PRB because it was not, presumably, medieval enough. To Dante Rossetti, Collinson wrote:

> Whit Monday.—Dear Gabriel, I feel that as a sincere Catholic, I can no longer allow myself to be called a P. R. B. in the brotherhood sense of the term, or to

> be connected in any way with the magazine. Perhaps this determination to withdraw myself from the Brotherhood is altogether a matter of feeling. I am uneasy about it. I love and reverence God's faith, and I love His holy Saints; and I cannot bear any longer the self-accusation that, to gratify a little vanity, I am helping to dishonor them, and lower their merits, if not absolutely to bring their sanctity into ridicule. –I cannot blame anyone but myself. Whatever may be my thoughts with regard to their works, I am sure that all the P R Bs have both written and painted conscientiously;–it was for me to have judged beforehand whether I could conscientiously, as a Catholic, assist in spreading the artistic opinions of those who are not. I reverence–indeed almost idolize–what I have seen of the works of the Pre-Raffaelle painters; [and this] chiefly because [they fill] my heart and mind with that divine faith which could alone animate them to give up their intellect and time and labor so as they did, and all for his glory.[30]

Collingson gently tells his PRB colleagues that their medievalism is a kind of game, that it lacks "reverence," and that it is invoked lightly. Collinson does not say that the medievalism of Pre-Raphael painters reflects a fashion, though he might have added that too.

The contemporary craze for restitution of old buildings–deplored by Ruskin as barbaric–and the desire for *new* medieval edifices have been discussed by Sir Kenneth Clark and other historians. In one phase the mid-nineteenth-century medievalism lent itself to Barry's Houses of Parliament. In another it informed works like Carlyle's *Past and Present* (1843) as a way of commenting on and criticizing modern life. Carlyle points to the lack of spiritual force in his contemporaries, to their false idols, and to their inhibiting and dehumanizing institutions, complete with "red-tape" (the nonce word he introduced in *Latter-Day Pamphlets*). Even Marx and Engels refer to medieval economic and social relations to clarify the alienation of workers in their own century, and Ruskin introduces a similar argument in *Pre-Raphaelitism* as well as in later works. The nostalgia for medieval culture led to a plethora of scholarly and polemical works. In 1850, for example, Anna Jameson published her *Legends of Monastic Orders* and A. W. Pugin published yet another of his apologies for neo-Gothic. Ruskin's defense of medieval art was and remains the best known.

Again, Ruskin himself categorically thinks of the Pre-Raphaelites as doing something different from the early masters. He ascribes the entire movement indeed to his own instructions given in the first volume of *Modern Painters* (1843).

> Eight years ago, in the close of the first volume of *Modern Painters*, I ventured to give the following advice to the young artists of England:–
>
> "They should go to nature in all singleness of heart, and walk with her labori-

> ously and trustingly, having no other thought but how best to penetrate her meaning; rejecting nothing, selecting nothing, and scorning nothing." Advice which, whether bad or good, involved infinite labour and humiliation in the following it. . . . It has, however, at last been carried out, to the very letter.[31]

Ruskin may be right. Certainly Patmore appreciated Ruskin, and the Pre-Raphaelites often discussed art with Patmore. Moreover, Ruskin himself came to befriend the Pre-Raphaelites and tried to influence them directly. But whereas Patmore wrote a laudatory review of *Seven Lamps* for the *North British Review* (February 1850), praising him, as Lewes and others praised him, for offering genuine standards in art criticism, Ruskin's name is conspicuously absent in *The Germ* and even in the private *Journal.* If the Pre-Raphaelites followed Ruskin, it was without fanfare. Interestingly, they also have little to say about Turner, whom Ruskin primarily discusses in *Pre-Raphaelitism* as well as in *Modern Painters*, and while for Ruskin "Pre-Raphaelitism and . . . Turnerism are one," the Pre-Raphaelites themselves seem unaware of the relationship.

Ruskin's admonition in *Modern Painters* nevertheless does coincide with the Pre-Raphaelites' aims. When Stephens, in "The Purpose and Tendency of Early Italian Art," thinks about medieval painting, he emphasizes vivid color, precise detail, and symbolic meaning. He acknowledges in the old masters a preeminence in "energy and dignity." The lesson to be learned from them is not idle copying, but the need for "originality of conception"; not "a dreary course of preparatory study," but a "bold" imaginative striving. Where then lies the medievalism, so important that it gave its name to the movement? For Stephens, it lies in the unconventionality and the lack of "coarseness" in medieval artists. They were humble, simple, earnest, and could thus be full of "passion and feeling." Modern artists need to find an equivalent for the discipline and the retirement of a monastery if they hope to find again "a more humble manner than has been practiced since the decline of Italian Art in the Middle Ages." According to Stephens, modern artists must provide "pure transcripts and faithful studies from nature, instead of feeble reminiscences from the Old Masters." The lesson from nature is a broad injunction to emphasize "the soul" more than "the hand" and to seek what amounts to "communion with nature."[32]

For the Pre-Raphaelites the communion can take a variety of forms. But Collinson notwithstanding, they *are* religious, in the sense of humble and reverent, in their approaches to the physical world. Hence they work as Ruskin urged artists to work—with accurate memories and as devoted scribes. One of the differences between them and the later Impressionists is that, while both groups effect a kind of "sun-painting," a brilliant recording of light and color, the Pre-Raphaelites want to catch the unchanging and permanent in their works rather than the transitory and therefore personal. Holman Hunt's famous *Scapegoat*, painted at the Dead Sea, while Hunt carried a gun under one arm to protect himself from hostile Arabs, is a case in point. Hunt was intent on absolute fidelity; he was ruthless with himself—and had, in fact, made a pilgrimage to do the painting—and ruthless with the goat, which died from exposure. And though art may be both accurate and symbolic, as several writers for *The Germ* assert, we can still appreciate the difficulty contemporary viewers had in understanding Hunt's pathetic animal obviously near to collapse, in a setting as carefully depicted as though it were a single furnished room. Part of the literalism in Hunt's painting results from the attempt to render the animal as if it had emerged from its biblical story. And what Hunt does to the poor goat, Millais almost does to Lizzie Siddal, who lies for hours in a cooling tub of water in imitation of the drowning Ophelia. Despite the claim to revere nature, Hunt's and Millais's and Rossetti's paintings are obviously literary in conception, no less anecdotal than so much of the academy work that the Brotherhood rejected.

The problem for the PRB was to define the new, which they saw as adherence to nature, as separate from the art of the recent past and at the same time to give it authority, to place it in a tradition. T. S. Eliot's arbitrary rejection of poetry since the Metaphysicals is a twentieth-century parallel, and Eliot, like the Pre-Raphaelites, had no trouble at all praising intervening artists.

An emphasis on tradition may take the direction of what Stephens calls "feeble reminiscences" from the Old Masters, or it may involve independence and "originality," using the Old Masters as spiritual more than purely technical guides. In discussing Dickens's attack on Millais, I mentioned the Pre-Raphaelite notion of a summer-dawn of time. To read *The Germ* is to see that they think of their own times whenever they invoke Raphael's predecessors, and also that they think of their times with a great deal of optimism. John Orchard, who was not technically a PRB member, but whose "Dialogue on Art" William Rossetti considered "really wonderful," had told Dante Rossetti that it was silly to adopt "the mode of thought and the practice of any preceding age."[33] Rossetti mentions no argument from his brother and offers none himself. The "Dialogue" takes place on the first day of spring, and the opening speaker, Kosmon, says:

> Great impulses are moving through man; swift as the steam-shot shuttle, weaving some mighty pattern, goes the new birth of mind. As yet hidden from eyes is the

> design: whether it be poetry, or painting, or music, or architecture, or whether it be a divine harmony of all, no manner of mind can tell.[34]

When Dickens introduced his "Preliminary Word" to *Household Words*, he carefully stressed the entertainment offered by his magazine. It came to its readers, he said, in "no utilitarian spirit." Now, Orchard's dialogue is not summed up in Kosmon's steam-shot shuttle speech, and Orchard's emphasis may not reflect utilitarian theories of progress, but the metaphors are exactly what people associated with the Utilitarians. And Orchard's view was not a single instance. In "Modern Giants" Stephens says:

> There is something else we miss; there is the poetry of the things about us; our railways, factories, mines, roaring cities, steam vessels, and the endless novelties and wonders produced every day; which if they were found only in the Thousand and One Nights, or in any poem classical or romantic, would be gloried over without end.[35]

Whether or not the other Pre-Raphaelites would have concurred with Stephens on the "poetry of things around us" (certainly they never painted railways and factories), Stephens expresses a common point of view of the time. His paean to the mechanical beauties of his age could have come from almost any poetry review from the early days of the *Westminster*, and it reads like an advertisement for the arts of the Great Exhibition for which Prince Albert, Sir Robert Peel, and Henry Cole were already preparing.

Within its Gothic court and its elaborate, ornately curved art-work, the Crystal Palace paid a common debt to the Middle Ages, exhibiting "gutta-percha" sideboards, foliated dinner ware, along with chairs, tapestries, and sundry other "useful" products that fairly writhed with decorative activity. Ruskin recognized in the Exhibition a universal love of pointless detail combined with a delight in efficient methods of production. He found no beauty in the "work of nations." Yet for Ruskin's readers the ornateness might seem to have met his own criteria for functional decoration; and Ruskin's admiration for the detail of medieval windows and sculpture was to invite an eclecticism perhaps not too far from the aesthetic-industrial muddle housed by Paxton's glass palace.

The Pre-Raphaelites also came close to advocating a doctrine of work. Stephens speaks of artists having to avoid authority and conventionality, and making sure that they have not "fritted away" "earnest thought . . . by a long, dreary course of preparatory study." At the same time he draws an analogy between artists and monks, advocating the discipline and retirement, the "patient devotedness" necessary to creation. But the sense of the artist's labor, though a matter of ambivalence for the Pre-Raphaelites as it was for Ruskin, involves a broader commitment to the stature of work which the Pre-Raphaelites shared with Lancashire factory owners and Thomas Carlyle. In his "Dialogue on Art," John Orchard presents differing points of view, without reconciling or allowing one to predominate (this was reserved for the second article, which Orchard did not live to write). He allows Kosmon to say: "Are not [the "mechanical arts"]—especially steam-power, chemistry, and the electric telegraph—more—eminently more—useful to man, more radically civilizers, than music, poetry, painting, sculpture, or architecture?" Kosmon sees a relationship between the artist and his society and expresses the widespread notion that "the career of one artist contains in itself the whole of art-history; its every phase is presented by him in the course of his life."[36] If Orchard himself sympathizes more with "Sophon" than with "Kosmon," he seems to share the assumption that the development of the arts parallels the development of society, and he admits—like Stephens in *Modern Giants*—the imaginative power inherent in steam, chemistry, electricity. His testimony qualifies the Pre-Raphaelite emphasis on what would seem to be escapes into the world of the past or the world of dreams. We might associate other Victorian painters—Turner, for example, in *Rain, Steam, and Smoke*, or Frith, in the painting of Paddington station—with the idealization of industry, but it was Ford Madox Brown who painted the famous *Work*, in which, ironically, the apostle of work, Carlyle, is represented as an idle onlooker.

For all their early isolation and hostile reception, the Pre-Raphaelites shared much with their contemporaries both in and out of the art world. Where, then, do we find their radicalism? The radical or revolutionary quality of the PRB lies in the group's intensity, in the transformation of common ideals into one ideal, which allows vague principles and expansive lists of immortals. The Pre-Raphaelites saw themselves as a new force, able to reopen the book of nature as it had not been opened for centuries, and able, too, to reject the social-political conformity of the Academy. To say that even Dickens came to be bored by the Royal Academy, or that scarcely anyone at the time with or without artistic pretensions failed to invoke nature, may remind us that Marx and other revolutionaries similarly reflect the preoccupations of their contemporaries and differ from them in passion or commitment. From our perspective a comparison of Marx and the Pre-Raphaelites is hyperbolic. For mid-century Englishmen, the group of young poets and painters might have seemed the more revolutionary.

3

> Why is it these pictures and essays [in *The Germ*] being so realistic, yet produce on the mind such a vague and dreamy sensation, approaching as it were the Mystic Land of a Bygone Age. . . ? There is in them the life I long for, and which never seems realizable in this life.—Thomas Dixon, "the working cork-cutter of Sutherland," in a letter to William Rossetti[37]

Thomas Dixon, who was to win passive recognition as Ruskin's "Working Man" in *Time and Tide*, serves to introduce this final note about *The Germ.* For in spite of the Pre-Raphaelite commitment to work, their appreciation of the promise in their times, their sense that great spirits were upon the earth, the effect of their paintings and poetry is perhaps the "vague and dreamy sensation" that Dixon describes. Dixon's "life that I long for, and which never seems realizable in this life," calls attention to the imaginary and sometimes visionary quality in the work of the Pre-Raphaelites, a quality divorced from mills and smoke, from the industrial, urban conditions of mid-nineteenth-century England. Christina Rossetti's "Dream Land" and Dante Rossetti's "Blessed Damozel" may come immediately to mind. When Dixon speaks of the "realistic" aspect of *The Germ*, he evidently means its specificity, and he seems surprised that "realistic" need not imply (as it had largely come to imply) a broad injunction to survey the modern world. Dixon ignores Stephens's and Orchard's protests about the poetry in machines or the energy of industrialization—for good reason. He senses behind the pronouncements of *The Germ* the Pre-Raphaelite disgust with ugliness and the association, made explicit by Ruskin, of ugliness with industrial growth. As René Wellek says: "Ruskin was one of the first to see industrialization in terms, not only of human suffering, but also of the blight it inflicts on art and free creativity."[38] All their protests about the poetry of mechanical things notwithstanding, the Pre-Raphaelites shared Ruskin's horror and acted on his assumptions.

The Pre-Raphaelite decision to omit politics from their magazine may have been a gesture toward commercial success or a tacit rejection of the political bias of other periodicals; but it was also a true reflection of the group's interests. The PRB was a revolutionary group with aesthetic rather than political principles. We can appreciate the energy behind *The Germ* by glancing at another short-lived periodical of 1850, which was, in intent, directed at men like Thomas Dixon, and which proclaimed itself as *The Red Republican.*

George Julian Harney was to *The Red Republican* what Dickens was to

Household Words. Before launching *The Red Republican* he had edited the Chartist *Northern Star* and later the *Democratic Review*, which had published commentaries by a variety of European intellectuals from Marx to Mazzini. Harney had been associated with the "Fraternal Democrats," a group of English radicals who joined French, Polish, Italian, and German exiles. As John Saville points out, Harney's relationships typify the international quality of early British radicalism, and Harney sought to bring to his readers the intellectual, revolutionary ferment of the continent.[39] He befriended Engels, who wrote for the *Democratic Review*, and Marx, whom he met on Marx's first visit to England in 1847. In their usual way, Marx and Engels were soon to spurn Harney for tolerating rival theories, but *The Red Republican* did publish, in Helen Macfarlane's translation, the first English version of the *Communist Manifesto.*

Harney's paper turned out to be little more commercially successful than *The Germ*, possibly because it shared certain attitudes with *The Germ.* Though committed to helping the working classes, it was almost as divorced from "the day to day struggles of the working people" as the magazine of the Pre-Raphaelites. Like *The Germ* it was largely theoretical, affirming certain "principles" in the face of the establishment, although its establishment was the "organizing hypocrisy" of the propertied classes rather than the aesthetic domination of the Royal Academy. Harney's commitment to political societies (like the Fraternal Democrats), his hope in an emancipating elite, his impatience with English provincialism and smugness, his flaunting of a name he knew would be, at the least, unpopular and misunderstood—all these might suggest the impetus behind *The Germ.* This is not to say that the small group of Pre-Raphaelites equaled a large working-class movement; rather that Harney himself scarcely reflected the movement, which, in its Chartist phase, was in disarray. Harney, like the Christian Socialist Kingsley, was, indeed, soon to give up active politics, and his rhetoric may reveal his isolation and ineffectuality. His proclamation in the first number of *The Red Republican* (June 22) is called "Our Name and Our Principles." The name, he says, is admittedly "imprudent," but the principles are time-honored. He reaches back to an address by Robespierre from the early days of the French Revolution, calling for a new order based on a new understanding, while quoting Robespierre's admonition to "fulfill the vows of Nature." Nature for *The Red Republican* as for *The Germ* is a call to arms as well as a self-evident principle of good. "The Golden Age, placed by blind tradition in the Past, *is before us.*"[40]

It may of course be historical coincidence that *The Germ* and *The Red*

Republican would share vocabulary or would assess their age in analogous ways or look with the same sort of optimism to the future. But if they expressed, in Sir Nikolaus Pevsner's words, "that unquestioning optimism, that yet unarrested drive, that naivety in overlooking bleak problems,"[41] in common with Crystal Palace England, they also spoke to the unattainable "life that I long for, and which never seems realizable" of Thomas Dixon. Although worlds apart in their ideals, the one exclusively aesthetic in content, the other stridently political, both *The Germ* and *The Red Republican* represent the views of self-appointed outsiders who saw themselves as, at once, underprivileged, prophetic, and indisputably right.

X

Postscripts

On the Eve of the Great Exhibition

> For, indeed, who knows anything about these matters now? And who, save fossils whose memory carries them back to the dark ages of the present century, or those curious investigators who like to stir up ashes of burnt out literary fires, would care to unearth these buried treasures? Who would care to read the old numbers of the defunct *Leader*, which Thornton Hunt and George Lewes mainly wrote . . .?—Elizabeth Lynn Linton, *My Literary Life* (1899)[1]

As this study draws to a close, I am aware of much left unsaid or unresolved. Clearly, no literary history that aims at broad description can do full justice to the demands of coherence on the one hand and to the demands of diversity, the acknowledgment of the forgotten and potentially significant, on the other. *Victorian Noon* has been a compromise. It has, in Elizabeth Linton's words, probably stirred up too many ashes, and it may seem to have done too little to provide sustaining theories. My intent, quite simply, has been to present materials as fully as space allowed, while offering generalizations in a more or less cumulative way, chapter by chapter. For these "postscripts," I want first to touch on conclusions already drawn and then to speculate about a final and possibly integrating question.

Throughout this essay I have pulled together works of a variety of writers in order to identify some central concerns in mid-century literature: the shift to autobiographical forms, with a consequent emphasis on the workings of memory; the tacit equation of poetic and novelistic processes, surprisingly without critical awareness of the parallels drawn; the application of religious questioning to literature, so that religious documents share with fiction and poetry both a retrospective account of a man or woman who has undergone a form of conversion and a way of dealing with the conversion through a body of shared metaphor; the preoccupation with terms such as *nature*, and the implications of those terms for attempts at verisimilitude—in photography, for example—and for new theories of *realism* formulated by critics like George Lewes.

I have tried to indicate that while mid-century critics still tend to denigrate fiction and to affirm expressive theories of poetry that seem primarily useful for lyric modes, fiction becomes the acknowledged epic of the time. For fiction can be seen as the implicit if inadequate realization of the appeal by Macaulay and others for a new type of literature, a literature appropriate for a new age and manifestly distinct from the utterances of "primitive" peoples or immature poets. Obviously this is to simplify. Discussions of poetry normally advocate the "creative" along with the "reflective" faculty, pointing to critical principles that are at best mixed. The poetry itself tends to be "dramatic" (in verse novels and dramatic monologues), not to mention elegiac, and it records, characteristically, "the dialogue of the mind with itself." Questions about the relative stature of fiction or of certain verse forms overlap with questions about the value of inherited traditions, ancient and modern, and lead to recurrent debates as to the place of literature in a society quite aware of its own anomalies.

Of the many unanswered questions raised in this essay, then, one seems to loom largest for a final chapter: whether there was an identifiable mid-century literary culture, or at least whether writers of the time thought so themselves. Since the term *culture* may beg the question, we could ask if the Pre-Raphaelites and Kingsley, Tennyson and Dickens, Arnold and Clough, Carlyle and Ruskin, might have agreed about the nature of the literary climate in which they wrote.

When G. M. Young looks back on mid-nineteenth-century English literature, he thinks of a time when there existed a sort of fraternity of writers, when young writers recognized the greatness of their elders and anticipated greatness of their own:

> Young men of 1850, reading with the proper avidity of youth, could have found most of their tastes, and most of their curiosities, satisfied by masterpieces published, since their birth, by men who had been pointed out to them in the streets. To watch Mr. Macaulay threading his way through the Piccadilly traffic, book in hand; to see Mr. Dickens running up the steps of the Athenaeum; to recognize the Laureate by his cloak and Mr. Carlyle by his shawl, were the peculiar joys of that time. The stonecutter by the Tiber, chipping out "Carmen composuit Q. Horatius Flaccus" on the memorial of the seculiar Games, must have had the same feeling that he too was living in a great age, peopled by Immortals.[2]

Well, this was a great age in literature. But was there such optimism about it at the time? Does Young perhaps confuse achievement with a sense of well-being, or equate a new confidence in economic prosperity with his own approximation of how men and women (actually he forgets the women) ought to have felt?

From our perspective, complicated by radically shifting assumptions about literature and a radically shrunken readership for literature, literary life in mid-nineteenth-century England may seem attractively unified and confident, just as literature in the age of Queen Anne might have seemed unified and confident to writers in the nineteenth century. In fact, it is never easy to be a writer, and it was far from easy at mid-century. Were George Meredith and Mark Rutherford, or Lewis Carroll and Frederic Harrison, or Leslie and Fitzjames Stephen, or Coventry Patmore and Walter Bagehot, entirely convinced that they lived among immortals? Patmore was soon to confide to William Allingham that the future belonged to the two of them—along with Matthew Arnold. Walter Bagehot remained more interested in Shelley than in his contemporaries, although he and his friend R. H. Hutton would soon edit and contribute to magazines that dealt fully with the literature of the time. Frederic Harrison, at Oxford, recorded 1850 as a dull year, with little of interest to read. And what of a self-proclaimed provincial like Charlotte Brontë, who visited Thackeray in 1850 (Thackeray slipped out of his own house to end the conversation), but who, as Elizabeth Gaskell realized, belonged with the strange characters peopling Haworth and the moors. Or William Barnes, the Dorset poet, who received his first real praise in 1850 from another provincial, William Allingham, and who lived apart as a country schoolmaster. Or George Borrow, who describes in *Lavengro* a depressing encounter with a London publisher—before allowing his hero to escape to remote parts of the kingdom. To a beginning writer like Margaret Oliphant or Edmund Yates (who found hope in Thackeray's *Pendennis*), literary life represented a possible but difficult profession.[3] Tennyson, whose cloak was in fact seldom seen in London, knew how difficult a literary career could be; so did the Brownings, living in a fairly typical exile; so did Carlyle and even Thackeray. None knew better than the young Arthur Clough.

This is not to deny among a younger generation a common respect for established writers. It is simply to suggest how carefully we need to sort out the relations between the intricacies of literary events and our own desire for historical coherence. Doubtless, for example, the Great Exhibition reflected and inspired a widespread optimism at mid-century. The trust in revived economic health and social stability, while far from universal, shows itself in newspaper editorials, omnibus reviews in journals, and in private correspondence, whether from ordinary citizens or from Queen Victoria herself. To Prince Albert and to Henry Cole, dedicated to the Great Exhibition, 1850 and the year to follow marked the high point of the century. They spoke of progress and achievement, peace and brotherhood. But we might remember that for Ruskin, who was not alone, the Crystal Palace and its contents offered a clear instance of values gone awry, of the shabby and tawdry promulgated in place of the beautiful, of taste perverted. "Show me what you like," as Ruskin said elsewhere, "and I will show you what you are."[4]

The taste of the exhibitors and the viewers at the Exhibition, discussed in Sir Nikolaus Pevsner's *High Victorian Design*, remains something of a mystery to modern readers of the Exhibition catalogue—the more so when we recall the popularity of *In Memoriam* among the visitors. How, to put this crudely, could so much ugliness be seen as beauty? What, excepting the Crystal Palace itself, has been remembered from the myriad objects of cutlery, furniture, statuary, gathered from the industrial world? The proud, relatively simple lines of Paxton's glass house, a last minute replacement for something that would have resembled a large warehouse, contrast utterly with the bric-a-brac within. It is of course coincidence, though an appropriate coincidence, that the word *Biedermeier*, taken from a work by the German Eichrodt, should have been coined in 1850. Commonly used to designate middle-class German taste from the era of Napoleon to the revolutions of 1848, the term has some application to those endless curves and flowers, the twistings and turnings of form in the Crystal Palace. And *Biedermeier* may serve, as Mario Praz has shown, to characterize general aesthetic developments in England as well as in Germany.[5] Whether gutta-percha sideboards or convoluted teaspoons can be linked with novels about domestic felicity or the desire for stasis among ordinary, middle-class heroes is dubious. Still, the emphasis on domestic happiness in *David Copperfield* or *Frank Fairlegh* or *Pendennis* implies limited aspirations coupled with rather stunted taste. One thinks of Pendennis, the *homme moyen sensuel*, succeeding in spite of inadequate talents, and hiding in lethargy as David Copperfield hides in work. Pendennis illustrates for Thackeray a political ideal of sluggish and safe reform, and Thackeray is sympathetic to his undistinguished hero, whose life he treats with an irony that is far from militant. It is Thackeray, not the fictional Pendennis, who writes a "May-Day Ode" to the Crystal Palace:

> Along the dazzling colonnade,
> Far as the straining eye can gaze,

Gleam cross and fountain, bell and vase,
In vistas bright;
And statues fair of nymph and maid,
And steeds and pards and Amazons,
Writhing and grappling in the bronze
In endless fight.

. . . .

Swell, organ, swell your trumpet blast,
March, Queen and Royal pageant, march
By splendid aisle and springing arch
Of this fair hall:
And see! above the fabric vast,
God's boundless Heaven is bending,
God's peaceful sunlight's beaming through,
And shines o'er all.[6]

The question of mid-century taste is obviously too complex to be subsumed in the imaginative worlds of writers of fiction or in the "writhing and grappling" contents of the Crystal Palace. It would have to address public and private architecture, the development of suburbs, the erection of those engineering masterpieces that Ruskin disallowed as architecture. Most London railway stations belong to the middle years of the nineteenth century. Barry and Pugin's Houses of Parliament neared completion by 1850; the great tubular bridge spanned the Menai Straits. A comprehensive discussion of taste would have to consider movements like the Gothic Revival, the uses of new materials for building, the plans of industrialists like Isambard Brunel, entertainments like the "Cyclorama." And the list would go on to book-binding and magazine advertisements, clothes and the wearing of beards. Even somewhat more manageable topics, such as those handled by John Steegman in *Victorian Taste*, are too large to be more than mentioned here. But one illustration may be pertinent. Steegman discusses the preferences in painting of Charles Eastlake and his intellectual wife, Elizabeth Rigby.[7] When Eastlake took over as director of the National Gallery, his preferences, allied to a great extent to those of his mentor, Prince Albert, helped to change British perceptions in the visual arts. Ruskin was right about English men and women having no easy way of estimating the qualities of either medieval or modern "Pre-Raphaelite" painting, and if Englishmen had to be educated to appreciate Turner, they also had to be educated to appreciate many painters, the works of whom became accessible only in the second half of the nineteenth century.

The important point is, however, that mid-century Englishmen either liked or were ready to like a great deal, in literature as well as in the visual arts. Their magazines report recent editions from France of Eugène Sue or Paul de Kock; they comment on English novelists in relation to Balzac (who died in 1850); they record from America works of Hawthorne, Bryant, Melville, above all Cooper and Washington Irving; novels by Elizabeth Sewell and Lady Chatterton crowd in with those of authors better remembered. Just as the *Art-Journal* is a fascinating hodgepodge of technological accounts, illustrations of poems from three centuries, reports of meetings, brief biographies and autobiographies of artists and architects, with etchings of old and contemporary paintings, so *Household Words* and the *Athenaeum*, the *Leader* and the *Examiner* suggest a reading public opening its arms to all and everything. If *Biedermeier* serves to characterize their tastes, it might indicate a pervasive and generous eclecticism, by which little would be excluded and new materials along with rediscoveries of older art would tumble indiscriminately together.

A term like *Biedermeier* may be provocative, but it is also inadequate, raising as many questions as it answers. While mid-century eclecticism posed problems for critics, poets, and novelists of the time, it reflected powerful intellectual and aesthetic movements, none susceptible of easy definition. To give one example: George Lewes quotes in the *Leader* Carlyle, applauding Carlyle's observation that "no age is Romantic to itself," that we turn from contemporary works to "the superficial trash" of times gone by.[8] Lewes tacitly approves the positive implications of the term *Romantic*, allowing it to express a variety of excellences he admires in his contemporaries. In the same months, Matthew Arnold describes for Arthur Clough the liabilities in Romantic traditions, regretting that his age cannot, alas, reproduce classical ideals, and thinking of classical both as a state of mind and as a standard of lost excellence. Arnold holds up classical models for emulation and directs his readers to modern European writers; Lewes objects to a slavish deference to classical writers but offers European contemporaries as his models, too. Both think of Wordsworth's influence as dangerous; both hold up Goethe as the paramount writer of the century, although Goethe epitomizes opposing virtues for each. Hence the dialogue about Romantic and Classic, common to literary discussions of the time, hints at the inadequacy of such terminology for a situation that no catch-all definitions or rhetorical alternatives could cover. To understand our own *and* mid-century difficulties with Procrustean definitions, we need to reapproach the eclecticism of the age from another angle.

If my own discussions have tacitly accepted a modern assumption of literature as *belles lettres*: poetry, fiction, drama, essays, Victorian readers would have included more histories in an account of literary achievement. George Gilfillan's comment that Macaulay and Dickens were the most popular writers of the day testifies to his own acceptance of Macaulay's literary importance—and he has in mind the first volumes of the *History of England* rather than the *Lays of Ancient Rome*—as well as the assumption that history *is* literature. History for mid-century readers could include a variety of works, from chronicles of ancient Greece to Harriet Martineau's record of events since Waterloo. The admiration for historical studies is anything but provincial. Strauss's *Life of Jesus* and other European books about the Bible or about religious belief among diverse civilizations usually found English reviewers. Articles in the *Quarterly* comment at length on scientific histories, on J. F. Blumenbach's anthropological works, for example, which are assumed to be at least as significant as the geological studies of Charles Lyell, and far more significant than such local popularizings as Hugh Miller's *Footprints of the Creator* (1850). Geology and anthropology are understood as largely historical sciences that explore human and prehuman development, and years before Darwin published *Origin of Species* (1859) some of the disquieting implications of Evolution have become common topics of discussion. Mackay's *Progress of the Intellect* shares with works on anthropology, ethnology, art history, and geology attempts to come to terms with an incalculably enlarged framework of human memory.

History in the sense of social and political narrative similarly interested English readers. Reviewers point to the example of Barthold Niebuhr; and possibly the most influential historian of the time is another German, Leopold von Ranke, who, as archivist for the Prussian state, had begun his monumental research in heretofore forgotten documents. To Henry Reeve, later editor of the *Edinburgh*, Ranke's *House of the Brandenburgs* warranted a careful assessment for British readers because it laid the groundwork for future endeavors.[9] Reeve's admiration for Ranke's precision points ahead to Lord Acton's appeal for "scientific" history as an alternative to the amateur work of British historians like Macaulay; and Reeve, who had studied in Germany, makes clear that the Germans are setting standards.

Allied to the political narratives of Ranke and Macaulay are the sociological studies of Comte, Marx, and Engels (in *The Condition of the Working Class in England*, 1843). And yet another kind of history may be seen in the works of Alexis de Tocqueville and John Ruskin. Tocqueville's *Ancien Régime* (1850), like the earlier *Democracy in America*, undertakes the comparison of civilizations. Tocqueville looks back to prerevolutionary

France in an attempt to define the nature of its civilization, the roots of its failure, the ways in which its institutions have survived. The same order of questions underlie British histories, like Carlyle's of the French Revolution, or Macaulay's, which emphasizes the Glorious Revolution a century earlier. But Ruskin is perhaps the historian who comes closest in spirit to Tocqueville. *Stones of Venice* (1851) combines art history with social history, and Venice becomes for Ruskin the civilization that speaks to other civilizations, that illuminates patterns in Rome or Athens or modern London. Ruskin's cultural history demonstrates the importance of historical perspective to men and women concerned about the standing of their own transitional age with historians to come.

The English at mid-century share with continental writers a relatively new historical interest, one even more pertinent for our discussion here. There had of course been a long tradition of classical literary studies, and histories of Greek and Roman literature continue to appear at mid-century. Book lists from Oxford and Cambridge, apart from staple works on religion, consist mainly of classical texts and exegeses. For that matter, histories of English literature reach at least as far back as Thomas Warton's in the eighteenth century, and Shakespearean as well as antiquarian studies remain popular. Still, Henry Hallam's *Introduction to the Literature of Europe during the Fifteenth, Sixteenth, and Seventeenth Centuries* (1837–39) represents a large step toward comprehensive and modern literary history. We have seen how Tennyson's friend and Henry Hallam's son, Arthur Hallam, typifies the growing reverence for Dante among his contemporaries; he also shares a broader interest in historical periods, defining literature in terms of its era. Another of Tennyson's friends, James Spedding, was to win a reputation for his protracted studies of Francis Bacon, and one of Tennyson's admirers, Charles Kingsley, lectured at Queen's College, London, about the desirability of English literature for educational purposes. Even in these random instances we can recognize the movement toward English studies as an acceptable and legitimate part of intellectual training.

The growing commitment to literary history and the relationship it bears to mid-century assessments of letters are evident in something as unlikely as *Notes and Queries*, which entered on its own long history in November 1849. According to its prospectus, *Notes and Queries* would offer "a most useful supplement to works already in existence—a treasury for enriching future editions of them—and an important contribution towards a more perfect history than we yet possess of our language, our literature, and those to whom we owe them."[10] Such a statement, basing its appeal on what is assumed to be widespread sympathy, invites several speculations. *Notes and Queries* represents both a voracious curiosity and a happy eclecticism. "When found, make note of": Captain Cuttle's maxim, prominent on the journal's title page, invites inquiry that will theoretically lead to a "more perfect history." But might not aimless inquiry also lead to the endless pigeonholes of a Mr. Casaubon, in which one fact rivals another, and from which emerges no coherent view whatever? There were arguments on either side. In France, a powerful advocate of historical materials was Hippolyte Taine, who would soon publish his *History of English Literature* (1856-59). Taine predicated literary interpretations on assessments of national and historical conditions. So, in a less exclusive way, did Sainte-Beuve, who began his *Causeries du lundi* in the months that saw publication of *Notes and Queries*.

Sainte-Beuve says that his models for the *Causeries* are English periodical essays, which he praises as exploratory and diffident. To Matthew Arnold, who damned English periodicals, and who started in these years to learn from Sainte-Beuve, the French critic represents all the standards and coherence lacking in English criticism, because Sainte-Beuve's sense of a "more perfect history," the understanding of the man and the moment, include the expectation of comprehensive judgments. Arnold might have censured *Notes and Queries* by quoting Sainte-Beuve: "For choose one must, because the primary conditions of good taste, after all has been understood, is to cease from endless voyaging and finally settle somewhere and take a stand."[11] The comment, from one of Sainte-Beuve's best-known essays, "What Is a Classic?" (1850), expresses an ideal for criticism which Arnold can espouse, an ideal at odds, however, with his understanding of English critical directions. For Arnold, the historical impulse can lead anywhere—witness Francis Newman and Bishop Colenso. Is the effect the inability to choose, the "endless voyaging" that speaks to a want of English culture? Arnold is not alone in coming to fear so.

Once again, George Lewes helps to define the problem. Modern lives lack, according to Lewes, a "common center." Because there is "no emanation from one common faith," there is the impossibility of the highest aesthetic achievement such as epic; more importantly, there is a general apprehension of something that he calls *anarchy*. With the work of Comte in mind, Lewes advocates a new "Social Science" to stabilize language (as Arnold was later to advocate an academy), and he complains about pseudo-philosophy, about untalented yet uncensured writers, and about a drama crippled by false principles.[12] He shares with Arnold great misgivings about the climate for literature. We might also remember in this context the works of men like Robert Mackay and Charles Radcliffe, whose criticisms are extreme but not untypical. By damning a pervasive *realism* (a term that can mean a range of ills from an exhaustively descriptive fictional art to a general nominalism in social and philosophic thought), these men charge that their society has lost, beyond "one common faith," the capacity to think mythically, to understand symbols, to conceive of and to express the elemental. They argue, as did Blake and Shelley before them, that intellectual anarchy begets a radical empiricism, itself a sign of failed imagination. Long before Arnold's writings of the 1860s, the terms *culture* and *anarchy* occur with surprising frequency, apparently because, whether political revolution is or is not imminent, apprehensions about cultural dissolution are widespread.

Possibly no one feared anarchy more than Carlyle. Always emphasizing the spiritual, or more often the lack of the spiritual in contemporary life, Carlyle anticipates Nietzsche in hoping for an outside authority, to whom obedience would prove as necessary as it was desirable. Whether writing "Characteristics" twenty years before, or speaking at mid-century about the life of his friend Sterling, Carlyle conceives of nineteenth-century life as chaotic, and through the chaos he imagines—to use his own recurrent figure—the contemporary pilgrim making his way. Carlyle suggests a further aspect of the anarchy feared by Lewes and Arnold, inasmuch as his language raises the specter of Babel: the breakdown of communication anticipated by Lewes in his call for Social Science.

As the monthly sections of *Latter-Day Pamphlets* appeared, critics received them with hostility. Carlyle's shots at Jesuitism, red-tape, model prisons, false heroes, Downing Street, and "Stump Orators" actually reflect the substance of innumerable contemporary complaints about a hypocritical and "veneering," society, the England of "Vanity Fair." What disturbs critics about *Latter-Day Pamphlets* is less Carlyle's censure than his manner. His anger is unforgivable because inappropriate for civilized discourse. Whereas Arnold by the time of *Latter-Day Pamphlets* can dismiss Carlyle as a "moral desperado," Lewes comes to his defense. He acknowledges that Carlyle is indeed irate, intemperate, irascible. But what, he asks, should we expect from a writer who has always scorned tolerance?[13] By supporting a writer proud of his intolerance and close, in the eyes of other critics, to the language of Babel (some said Billingsgate), Lewes anticipates the arguments of John Stuart Mill's "On Liberty" (1859), upholding the rights of a minority and fearing a tyrannical majority. We have the anomaly, nonetheless, of an English Democrat pleading for an anti-Democrat and overlooking in Carlyle what he identifies as a disintegrating force in his time.

Possibly it disturbed Lewes less than it disturbed other commentators that Carlyle, strong apologist for men-of-letters, should lose his manners when the higher journalism appeared to be coming of age. For the pride in journalism to a great extent rested on the issue of tone. How important an appropriate tone of reviewing had become can be seen in the response of Dickens's *Household Narrative* to the death (in 1850) of Francis Jeffrey, early dean of reviewers for the *Quarterly*, who had treated Keats and others "so savage and tartarly." Dickens (or his colleague) says that since the early years of the century Jeffrey had mended his ways, had allowed what Stuart Tave would call "the amiable humorist" to come through, and had therefore died amid the love and respect of fellow writers.[14] (Croker, the other *bête noire* of the English Romantic poets, lived on until 1857, still working on his study of the French Revolution.)

It may well be desirable to advocate good literary manners, and certainly the general level of discourse in mid-century magazines was higher than it had been in the early days of *Edinburgh* and *Quarterly*, or even a generation later in the early days of *Fraser's*. Carlyle, however, raises a more profound issue than tolerance or good manners. He had always paraded as a sort of German-Scottish version of the Old Testament prophets, expressing himself categorically in his either-or rhetoric. (*Past and Present*, 1843, is contemporaneous with Kierkegaard's *Either-or*.) But *Latter-Day Pamphlets* are peculiarly absolute in their manner, far more so, for instance, than the *Life of Sterling* (1851), which pays public homage to a friend. If we think by contrast of Arnold's later suavity, his "kid-glove" style, and his often patronizing repetitions, or of John Henry Newman's subtle modulations, the shifts in tone that reflect a shift in audience ("Christ upon the Waters" as opposed to *Lectures on Certain Difficulties*), we can appreciate that Carlyle is not persuading but rather shouting at his audience: an Amos come to make his point, too impatient to argue. Granting a public conscience to this man-of-letters, is there any longer a sure sense of a public there to listen? Does Carlyle not accept himself as a voice in the wilderness, more likely than not to be misunderstood? Implicitly he deflates the rhetoric of men like John W. Kaye about the stature of "the fourth estate," as well as the remark by John Henry Newman about the concerted impact of the fourth estate. For if few periodicals represent Roman Catholic persuasions (the *Dublin* and the admirable *Rambler* are exceptions), if they tend from Newman's point of view toward a "liberal" position, are they as a whole any more coherent than the various interests they represent? In terms of critical judgments they certainly are not.

Once more, I am not arguing the lack of critical generosity among critics of the time or a failure to see that many of their contemporaries deserve their praise. We know with what adulation Charles Kingsley and others received *In Memoriam*; we know how many readers welcomed *David Copperfield*—and with what gratitude. Reviewers did strenuously object to the Newman brothers and to the Pre-Raphaelites, but such extreme censure was rare. So to say that critics of the time are apprehensive about their society and about the place of literature in their society is not to say that there was a hostile literary climate. Writers disagreed, debated, argued, reviewed each other, kept up literary gossip. The problem lay in finding standards. Not only does the critical theory of the time tend to honor modern works with assumptions appropriate for different kinds of literary excellence (as we have seen in earlier chapters), critics themselves are aware that something is amiss. Hence, Ruskin's appeal for the few stoical lamps to light up a cultural darkness, and Kingsley's cry for greater sincerity, and Arnold's hope for a redeeming classicism.

As Arnold himself illustrated, the shape of later criticism seems determined by shared perceptions at mid-century. There is in Arnold's formulations (as there is analogously in those of Ruskin and Newman, and in the shrewd commentaries of Richard Simpson)[15] a self-imposed reasonableness in the face of cultural threats—threats manifest in men like Carlyle and Kingsley, who seem out of control. In Arnold's struggle—about to begin in these years—to define the function of criticism we can appreciate a crisis facing men-of-letters. For whether there is or can be a healthy literary climate seems to depend on insoluble but unavoidable questions: What is a literary work? What are its limits? What is its genesis? Is there a way of defining its value? or its relationship to society? or its autonomy or authenticity? Needless to say, such questions remained unanswered, remained to some extent unformulated. But they lie behind mid-century estimates of literature just as they haunt the literature itself.

I don't presume here to account for all the doubts and misgivings in mid-century writers. We are considering phenomena for which there can be no simple explanations. The revolutions of 1848 had reminded men and women of potentially huge social changes; unsolved social problems evidently called for attention; and there was widespread recognition of class tensions and of the failure of education in a society only half literate. Yet while one can point to this or that example of social conscience, to Carlyle, say, or Kingsley, the writers I have dealt with in this book do not seem at mid-century primarily concerned with political and social issues. Nearly all are preoccupied with individual crises of identity or faith, with the autobiographical account of themselves as pilgrims. The crises elaborated by Francis Newman or Alfred Tennyson, Robert Browning or Arthur Clough, bear on social issues, but they seem to have more profound causes. Religion, as we have seen so often, has to be one of the causes; the new science is probably another.

We might briefly reconsider the impact of scientific thinking, turning again to Charles Kingsley. Kingsley identifies Alton Locke in relation to the new sociology (class struggles, historical necessity, statistics), but he speaks also of Alton's inexplicable longings, his sense of an order beyond the circumstances of history. Alton tries to depict his mature self in terms of his pathetic journey from a Dissenting home, through slop tailor work, Chartism, love, and final, exiled defeat. But his most powerful self-perception may come in the unexplained dream of himself adopting various forms of life in a long, evolutionary process. Like so many of the retrospective, elegiac writers of his time, Alton is disturbed by thoughts of Evolution, which place the development of his own life in dwarfing perspective.

Kingsley's contemporaries emphasized geology and other sciences synthesized in evolutionary theories; they were not unaware of chemistry and physics. Dickens hoped to lure Michael Faraday into writing a popular series of articles for *Household Words*, and Faraday was busy in 1850 with his experiments on light and lecturing on his findings. Like Wordsworth and Dickens and Ruskin, J. P. Joule, another physicist, spent time in the Alps, using Swiss waterfalls to demonstrate the conversion of energy in the form of heat. Science, coincidentally, owes the Second Law of Thermodynamics to the year 1850, and many scientists were at work on what the German Clausius would soon call *entropy*. Now, while there may be no direct connection between the common usage of the word *waste* in mid-century literature and the study of entropy by contemporary scientists, there are apt metaphoric connections.

For David Copperfield, the first remembered impression of his Alpine experience is beneficent; so, in "The Lamp of Memory," is Ruskin's recollection in the Jura. Both writers come to link the mountain loneliness with human isolation; both formulate a nightmare world potentially devoid of life and hope. Just as Kingsley allows Alton Locke the unflattering dream about his possible evolution, so Dickens and Ruskin posit a spatial equivalent among the mountains. The sublime vision takes place, but tied to a vision of physical and psychic waste. Waste land and waste water—Dickens connects the two in a late Retrospect—often fuse in a writer's sense of a world hostile to civilization. We have seen Browning and his dream of the rasping German professor, emblem of an ultimate loneliness in a world committed to scientific rigor; and Tennyson, for whom science becomes at best a threat to love and belief; and Francis Newman, whose autobiography is a lonely assessment of his life in terms of the new science.

At various times I have tried to equate a growing autobiographical consciousness with both a heightened self-awareness and a disturbing realization of human frailty. Even Charlotte Brontë, urging her heroine to independence, allows Jane Eyre repeated visions of physical waste, and Jane speaks appropriately of "imagination's boundless and trackless waste" (chapter 16).[16] Ruskin proposes tradition in the form of monuments of art as a barrier against the waste. Carlyle imagines his modern pilgrim traversing the "Waste of Time." Clough tells of internal struggles with a modern Mephisto, a satirist of his "poetical self." Matthew Arnold writes haunting lyrics about an estranging sea or about desolate mountain spaces. In "Stanzas from the Grande Chartreuse," Arnold's perception of himself as caught between two worlds, the one dead, the other powerless to be born, conflates the historical with the religious and scientific, and Arnold's "trackless waste" is the Alps.

It is not science alone that generates feelings of sadness and isolation at mid-century, although science plays its part. Nor is the loss we read about restricted to Englishmen. David Masson, the Scottish critic, wrote in his "Wordsworth" essay (1850) that "new intellectual dispensations are like atmospheres; they overhang all countries at once."[17] This would certainly seem true of the obsessions with science, history, declining faith—and melancholia. In Melville's *Moby Dick* (1851), Ishmael goes to sea rather than put a bullet through his head. Baudelaire works at the lyrics that will result in *Les Fleurs du Mal* (1857); Flaubert tortures himself with Emma Bovary and all that she represents. In Russia, Dostoyevski experiences the exile and imprisonment that he will describe in *House of the Dead*. So much literature of the time grows out of and explores what Søren Kierkegaard calls "despair." And despair in Kierkegaard's 1850 book is *The Sickness unto Death*, the ultimate malady of the sensitive writer made aware in difficult times of the shrunken nature of faith and of calling.[18]

If we speculate a final time about the complex and often contradictory directions of mid-century literature, we might conclude with a few tentative observations. In the first place, then, there seems to be a disparity between the economic or political climate and the recurrent themes of the literature. A sense of unease, of potential Babel or anarchy, is not merely characteristic of a few writers, but rather a pervasive quality, a necessary complement to the new, irrepressible optimism symbolized by the Great Exhibition and invoked too often to summarize the times.

Moreover, while there is perhaps no such entity as a collective frame of mind—within a nation or across an age—we might well follow David Masson's hint and think of English writers not so much reflecting their own, local situation, complex as that may be, but expressing ideas, feelings, and apprehensions that they hold in common with writers abroad. Except incidentally, I have not made such connections in this study—and have in a sense kept my own work more provincial than the interests of Arnold, Lewes, and their contemporaries warrant. But comparative studies of literature focusing on limited periods of time could tell us much about the sociology of literature, about the ways that literature does or does not reflect its society.

One conclusion that I would not have expected at the beginning of this study has been evident in the last few pages. It is that mid-century writers, although excessively conscious about literary changes, about traditions, periods, and "the spirit of the age," share no perspective about what we might call *modernity*. Writers are aware, we could say, of their own contemporaneity, though unsure as to the nature of their accomplishment. The Pre-Raphaelites perhaps come closest to an assertion of modernity, but the Pre-Raphaelites publish a magazine surprisingly in tune with common taste of the day. An extraordinary awareness of time, a preoccupation with posterity, and a generous eclecticism lead to no easy historical categories—for them or for us. What might be explored is how far England differs in this from the United States, with its New England "American Rennaissance,"[19] or from the Russia of Tolstoi and Dostoyevski and Gogol, or the France of Baudelaire and Sainte-Beuve. We can at least say that there is in England no distinct literary school or movement—of the sort hoped for by defenders of *The Germ*—and no self-conscious attempt at a national literature. Certain provincialisms there obviously are and certain pruderies, as Thackeray complains in the preface to *Pendennis*, but these are not in any important sense the defining characteristics of the literature, and they are not held up by contemporaries as ideals to be attained. Later decades were to see rigorous standards of moral propriety with their effects in self-censure and aesthetic compromises. These were not yet central concerns at mid-century.

Having argued a kind of critical unsurety, a sense of inadequate standards, and an eclecticism that borders on chaos, I want finally to come back to the remarks of G. M. Young about the contemporary assessment of mid-century literature. Earlier, I spoke about the feeling apparently shared by Dickens and the Pre-Raphaelites, a feeling that there were indeed modern giants and that the age, with all its problems, could boast abundant talent. We might put this another way. For in spite of their reservations about the climate for literature, mid-century writers knew that great spirits were among them. If we bear in mind their doubts, if we remember their repeated expressions of isolation and their sense of false directions, we can still recognize a kind of muted pride. Dickens, like most of his countrymen, admired Tennyson; and Tennyson, though ambivalent about fiction, attended Dickens's banquet to celebrate the completion of *David Copperfield*. We might imagine them sitting with a larger group, aware—in a moment of generous foresight—that across the years their own names and the names of Wordsworth, Thackeray, Carlyle, Macaulay, Ruskin, the Brontës, the Brownings, the Newmans, Arnold, Clough, Kingsley, and the Rossettis would have to be remembered.

Notes

Preface

1. G. M. Young, "The Victorian Noon-Time," *Victorian Essays*, ed. W. D. Hancock (London: Oxford University Press, 1962).

I

1. Sir Nikolaus Pevsner, *High Victorian Design: A Study of the Exhibits of 1851* (London: Architectural Press, 1951), p. 17.
2. Thomas Carlyle, "The Present Time," *Latter-Day Pamphlets* (New York: Clarke, n.d.), p. 6.
3. Charles Dickens, "A Preliminary Word," *Household Words*, 30 March 1850, p. 1.
4. Quoted in Asa Briggs, *The Age of Improvement* (New York: David McKay, 1962), p. 25.
5. See, for example, *The Letters of Queen Victoria*, ed. E. F. Benson and R. B. Esher (London: Longmans, 1907); and *The Greville Memoirs, 1814–1860*, ed. Lytton Strachey and Roger Fulford (London: Macmillan, 1938), vol. 6.
6. Briggs, *The Age of Improvement*, p. 395.
7. Quoted in Pevsner, *High Victorian Design*, p. 16.
8. George R. Porter, *The Progress of the Nation*, a new edition (London: Knight, 1851), p. 1.
9. *Punch: or the London Charivari* 18 (1850): iv.
10. John Stores Smith, *Social Aspects* (London: Chapman, 1850), p. 167. Chapman, soon to engage George Eliot to edit the *Westminster*, was an active mid-century publisher. Among his important books were Robert Mackay's *Progress of the Intellect* and Francis Newman's *Phases of Faith*.
11. Carlyle, *Latter-Day Pamphlets*, p. 48.
12. See the introductory essays by Eileen Yeo and E. P. Thompson, in *The Unknown Mayhew* (New York: Pantheon, 1971). Another important document was reissued in 1850: Charles Hall's *The Effects of Civilization on the People in European States*, which had been virtually ignored for half a century.
13. Briggs, *The Age of Improvement*, p. 410.
14. *The Poems of Matthew Arnold*, ed. Kenneth Allott (London: Longmans, 1965), p. 228.
15. T. S. Eliot, "*In Memoriam*," *Ancient and Modern Essays* (London: Faber, 1936), p. 181.
16. Hallam Lord Tennyson, *Alfred Lord Tennyson: A Memoir* (London: Macmillan, 1898), 1: 304–5; James Knowles, in the *Nineteenth Century* 33 (1893): 182; quoted in *The Poems of Tennyson*, ed. Christopher Ricks (London: Longmans, 1969), p. 859.
17. Quoted in Humphry House, "Wordsworth's Fame," *All in Due Time* (London: Rupert Hart-Davis, 1955), p. 40.
18. The *O.E.D.* cites only one late eighteenth century use of the term.
19. "The Triumph of Love," *The Art-Journal*, January 1850, p. 9.

20. See, for example, *John Ruskin*, ed. E. T. Cook and Alexander Wedderburn (London: George Allen, 1904), 9:14 and 24:203–4. See also René Wellek, *A History of Modern Criticism, 1750–1950: The Age of Transition* (New Haven: Yale University Press, 1965), pp. 147–48.

21. Charles Kingsley, "On English Literature," *Introductory Lectures Delivered at Queen's College London* (1849), p. 57; "On English Composition," p. 33.

22. Thomas Carlyle, "The Hero as Man of Letters," *Heroes, Hero-Worship, and the Heroic in History* (New York: Clarke, n.d.), p. 148.

23. The recognition of the importance of periodical literature can be seen in the founding of the Research Society on Victorian Periodicals, which publishes the *Victorian Periodicals Newsletter*, and in the *Wellesley Index to Victorian Periodicals*, a work I find invaluable. Without listing each borrowing, I have used the *Wellesley Index* for many attributions.

24. See Leslie Marchand, *The Athenaeum: Mirror of Victorian Culture* (Chapel Hill: University of North Carolina Press, 1941) for a discussion of the *Athenaeum*'s history, contributors, policies. Allvar Ellegard's *The Readership of the Periodical Press in Mid-Victorian Britain* (Göteborg: Universitets Arsskrift, 1957) is a good guide to circulation figures, etc.

25. The "Receipts" can be found in *The George Eliot Letters*, ed. Gordon S. Haight (New Haven: Yale University Press, 1955), 8:369–70.

26. [J. W. Kaye], "Pendennis and the Literary Profession," *North British Review*, August 1850, pp. 199–200. Kaye's identification is thanks to the *Wellesley Index*.

27. For a survey of the literary profession, see, for example, John Gross's *The Rise and Fall of the Man of Letters* (London: Weidenfeld and Nicolson, 1969).

28. W. M. Thackeray, *Letters and Private Papers*, ed. Gordon Ray, 4 vols. (Cambridge: Harvard University Press, 1945), 2:636.

29. See, for example, Kellow Chesney, *The Anti-Society* (Boston: Gambit, 1970), chap. 1.

30. Martha Vicinus, *The Industrial Muse* (Bloomington: Indiana University Press, 1974), p. 1.

31. See John W. Dodds, "1849: Authorship and the Reading Public," *The Age of Paradox: A Biography of England, 1841–1851* (New York: Rhinehart, 1952), p. 374.

32. Louis James, *Fiction for the Working Man, 1830–1850* (London: Oxford University Press, 1963), *passim.*

33. On the matter of literacy, see Vicinus, *The Industrial Muse*, p. 26, and Lawrence Stone, "Literacy and Education in England, 1640-1900," *Past and Present* 42 (1969): 118–26.

34. See Richard D. Altick, "From Aldine to Everyman: Cheap Reprint Series of the English Classics, 1830–1906," *Studies in Bibliography*, ed. Fredson Bowers (Charlottesville: University of Virginia Press, 1958). See also Altick's *The English Common Reader* (Chicago: The University of Chicago Press, 1957).

35. "The Stage As It Is in 1850," *Bentley's Miscellany* 27 (1850): 300.

36. [George Lewes], unsigned article in the *Leader* 1 (1850); rpt. *Literary Criticism of G. H. Lewes*, ed. Alice R. Kaminsky (Lincoln: University of Nebraska Press, 1964), p. 146.

37. See Allardyce Nicoll, *A History of Early Nineteenth-Century Drama, 1800–1850* (Cambridge: Cambridge University Press, 1930).

II

1. Thomas Shaw, *Outlines of English Literature* (London: 1849; new American edition, Philadelphia: Tuckerman, 1859), p. 416.

2. [George Lewes?], "Death of Bowles," *Leader* 1 (1850): 86. The concerns and phraseology here, as in so many *Leader* reviews, suggest Lewes, who contributed a great deal. The Receipt Book implies at times almost single-handed production of the magazine. On Lewes's criticism see Morris Greenhut's "Lewes and the Classical Tradition in English Criticism," *Review of English Studies* 24 (1948) and Alice R. Kaminsky, *George Lewes as Literary Critic* (Syracuse: Syracuse University Press, 1968).

3. T. L. Peacock, "The Four Ages of Poetry," *Works of Thomas Love Peacock*, ed. H. F. B. Brett-Smith and C. E. Jones, 10 vols. (London: Constable, 1934), 8:20–21.

4. I rely here on M. H. Abrams's *The Mirror and the Lamp: Romantic Theory and the Critical Tradition* (1953; rpt. New York: W. W. Norton, 1958), pp. 144–47.

5. William Wordsworth, *The Prose Works*, ed. W. J. B. Owen and J. W. Smyser, 3 vols. (Oxford: Clarendon, 1974), 3:65.

6. [Aubrey De Vere], "Landor's Poetry," *Edinburgh Review* 92 (1850): 410-30.

7. Alba Warren, *English Poetic Theory, 1825-1865* (Princeton: Princeton University Press, 1950), pp. 4-5.

8. Thomas Babington Macaulay, "Milton," *Critical and Miscellaneous Essays*, 2 vols. (London: Dent, 1966), 1:155. Cited hereafter by page in the text.

9. Quoted in John Clive's "The *Edinburgh Review*: The Life and Death of a Periodical," *Essays in the History of Publishing*, ed. Asa Briggs (London: Longman, 1974), p. 124.

10. Jeremy Bentham, *The Rationale of Reward*, ed. John Bowring, *Works* (London: 1843; rpt. New York: Russell and Russell, 1962), 2:263.

11. Cf. Coleridge's concern for "language mechanized . . . into a barrel-organ" in chapter 2 of *Biographia Literaria*, ed. J. Shawcross (London: Oxford University Press, 1907; rpt. 1962), p. 25; and Tennyson's "sad mechanic exercise" in *In Memoriam* 5, *Poems*, p. 868.

12. John Orchard, "A Dialogue on Art," *The Germ*, ed. W. M. Rossetti (1899; rpt. New York: AMS Press, 1968), p. 99.

13. J. S. Mill, *On Bentham and Coleridge*, ed. F. R. Leavis (London: Chatto and Windus, 1950), p. 106.

14. Raymond Williams, *Culture and Society, 1780-1950* (New York: Columbia University Press, 1958), p. 52.

15. *The Letters of Matthew Arnold to Arthur Hugh Clough*, ed. H. F. Lowry (Oxford: Clarendon, 1932; rpt. 1968), p. 99.

16. [George Lewes], "Death of Bowles," *Leader* 1:86.

17. *Life and Letters of Lord Macaulay*, ed. G. O. Trevelyan, 2 vols. in 1 (New York: Harper, 1875), 2:239; Arthur Bryant, *Macaulay* (New York: Appleton, 1933), p. 140.

18. George Gilfillan, *A Second Gallery of Literary Portraits* (Edinburgh: James Hogg, 1850), p. 119.

19. On Vico's impact on English thought see Max Frisch's introduction to Giambattista Vico, *Autobiography*, trans. M. H. Fisch and T. G. Bergin (Ithaca: Cornell University Press, 1944) and *Giambattista Vico: An International Symposium*, ed. G. Tagliacozzo and H. V. White (Baltimore: The Johns Hopkins University Press, 1969). See also P. W. Day, *Matthew Arnold and the Philosophy of Vico* (Auckland: University of Auckland Press, 1964).

20. See, for example, P. Demetz, *Marx, Engels, and the Poets* (Chicago: The University of Chicago Press, 1965). For a background of Marx in England, see Isaiah Berlin, "Exile in England: The First Phase," *Karl Marx, His Life and Environment* (New York: Oxford University Press, 1966).

21. Herbert Spencer, *Autobiography*, 2 vols. (New York: Appleton, 1904), 1:360. J. D. Y. Peel's *Herbert Spencer: The Evolution of a Sociologist* (New York: Basic Books, 1971) offers an excellent discussion of *Social Statics.*

22. Thomas Carlyle, *Heroes, Hero-Worship, and the Heroic in History* (New York: Clarke, n.d), p. 33.

23. Harriet Martineau, *A History of the Thirty Years' Peace, 1816-1846*, 4 vols. (London: George Bell, 1878 ed.), 4:637.

24. *Two Notebooks of Thomas Carlyle*, ed. Charles Eliot Norton (1898; rpt. Mamaroneck, N.Y.: Paul P. Appel, 1972), p. 151.

25. G. S. R. Kitson-Clark, "The Romantic Element, 1830-1850," in *Studies in Social History*, ed. J. H. Plumb (1955; rpt. Freeport, N.Y.: Books for Libraries Press, 1969), p. 215.

26. See, for example, Lewes's review of *The Prelude, Leader* 1, 17 August 1850; rpt. *Literary Criticism of G. H. Lewes*, ed. Alice R. Kaminsky (Lincoln: University of Nebraska Press, 1964), pp. 78-84. For this principle as for much else, Lewes is specifically indebted to Carlyle.

27. Thomas Carlyle, "The State of German Literature," *Critical and Miscellaneous Essays* (Chicago: Clarke, n.d.), 3:67.

28. Carlyle, *Heroes, Hero-Worship, and the Heroic in History*, p. 76. Cited hereafter by page in the text.

29. Thomas Carlyle, "Signs of the Times," *Critical and Miscellaneous Essays*, 3:12.

30. As he grew older, Carlyle himself became more skeptical about all art, and he was never sanguine about the novel. See below and chapter 7.

31. Patricia Ball, "Sincerity: The Rise and Fall of a Critical Term," *Modern Language Review* 59 (1964): 3. See also Lionel Trilling's *Sincerity and Authenticity* (Cambridge: Harvard University Press, 1971).

32. Letter to John Brown, 11 May 1848. Quoted in John W. Dodds, "Thackeray's Irony," *Thackeray: A Critical Portrait* (Toronto: University of Toronto Press, 1941), p. 114.

33. Ball, "Sincerity," pp. 3–4.

34. [J. Westland Marston], "*In Memoriam*," *Athenaeum*, 28 March 1850; quoted and identified in Leslie Marchand, *The Athenaeum: Mirror of Victorian Culture* (Chapel Hill: University of North Carolina Press, 1941), p. 278.

35. An indication of the currency of the term *power* is Ruskin's reliance on it. The entire second section of pt. I, vol. I of *Modern Painters* treats "Of Power."

36. J. S. Mill, "Nature," *Three Essays on Religion* (1874), in *The Philosophy of John Stuart Mill*, ed. Marshall Cohen (New York: Modern Library, 1961), p. 445.

37. [Charles Kingsley], review of *In Memoriam, Fraser's Magazine* 12 (September 1850): 217; rpt. *Miscellanies* (1859). Identified in the *Wellesley Index*.

38. It did apply. In *Barchester Towers* (1857), Trollope compares his art of characterization with the potential of photography and the daguerreotype (chapter 20).

39. Bryan Waller Procter, "On English Poetry," quoted in Warren, *English Poetic Theory*, p. 13.

40. [Aubrey De Vere], "Taylor's *Eve of Conquest*," *Edinburgh Review* 99 (1849): 363–65.

41. Ibid., 360–61.

42. Ibid., 361.

43. See Abrams, *The Mirror and The Lamps*, chap. 4; and Abbie Findlay Potts, *The Elegiac Mode: Poetic Form in Wordsworth and Other Elegists* (Ithaca: Cornell University Press, 1967).

44. Bulwer-Lytton offers another exception. Bulwer saw himself adapting his Byronic heritage to the new age, in which fiction rather than poetry had become the dominant form. See Allan Conrad Christensen, *Edward Bulwer-Lytton: The Fiction of New Regions* (Athens: University of Georgia Press, 1976), chap. 1.

45. Tennyson, quoted in Geoffrey Tillotson, *Criticism and the Nineteenth Century* (London: Athlone, 1951), p. 213.

III

1. "In Memoriam," *Tait's Edinburgh Magazine*, August 1850; rpt. *Tennyson: In Memoriam: A Casebook*, ed. John Dixon Hunt (London: Macmillan, 1970), p. 84.

2. "In Memoriam," *Ainsworth's Magazine: A Miscellany of Romance, General Literature, and Art* 17 (1850): 558.

3. See Basil Willey, "Tennyson," *More Nineteenth-Century Studies* (1956; rpt. New York: Harper, 1966), p. 79.

4. Edgar Finley Shannon, Jr., *Tennyson and the Reviewers* (Cambridge: Harvard University Press, 1952), p. 163.

5. Harold G. Merriam, *Edward Moxon: Publisher of Poets* (New York: Columbia University Press), p. 176.

6. Ibid., p. 148.

7. George Gilfillan, *A Second Gallery of Literary Portraits* (Edinburgh: James Hogg, 1850), p. 215.

8. Robert and Elizabeth Watson, *George Gilfillan: Letters and Journals, with a Memoir* (London: Hodder and Stoughton, 1892), p. 140.

9. Gilfillan, *A Second Gallery*, p. 214.

10. E. D. H. Johnson, *The Alien Vision of Victorian Poetry* (Princeton: Princeton University Press, 1952), pp. ix–x.

11. Edward Fitzgerald, *Letters and Literary Remains* (London: Macmillan, 1889), quoted in *The Poems of Tennyson*, ed. Christopher Ricks (London: Longman, 1969), p. 856.

12. [W. E. Gladstone], "Works and Life of Giacomo Leopardi," *Quarterly Review* 86 (1850): 310.

13. John Ruskin, *Modern Painters*, 3, *Works*, ed. E. T. Cook and Alexander Wedderburn (London: George Allen, 1903), 5:205.

14. Quoted in T. Herbert Warren, "Tennyson and Dante," *Essays of Poets and Poetry Ancient and Modern* (London: 1906; rpt. London: Kennicat, 1970), p. 261.

15. Hallam Lord Tennyson, *Alfred Lord Tennyson: A Memoir* (London: Macmillan, 1898), p. 304.

16. Quoted in *Poems of Tennyson*, p. 859.

17. Jerome Buckley, *Tennyson: The Growth of a Poet* (1960; rpt. Boston: Houghton Mifflin, 1965), p. 119.

18. Warren, "Tennyson and Dante," p. 251.

19. Arthur Hallam, "On Some Characteristics of Modern Poetry, and on the Lyrical Poems of Alfred Tennyson," rpt. in Hunt, ed., *Tennyson: a Casebook*, pp. 56-57.

20. Valerie Pitt, *Tennyson Laureate* (Toronto: University of Toronto Press, 1963), p. 114. See also E. B. Mattes, *In Memoriam: The Way of a Soul* (New York: Exposition Press, 1951), on Tennyson and Hallam.

21. Tennyson, "To Dante," *Poems*, p. 1192.

22. W. S. Landor, "Dante," *Fraser's Magazine* 12 (1850): 685, in *Poems*, selected, intro. Geoffrey Grigson (Carbondale: Southern Illinois University Press, n.d.), p. 180.

23. See William De Sua, *Dante into English* (Chapel Hill: University of North Carolina Press, 1964) and Werner Friedrich, *Dante's Fame Abroad* (Chapel Hill: University of North Carolina Press, 1950).

24. "Article I," *Quarterly Review* 171 (1850): 11.

25. Thomas Babington Macaulay, "Milton," *Critical and Miscellaneous Essays*, 2 vols. (London: Dent, 1966), 1:164.

26. [Richard Church], "Dante," *Christian Remembrancer* (1850): 3; rpt. *Essays and Reviews* (1854).

27. Ibid., 76.

28. Ibid., 39.

29. Ibid., 43. While I emphasize Carlyle's influence, most of what Carlyle, Macaulay, Church, and other early Victorian writers say about Dante had been anticipated in the lectures and writings of Coleridge.

30. Ibid., 39.

31. Herbert Lindenberger, *On Wordsworth's Prelude* (Princeton: Princeton University Press, 1963), pp. 272-73. Matthew Arnold argues similarly in "Wordsworth," saying that, in the 1840s "Tennyson drew to himself and away from Wordsworth, the poetry-reading public." *Complete Prose Works*, ed. R. H. Super (Ann Arbor: University of Michigan Press, 1973), 9:37.

32. Quoted in Lindenberger, *On Wordsworth's Prelude*, p. 277. That many magazines chose not to review *The Prelude* may be attributable to the sense that, after a flood of obituaries, the public had had enough Wordsworth.

33. Ibid.

34. Ibid., p. 277.

35. Ibid., p. 276.

36. [Charles Kingsley], review of *The Prelude, Fraser's Magazine* 12 (1850): 124. There were favorable reviews in *Ainsworth's* and *Household Narrative*, among popular magazines. Brimley's review in *Fraser's* (see below) was very favorable, and Masson and other readers admired *The Prelude*.

37. [Charles Kingsley], review of *In Memoriam, Fraser's Magazine* 12 (1850): 217.

38. George Lewes, "Wordsworth's *Prelude*," *Leader*, 10 August 1850; rpt. *Literary Criticism of G. H. Lewes*, ed. Alice R. Kaminsky (Lincoln: University of Nebraska Press), pp. 78-84.

39. George Brimley, "Wordsworth," *Fraser's Magazine* 13 (June-July 1851): 120, 148.

40. Kingsley, "*In Memoriam*," 217.

41. Charles Williams, *The Figure of Beatrice* (New York: Noonday, 1961), p. 13.

42. Josephine Miles, "Poetry of the 1840's," *The Primary Language of Poetry in the 1740's and 1840's* (Berkeley and Los Angeles: University of California Press, 1950), p. 258.

43. Ibid., p. 258.

44. Ibid., p. 263.
45. D. G. James, "Wordsworth and Tennyson," *Proceedings of the British Academy* 36 (1950):127.
46. Karl Weintraub, "Autobiography and Historical Consciousness," *Critical Inquiry* 1, no. 4 (June 1975): 821.
47. James, "Wordsworth and Tennyson," p. 119.
48. Thomas Carlyle, *Heroes, Hero-Worship, and the Heroic in History* (New York: Clarke, n.d.), p. 160.
49. Ibid., p. 86.
50. *Poems of Tennyson*, p. 946.
51. William Wordsworth, *The Prelude*, ed. E. de Selincourt and H. Darbishire (Oxford: Clarendon, 1959), p. 481.

IV

1. William Michael Rossetti, "*The Bothie of Tober-na-Vuolich*," *The Germ*, ed. W. M. Rossetti (1899; rpt. New York: AMS Press, 1965), p. 34.
2. Carl G. Jung, *Memories, Dreams, Reflections*, recorded and ed. Aniela Jaffé, trans. Richard and Clara Winston (New York: Pantheon, 1961), pp. 4–5.
3. *The Letters of Matthew Arnold, 1848–1888*, ed. George W. E. Russell, 2 vols. (London: Macmillan, 1895), 2:9.
4. Rossetti, "*The Strayed Reveller; and other Poems*," *The Germ*, p. 84.
5. The exception was George J. Cayley's *Sir Reginald Mohun*, originally to have been reviewed by Clough.
6. Rossetti, "*The Strayed Reveller*," *The Germ*, p. 84.
7. See, for example, *The Letters of Matthew Arnold to Arthur Hugh Clough*, ed. H. F. Lowry (Oxford: Clarendon, 1932; rpt. 1968), p. 120.
8. Rossetti, "*The Strayed Reveller*," *The Germ*, p. 85.
9. Lawrence Durrell, *Balthazar* (New York: Dutton, 1968), p. 245.
10. [Charles Kingsley], "The Strayed Reveller and Other Poems" *Fraser's Magazine* 29 (1849): 566; rpt. *Matthew Arnold: The Critical Heritage*, ed. Carl Dawson (London: Routledge & Kegan Paul, 1973), pp. 41–46. See also W. E. Aytoun, unsigned review, *Blackwood's Magazine* 66 (1849): 340–46. Aytoun describes Arnold as though he were a "spasmodic," a term he soon applied to Alexander Smith.
11. Matthew Arnold, "Wordsworth," *Complete Prose Work* ed. R. H. Super (Ann Arbor: University of Michigan Press, 1973), 9:53.
12. *Poems of Matthew Arnold*, ed. Kenneth Allott (London: Longman, 1965), p. 226.
13. Quoted in ibid., p. 226.
14. Ibid., p. 227. Arnold's mentor, Sainte-Beuve, quotes the passage from Eckermann in "What Is a Classic" (October 1850). *The Literary Criticism of Sainte-Beuve*, ed. E. R. Marks (Lincoln: University of Nebraska Press, 1971), pp. 89–90.
15. *Unpublished Letters of Matthew Arnold*, ed. Arnold Whitridge (New Haven: Yale University Press, 1923), p. 17.
16. Charles Mackay, *Egeria; or the Spirit of Nature, and Other Poems* (London: David Bogue, 1850), p. xx.
17. Ibid., p. 2.
18. For a discussion of Arnold's treatment of nature, see, for example, Dwight A. Culler, *Imaginative Reason: The Poetry of Matthew Arnold* (New Haven: Yale University Press, 1966).
19. Arnold, *Letters to Clough*, p. 120.
20. Charles Radcliffe, *Proteus; or the Unity of Nature* (1850; 2d ed., London: Macmillan, 1877), pp. 7–9.
21. Arnold, *Letters to Clough*, p. 71.
22. *Letters of Matthew Arnold*, 1:5.
23. Arnold, *Letters to Clough*, p. 107.
24. Kathleen Tillotson, "Rugby 1850: Arnold, Clough, Walrond, and *In Memoriam*," *Mid-Victorian Studies* (London: Athlone, 1965), p. 183.

25. *The Poems of Tennyson*, ed. Christopher Ricks (London: Longman, 1969), pp. 911-12.
26. See above, note 23.
27. Ibid., p. 145. Like his attitude to Wordsworth's poetry, Arnold's feelings for Clough are ambivalent. He says, for example, (p. 129): "I really have clung to you in spirit more than to any man—and have never seriously been estranged from you." This is in 1853.
28. Ibid., p. 96.
29. Ibid., p. 99.
30. *The Correspondence of Arthur Hugh Clough*, ed. Frederick L. Mulhauser (London: Oxford University Press, 1957), 1:287.
31. Arthur Hugh Clough, "Recent English Poetry" (1853), *Selected Prose Works*, ed. B. B. Trawick (University, Ala.: Alabama University Press, 1964), p. 163.
32. Ibid., p. 144.
33. Arnold, *Letters to Clough*, p. 99.
34. Rossetti, *"The Bothie of Tober-na-Vuolich," The Germ*, p. 34.
35. Ibid., p. 34.
36. Ibid., p. 20.
37. Ibid., p. 44.
38. In *The P. R. B. Journal: William Michael Rossetti's Diary of the Pre-Raphaelite Brotherhood, 1849–1853*, ed. William E. Fredeman (London: Oxford University Press, 1975), pp. 130–54.
39. But see the comparative figures in Josephine Miles's charts ("Poetry of the 1840's, *The Primary Language of Poetry* [Berkeley and Los Angeles: University of California Press, 1950]), which indicate a kind of "classical moderation" in both poets.
40. William Makepeace Thackeray, letter to Clough, in *The Correspondence of Arthur Hugh Clough*, p. 228.
41. *The Poems of Arthur Hugh Clough*, ed. F. L. Mulhauser (London: Oxford University Press, 1974), p. 249. Cited hereafter by page in the text.
42. Asa Briggs, *The Age of Improvement* (New York: David McKay, 1962), p. 410.
43. Evelyn Greenberger, *Arthur Hugh Clough: The Growth of a Poet's Mind* (Cambridge: Harvard University Press, 1970), pp. 170–71.
44. For a sympathetic but overly optimistic discussion of Clough's beliefs, see Michael Timko, *Innocent Victorian: The Satiric Poetry of Arthur Hugh Clough* (Athens: Ohio University Press, 1963.
45. Søren Kierkegaard, *Journals*, quoted in Walter Lowrie, *Kierkegaard* (1938; rpt. New York: Harper, 1962), 2:416.
46. Jerome Buckley mentions Kierkegaard's *Concluding Scientific Postscript* as "an unexpected yet oddly apposite gloss on the faith of *In Memoriam* . . . ," *Tennyson: The Growth of a Poet* (1960; rpt. Boston: Houghton Mifflin, 1965), p. 125.
47. Kierkegaard, *Journals*, quoted in Lowrie, 2:450.
48. Kierkegaard, *Either/Or*, trans. D. F. and L. M. Swenson, 2 vols. (Princeton: Princeton University Press, 1959), 1: 19.
49. Kierkegaard, *Journals*, quoted in Lowrie, 2: 416.
50. Kierkegaard, *Christian Discourses*, quoted in Lowrie, 2:456.
51. Walter E. Houghton, *The Poetry of Clough: An Essay in Revelation* (New Haven: Yale University Press, 1963), pp. 160–61.
52. J. W. von Goethe, *Werke* (Frankfurt: Insel, 1966), p. 16.
53. [George Lewes], "Pendennis," *Leader*, 21 December 1850, p. 929.
54. Greenberger, *Clough*, p. 177.
55. Harriet Martineau, *Autobiography*, 2 vols. (Boston: Chapman, 1878), 2:28.
56, Benedetto Croce, *Guide to Aesthetics*, trans., intro. Patrick Romanell (New York: Library of Liberal Arts, 1965), p. 44.
57. David M. Moir, *Sketches of the Poetical Literature of the Past Half Century* (1851; 3d ed., Edinburgh: Blackwood, 1856), p. 280.
58. William Rossetti, "*Christmas-Eve and Easter-Day*," *The Germ*, p. 186.
59. Ibid., p. 188.
60. Ibid., p. 192.
61. Robert Browning, *Poetical Works* (London: Oxford University Press, 1905; rpt. 1960), p. 97.

62. Robert Langbaum, *The Poetry of Experience: The Dramatic Monologue in Modern Literary Tradition* (1957; rpt. New York: Norton, 1963), p. 81.

63. [George Lewes], *Leader*, 30 March 1850, p. 13.

64. *Letters of Robert and Elizabeth Barrett Browning* (Cambridge: Belknap, 1969), 2: 731-32. Letter of May 25, 1846.

65. William Irvine and Park Honan, *The Book, the Ring, and the Poet: A Biography of Robert Browning* (New York: McGraw Hill, 1974), p. 261.

66. Letter of October 1849, quoted in ibid., p. 263.

67. J. Hillis Miller, *The Disappearance of God: Five Nineteenth-Century Writers* (Cambridge: Belknap, 1963), p. 104.

68. Ibid., p. 109. For another approach to the question of Browning's poetic voices, see Barbara Melchior, *Browning's Poetry of Reticence* (London: Oliver and Boyd, 1968).

69. *Letters of Robert and Elizabeth Barrett Browning*, 2:73; The text of the letter allows several variant readings.

70. Miller, *Disappearance of God*, p. 97.

71. Jung, *Memories, Dreams, Reflections, passim.*

72. Browning, *Poetical Works*, p. 406. Cited hereafter by page in the text.

73. Lewes, *Leader*, 27 April 1850, p. 111.

74. Ibid.

75. Anonymous review, *Spectator* 23, (6 April 1850): 329; rpt. *Browning: The Critical Heritage*, ed. D. Smalley and Boyd Litzinger (London: Routledge, 1970), p. 139.

76. Anonymous review, *Athenaeum*, 6 April 1850, pp. 370-71; rpt. *Browning: The Critical Heritage*, p. 138.

77. See, for example, Ian Jack, *Browning's Major Poetry* (Oxford, Clarendon, 1973), p. 127.

78. William Clyde De Vane, "The Virgin and the Dragon," *Yale Review*, 37 (September 1947): 35.

79. Thomas Hardy, *Tess of the d'Urbervilles*, ed. Scott Elledge (New York: Norton, 1965), p. 98.

80. Since, as Ian Watt argues, the "inward" nature of Puritanism lies behind fiction like Defoe's, Browning's "novelistic" tendencies have historical precedent (see chapter 7 below). Ian Watt, *The Rise of the Novel: Studies in Defoe, Richardson, and Fielding* (London: Chatto and Windus, 1960), pp. 78-80. See also E. LeRoy Lawson, *Very Sure of God: Religious Language in the Poetry of Robert Browning* (Vanderbilt: University of Tennessee Press, 1974).

81. Robert Browning, *Browning's Essay on Shelley, etc.* [Percy reprints no. 3], ed. H. F. B. Brett-Smith (Boston: Houghton Mifflin, 1921), p. 68.

82. Ibid., p. 86.

83. For an excellent analysis of Browning's essay see Philip Drew, *The Poetry of Robert Browning: A Critical Introduction* (London: Methuen, 1970), pp. 3-11.

84. Here I disagree with Masao Myoshi who finds Browning's "apologia" an unrealized "syllabus for moral commitment." *The Divided Self: A Perspective on the Literature of the Victorians* (New York: New York University Press, 1969), pp. 159-60. Myoshi discounts the "visions" and underemphasizes Browning's sense of "moral experience."

85. [George Lewes], *Leader*, 27 April 1850, p. 111.

86. Croce, *Guide to Aesthetics*, p. 44.

87. Browning, *Shelley*, p. 67.

88. I have taken the phrase "England's most distinguished historicist" from Miller, *The Disappearance of God*, p. 108.

V

1. Thomas Carlyle, "Jesuitism," *Latter-Day Pamphlets* (New York: Clarke, n.d.), p. 292.

2. John Stuart Mill, "The Church of England," *Westminster Review* 53 (1850): 89.

3. See U. C. Knoepflmacher's edition of Newman's *Phases of Faith* (New York: Humanities Press, 1970), intro., p. 9.

4. *The George Eliot Letters*, ed. Gordon Haight (New Haven: Yale University Press, 1954), 1:282. The date of the letter is May 1849.

5. Ibid., 1:282n.
6. Knoepflmacher, ed., *Phases*, p. 10.
7. Basil Willey, *More Nineteenth-Century Studies: A Group of Honest Doubters* (New York: Columbia University Press, 1956). Chapter 1 is devoted to Francis Newman.
8. John Henry Newman, *Apologia pro Vita Sua*, ed. David J. DeLaura (New York: Norton, 1968), p. 40.
9. For a discussion of *Contributions*, see William Robbins's excellent study *The Newman Brothers: An Essay in Comparative Biography* (Cambridge: Harvard University Press, 1966), esp. chap. 1.
10. See K. S. Inglis, "Patterns of Religious Worship in 1851," *Journal of Ecclesiastical History* (1960): 74-86.
11. *The Letters of Matthew Arnold to Arthur Hugh Clough*, ed. H. F. Lowry (Oxford: Clarendon, 1932; rpt. 1968), p. 75. The letter is dated 8 March 1848.
12. Mill, "The Church of England," p. 96.
13. Ibid., p. 88.
14. Letter of April 11, 1851, quoted in John Morley, *The Life of William Ewart Gladstone*, 3 vols. (London: Macmillan, 1903), 3:387.
15. For Russell's views, see *English Historical Documents, 1833-1874*, ed. G. M. Young and W. D. Hancock (New York: Oxford University Press), pp. 367-68.
16. John W. Dodds, *The Age of Paradox* (New York: Rhinehart, 1952), p. 361.
17. Francis William Newman, *Phases of Faith; or Passages from the History of My Creed* (London: Chapman and Hall, 1850), pp. iii-iv. For convenience, future references in the text are to the recent Knoepflmacher edition.
18. Knoepflmacher, ed., *Phases*, p. 14.
19. Quoted in Robbins, *The Newman Brothers*, p. 113.
20. Robert William Mackay, *The Progress of the Intellect, As Exemplified in the Religious Development of the Greeks and Hebrews* (London: Chapman, 1850), pp. xi-xii.
21. W. M. Thackeray, *The History of Pendennis*, ed. Donald Hawes, intro. J. I. M. Stewart (Baltimore: Penguin, 1972), p. 649.
22. *The Rambler: A Catholic Journal and Review* 5-6 (1850): 3.
23. Thomas Carlyle, "Jesuitism," pp. 286-87.
24. John Henry Newman, *Lectures on Certain Difficulties Felt by Anglicans in Submitting to the Catholic Church* (1850; rpt. Dublin: J. Duffy, 1857), p. 163. Future references cited by page in the text.
25. *The Rambler*, p. 64.
26. If few heeded Newman's call, many did nevertheless listen with pleasure. The critic Richard Holt Hutton, looking back on the lectures (in *Cardinal Newman* [London: Methuen, 1891], pp. 207-8), wrote: "I shall never forget the impression which his voice and manner, which opened upon me for the first time in these lectures, made upon me."
27. Thomas Vargish, *Newman: The Contemplation of Mind* (Oxford: Clarendon, 1970), p. 11. See also George Levine's fine account of Newman as autobiographer in *The Boundaries of Fiction: Carlyle, Macaulay, Newman* (Princeton: Princeton University Press, 1968).
28. Arthur Clough, "Wordsworth," *Selected Prose Works*, ed. B. B. Trawick (University, Ala.: Alabama University Press, 1964), p. 117: "You may trace in [Wordsworth] . . . a spiritual descent from the Puritans."
29. Robert Vaughan, *The Age and Christianity* (London: Johnson and Walford, 1849), pp. v-vi.
30. George Saintsbury, *A Consideration of Thackeray* (1931; rpt. New York: Oxford University Press, 1968), p. 187; also Kathleen Tillotson, "Yes, in the Sea of Life," in *Mid-Victorian Studies* (London: Athlone, 1965), pp. 157-79.
31. Thackeray, *Pendennis*, pp. 177-78.
32. "Letters," *Leader*, 25 May 1850, p. 180.
33. Karl Marx, *Selected Writings in Sociology and Social Philosophy*, ed. T. B. Bottomore and M. Rubel (1956; rpt. Hammondsworth: Penguin, 1963), p. 177.
34. Quoted in Erich Eyck, *Gladstone*, trans. Bernard Miall (1938; rpt. New York: Augustus Kelley, 1968), p. 55.
35. A. W. Benn, *History of English Rationalism in the 19th Century*, quoted in Robbins, *The Newman Brothers*, p. 112.

36. The Knoepflmacher edition includes Newman's later and more polemical chapters, which rebut critics and take him further in his lonely pursuits.
37. [George Lewes], *Leader*, 18 May 1850, p. 181; 25 May 1850, p. 206.
38. Arnold, *Letters to Clough*, p. 115.
39. Lionel Trilling, *Matthew Arnold* (1939; new ed. New York: Columbia University Press, 1949), pp. 168–72.
40. See David J. DeLaura, "Newman and the Center of the Arnoldian Vision," *Hebrew and Hellene in Victorian England* (Austin: University of Texas Press, 1969).
41. John Henry Newman, "Christ upon the Waters" (27 October 1850), in *Sermons and Discourses 1839–1857*, ed. C. F. Harrold (London: Longmans, 1949), p. 332.
42. Matthew Arnold, *Complete Prose Works*, ed. R. H. Super (Ann Arbor: University of Michigan Press, 1973), 5:31–32.
43. Arnold, *Letters to Clough*, p. 86.
44. Clough, "Newman's *The Soul*," *Selected Prose Works*, p. 277.

VI

1. Marcel Proust, "John Ruskin," in *Marcel Proust: A Selection from His Writings*, ed. Gerard Hopkins (London: Wingate, 1948), p. 96.
2. John Ruskin, "Introduction," *Modern Painters, Works*, ed. E. T. Cook and Alexander Wedderburn (London: George Allen, 1903), 1:84.
3. Proust, "Ruskin," p. 78.
4. John Ruskin, *The Seven Lamps of Architecture* (New York: Noonday, 1969), p. 167.
5. Ibid., pp. 168–69.
6. Charles Radcliffe, *Proteus; or the Unity of Nature* (1850; 2d ed., London: Macmillan, 1877), p. 187.
7. For a detailed study of Ruskin's aesthetics, see George P. Landow, *The Aesthetical and Critical Theories of John Ruskin* (Princeton University Press, 1971). I wrote this chapter before seeing Jay Fellows's *The Autobiographical Impulse in John Ruskin* (Baltimore: The Johns Hopkins University Press, 1975).
8. Ruskin, *Seven Lamps*, p. 169.
9. Frances A. Yates, *The Art of Memory* (Chicago: The University of Chicago Press, 1966), p. 1. My discussion of the artificial memory is drawn from Yates. See also Walter J. Ong, S.J., *Rhetoric, Romance, and Technology* (Ithaca: Cornell University Press, 1971), chap. 4, "Memory as Art."
10. In chapter 7 of *Biographia Literaria*, ed. J. Shawcross (London: Oxford University Press, 1907; rpt. 1962), Coleridge refers to the "Arts of Memory," 1:73.
11. Alfred North Whitehead, *Science and the Modern World* (New York: Macmillan, 1928), p. 27.
12. Charles Dickens, *David Copperfield*, ed. George H. Ford (Boston: Houghton Mifflin, 1958), p. 269. Cited hereafter by page in the text.
13. Coleridge, *Biographia Literaria*, 2:101.
14. See, for example, the comments in Coleridge's Lecture X (1818) in *Coleridge's Miscellaneous Criticism*, ed. Thomas R. Raysor (London: Constable, 1936). In *The Friend*, ed. Barbara Rooke (London: Routledge & Kegan Paul, 1969) Coleridge speaks of the man of genius carrying on "the feelings of childhood into the powers of manhood" by combining "the child's sense of wonder and novelty with the apperances which every day . . . had rendered familiar," pp. 109–10.
15. Thomas Carlyle, "The Hero as Poet," *Heroes, Hero-Worship, and the Heroic in History* (New York: Clarke, n.d.), p. 91.
16. David Masson, "Thackeray and Dickens," *North British Review*, May 1851, p. 39.
17. See Gwendolyn B. Needham, "The Undisciplined Heart of David Copperfield," *Nineteenth-Century Fiction* 2 (1954): 81–107, and Barbara Hardy, "Change of Heart in Dickens's Novels," *Victorian Studies* 5 (1961): 49–67.
18. Thomas Shaw, *Outlines of English Literature* (London: 1849; new American edition, Phila-

delphia: Tuckerman, 1859), pp. 388-418. Shaw was professor of English at the St. Petersburg Lyceum.

19. See, for example, *The Letters of Charles Dickens*, ed. Madeleine House, Graham Story, and Kathleen Tillotson (Oxford: Clarendon, 1974), 3:57, 211.

20. *Household Narrative of Current Events (for the Year 1850. . . , Conducted by Charles Dickens* (London: 1850), p. 167.

21. Angus Wilson, "Dickens on Children and Childhood," *Dickens 1970: Centenary Essays*, ed. Michael Slater (New York: Stein and Day, 1970), p. 220.

22. See *Household Narrative*, pp. 82-83: "the terrific storm . . . on the last two days of March." Note the "despatch from Margate": "the wreck was covered at high-water, and. . .two bodies had been picked up off the sands."

23. Carlyle, "The Hero as Man-of-Letters," *Heroes, Hero-Worship, and the Heroic in History*, p. 149.

24. J. S. Mill, *Principles of Political Economy*, quoted in Basil Willey, *Nineteenth-Century Studies* (New York: Columbia University Press, 1956), p. 160.

25. The following unnumbered quotations are from chapter 58, pp. 620-25.

26. William Wordsworth, *The Prelude*, ed. E. de Selincourt and H. Darbishire (Oxford: Clarendon, 1959), p. 207. The following quotations are from book 6, pp. 203-15.

27. For a discussion of *Copperfield* and *Great Expectations*, see, for example, H. M. Daleski, *Dickens and the Art of Analogy* (New York: Schocken, 1970), pp. 241-42.

28. George Brimley, "Wordsworth," *Fraser's Magazine* 13 (June-July): 104-5.

29. See Graham Greene, "The Burden of Childhood," *Collected Essays* (New York: Viking, 1969), p. 127. Greene speaks appropriately of "the music of memory" in *Copperfield.*

30. The phrase is from William Empson's *Some Versions of Pastoral* (New York: New Directions, 1960), p. 249. See also Peter Coveney, "The Child in Dickens," *Poor Monkey: The Child in Literature* (London: Rockliff, 1957).

31. G. K. Chesterton, *Charles Dickens* (1906; rpt. New York: Schocken, 1965), p. 195.

32. Quoted in Yates, *The Art of Memory*, p. 9.

33. Susanne Langer, *Mind: An Essay on Human Feeling* (Baltimore: The Johns Hopkins University Press, 1972), 2:339.

34. George Orwell, "Charles Dickens," *A Collection of Essays* (1946; rpt. New York: Harcourt Brace, n.d.), pp. 72-73.

35. I draw the term *concrete memory* from Paul Brockelman, "Of Memory and Things Past," *International Philosophical Quarterly* 15 (1975): 309-25.

36. Northrop Frye, *The Anatomy of Criticism* (Princeton: Princeton University Press, 1957), pp. 34, 38, and *passim.*

37. See the autobiographical material in John Forster, *The Life of Charles Dickens* (2d ed., London: Chapman and Hall, 1872) 1: chap. 1 and 2. Also Edgar Johnson, *Charles Dickens: His Triumph and Tragedy* (New York: Simon and Schuster, 1952), 2:661-62.

38. Ruskin, *Modern Painters, Works*, 1:30-31.

VII

1. Thomas Shaw, *Outlines of English Literature* (London: 1849; new American edition, Philadelphia: Tuckerman, 1859), p. 375.

2. David Masson, "Thackeray and Dickens," *North British Review*, May 1851, p. 30.

3. Anonymous review, *Prospective Review* 7 (1851): 158.

4. See John Dodds, *The Age of Paradox* (New York: Rhinehart, 1952), p. 365.

5. William Bell Scott, *Autobiographical Notes*, ed. W. Minto (1893; rpt. New York: AMS Press, 1970), 1:251.

6. See G. S. R. Kitson-Clark, "The Romantic Element, 1830-1850," in *Studies in Social History*, ed. J. H. Plumb (1955; rpt. Freeport, N.Y.: Books for Libraries Press, 1969), p. 225.

7. *Prospective Review*, p. 159.

8. Shaw, *Outlines*, p. 375.

9. Eliot Warburton, *Reginald Hastings; or a Tale of the Troubles in 164-*, 3 vols. (London: Colbourn, 1850), p. 9.

10. For a useful survey of mid-Victorian theories of fiction, see Richard Stang, *The Theory of the Novel in England, 1850–1870* (New York: Columbia University Press, 1959).
11. See "George Meredith," in ibid., pp. 34–39.
12. Ian Watt, *The Rise of the Novel* (London: Chatto and Windus, 1960), p. 15.
13. Ibid., p. 21.
14. Ibid., p. 21.
15. Edward Bulwer-Lytton, *The Caxtons: A Family Picture* (London: Blackwood, 1849). For a discussion of Bulwer's critical theories and a fine defense of him as a pioneer rather than a mere follower of trends, see Allan Conrad Christensen's *Edward Bulwer-Lytton: The Fiction of New Regions* (Athens: University of Georgia Press, 1976).
16. See Harvey Peter Sucksmith, *The Narrative Art of Charles Dickens* (London: Oxford University Press, 1970) on the "introverted vision" in Victorian literature.
17. *Prospective Review*, p. 162.
18. See Elizabeth Haldane, *Mrs. Gaskell and Her Friends* (1930; rpt. Freeport, N.Y.: Books for Libraries), p. 79.
19. Nathaniel Hawthorne, *The Scarlet Letter*, ed. Thomas E. Connolly (New York: Penguin, 1970), pp. 35-36.
20. See William F. Grayburn, "George Borrow's German Interests," *Anglo-German Cross-Currents*, ed. P. A. Shelley and O. A. Lewis (Durham: University of North Carolina Press, 1962), p. 226.
21. Thomas Carlyle, "Diderot," *Critical and Miscellaneous Essays*, 1:114.
22. Kathleen Tillotson, *Novels of the Eighteen-Forties* (Oxford: Clarendon, 1954), p. 155.
23. Charlotte Yonge's immense popularity was soon to come with *The Heir of Redclyffe*, begun in 1850. See Margaret Mare and Alicia C. Percival, *Victorian Best-Seller: The World of Charlotte M. Yonge* (New York: Kennikat, 1947), pp. 134-35.
24. Thomas Prest [?], *The Maniac Father; or the Victim of Seduction* (London: 1850), p. 4.
25. William M. Thackeray, Preface, *The History of Pendennis* (New York: Charles Scribner's Sons, 1904), 1:13.
26. Ibid.
27. Charles Dickens, *David Copperfield*, ed. George H. Ford (Boston: Houghton Mifflin, 1958), p. 3.
28. G. P. R. James, *The Old Oak Chest: A Tale of Domestic Life*, 3 vols. (London: T. C. Newby, 1850), pp. 1-2.
29. Anthony Trollope, *The Noble Jilt, a Comedy*, ed. Michael Sadleir (London: Constable, 1923), p. viii. Trollope wrote *The Noble Jilt* in 1850. He later used the plot for *Can You Forgive Her.*
30. Wilkie Collins, *Antonina; or the Fall of Rome: A Romance of the Fifth Century* (London: Bentley, 1850), pp. x–xi.
31. Warburton, *Reginald Hastings*, p. v.
32. Anthony Trollope, *Autobiography* (New York: Dodd, Mead, 1916), chap. 6, p. 96.
33. Bulwer-Lytton, *The Caxtons*, p. v.
34. Warburton, *Reginald Hastings*, p. vi.
35. Robert Hunt, "Photography on Glass Plates," *Art-Journal* 12 (1850): 40.
36. See, for example, Aaron Scharf, *Art and Photography* (London: Allen Lane, 1969).
37. Harriet Martineau, *A History of the Thirty Years' Peace, 1816–1846*, 4 vols. (London: George Bell, 1878 ed.), 4:442–43.
38. See, for example, Scott, *Autobiographical Notes*, 1:279.
39. Mayne Reid, *The Rifle Ranges; or Adventures of an Officer in Southern Mexico*, 3 vols. (London: William Shoberl, 1850), p. viii.
40. Quoted in George H. Ford, *Dickens and His Readers* (1955; rpt. New York: Norton, 1965), p. 171.
41. Richard Henry Horne, *The Poor Artist; or Seven Eye Sights and One Object* (London: J. Van Voorst, 1850), p. 96.
42. Robert Mackay, *The Progress of the Intellect* (London: Chapman and Hall, 1850), p. 4.
43. In *Thackeray and the Form of Fiction* (Princeton: Princeton University Press, 1964), John Loofbourow discusses Thackeray's pastoralism in terms of neoclassical conventions, but he over-

looks both the widespread interest in eighteenth-century modes and the fact that Thackeray's pastoral leanings are characteristic of the fiction of the age.

44. Elizabeth Gaskell, *The Moorland Cottage*, in *Cranford and Other Tales* (1904; rpt. New York: AMS Press, 1972), p. 267. In *Cranford* (1851-53), Mrs. Gaskell writes another sort of pastoral, or idyll, which describes the matriarchal community of the Misses Jenkyns in rural, early nineteenth-century Cheshire.

45. Frances Trollope, *Petticoat Government* (New York: Harper and Bros., 1850), p. 159.

46. Collins, *Antonina*, p. xii.

47. Tillotson, *Novels of the Eighteen-Forties*, pp. 92-93.

48. [George Lewes], "Shirley: A Tale," *Edinburgh Review* 91 (October 1849-April 1850): 158. Identification is thanks to the *Wellesley Index*.

49. Charlotte Brontë, 1850 Preface to *The Professor*, quoted in Tillotson, *Novels of the Eighteen-Forties*, pp. 84-85.

50. Francis E. Smedley, *Frank Fairlegh* (London: Routledge, 1850), p. vi.

Cf. Thackeray in the preface to *Pendennis*: "Since the author of *Tom Jones* was buried, no writer of fiction among us has been permitted to depict. . . a MAN. We must drape him. . .etc." p. 34. As for Smedley, theories about realistic portrayal are involved with questions of prudery.

51. Mario Praz, *The Hero in Eclipse in Victorian Fiction*, trans. Angus Davidson (New York: Oxford University Press, 1956).

52. Tillotson, *Novels of the Eighteen-Forties*, p. 131, and *passim*.

53. Edmund Yates, *Fifty Years of London Life* (New York: Harper, 1885), pp. 142-43.

54. Richard Henry Horne, *The Dreamer and the Worker* (London: Henry Colburn, 1851), p. iv.

55. Thackeray, *Pendennis*, p. 33.

56. For discussions of the "reader" in mid-century fiction, see, for example, John Butt and Kathleen Tillotson, *Dickens at Work* (London: Methuen, 1963); Ford, *Dickens and His Readers*; and Sylvère Monod, "The Thirty 'Readers' of *Jane Eyre*," in *Jane Eyre*, ed. Richard J. Dunn (New York: Norton, 1971).

VIII

1. Charles Kingsley, *His Letters, and Memories of His Life, Edited by His Wife*, intro. Maurice Kingsley, 2 vols. (Boston: Little, Brown, 1900), 1:212.

2. Quoted in Thomas Hughes, "Prefatory Memoir," Charles Kingsley, *Alton Locke: Taylor and Poet* (Boston: Little, Brown, 1900), p. 14.

3. [J. M. Ludlow], "The New Idea," *The Christian Socialist*, no. 1 (1850): 1.

4. G. M. Young, "Sophist and Swashbuckler," *Victorian Essays*, ed. W. D. Hancock (London: Oxford University Press, 1962), pp. 151-52.

5. Ibid., p. 151.

6. Hughes, "Prefatory Memoir," pp. 20-21.

7. Letter of 1843, quoted in Susan Chitty, *The Beast and the Monk: A Life of Charles Kingsley* (New York: Mason & Charter, 1975), p. 59.

8. Ibid.

9. See ibid., chaps. 3 and 4. I am indebted to her study and to Robert B. Martin's *The Dust of Combat: A Life of Charles Kingsley* (London: Faber and Faber, 1959) for biographical information. Brenda Colloms's *Charles Kingsley* (London: Constable, 1975) came to my attention after this chapter had been written.

10. Letter of 1845, quoted in Martin, *The Dust of Combat*, p. 71.

11. [Charles Kingsley], "Why Should We Fear the Romish Priests?" *Fraser's Magazine* (1848), quoted in Martin, *The Dust of Combat*, p. 76.

12. Letter of 1840, quoted in Chitty, *The Beast and the Monk*, p. 58.

13. Letter of 1843, quoted in ibid., p. 52. Kingsley may remind us how much mid-century literature (Tennyson, Dickens, Arnold, etc.) is concerned with the importance of male friendships.

14. Charles Kingsley, "Chalk Stream Studies," *Prose Idylls New and Old* (London: Macmillan, 1873). See Chitty, *The Beast and the Monk*, pp. 52-53.

15. Quoted in Martin, *The Dust of Combat*, pp. 128-29.

16. Ibid., p. 91.
17. John Stores Smith, *Social Aspects* (London: 1850).
18. Charles Kingsley, "Cheap Clothes and Nasty," in *Alton Locke*, 1:94-95.
19. Kingsley, *Letters and Memories*, 1:132.
20. Quoted by Hughes, "Prefatory Memoir," pp. 28-29.
21. Letter to J. M. Ludlow, ibid., pp. 16-17.
22. See, for example, Robert Knox's notorious *The Races of Man* (London: 1850), which reflected contemporary interests but incensed most reviewers with its Gobineau-like theories.
23. Kingsley, "Cheap Clothes and Nasty," 1:76.
24. Charles Kingsley, "Preface to the Undergraduates of Cambridge," in *Alton Locke*, 1:102.
25. See Hughes, "Prefatory Memoir," p. 54.
26. Frederic Harrison, *Forum* (1895), quoted in Chitty, *The Beast and the Monk*, p. 134.
27. S. T. Coleridge, *The Friend*, ed. Barbara Rooke (London: Routledge & Kegan Paul, 1969), p. 106.
28. Benjamin Disraeli, "Preface to the Fifth Edition," *Coningsby: Or the New Generation* (London: Longmans, 1919), pp. vii-viii.
29. Quoted in Martin, *The Dust of Combat*, p. 93.
30. J. M. Ludlow, letter of 1848, ibid., p. 92.
31. Quoted in ibid., p. 95.
32. Thomas Cooper, "To the Young Men of the Working Classes," quoted in Martha Vicinus, *The Industrial Muse* (Bloomington: Indiana University Press), p. 1.
33. Kingsley, *Alton Locke*, 1: 151. Cited hereafter by volume and page in the text.
34. Letter to Fanny, quoted in Chitty, *The Beast and the Monk*, p. 137.
35. Letter to Ludlow, 1848, quoted in Martin, *The Dust of Combat*, p. 92.
36. Quoted in Paul Brockleman, "Of Memory of Things Past," *International Philosophical Quarterly* 15 (1975): 320.
37. Carlyle, letter of 31 October 1850, in Kingsley, *Letters and Memories*, 1:206-7.
38. See also the brief discussion of *Alton Locke* in Raymond Williams, *Culture and Society, 1780-1950* (New York: Columbia University Press, 1958), pp. 100-02.
39. William Empson, *Some Versions of Pastoral* (New York: New Directions, 1960), chap. 1.
40. Georg Lukács, *The Historical Novel*, trans. H. and S. Mitchell (Boston: Beacon Press, 1963). See esp. chapter 1.

IX

1. William Michael Rossetti, *The Germ: Thoughts Towards Nature in Poetry, Literature and Art* (1899; rpt. New York: AMS Press, 1965), pp. 10-11. See also *The Germ: A Pre-Raphaelite Little Magazine*, ed. R. S. Hosman (Coral Gables: University of Florida Press, 1970).
2. Harry Stone, ed., intro. to Charles Dickens, *Uncollected Writings from Household Words*, 2 vols. (Bloomington: Indiana University Press, 1968), 1:13.
3. *Household Words: A Weekly Journal*, "Conducted by Charles Dickens," no. 1 (30 March 1850): 1.
4. *Household Words: A Weekly Journal 1850-1859. . .*, compiled by Anne Lohrli (Toronto: University of Toronto Press, 1973), *passim*.
5. Walter Graham, *English Literary Periodicals* (New York: Nelson & Sons, 1930), pp. 296-97.
6. Lohrli, comp., *Household Words*, p. 58.
7. Quoted in Stone, ed., *Uncollected Writings*, p. 16.
8. Rossetti, *The Germ*, p. 20.
9. Ibid., unnumbered Contents page, with information from pp. 20-23.
10. Ibid., pp. 18-19.
11. Quoted in Rossetti in ibid., p. 13.
12. Ibid., pp. 14-15.
13. Quoted in William Gaunt, *The Pre-Raphaelite Dream* (New York: Schocken Books, 1966), p. 46.
14. Ibid. See Herbert Sussman, "The Language of Criticism and the Language of Art: The Re-

sponse of Victorian Periodicals to the Pre-Raphaelite Brotherhood," *Victorian Periodicals Newsletter*, 19 (March 1973): 21–28.

15. [Charles Dickens], "Old Lamps for New Ones," *Household Words*, 15 June 1850, pp. 265–66.

16. Edgar Johnson, *Charles Dickens, His Triumph and Tragedy* (New York: Simon and Schuster, 1952), 2:1131.

17. Quoted in Gaunt, *The Pre-Raphaelite Dream*, p. 84.

18. David Masson, "Thackeray and Dickens," *North British Review*, May 1851, p. 39.

19. The charge came from the conservative *Quarterly*. Quoted in George H. Ford, *Dickens and His Readers* (1955; rpt. New York: Norton, 1965), p. 102.

20. See William Bell Scott, *Autobiographical Notes*, ed. W. Minto (1893; rpt. New York: AMS Press, 1970), 1:277–28.

21. "John Seward" [George Stephens], "The Purpose and Tendency of Early Italian Art," *The Germ*, p. 63.

22. William Michael Rossetti, "*The Bothie of Tober-na-Vuolich*," *The Germ*, p. 34.

23. "Laura Savage" [George Stephens], "Modern Giants," *The Germ*, p. 169.

24. John Steegman, *Victorian Taste: A study of the Arts and Architecture from 1830 to 1870* (Cambridge, M.I.T. Press, 1971), p. 154.

25. Quoted in Rossetti, *The Germ*, p. 16.

26. Stephens, "Purpose and Tendency," p. 64.

27. Steegman, *Victorian Taste*, p. 160.

28. *The Pre-Raphaelite Journal; William Michael Rossetti's Diary of the Pre-Raphaelite Brotherhood*, 1849–1853, ed. William E. Fredeman (London: Oxford University Press, 1975), p. 107.

29. John Ruskin, "Pre-Raphaelitism," in *Lectures on Architecture and Painting, with Other Papers* (London: George Allen, 1904), 12:357n.

30. *Pre-Raphaelite Journal*, p. 71.

31. Ruskin, "Pre-Raphaelitism," p. 339.

32. Stephens, "Purpose and Tendency," pp. 58–59.

33. *Pre-Raphaelite Journal*, p. 11.

34. John Orchard, "A Dialogue on Art," *The Germ*, p. 147.

35. Stephens, "Modern Giants," p. 170.

36. Orchard, "A Dialogue," p. 148.

37. Quoted in Gaunt, *The Pre-Raphaelite Dream*, p. 91.

38. René Wellek, *A History of Modern Criticism, 1750–1950: The Age of Transition* (New Haven: Yale University Press, 1965), 3: 148.

39. *The Red Republican* and *The Friend of the People*, ed. and intro. John Saville (London: Merlin, 1966), p. vii.

40. Ibid., pp. 4–5.

41. Sir Nikolaus Pevsner, *High Victorian Design: A Study of the Exhibits of 1851* (London: Architectural Press, 1951), p. 17.

X

1. Elizabeth Lynn Linton, *My Literary Life* (London: Hodder & Stoughton, 1899), pp. 28-29.

2. G. M. Young, *Victorian Essays*, ed. W. D. Hancock (London: Oxford University Press, 1962), pp. 133-34.

3. See *The Autobiography and Letters of Mrs. M. O. W. Oliphant*, ed. H. Coghill (New York: Dodd, Mead, 1899), pp. 151–52.

4. John Ruskin, *Works*, 18:434–45. Ruskin often makes the equation: see *Works*, 3:71-72; 109–10; 4:55–56. Jerome Buckley uses the above quotation as an epigraph for *The Victorian Temper* (Cambridge: Harvard University Press, 1951).

5. Mario Praz, *The Hero in Eclipse in Victorian Fiction*, trans. Angus Davidson (New York: Oxford University Press, 1956), *passim*.

6. W. M. Thackeray, *Ballads and Tales* (New York: Scribner's, 1904), pp. 44–55. For a study

of Thackeray's political ideals, see Avrom Fleishman, "Thackeray: Beyond Whig History," *The English Historical Novel* (Baltimore: The Johns Hopkins University Press, 1971).

7. Eastlake had published several art histories, and his wife had written a variety of art and literature reviews, including the notorious attack on *Jane Eyre* for the *Quarterly Review* (December 1848).

8. [George Lewes], *Leader*, 21 December 1850, p. 929.

9. [Henry Reeve], "Ranke's *House of Brandenburg*," *Quarterly Review* 86 (1850): 337-38.

10. *Notes and Queries: A Medium of Intercommunication*. . .1 (3 November 1849): 1.

11. "What Is a Classic?" *The Literary Criticism of Sainte-Beuve*, ed. E. R. Marks (Lincoln: University of Nebraska Press, 1971), p. 96.

12. [George Lewes], *Leader*, 4 May 1850, p. 133; 11 May 1850, p. 159.

13. [George Lewes], *Leader*, 30 March 1850, p. 12.

14. Charles Dickens [?], *Household Narrative*, February 1850, p. 47.

15. For a discussion of Simpson and the liberal Catholic press—Simpson began writing for the *Rambler* in 1850—see *Richard Simpson as Critic*, ed. David Carroll (London: Routledge & Kegan Paul, 1977).

16. Charlotte Brontë, *Jane Eyre*, ed. Richard J. Dunn (New York: Norton, 1971), p. 140.

17. David Masson, "Wordsworth," *North British Review* 13 (1850): 475.

18. Again, Kierkegaard can be of great use to a reader of mid-nineteenth-century literature. See *The Sickness unto Death*, trans. Walter Lowrie (1941; rpt. New York: Anchor, 1954). Kierkegaard is not the less representative for setting himself apart. He says of Descartes: "He did not cry 'Fire!' nor did he make it a duty for everyone to doubt; for Descartes was a solitary thinker, not a bellowing night-watchman; he modestly admitted that his method had importance for him alone. . ." pp. 22–23.

19. See F. O. Matthiessen, *American Renaissance: Art and Expression in the Age of Emerson and Whitman* (New York: Oxford University Press, 1941).

Index

Abrams, M. H., 242(n.4), 244(n.43)
Acton, William, 230
Adamson, Robert, 168; calotype by, 148
Ad Herrenium, 137-38
Ainsworth, Harrison, 166
Ainsworth's Magazine, 136, 206, 244(n.2), 245(n.36)
Albert, Prince Consort, 3, 4, 8, 219, 227, 228
Alienation, 7, 83-84, 107, 111, 112, 118, 216
Allingham, William, 2, 79, 84, 205, 226
Allott, Kenneth, 68, 71, 241(n.14), 246(n.12)
Altick, Richard, 242(n.34)
Anglican Church, 3, 114, 198
Anglicanism, 106, 109, 114, 120, 182
Arnold, Matthew, xiv, 1, 13, 64-82, 84, 96, 122, 125, 156, 190, 226, 237, 238, 239, 241(n.14), 243(n.15), 246(nn.3, 7, 10, 12, 15, 19-24), 250(nn.38-40, 42-43); on anarchy, 233, 235; and autobiography, 8, 127; and the Brownings, 66, 97, 101, 117; and Byron, 68-69; and Carl Jung, 64, 74-75; Charles Kingsley on, 79, 180, 185; and classicism, 40, 68, 72, 229, 235; and Clough, 66, 75, 76-80, 86, 121-22, 229, 247(n.27), 253(n.13); critical principles of, 40, 64-65, 72-75, 161, 232; on culture, 120, 235; on fiction, 161; on Francis Newman, 78, 116, 119-22; and Goethe, 68-69, 74; and John Henry Newman, 116, 117, 120-21; on modern poetry, 25, 27, 39, 66, 69, 74-75, 78-80, 225; and nature, 49, 67-76, 117, 118, 246(n.18); on periodical literature, 11, 120, 232; photograph of, 59; on Romantic poets, 24-25, 67-68, 94, 101; and Sainte-Beuve, 232, 246(n.14); and self-consciousness in literature, 65, 69, 86; and Tennyson, 39, 48, 64, 76, 77-78, 116; W. M. Rossetti's criticism of, 66-67, 73, 206, 246(nn.4, 6, 8); on Wordsworth, 67-70, 131, 245(n.31), 246(n.11); and the *Zeitgeist*, 24, 74, 80; "Balder Dead," 71; *Culture and Anarchy*, 120, 233; "Dover Beach," 67, 97, 117; *Empedocles on Etna*, 67, 70, 72-76, 79, 80, 89, 96, 97; "The Forsaken Merman," 72; *Friendship's Garland*, 120; *Literature and Dogma*, 107; "To Marguerite—Continued," 67, 70-72, 74, 117, 249(n.30); "My Countrymen," 120; Obermann poems, 69, 72-73, 76, 89; *Poems* (1853), 67, 69, 72-75; *Poems* (1867), 67, 73; "Quiet Work," 76; "Resignation," 72; *St. Paul and Protestantism*, 107; "The Scholar Gipsy," 67, 81; "Stanzas from the Grande Chartreuse," 97, 237; *The Strayed Reveller*, 1, 66, 79, 97, 246(nn.4, 6, 8, 10); "Wordsworth," 245(n.31)
Arnold, Thomas, 26, 77, 79, 107, 180
Artificial memory, 126-28. *See also* memory
Art-Journal, 9, 167, 229, 241(n.19), 252(n.35)
Athenaeum, xiii, 10, 47, 98, 109, 205, 229, 242(n.24), 244(n.34), 248(n.76)
Augustine, Saint, 100
Austen, Jane, 154, 155
Autobiography, xiii, 64, 86, 133-35, 159-67, 224, 236, 250(n.7); and Browning, 100-101, 103; and Dante, 45-48, 50; and Dickens, 127-43; and fiction, 8-9, 159-66; and historicism, 50, 166, 246(n.46); as literature, 19; and mid-nineteenth-century poetry, 64, 177; and the Newman brothers, 105-6, 108-16; and Wordsworth, 45-48, 50
Aytoun, William, 8, 246(n.10)

Babbitt, Irving, 25-26
Bacon, Sir Francis, 20, 214, 231
Bagehot, Walter, 2, 82, 226
Bailey, Philip, 30, 99, 156
Ball, Patricia, 30-31, 244(nn.31, 33)
Balzac, Honoré de, xii, 229
Bannerman, Patrick, 43
Barnes, William, 226
Barry, Sir Charles, 216, 228
Bohn, Henry, 90

Borrow, George, 155; autobiographical fiction by, 8, 160; on fiction and painting, 171; and Goethe, 162, 252(n.20); *Lavengro*, 8, 160, 171, 172, 178, 226
Bottomore, T. B., 249(n.33)
Bowers, Fredson, 242(n.34)
Brett-Smith, H. F. B., 242(n.3), 248(n.81)
Briggs, Asa, 3, 6, 66, 83, 241(nn.4, 6, 13), 243(n.9), 247(n.42)
Brimley, George, 47, 136, 245(n.39), 251 (n.28)
British Quarterly Review, 187
Broad Church Movement, 107, 181, 186
Brockelman, Paul, 251(n.35), 254(n.36)
Brontë, Charlotte, xiv, 2, 155, 160, 256 (n.7); and autobiographical fiction, 158; on fiction, 174; and G. H. Lewes, 158, 166-67; portrait of, 149; *Jane Eyre*, 2, 158, 162, 173-74, 175, 178, 194, 199, 226, 237, 253(n.56), 256(n.16); *The Professor*, 174, 253(n.49); *Shirley*, 173, 176, 253(n.48)
Brontë, Emily, 2, 155, 160, 177, 239; *Wuthering Heights*, 2, 162
Brown, Ford Madox, 206, 207, 213, 220
Brown, John, 244(n.32)
Browning, Elizabeth Barrett, 1, 36, 92, 204, 214, 248(nn.64, 69); religious views of, 99-100; on Robert Browning, 94-97; *Sonnets from the Portuguese*, 1, 39, 42
Browning, Robert, xiii, xiv, 1, 7, 8, 13, 19, 37, 40, 48, 49, 63, 66, 73, **92-104**, 105-6, 122, 125, 127, 131, 156, 214, 236, 239, 248(nn.64-65, 68, 69, 72, 75-84, 87); artistic ideals of, 95-96; dramatic monologues of, 102-3; fame of, 37; historicism of, 103-4, 167, 178; novelistic tendencies in, 104, 178; portrait of, by D. G. Rossetti, 60; and the Pre-Raphaelites, 81-82, 206, 212; religious views of, 97-101, 112; style of, 92-98; *Bells and Pomegranates*, 97; "Bishop Blougram's Apology," 97; "Childe Roland," 51; *Christmas-Eve and Easter-Day*, 1, 7, 63, 65, 84, **93-104**, 106, 110, 247(nn.58, 84); *Dramatic Lyrics*, 102; "Essay on Shelley," 40, 101-2, 248(nn.81, 87); *Men and Women*, 97, 102; *Pauline*, 103; *The Ring and the Book*, 103; Sordello, 93
Brunel, Isambard, 228
Bryant, Arthur, 243(n.17)
Bryant, William Cullen, 48, 229
Buckley, Jerome, xiv, 40, 245(n.17), 247 (n.46), 255(n.4)
Bulwer-Lytton, Edward, 15, 177, 244(n.44); and autobiographical fiction, 160; on fiction and the age, 244(n.44), 252(n.15); *The Caxtons*, 8, 160, 167, 252(nn.15, 33)
Bunyan, John, 44, 100, 116
Burns, Robert, 200
Butler, Arthur, 77
Butler, Samuel (author of *Sir Hudibras*), 63, 98, 99
Butt, John, 253(n.56)
Byron, George Gordon, 17, 25, 36, 182, 189, 214, 244*n*; Arnold on, 68, 79; and Clough, 79, 85, 91; *Childe Harold*, 46, 80, 85, 132; *Don Juan*, 18; *English Bards*, 18; *Manfred*, 46

Caldwell, Calder, 207
Carlyle, John A., 43
Carlyle, Thomas, 6, 13, **27-35**, 39, 41, 66, 125, 132, 183, 213, 220, 225, 237, 239; and Browning, 98; critical vocabulary of, 29-34; on Dante, 29, 43-44, 48, 50, 51; as defender of imaginative literature, 28-30, 50, 163; and Dickens, 5-6, 35, 130-31, 160, 165, 197; and *epos*, 45; on fiction, 30, 35, 163, 176, 243(n.30); George Lewes on, 229, 233; influence of, 27, 131, 163-64; on J. S. Mill, 23; and Kingsley, 1, 163, 185, 187, 197-98, 200-201, 254 (n.37); and Macaulay, 21, 28-29; medallion of, by Thomas Woolner, 57; on men-of-letters as heroes, xiv, 5, 10, 11, 34, 69, 130, 175; and nature, 32-34; and Romantic conventions, 29-33; and self-consciousness, 8, 65, 161, 178; and sincerity, 30-31; as social critic, 5, 130, 187, 201, 233; and Tennyson, 162; and "Wertherism," 198; "Characteristics," 233; "Diderot," 162, 163, 252(n.21); *French Revolution*, 201, 231; *Heroes and Hero-Worship*, 9, 28-29, 50, 242(nn.22, 28), 243(nn.22, 28), 250(n.15), 251(n.23); *Latter-Day Pamphlets*, 1, 5, 27, 39, 105, 113-14, 216, 233, 248(n.1), 249(n.23); *Life of Sterling*, 233, 234; *Past and Present*, 2; *Sartor Resartus*, 130, 162, 194; "Signs of the Times," 243(n.29)
Carnegie, Andrew, 27
Carroll, David, 256(n.15)
Carroll, Lewis. *See* Dodgson, Charles
Cary, Henry (translator), 43
Catholicism, Roman, 97, 109, 118, 120, 121, 183, 184, 186, 210, 215-16, 234
Cayley, George J., 246(n.5)
Census of 1851, 107, 181, 249(n.10)
"Charlotte Elizabeth." *See* Tonna, Mrs. Charlotte Elizabeth
Chartism, 3, 179-80, 181, 222, 236

Chapman, George, 241(n.10)
Chaucer, Geoffrey, 78, 80, 214
Chesney, Kellow, 242(n.29)
Chesterton, G. K., 137, 140, 251(n.31)
Chesterton, Lady Henrietta, 168, 229
Chisolm, Mrs. Caroline, 205
Chitty, Susan, 253(nn.9, 12-14), 254(n.34)
Christ, 38, 63, 179, 189, 210, 214
Christensen, Allan Conrad, 244(n.44), 252 (n.15)
Christian Remembrancer, 44, 245(n.26)
Christian Socialist, 10, 179, 180, 186, 205, 253(n.3)
Christian Socialists, 191, 193, 222
Christie, John, 83
Church, Richard, 44-45, 47, 51, 104, 129, 245(nn.26-30)
Clark, Sir Kenneth, 216
Clausius, Rudolf, 236
Clio, muse of history, 51
Clive, John, 243(n.9)
Clough, Arthur, xiii, 1, 7, 8, 19, 24, 48, 49, 63, 66, 72, 73, 75, **76-91**, 97, 99, 107, 116, 121, 156, 206, 214, 225, 229, 236, 239, 243(n.15), 246(nn.19, 21, 23), 247 (nn.33, 41), 249(n.11), 250(n. 38); as dramatic elegist, xiii, 85; on Francis Newman, 121-22; and Goethe, 87-91; and Kierkegaard, 85-88, 90; and Matthew Arnold, 66, 75, 77-80, 247(n.27); novelistic tendencies of, 104, 157; religious views of, 85-87, 89, 112, 115, 247(n.44); as satirist, 8, 87-89, 91, 247(n.44); *Amours de Voyage*, 80, 84-85; *The Bothie of Tober-na-Vuolich*, 79-81, 82, 89, 91, 247 (n.34); *Dipsychus*, 7, 51, 63-64, 80, 84, 85-91, 103; "Easter Day Naples, 1849," 77, 80, 83, 84, 97, 100; "Epi-Strauss-ion," 84, 97; "Wordsworth," 249(n.28)
Coghill, H., 255(n.3)
Cohen, Marshall, 244(n.36)
Cole, Henry, 3, 219, 226
Colenso, John William, 120, 232
Coleridge, Samuel Taylor, 16, 18, 23, 24, 28, 34, 106, 135, 206; on Dante, 128, 245*n*; on imagination, 40, 50, 154, 169; influence of, on Christian Socialists, 186; on memory, 125, 126, 250(n.10); on Wordsworth, 45, 128, 138; *Biographia Literaria*, 243(n.11), 250(n.10); *On the Constitution of Church and State*, 186; *Dejection*, 133; *Essays on His Times*, alluded to, 2; *The Friend*, 192, 254(n.27)
Collins, Wilkie, 160, 204; on fiction and painting, 171-72, 177; *Antonina; or the Fall of Rome*, 166-67, 171-72, 252(n.30), 253 (n.46); *Rambles beyond Railways*, 172; *The Woman in White*, 172
Collinson, James, 207, 215-16
Colloms, Brenda, 253(n.9)
Communist Manifesto, 1, 222
Comte, Auguste, 26-27, 110, 230, 232
Connolly, Thomas E., 252(n.19)
Conrad, Joseph, 132
Contemporary Review, 10
Cook, E. T., 242(n.20), 245(n.13), 250(n.2)
Cooper, James Fenimore, 229
Coveney, Peter, 251(n.30)
Crabbe, George, 200
Croce, Benedetto, 92, 97, 103, 247(n.56), 248(n.86)
Croker, John Wilson, 234
Crome, John, 171
Cruikshank, George, 149
Crystal Palace, xiv, 3-4, 219, 223, 227-28; views of, 54-56
Culler, Dwight A., 246(n.18)
Culture, at mid-nineteenth century, 21, 23, 116, 225, 232

Daguerre, Louis Jacques, 33, 168
Daily News, 204
Daily Telegraph, 10
Daleski, H. M., 251(n.27)
Dallas, Eneas Sweetland, 161
Dante, Alighieri, xiii, 37, 39, **40-51**, 90, 100, 104, 116, 214, 245(nn.23, 26); Carlyle on, 29, 43-44, 48, 50-51; and English poetry, 8, 37, 40, 42-51, 245(nn.23, 29); Landor's poem about, 43, 245(n.22); Richard Church on, 44-45, 47, 51, 104, 245(nn.26-30); and Tennyson, 8, 38, 39, 40-51, 245 (nn.14, 18, 21, 31); and Wordsworth, 37, 40, 44-51, 128-29; *The Divine Comedy*, 8, 29, 39, 40-51, 81; *Vita Nuova*, 215
Darbishire, Helen, 246(n.51), 251(n.26)
Darwin, Charles, 27, 230
Davidson, Angus, 253(n.51), 255(n.5)
Dawson, Carl, 246(n.10)
Day, P. W., 243(n.19)
Defoe, Daniel, 158, 159, 160, 248(n.80)
de Kock, Paul, 229
DeLaura, David, 250(n.40)
Demetz, P., 243(n.20)
Democratic Review, 222
De Quincey, Thomas, 2, 35
Descartes, René, 159, 160, 256(n.18)
de Selincourt, Ernest, 246(n.51), 251(n.26)
De Sua, William, 245(n.23)
de Tocqueville, Alexis, 230-31
De Vane, William Clyde, 98, 248(n.78)
De Vere, Aubrey, 20, 21, 33-35, 158, 161,

De Vere, Aubrey (*continued*)
243(n.6), 244(n.40)
Deverell, Walter, 207
Dickens, Charles, xiii, xiv, 2, 3, 13, 20, 35, 45, 80, 111, **123-43**, 158, 177, 188, 220, 225, 236, 251(nn.19-21, 30-31, 34); and autobiographical fiction, 134-37, 251(n.37); characterization in, 139-42, 251(n.30); and the drama, 15; and memory, 127-30, 137-38, 141-43, 251(n.29); photograph of, 145; popularity of, 26, 230, 235; and the Pre-Raphaelites, xiii, 203-12, 215, 218; realism in, 129-30, 158, 172, 199; relation of, to Carlyle, 5, 130-31, 193, 197, 199; relation of, to Kingsley, 188, 195, 197-200; and Ruskin, 123-27, 135, 143, 236; and Thackeray, 1, 5, 8, 140, 153-56, 165, 251(n.2); and Wordsworth, 127, 131-43; *All the Year Round*, 205; *Bleak House*, 5, 80, 136; *David Copperfield*, xiii, 1, 5, 8, 10, 15, 25, 32, 109, 110, 111, 112, 117, **123-43**, 145, 146, 153-54, 157, 160, 161, 164-66, 167, 170, 172, 173, 175, 193, 194-95, 199, 210, 211, 227, 235, 236, 239, 250(nn.12, 17), 251(n.27), 252(n.27); *Dombey and Son*, 5, 153; *Great Expectations*, 136; *Household Narrative* (edited by), xiii, 131, 234, 245(n.36), 251(nn.20, 22), 256(n.14); *Household Words* (edited by), xiv, 2, 3, 5, 10, 12, 15, 169, 170, 203-6, 212, 215, 219, 221-22, 229, 236, 241(n.3), 254(nn.3-4, 6), 255(n.15); *Oliver Twist*, 195, 199; *Our Mutual Friend*, 213; *Pictures from Italy*, 133
Diderot, Denis, 162
Disraeli, Benjamin, 2, 7, 155, 188, 189, 192; *Coningsby*, 2, 192, 254(n.28); *Sybil*, 2, 7, 192, 194; *Tancred*, 2
Dixon, Thomas, 221, 223
Dodds, John, xiii, xiv, 109, 242(n.31), 244(n.32), 249(n.16), 251(n.4)
Dodgson, Charles (Lewis Carroll), 2, 226
Donne, John, 99
Donne, W. B., 39
Don Quixote, 175
Dostoyevski, Fyodor, 87, 237, 238
Drama, at mid-nineteenth century, 14-15
Drew, Philip, 248(n.83)
Dryden, John, 21
Dublin Review, 234
Dunn, Richard J., 253(n.56), 256(n.16)
Durrell, Lawrence, 66, 246(n.9)
Dyce, William, 213

Eastlake, Charles, 215, 228, 256(n.7)
Eckermann, Johann, 68, 90, 246(n.14)
Edinburgh Review, 10, 26, 46, 208, 230, 234, 244(n.40), 253(n.48)
Eichrodt, Ludwig, 227
Eliot, George (Marian Evans), 2, 10, 158, 242(n.25), 248(n.4); and Charlotte Brontë, 177; on fiction and painting, 172-73; on Francis Newman, 105; *Middlemarch*, 171, 172-73
Eliot, T. S., 24, 26, 125, 218; and Arnold, 85; and Clough, 91; on Tennyson, 7, 241(n.15); *The Waste Land*, 19, 125
Eliza Cook's Journal, 10
Ellegard, Allvar, 242(n.24)
Elliott, Ebeneezer, 13
Emerson, Ralph Waldo, xii, 214
Empirical philosophers, English, 159
Empson, William, 201, 251(n.30), 254(n.39)
Engels, Friederich, 6, 44, 186-87, 216, 230
English Review, 99
Entropy, 236
Epos, 45, 104, 173
Esher, R. B., 241(n.5)
Essays and Studies, 107
Evangelicalism, 46, 100-101, 109, 114, 115, 119
Evolution, theories of, 20, 187, 198-99, 236
Examiner, xiii, 2, 46, 229
Eyck, Erich, 249(n.34)

Faraday, Michael, 236
Faulkner, William, 138
Fellows, Jay, 250(n.7)
Fichte, Johann Gottlieb, 28
Fielding, Henry, 162, 165, 170, 171, 248
Fisch, M. H., 243(n.19)
Fitzgerald, Edward, 39, 42, 244(n.11)
Fleishman, Avrom, 256(n.6)
Flemish painting (in relation to fiction), 172, 199
Ford, George H., 250(n.12), 252(n.40), 255(n.19)
Forster, E. M., 15
Forster, Jane Arnold, 69, 76
Forster, John, 251(n.37)
Fortnightly Review, 10
Fourth Estate, 11, 234
Fox, George, 115
Fraser's Magazine, 46, 68, 180, 184, 206, 213, 234, 244(n.37), 245(nn.22, 36-37), 251(n.28), 253(n.11)
Fraternal Democrats, 222
Fredeman, William E., 247(n.38), 255(n.28)
Freud, Sigmund, 19
Friedrich, Werner, 245(n.23)
Frith, William, 220
Froude, James Anthony, 107

Frye, Northrop, 142, 251(n.36)
Fulford, Roger, 241(n.5)

Gaskell, Elizabeth, 2, 6, 155, 204, 226; *Cranford*, 253(n.44); *Lizzie Leigh*, 170, 205; *Mary Barton*, 170, 194, 197, 199; *The Moorland Cottage*, 161, 170, 172, 188, 253(n.44)
Gaunt, William, 254(n.13), 255(nn.17, 37)
Germ, The, xiv, 1, 10, 12, 22, 32, 63, 81, 92, **203-23**, 238, 243(n.12), 246(nn.1, 4, 6, 8), 247(nn.34, 58), 254(nn.1, 8), 255 (nn.21-23, 25, 34); contents of, 207-8; founding of, 203-7; reception of, 208-11; title page from, 150
Gide, André, 87
Gilfillan, George, 26, 230; on Tennyson, 38-39, 42, 66; *Second Gallery of Literary Portraits*, 38, 244(nn.7, 9)
Gissing, George, 202
Gladstone, William Ewart, 3, 108, 118, 126, 244(n.12); as journalist, 10-11, 40
Gobineau, Joseph, 254(n.22)
Godwin, William, 162
Goethe, Johann Wolfgang von, xiii, 25, 46, 198, 214, 247(n.52); and Arnold, 68-70, 74, 77, 229; and Clough, 77, 87, 90-91; *Dichtung and Wahrheit*, 162; *Faust*, 73, 74, 87, 90-91; *Werther*, 132; *Wilhelm Meister*, 35, 44, 68-69, 132
Gogol, Nikolai, 238
Goldsmith, Oliver, 160
Goncourt brothers, 202
Gorham Controversy, 106, 108, 115
Gosse, Edmund, 106, 194
Graham, Walter, 205, 254(n.5)
Grayburn, William F., 252(n.20)
Great Exhibition, xiv, 3-4, 8, 12, 219, 224, 236
Greenburger, Evelyn, 83, 90, 247(nn.43, 54)
Greene, Graham, 251(n.29)
Greenhut, Morris, 242(n.2)
Greville, Charles Cavendish, 108, 241(n.5)
Grigson, Geoffrey, 245(n.22)
Gross, John, 242(n.27)
Guardian, 208

Haight, Gordon, 242(n.25), 248(n.4)
Haldane, Elizabeth, 252(n.18)
Hall, Charles, 241(n.12)
Hallam, Arthur, 39, 40-42, 51, 67, 231, 245 (n.19)
Hallam, Henry, 231
Hancock, W. D., 241(n.1), 249(n.15), 253 (n.4)
Hardy, Barbara, 250(n.17)
Hardy, Thomas, 2, 71, 99, 172, 248(n.79)
Harney, George, 11, 13; and the *Red Republican*, 221-23
Harrison, Frederic, 2, 78, 191, 226, 254(n.26)
Harrold, C. F., 250(n.41)
Hawthorne, Nathaniel, xii, 161-62, 229, 252 (n.19)
Hawes, Donald, 249(n.19)
Haydon, Benjamin, 171, 214
Hazlitt, William, 43
Hegel, Georg Wilhelm, 26
Herodotus, 21
High Church Movement, 107, 181
Hill, David, 168; calotype by, 148
Historiography, 26-27, 33, 50
History (and historicism), 33, 51, 73, 113, 127, 129, 156, 162, 230-32, 236, 237; and autobiography, 43-45, 50, 109-10, 114, 158, 166-67, 220, 246(n.46); and biography, 32, 98, 119; in Browning, 101-4; and Carlyle, 27-30, 32, 162; and fiction, 103-4, 158, 165-78, 256(n.6); and literary development, 21-27, 231-33; as literature, 35, 230; and Macaulay, 21-27, 162-68; and the Newman brothers, 109-10, 114, 119
Hogarth, William, 171, 172, 177, 214
Hogg, James, 162
Homer, 40, 214
Honan, Park, 95, 248(n.65)
Hood, Thomas, 200, 214
Hopkins, Gerard, 250(n.1)
Horace, 225
Horne, Richard Henry, 168-69, 175, 204, 252(n.41), 253(n.54)
Hosman, R. S., 254(n.1)
House, Humphry, 241(n.17)
House, Madelaine, 251(n.19)
Household Narrative. See Dickens
Household Words. See Dickens
Hughes, Thomas, 182, 186, 253(nn.2, 6), 254(nn.20, 25)
Hulme, T. E., 26
Hunt, F. Knight, 11
Hunt, Holman, 12, 168, 206, 208, 210, 214, 215, 218; portrait of D. G. Rossetti by, 150
Hunt, Leigh, 2, 10, 35, 36, 205, 214
Hunt, John Dixon, 244(n.1), 245(n.19)
Hunt, Robert, 167, 252(n.35)
Hunt, Thornton, 16, 205, 224
Hutton, Richard Holt, 226, 249(n.26)
Huxley, Thomas Henry, 39

Imagination, 20, 71, 73, 86, 89, 166, 237; and Carlyle, 28, 50, 129; Coleridge on, 40, 50; and Dickens, 128-30, 134, 141-43; and

Imagination (*continued*)
memory, 125; mid-nineteenth century views on, 20–21, 49–50, 74–75, 111, 125, 154, 169; and Wordsworth, 49, 128–30, 134–35, 169
Inglis, K. S., 249(n.10)
Irvine, William, 95, 248(n.65)
Irving, Washington, 229

Jack, Ian, 248(n.77)
Jaffé, Aniela, 246(n.2)
James, D. G., 49, 246(nn.45, 47)
James, G. P. R., 164, 165–66, 177, 252(n.28)
James, Henry, 158
James, Louis, 14, 242(n.32)
Jameson, Anna, 216
Jeffrey, Francis, 234
Jeremiah, 179, 182, 190
Jerrold, Douglas, 14
Jerrold, William Blanchard, 204
Jewsbury, Geraldine, 204
Job, 107, 214
Johnson, Edgar, 251(n.37), 255(n.16)
Johnson, E. D. H., 39, 244(n.10)
Johnson, Samuel, 155
Jones, C. E., 242(n.3)
Joule, J. P., 236
Journal of Design, 10
Joyce, James, 136, 138, 154
Jung, Carl, 64, 74–75, 96, 246(n.2), 248 (n.71)

Kaminsky, Alice, 242(n.2), 245(n.38)
Kant, Immanuel, 18
Kay, Joseph, 5
Kaye, J. W., 11, 164, 234, 242(n.26)
Kay-Shuttleworth, Sir James, 6
Keats, John, 17, 28, 34, 40–41, 71, 214, 234
Keble, John, 19, 107
Kierkegaard, Søren, 85–86, 88, 90–91, 112, 234, 237, 247(nn.45–50), 256(n.18)
Kingsley, Charles, xiv, 6, 46, 107, 160, **179–202**, 213, 225, 253(nn.2, 4, 9, 13); and Carlyle, 1, 163, 187, 193, 194, 197–98, 200–201; and Chartism, 179–80, 188–90; as Christian Socialist, 179, 187, 191, 193, 194, 196, 222; and the *Christian Socialist*, 10, 179, 180, 186, 205; and Dickens, 188, 195, 197–200; on English literature, 9, 199, 231; as feminist, 184–85; on Francis Newman, 185–86; as index to the times, xiv, 179–81; on John Henry Newman, 108, 115, 180, 183, 184–85, 253(n.11); on Matthew Arnold, 66, 79, 246(n.10); as Parson Lot, 179, 180, 190; religious beliefs of, 183–84; reputation of, 180–81; on Tennyson, 46–48, 200, 235, 244(n.37); on Wordsworth, 9, 32, 46–48, 200, 245(nn.36–37); *Alton Locke*, 1, 175, 180, 182, 190–91, 192, **194–204**, 253(n.2), 254(nn.18, 24, 38); "Cheap Clothes and Nasty," 1, 180, 182, 195, 254(nn.18, 23); *Elizabeth of Hungary*, 183; *Lectures at Queen's College*, 231, 242(n.21); *Politics for the People*, 180, 186, 192, 196; *Prose Idylls*, 253(n.14); *Water Babies*, 163; *Yeast*, 180, 182, 192, 193–94, 196
Kingsley, Frances Grenfell, 183–84, 194, 253 (n.1), 254(n.34)
Kingsley, Maurice, 253(n.1)
Kitson-Clark, G. S. R., 28, 29, 243(n.25), 251(n.6)
Knight, Charles, 14
Knoepflmacher, U. C., 109, 248(n.3), 249 (nn.6, 17), 250(n.36)
Knowles, James, 241(n.16)
Knox, Robert, 254(n.22)

Lamartine, Alphonse de, 155
Landor, Walter Savage, 2, 20, 33, 43, 204, 214, 243(n.6); "Dante," 43, 245(n.22)
Landow, George P., 250(n.7)
Langbaum, Robert, 94, 248(n.62)
Langer, Susanne, 138, 251(n.33)
Lansdowne, Lord, 7, 66
Laurence, Samuel, portrait of Tennyson by, 57; portrait of Thackeray by, 58
Lawrence, D. H., 185
Lawson, E. LeRoy, 248(n.80)
Leader, 10, 16, 90, 94, 98, 117–18, 119, 186, 187, 224, 229, 247(n.53), 248(nn.73, 85), 249(n.32), 250(n.37), 256(nn.8, 12, 13)
Leech, John, 210
Leigh Hunt's Journal, 10
Leopardi, Giacomo, 10, 40, 244(n.12)
Lessing, Gotthold, 212
Lever, Charles, 155
Lewes, George, xiv, 34, 90, 187, 233, 238, 248 (n.63), 256(n.8); on anarchy, 232–34; on Browning, 94, 98, 102, 158, 248(nn.63, 73, 85); on Carlyle, 225, 233; on Charlotte Brontë, 176–77, 253(n.48); on Comte, 26, 232; on the drama, 14–15; drawing of, by Thackeray, 58; on fiction, 35, 176, 242 (n.2); on Francis Newman, 105, 119; and the *Leader*, 10, 16–17, 90, 94, 119, 205, 224, 225, 229, 242(n.2); on the literary profession, 11, 233–34; on poetry, 16–17, 28, 81; on realism, 98, 129, 158, 225; on Tennyson, 36, 47, 158; on Thackeray, 247(n.53); on William Bowles, 16–17, 21, 24, 36, 242(n.2); on Wordsworth, 32, 119,

Lewes, George (*continued*)
128, 158, 177, 245(n.38); *Life of Goethe*, 90; *The Noble Heart*, 14
Lewis, O. A., 252(n.20)
Lindenberger, Herbert, 45-46, 245(nn.31-35)
Linton, Elizabeth Lynn, 204, 224, 255(n.1)
List of Immortals (Pre-Raphaelite), 214-15
Litzinger, Boyd, 248(n.75)
Locke, John, 176
Lohrli, Anne, 254(n.4)
London Catalogue, 108
Loofbourow, John, 252(n.43)
Lovejoy, Arthur, xii
Lowrie, Walter, 247(nn.45, 47, 49-50)
Lowry, Howard Foster, 246(n.7)
Lucian, 162
Ludlow, J. M.: on Kingsley, 179, 180, 186, 193, 194, 253(n.3), 254(nn.21, 30, 35)
Lukács, Georg, 201, 254(n.40)
Luther, Martin, 179
Lyell, Sir Charles, 9, 77-78, 110, 230

Macaulay, Thomas Babington, **21-26**, 35, 243 (n.17); on Dante, 28-29; 43-44, 245 (n.29); on Dickens, 25, 128; on literature and progress, 22-24, 29, 41; on poetry, 22-25, 29; style of, 21; on Wordsworth, 25, 128, 130; *History of England*, 2, 26, 230; *Lays of Ancient Rome*, 230; "Milton," 21-26, 243(n.8), 245(n.25)
"McCandlish Children," reproduction of, 148
Macfarlane, Helen, 222
Machiavelli, 21
Mackay, Charles, 32, 69-70, 246(n.16)
Mackay, Robert, 11, 169, 230, 233, 241(n.10), 249(n.20), 252(n.42)
Macready, William Charles, 14
Malthus, Thomas, 117
Mann, Thomas, 87
Manning, Henry, 3, 97, 108, 183
Mansfield, Charles, 185, 186
Marchand, Leslie, 242(n.24), 244(n.34)
Mare, Margaret, 252(n.23)
Marks, E. R., 246(n.14), 256(n.11)
Marryat, Frederick, 163
Marston, J. Westland, 244(n.34)
Martin, Robert, 186, 193, 253(nn.9-10, 15), 254(n.29)
Martineau, Harriet, 26, 27, 204; as historian, 168, 230; *Autobiography*, 91, 247(n.55); *History of the Thirty Years' Peace*, 27, 243 (n.23), 252(n.37)
Martineau, James, 119
Marx, Karl, 6, 44, 118, 186, 190, 222, 230; on alienation, 118, 216; on the arts, 26-27; and Hegel, 26; and Kingsley, 189; and the Pre-Raphaelites, 220; *Communist Manifesto*, 6, 186, 189, 222
Marxist theories of literature, 201
Masson, David, 11-12, 83, 238; on Dickens and Thackeray, 129, 153-54, 157, 177-78, 210, 250(n.16), 251(n.2); on Wordsworth, 153, 237, 245(n.36), 256(n.17)
Mattes, E. B., 245(n.20)
Matthiessen, F. O., 256(n.19)
Maurice, Frederick Denison, 10, 46, 179, 186
Mayhew, Henry, 6, 168, 188, 213; *London Labour and London Poor* articles by, 6, 180, 241(n.12)
Mazzini, Giuseppi, 87, 222
Medievalism, 211, 213-17
Melchior, Barbara, 248(n.68)
Melpomene, muse of tragedy, 51, 63
Melville, Herman, xii, 91, 160, 162, 229, 237
Memory, uses and theories of, xiii, 123-31, 136-39; "biographical memory," 138; and Dickens, 127-43; and fiction, 159-61, 168; "flashback memory," 138; and imagination, 125, 128-29; and Ruskin, xiv, 40, 123-27, 135; and Tennyson, 51; and Wordsworth, 51, 123-24, 126-43
Meredith, George, 1, 42, 156, 204, 226; on fiction, 158-59, 252(n.11)
Merriam, Harold G., 244(n.5)
Miall, Bernard, 249(n.34)
Miles, Josephine, 48-49, 245(nn.42-43), 246(n.44)
Mill, John Stuart, 2, 10, 35, 39, 184; on Bentham and Coleridge, 33; on nature, 32, 132-33, 135, 244(n.36); on poetry, 23, 24, 35, 158; *Autobiography*, 23, 109, 111, 132-33; "The Church of England," 105, 107-8, 248(n.2), 249(n.12); "On Liberty," 233; *Principles of Political Economy*, 132-33, 135, 251(n.24); *Three Essays on Religion*, 244(n.36)
Millais, John Everett, 12, 206, 208-10, 215, 218
Miller, Hugh, 230
Miller, J. Hillis, 95-96, 248(nn.67, 70, 88)
Milsand, Joseph, 93-94, 97, 103
Milton, John, 21, 25, 26, 75, 99, 199, 200, 214, 243(n.8), 245(n.25)
Minto, W., 255(n.20)
Mitchell, H., 254(n.40)
Mnemosyne, muse of memory, 51
Moir, David, 92-93, 95, 247(n.57)
Monod, Sylvère, 253(n.56)
Montgomery, Robert, 21
Morell, J. D., 110
Morley, Henry, 204
Morley, John, 249(n.14)
Morning Chronicle, 5, 10, 69, 180, 186

Morris, William, 2, 39
Moxon, Edward, 37, 102, 244(n. 5)
Mudie's Circulating Library, 14
Mulhauser, Frederick, 247(n. 30)
Myoshi, Masao, xiv, 248(n. 84)
Myth and mythology, xiv, 28, 100, 111, 169

Napoleon (Bonaparte), 227
National Gallery (London), 215, 228
Nature, xiii, xiv, 32-33, 117-18, 136-38, 167-73, 225, 224*n*; and Arnold, 49, 67-76, 117-18, 246(nn. 16, 18); and Carlyle, 32-33; and Clough, 77-78, 89-90; and Dickens, 32, 133-40, 170, 211; and fiction, 9, 118, 165, 167-73, 177; and mid-nineteenth-century poetry, 49, 68-70, 77-78, 118; and Ruskin, 33, 49, 123-26, 135, 215; and the Pre-Raphaelites, xiv, 211, 213, 216-18, 222; and Tennyson, 49-50, 77-78; and Wordsworth, 9, 12, 32, 33, 47-49, 67, 69-70, 74, 133-35
Nazarenes (German artists), 213
Needham, Gwendolyn, 250(n. 17)
Newman, Francis William, xiii, 78, **105-22**, 235; Arnold on, 119-21, 122; autobiographical writing of, 2, 7, 106, 109-12; and Browning, 112; and *David Copperfield*, 109, 111, 112, 118; and George Henry Lewes, 119, 122; and the Higher Criticism, 109; and John Henry Newman, 7, 106-16, 119; photograph of, 60; reputation of, 105-6; and science, 110, 237; *Contributions to the Early History of the Late Cardinal Newman*, 106; *Iliad* translation, 119; *Phases of Faith*, 2, 7, 107, 108-12, 119, 122, 185, 186, 249(n. 17), 250(n. 36); *The Soul*, 84, 105, 106, 118, 121, 122, 179, 185, 186, 190, 250(n. 44)
Newman, John Henry, xiii, xiv, 35, 97, **105-22**, 185, 235; and Anglicanism, 106, 114-15; autobiographical writing of, 114-16; and Carlyle, 113, 183; and Charles Kingsley, 108, 115, 180, 183-85, 253(n. 11); and Evangelicalism, 115; and the Oxford Movement, 3, 107, 114, 115; on periodical literature, 11, 120; portrait of, 60; and *The Rambler*, 11, 113, 114; *Apologia pro Vita Sua*, 106, 108, 113, 114-15; *On Certain Difficulties Felt by Anglicans*, 2, 7, 108, 113-16, 234, 249(n. 24); "Christ upon the Waters," 113-16
New Testament, 41, 116, 179, 198
Nicoll, Allardyce, 242(n. 37)
Niebuhr, Barthold, 33, 230
Niepce, Nicéphore, 33
Nietzsche, Friedrich, 29, 233
Nightingale, Florence, 84
Nonsense verse, 31
North American Review, 79
North British Review, 217, 242(n. 26), 256 (n. 17)
Northern Star, 222
Norton, Charles Eliot, 243(n. 24)
Notes and Queries, 10, 231-32, 256(n. 10)

Old Testament, 179, 199, 234
Oliphant, Margaret, 226
Ong, Walter J., 250(n. 9)
Orchard, John, 22-23, 24, 207, 218-21, 243 (n. 12), 255(nn. 34, 36)
Orwell, George, 140, 251(n. 34)
Owen, Robert, 186
Owen, W. J. B., 243(n. 5)
Oxford Movement, 3, 106, 114, 181

Paracelsus, 96
Pastoralism and pastoral conventions, 80, 124; in fiction, 6, 118, 133, 170-71, 198, 200-201, 252(n. 43), 253(n. 44); in poetry, 80, 118, 124-25, 133
Pater, Walter, 2
Pathetic fallacy, 49
Patmore, Coventry, 10, 204, 212, 214, 215; love poems of, 42; on *Macbeth*, 207, 215; on modern poetry, 161, 226; and the Pre-Raphaelites, 81, 212, 214, 218; on Ruskin and criticism, 217
Paxton, Joseph, 12, 219, 227
Peacock, Thomas L., 84, 175; on the poetry of his age, 17-18, 21, 22, 29, 242(n. 3)
Peel, J. D. Y., 243(n. 21)
Peel, Sir Robert, 2, 3, 219
Percival, Alicia, 252(n. 23)
Petrarch, 46
Petronius Arbiter, 158
Pevsner, Sir Nikolaus, 1, 223, 241(n. 1), 255 (n. 41)
Phillpotts, bishop of Exeter, 108
Photography, 9, 33, 126, 168, 199, 211
Pitt, Valerie, 41, 245(n. 20)
Pius IX, 3, 108
Plato, 20, 25, 41, 125, 162
Plumb, J. H., 243(n. 25), 251(n. 6)
Poe, Edgar Allan, xii, 19, 214
Political Instructor, 155
Porter, G. R., 4, 241(n. 8)
Positivism (of Comte), 26-27, 110
Potts, Abbie Findlay, 244(n. 43)
Pound, Ezra, 26, 91
Power (as a critical term), 31-32, 41, 44, 49, 95, 129, 135, 170
Praz, Mario, 227, 253(n. 51), 255(n. 5)

Pre-Raphaelites, xiii, 2, 168, **203-23**, 228; on Browning, 92-93, 211-12; and Dante, 43, 81, 215; and the Great Exhibition, 219, 223; List of Immortals of, 214; and Marx, 220; medieval interests of, 213-18; and nature, xiv, 211, 213, 216-18, 222; and Patmore, 81, 212, 214, 218; and photography, 168, 211; reception of, at mid-nineteenth century, 235, 254-55(n.14); revolutionary ideas of, 213, 220; and Ruskin, 12, 33, 215-17, 221, 255(n.29); *Pre-Raphaelite Journal*, 214, 247(n.38), 255(nn.28, 30, 33). See also *Germ, The*
Prest, Thomas, 13, 155, 156, 163, 164, 252 (n.24)
Procter, Bryan Waller, 33, 244(n.39)
Progress, ideas of, 22, 29, 92, 187, 218-19, 223, 227
Prospective Review, 154, 155, 159, 161, 251 (nn.3, 7)
Proust, Marcel, 123-24, 138, 139, 250(nn.1, 3)
Public Library Act (1850), 14
Pugin, A. W., 216
Punch, xiv, 4, 53, 206, 241(n.9)
Puritanism, 29, 101, 248(n.80)

Quarterly Review, 4, 20, 43, 217, 230, 234, 245(n.24), 255(n.19), 256(n.7)
Quillinan, Edward, 68
Quintilian, 126

Rabelais, François, 158
Radcliffe, Charles Bland, 74-75, 76, 111, 125, 128, 169, 233, 250(n.6)
Rambler: A Catholic Journal and Review, 11, 113, 114, 239
Ranke, Leopold von, 33, 230, 256(n.9)
Ray, Gordon, 242(n.28)
Raysor, Thomas R., 250(n.14)
Realism and the realistic, 129, 221, 225, 233; in Browning, 98; and Dickens, 129, 159; in fiction, 98, 158-59, 168, 173, 177, 233; George Lewes on, 98, 129, 158, 177, 225; and poetry, 20, 81, 98; and Thackeray, 140, 210
Red Republican, 6, 13, 187, 205, 221-23, 255(n.39)
Reeve, Henry, 33, 166, 230, 256(n.9)
Reid, Mayne, 155, 164, 168, 177, 252(n.39)
Research Society on Victorian Periodicals, 242(n.23)
Richardson, Samuel, 159, 248(n.80)
Ricks, Christopher, 241(n.16), 244(n.11), 247(n.25)
Rigby, Elizabeth (Mrs. Charles Eastlake), 228
Robbins, William, 249(n.9)
Robespierre, Maximilien de, 222
Robinson, Henry Crabb, 68
Rogers, Henry, 119
Romanell, Patrick, 247(n.56)
Romanticism, xiv, 9, 19, 20, 23, 25, 27-28, 30, 31, 67-69, 91, 92, 101, 115, 160, 229
Rooke, Barbara, 250(n.14), 254(n.27)
Rookeries (London slums), 3, 12
Rossetti, Christina, 207, 221
Rossetti, Dante Gabriel, 1, 12, 156, 214, 215; and Catholicism in the PRB, 210, 215-16; and Dante, 43, 214-15; and Elizabeth Siddal, 215; and *The Germ*, 203-6; portrait of, by Holman Hunt, 150; portrait of Browning by, 60; and the PRB, 203, 206, 209; "An Autopsychology" ("St. Agnes of Intercession"), 207; "The Blessed Damozel," 1, 207, 221; "Dante in Exile," 215; "Hand and Soul," 208; "My Sister's Sleep," 207
Rossetti, Gabriele, 41, 43
Rossetti, William Michael, 11, 208, 214, 218, 243(n.12); on Arthur Clough, 81-82, 85-86, 91, 206, 211, 246(n.1), 247(nn.34-37), 255(n.22); on Browning, 81, 85-86, 92-93, 98, 102, 206, 247(nn.58-60); on Dante, 43, 81, 214; as editor of *The Germ*, 206-8, 254(n.1); on *The Germ*, 203; on Matthew Arnold, 65-66, 73, 206, 246 (nn.4, 6, 8); on modern poetry, 65-66, 80-82, 93, 118, 161, 206; "Fancies at Leisure," 207; "Mrs. Holmes Grey," 81; *The P. R. B. Journal* (Rossetti's diary), 247 (n.38), 255(nn.28, 30, 33)
Rousseau, Jean-Jacques, 44, 115
Routledge, George, 14
Royal Academy, 12, 168, 209, 210, 211, 221, 222
Rubel, M., 249(n.33)
Ruskin, Effie, 209
Ruskin, John, 11, 12, 13, 34, 39, 40, 43-44, 87, 129, 169, 213, 225; and autobiography, 9, 242(n.20), 250(n.7); and Carlyle, 33, 40; on *creative* and *reflective* poets, 41, 127; drawing by, 147; on fiction, 163; on industrialization, 221; on memory, 40, 124-27; on nature, 33, 49, 124, 135; Proust's homage to, 123; on taste, 227; on Turner, 9, 33, 125, 212, 228; and Wordsworth, 33, 40, 124-25; *The King of the Golden River*, 2, 149, 163, 169; *Modern Painters*, 33, 39, 40, 123, 217, 244(n.35), 245(n.13), 250(n.2), 251(n.38); *Praeterita*, 39, 123, 143; *Pre-Raphaelitism*, 215, 219, 255(nn.29, 31); "Of Queens' Gardens,"

Ruskin, John (*continued*) 184; *The Seven Lamps of Architecture* (and "The Lamp of Memory"), xiv, 2, 123–27, 129, 130, 131, 142–43, 217, 235, 236, 250 (nn.4, 5, 8); *Stones of Venice*, 2, 87, 123, 230–31; *Time and Tide*, 221
Russell, George W. E., 246 (n.3)
Russell, Lord John, 3, 108, 249 (n.15)
Rutherford, Mark. *See* White, W. H.

Sadleir, Michael, 166, 252 (n.29)
Sainte-Beuve, Charles Augustine, 232, 238, 246 (n.14), 256 (n.11)
Saintsbury, George, 117, 249 (n.30)
Saturday Review, 10
Saville, John, 222, 255 (n.39)
Scharf, Aaron, 252 (n.36)
Schiller, Johann Christoff, 28
Scott, Sir Walter, 5, 14, 17, 36, 46, 80; influence of, on mid-nineteenth-century fiction, 140, 155, 165–66, 177, 201
Scott, William Bell, 156, 207, 210, 251 (n.5), 252 (n.38)
Self-consciousness (in literature), 65, 66, 74, 103–4, 118, 161, 164, 176, 177, 178, 206
Sellwood, Emily (Tennyson), 36
Sénancour, Etienne, 66, 69
Sewell, Elizabeth, 229
Shakespeare, William, 33, 35, 40, 157, 199, 206, 214, 215
Shannon, Edgar Finley, Jr., 37, 244 (n.4)
Shaw, Thomas, 16, 131, 153, 157, 176, 242 (n.1), 250–51 (n.18)
Shawcross, John, 243 (n.11), 250 (n.10)
Shelley, P. A., 252 (n.20)
Shelley, Percy Bysshe, 28, 38, 40, 41, 64, 214, 226, 233; and Browning, 92, 96, 101–2, 248 (nn.81–83, 87); debate of, with Peacock, 18, 21; on utilitarianism, 18, 22, 31; *Defense of Poetry*, 18, 21; *Epipsychidion*, 102
Siddal, Elizabeth, 215, 218
Sidney, John, 205
Sidney, Samuel, 205
Silone, Ignazio, 199, 202
Silver-fork fiction, 170
Simonides, 126
Simpson, Richard, 235, 256 (n.15)
Sincerity (as a critical principle), 29, 30–31, 165, 244 (nn.31, 33)
Slater, Michael, 251 (n.21)
Smalley, Donald, 248 (n.75)
Smedley, Francis, 8, 149, 174, 227, 253 (n.50)
Smith, Albert, 204
Smith, Alexander, 30, 79
Smith, John Stores, 4, 187, 241 (n.10), 254 (n.17)
Smith, W. H., 13, 14
Smollett, Tobias, 159, 160, 171
Smyser, J. W., 243 (n.5)
Social realism, Russian, 202
Sophocles, 66
Spasmodic verse, 8, 30, 94, 246 (n.10)
Spectator, 10, 98, 205, 208
Spedding, James, 231
Spencer, Herbert, 2, 27, 187, 243 (n.21)
Sprat, Thomas, 22
Stang, Richard, 252 (n.10)
Stanley, Arthur, 121
Steegman, John, 212–13, 228, 255 (nn.24, 27)
Stephen, James Fitzjames, 226
Stephen, Leslie, 2, 226
Stephens, George, 206, 207, 211–212, 217, 219–21, 255 (nn.21, 26, 32, 35)
Sterling, John, 233
Sterne, Laurence, 159, 160
Stewart, J. I. M., 249 (n.31)
Stone, Harry, 254 (nn.2, 7)
Stone, Lawrence, 242 (n.33)
Story, Graham, 251 (n.19)
Strachey, Lytton, 241 (n.5)
Strauss, David Friedrich, 2, 89, 97, 105, 110, 179, 230
Sucksmith, Harvey Peter, 252 (n.16)
Super, R. H., 245 (n.31), 250 (n.42)
Sussman, Herbert, 254–55 (n.14)
Swenson, D. F., 247 (n.48)
Swinburne, Algernon Charles, 2

Tagliacozzo, G., 243 (n.19)
Taine, Hippolyte, 92, 232
Tait's Edinburgh Magazine, 36, 244 (n.1)
Talbot, William Henry Fox, 33, 168
Tave, Stuart, 234
Taylor, Harriet, 184
Taylor, Henry, 33, 244 (n.40)
Tennyson, Alfred Lord, xiii, xiv, 7, 13, 19, **36–51**, 65, 101, 111, 127, 131, 156, 214, 226, 241 (n.16), 244 (nn.3–4, 11), 245 (nn.14–21), 246 (nn.45, 47, 24); and Arnold, 76–78; and Arthur Hallam, 40–42, 231, 245 (nn.15, 19–20); and autobiography, 50, 64, 95; and Carlyle, 162; and Clough, 77–78, 214; and Dante, 8, 40–51, 90, 245 (nn.14, 18, 21); as a "democratic poet," 200; on fiction, 35, 80, 244 (n.45); and the Laureateship, 36, 38; on love, 41–42; portrait of, by Samuel Laurence, 57; and the PRB, 81; and realism, 140; reputation of, at mid-nineteenth century, 5, 36–38, 46–48, 92, 99, 225, 239,

Tennyson, Alfred Lord (*continued*) 244(n.4); style of, 48-50, 116, 117, 243 (n.11); and Wordsworth, 32, 37, 41-51, 245(n.31), 246(nn.45, 47); "To Dante," 42, 245(n.21); "Dora," 48; *In Memoriam*, 1, 7, 36-51, 67, 77-78, 95, 227, 235, 241 (n.15), 243(n.11), 244(nn.34, 37, 1-2), 245(nn.20, 37, 40), 247(n.46); *Poems* (1842), 37; *The Princess*, 37

Tennyson, Hallam Lord, 241(n.16), 245(n.15)

Thackeray, William Makepeace, xiv, 35, 83, 155, 239, 249(n.30); on Arthur Clough, 82, 247(n.40); and autobiography, 164; and Charlotte Brontë, 226; and Dickens, 1, 5, 8, 10, 80, 140, 153-56, 165; drawings by, 58, 59; and eighteenth-century fiction, 160, 252-53(n.43); George Lewes on, 90, 247 (n.53); and Kingsley, 194; narrative art of, 8, 164-65, 172, 177; and the Newman brothers, 112, 249(n.21); and pastoral fiction, 6, 170, 252-53(n.43); popularity of, 1, 5, 35, 155-56, 167; portrait of, by Samuel Laurence, 58; on the profession of letters, 11, 175; and realism, 140; and self-consciousness in literature, 164; *Ballads and Tales*, 255(n.6); *English Humourists*, 160; *Henry Esmond*, 8; *Kicklebury's on the Rhine*, 1; "May-Day Ode," 227-28; *Pendennis*, 1, 8, 11, 14, 112, 117, 129, 140, 148, 153-54, 157, 161, 164, 167, 170, 172, 175-76, 178, 193, 210, 214, 226, 238, 242 (n.26), 247(n.53), 249(nn.21, 31), 252 (n.25), 253(nn.50, 55); *Vanity Fair*, 1, 8, 80, 83, 153, 233

Thirty-Nine Articles, 82, 112

Thompson, E. P., 241(n.12)

Thousand and One Nights, 219

Tillich, Paul, 109

Tillotson, Geoffrey, xiv, 244(n.45)

Tillotson, Kathleen, xiv, 77, 163, 172, 246 (n.24), 249(n.30), 252(n.22), 253(nn.47, 52, 56)

Times (London), 10, 47, 209

Timko, Michael, 247(n.44)

Tolstoi, Count Leo, 161, 238

Tonna, Mrs. Charlotte Elizabeth ("Charlotte Elizabeth"), 155

Tractarians, 3, 107, 114-15, 181

Trawick, B. B., 247(n.31), 249(n.28)

Trevelyan, George Otto, 243(n.17)

Trilling, Lionel, 120, 244(n.31), 250(n.39)

Trollope, Anthony, 2, 84, 170, 210; and historical fiction, 167, 177; and serial publication, 157; *Autobiography*, 167, 252 (nn.29, 32); Barchester novels, 2; *Can You Forgive Her?*, 252(n.29); *The Noble Jilt*, 252(n.29); *La Vendée*, 2, 166-67

Truth (as a critical term), 33-35, 162-66, 169, 178, 196, 202

Tupper, George, 203

Tupper, Martin, 17, 30, 36

Turner, J. M. W., 9, 12, 33, 212, 217, 220, 228; "Yarmouth Sands," 147

Utilitarians, 18, 20, 26, 31, 44, 92, 101, 198, 204, 219

Vargish, Thomas, 215, 249(n.27)

Vaughan, Robert, 116, 249(n.29)

Vergil, 26, 42

Vicinus, Martha, 12-13, 242(nn.30, 33)

Vico, Giambattista, 26, 243(n.19)

Victoria, queen of England, 15, 16, 227, 228, 241(n.5)

Walrond, Theodore, 246(n.24)

Warburton, Eliot, 8, 157, 166-67, 177, 178, 251(n.9), 252(nn.31, 34)

Warren, Alba, 20, 243(n.7), 244(n.39)

Warren, T. Herbert, 245(nn.14, 18)

Warton, Thomas, 231

Watson, Elizabeth, 244(n.8)

Watson, Robert, 244(n.8)

Watt, Ian, 159-60, 248(n.80), 252(nn.12-14)

Wedderburn, Alexander, 242(n.20), 245(n.13), 250(n.2)

Weintraub, Karl, 50, 246(n.46)

Wellek, René, 221, 242(n.20), 255(n.38)

Wellesley Index to Victorian Periodicals, 10, 242(nn.23, 26), 244(n.37), 253(n.48)

Westminster Review, 10, 20, 107, 219, 248 (n.3)

White, H. V., 243(n.19)

White, William Hale (Mark Rutherford), 194, 226

Whitehead, Alfred North, 127, 250(n.11)

Whitridge, Arnold, 246(n.15)

Willey, Basil, 106, 244(n.3), 249(n.7), 251 (n.24)

Williams, Charles, 48, 245(n.41)

Williams, Raymond, 243(n.14), 254(n.38)

Wills, William Henry, 204

Wilson, Angus, 131, 251(n.21)

Winston, Clara, 246(n.2)

Winston, Richard, 246(n.2)

Wiseman, Nicholas, 3, 97, 108, 114

Woolner, Thomas, 206, 207, 212; medallion of Carlyle by, 52

Wordsworth, William, xiii, xiv, 16, 17, 22, **36-51**, 67-70, 89, 101, **123-43**, 178, 214, 236, 237, 239, 244(n.43), 245(nn.31-39); and autobiography, 45, 47, 50, 64, 115 (*see also* memory); and childhood, 25,

Wordsworth, William (*continued*)
136–39; and Clough, 89, 115, 249(n. 28); Coleridge on, 45, 128, 138; and Dante, 43–48; and Dickens, 127–43, 160, 200; fame of, 35, 36, 45–47, 92 (*see also* influence); George Lewes on, 32, 119, 128, 158, 177, 245(n.38); on imagination, 49–50, 134; influence of, 9, 19, 25, 28, 34, 41, 67, 131, 170; J. S. Mill on, 23–24; and Kingsley, 9, 46–47, 200, 201; Matthew Arnold on, 67–70, 90; and memory, 40, 45, 50–51, 124, 126–27, 138–39, 142–43, 161; and nature, 9, 12, 32, 47–49, 67, 69–70, 74, 133–35; and power, 31, 44; on religion and poetry, 19; and Ruskin, 33, 40, 124–25; and sincerity, 30; and Tennyson, xiii, 32, 37, 41–51, 245(n.31), 246(n.45); vocabulary of, 49; "Upon Epitaphs," 30; *The Excursion*, 40; *Intimations Ode*, 133; *Lyrical Ballads*, 131, 138, 140, 142, 200; *Michael*, 67, 138–39, 142, 170; "Nutting," 137; *The Prelude*, 1, 25, 37, 43–51, 109, **123–43**, 153, 158, 243(n. 26), 245(nn.31–38), 246(n. 51), 251(n. 26); *The Recluse*, 45, 135; "Tintern Abbey," 126

Yates, Edmund, 204, 226, 253(n. 53)
Yates, Frances, 126, 175, 250(n. 9), 251 (n.32)
Yeats, William Butler, 74
Yeo, Eileen, 241(n. 12)
Yonge, Charlotte, 163, 252(n. 23)
Young, G. M., xi, 180–81, 225–26, 239, 241 (n.1), 249(n.15), 253(nn. 4–5), 255(n. 2)

Zeitgeist, 24, 74, 79, 85, 87

The Johns Hopkins University Press

This book was composed in Aldine Roman text with Garamond display type by Horne Associates, Inc., from a design by Alan Carter. It was printed and bound by Universal Lithographers, Inc.

Library of Congress Cataloging in Publication Data

Dawson, Carl.
Victorian noon.

Includes bibliographical references and index.
1. English literature–19th century–History and criticism. I. Title.
PR461.D35 820'.9'008 78-13939
ISBN 0-8018-2110-X